T0394049

The Ukraine Conflict

It is not hyperbole to suggest that the foundations of post–cold war security in Europe have been badly damaged by the conflict in Ukraine since 2014. Russia's annexation of Crimea and intervention in eastern Ukraine appear to have created a 'simmering' conflict, which may take years to resolve and have profound consequences for the European security environment. This volume explores the various political, economic and social aspects of these profound changes and their wider significance for Europe, bringing together contributions by scholars from across the continent and in various disciplinary fields to offer an authoritative, in-depth examination of the complex causes of the Ukraine crisis and the consequences for Ukrainian statehood, Ukraine's relations with Russia, Russia's own domestic governance and Russia's relations with Europe.

This book was originally published as a special issue of *Europe-Asia Studies*.

Derek Averre is a Reader and former Director of the Centre for Russian, European and Eurasian Studies, University of Birmingham, UK. He is a Russian foreign/security policy specialist with 25 years' experience in the field.

Kataryna Wolczuk is Professor of East European Politics at the Centre for Russian, European and Eurasian Studies, University of Birmingham, UK.

Routledge Europe-Asia Studies Series
A series edited by Terry Cox
University of Glasgow

The **Routledge Europe-Asia Studies Series** focuses on the history and current political, social and economic affairs of the countries of the former 'communist bloc' of the Soviet Union, Eastern Europe and Asia. As well as providing contemporary analyses it explores the economic, political and social transformation of these countries and the changing character of their relationships with the rest of Europe and Asia.

Please find a full list of titles in this series at https://www.routledge.com/Routledge-Europe-Asia-Studies/book-series/REAS

Recent titles in this series include:

EU Conditionality in the Western Balkans
Edited by Florian Bieber

Reflections on 1989 in Eastern Europe
Edited by Terry Cox

Russia and the World
The Internal-External Nexus
Edited by Natasha Kuhrt

Civil Society and Social Capital in Post-Communist Eastern Europe
Edited by Terry Cox

New Media in New Europe-Asia
Edited by Vlad Strukov, Jeremy Morris and Natalya Rulyova

Many Faces of the Caucasus
Edited by Nino Kemoklidze, Cerwyn Moore, Jeremy Smith and Galina Yemelianova

Explaining Policy Change in the European Union's Eastern Neighbourhood
Edited by Julia Langbein and Tanja A. Börzel

Transition Economies after 2008
Responses to the Crisis in Russia and Eastern Europe
Edited by Martin Myant and Jan Drahokoupil

Self-Determination after Kosovo
Edited by Annemarie Peen Rodt and Stefan Wolff

State against Civil Society
Contentious Politics and the Non-Systemic Opposition in Russia
Edited by Cameron Ross

The State of Democracy in Central and Eastern Europe
A Comparative Perspective
Edited by Ramona Coman and Luca Tomini

The Ukraine Conflict
Security, Identity and Politics in the Wider Europe
Edited by Derek Averre and Kataryna Wolczuk

Russian Modernisation
Structures and Agencies
Edited by Markku Kivinen and Terry Cox

The Ukraine Conflict

Security, Identity and Politics in the Wider Europe

Edited by
Derek Averre and Kataryna Wolczuk

LONDON AND NEW YORK

First published 2018
by Routledge
2 Park Square, Milton Park, Abingdon, Oxon, OX14 4RN, UK

and by Routledge
711 Third Avenue, New York, NY 10017, USA

Routledge is an imprint of the Taylor & Francis Group, an informa business

Chapters 1–7 & 9–12 © 2018 University of Glasgow
Chapter 8 © Rilka Dragneva & Kataryna Wolczuk, originally published
as Open Acess

British Library Cataloguing in Publication Data
A catalogue record for this book is available from the British Library

ISBN 13: 978-1-138-04743-3

Typeset in Times
by diacriTech, Chennai

Publisher's Note
The publisher accepts responsibility for any inconsistencies that may have arisen
during the conversion of this book from journal articles to book chapters, namely
the possible inclusion of journal terminology.

Disclaimer
Every effort has been made to contact copyright holders for their permission to
reprint material in this book. The publishers would be grateful to hear from any
copyright holder who is not here acknowledged and will undertake to rectify any
errors or omissions in future editions of this book.

Contents

CONTENTS

Citation Information

The chapters in this book were originally published in *Europe-Asia Studies*, volume 68, issue 4 (June 2016). When citing this material, please use the original page numbering for each article, as follows:

Chapter 1
Introduction: The Ukraine Crisis and Post-Post-Cold War Europe
Derek Averre & Kataryna Wolczuk
Europe-Asia Studies, volume 68, issue 4 (June 2016) pp. 551–555

Chapter 2
The Maidan in Movement: Diversity and the Cycles of Protest
Olga Onuch & Gwendolyn Sasse
Europe-Asia Studies, volume 68, issue 4 (June 2016) pp. 556–587

Chapter 3
National Identity in Ukraine: Impact of Euromaidan and the War
Volodymyr Kulyk
Europe-Asia Studies, volume 68, issue 4 (June 2016) pp. 588–608

Chapter 4
The Ukrainian Party System before and after the 2013–2014 Euromaidan
Kostyantyn Fedorenko, Olena Rybiy & Andreas Umland
Europe-Asia Studies, volume 68, issue 4 (June 2016) pp. 609–630

Chapter 5
The Donbas in 2014: Explaining Civil Conflict Perhaps, but not Civil War
Andrew Wilson
Europe-Asia Studies, volume 68, issue 4 (June 2016) pp. 631–652

Chapter 6
A Perfect Storm; Or What Went Wrong and What Went Right for the EU in Ukraine
Hiski Haukkala
Europe-Asia Studies, volume 68, issue 4 (June 2016) pp. 653–664

For any permission-related enquiries please visit:
http://www.tandfonline.com/page/help/permissions

Notes on Contributors

Derek Averre is a Reader and former Director of the Centre for Russian, European and Eurasian Studies, University of Birmingham, UK. He is a Russian foreign/security policy specialist with 25 years' experience in the field.

Richard Connolly is a Senior Lecturer at the Centre for Russian, European and Eurasian Studies, University of Birmingham, UK.

Lance Davies is a post-doctoral researcher in the School of Politics and International Relations, University of Nottingham.

Rilka Dragneva is Reader in Law, Development and Regional Integration, School of Law, University of Birmingham, UK.

Kostyantyn Fedorenko is a Junior Research Fellow at the Institute for Euro–Atlantic Cooperation in Kyiv, Ukraine.

Hiski Haukkala an Associate Professor of International Relations at the School of Management at the University of Tampere, Finland, a Special Adviser at the Unit for Policy Planning and Research at the Ministry for Foreign Affairs of Finland and a Visiting Professor at the College of Europe in Natolin, Warsaw. He has also worked at the Finnish Institute of International Affairs and the University of Turku.

Volodymyr Kulyk is Head Research Fellow at the Institute of Political and Ethnic Studies, National Academy of Sciences of Ukraine.

Olga Onuch (DPhil, Oxford) is an Assistant Professor (Lecturer) in Politics at the University of Manchester, UK, and is an Associate Member in Politics at Nuffield College, at the University of Oxford, UK.

Tatiana Romanova is an Associate Professor at St. Petersburg State University, Russia, since 2002, Jean Monnet Chair since 2011, and Director of the Jean Monnet Centre of Excellence since 2015.

Olena Rybiy is an analyst at the Civil Network OPORA and a Senior Lecturer at the National University of Kyiv-Mohyla Academy, Kyiv, Ukraine.

Gwendolyn Sasse is Professor of Comparative Politics in the Department of Politics and International Relations and the School of Interdisciplinary Area Studies at the University of Oxford, UK.

Marco Siddi is a Senior Research Fellow at the Finnish Institute of International Affairs, Finland, and Associate Researcher at the University of Cagliari, Italy.

Andreas Umland is a Senior Research Fellow at the Institute for Euro–Atlantic Cooperation, Kyiv, Ukraine.

Andrew Wilson is Professor in Ukrainian Studies at University College London, UK.

Kataryna Wolczuk is Professor of East European Politics at the Centre for Russian, European and Eurasian Studies, University of Birmingham, UK.

Introduction: The Ukraine Crisis and Post-Post-Cold War Europe

DEREK AVERRE & KATARYNA WOLCZUK

NOBODY COULD HAVE FORESEEN THAT THE TURMOIL WHICH erupted on the streets of Kyiv in late 2013—which became known as the Euromaidan—would soon lead to what has been regarded as the collapse of the post-Cold War regional order in the wider Europe. It bears remembering that the Euromaidan was essentially a domestic affair, reflecting the rejection by most Ukrainians of their corrupt and ineffective political elites, embodied in the person of President Viktor Yanukovych. However, Yanukovych's ignominious flight from Ukraine and the subsequent change of government in Kyiv triggered a sequence of events—the territorial annexation of Crimea by Russia and the war in the Donbas—the reverberations of which are likely to be felt in Europe and beyond for some time to come. These events have highlighted a fundamental shift, both in Ukraine's relationship with Russia and—with unpredictable implications for the future of European security—Russia's own relations with Europe. At this stage we can say with some certainty that the post-post-Cold War Europe[1] is upon us but it is unclear what kind of order will emerge from the current tensions. The profound domestic and international implications of these ongoing developments present a major challenge to scholars specialising in Russia and Eastern Europe.

Amidst fast-changing events we need to consider the longer-term perspective in order to contextualise developments, both in Ukraine's domestic politics and in its relations with Russia and Russia's relations with the EU. Like most newly independent states which emerged from the collapse of the USSR, Ukraine was largely *terra incognita* in the early 1990s. Apart from domestic politics, scholarly research focused on two aspects. The first was nationalism, identity and language issues (Kuzio & Wilson 1994; Arel 1996; Wilson 1996; Janmaat 1999; Kuzio 1998; Wanner 1998; Wolczuk 2000) as well as the ethnic, linguistic and regional

The guest co-editors gratefully acknowledge the financial contribution provided by the Centre for East European Language Based Area Studies (CEELBAS) and the University of Birmingham for a workshop held at the University of Birmingham to discuss drafts of the essays in this collection in March 2015.

[1]Michael Smith has referred to the 'post-post-post Cold War' period; in his view, the post-Cold War order was defined by the collapse of the Soviet Union and the predominance of the US, the post-post-Cold War order by recognition of the US's power limitations, and the post-post-post-Cold War order by 'the emergence of rising powers and their much more active (re-)engagement in world affairs' (Smith 2013, p. 660). However, within the confines of the European continent, we suggest that the annexation of Crimea and the war in Eastern Donbas may be seen as marking the end of the post-Cold War period in Europe.

diversity of Ukraine (Solchanyk 1994; Pirie 1996; Sasse 1996; Shulman 1998; Zhurzhenko 2002). Second, research on Ukraine's foreign policy in the first post-Soviet decade (D'Anieri 1995, 1997; Laba 1995; Larrabee 1996; Bukkvoll 1997; Garnett 1997; Moroney *et al.* 2002; Sherr 2002; Wolczuk 2003) demonstrated the extremely precarious position Ukraine occupied between two integrating blocs—the EU on the one hand, and Russia's projects to reintegrate in some form the Soviet successor states on the other. Greater interest in Ukraine's domestic politics was inspired by the 2004 Orange Revolution (Åslund & McFaul 2005; Wilson 2005; D'Anieri 2006). However, its failure to bring about lasting change led to diminishing interest in Ukrainian politics and foreign policy by the time Yanukovych came to power in 2010.

In similar fashion, Russia's policy towards its 'near abroad' (as it was then called) was studied extensively in the 1990s and early 2000s (Lester 1994; Lieven 1999; Bukkvoll 2001; Tsygankov 2001), but interest declined thereafter (with the exceptions of Dragneva and de Kort (2007), Dusseault (2007) and Malfliet *et al.* (2007)). This changed to an extent with Russia's intervention in Georgia over the latter's invasion of South Ossetia in 2008; still, more attention was paid to the security implications of Moscow's decision to intervene (Allison 2009) than to Russia's renewed push for integration (Dragneva & Wolczuk 2012, 2013; Vinokurov & Libman 2012). It should therefore come as no surprise that, while Ukraine's relations with Russia and its place in Russia-led regional integration projects lie at the root of the 2014 crisis, expertise on these topics had become rather scarce. Again, while Russia's relations with the EU had been extensively explored, relatively few scholars had examined Russia's and the EU's respective policies towards the 'common neighbourhood' (Averre 2009; Haukkala 2009, 2011; Zagorsky 2011; Moshes 2013) or the role of domestic Ukrainian politics in the country's relations with Russia and the EU (Gnedina & Sleptsova 2012; Kuzio 2012; Puglisi 2008; Wolczuk 2009).

This edited collection, drawing on contributions by scholars from across Europe who bring to bear their considerable expertise in various disciplinary fields, seeks to redress the gaps described above by offering a set of essays that, taken together, constitute a multifaceted, yet coherent, in-depth examination of the complex causes and consequences of the Ukraine crisis for domestic developments in Ukraine, Ukraine's relations with Russia and Russia's relations with Europe in the context of their common neighbourhood.[2]

The contributions fall into three broad sections. The first four articles focus on domestic developments in Ukraine, using extensive empirical research. Olga Onuch and Gwendolyn Sasse examine in considerable depth the dynamics of the Euromaidan protests. Based on the *EuroMaidan Protest Participant Survey*, they trace the actors, claims and frames of each phase in the protest cycle. They emphasise the diversity of actors, and the multi-dimensional, shifting and contingent nature of the protests in the build-up towards the violent denouement of the Maidan. Volodymyr Kulyk offers a subtle analysis of the changes in Ukrainian national identity that have become apparent as a result of the Euromaidan and Russia's policy towards Ukraine. Drawing on data from focus groups and public opinion surveys, he argues that national identity in Ukraine is expressed in a much more overt way and is accompanied by an increased sense of alienation from Russia, although the embrace of Ukrainian nationalism is not unconditional. Kostiantyn Fedorenko, Olena Rybiy and Andreas Umland investigate the evolution of the Ukrainian party system, assessing the changes since the Euromaidan protests

---

[2]Among individual empirical contributions to scholarship on the Ukraine crisis see Burke-White (2014), Allison (2014), Freedman (2014a, 2014b, 2015), Wilson (2014), Sakwa (2015a, 2015b), Tsygankov (2015), Yost (2015) and Forsberg (2016).

in the context of longer-term trends. Drawing on comprehensive empirical data they argue that, despite notable advances in democratisation as a result of the revolutionary events of 2013–2014, the essential features of Ukraine's party system have not changed: the legislative, ideological and organisational foundations of the Ukrainian party-political landscape and parliamentary politics remain fragile and volatile. In the final contribution in this section, Andrew Wilson assesses the role of various factors in the conflict in eastern Ukraine. He suggests that historical and identity factors, economic problems and alienation from the new government in Kyiv form only part of the explanation accounting for the eruption of separatism in the Donbas in the spring of 2014 and draws attention to the effects of 'Russian sponsorship' and the role of local elites in supporting the separatist agenda.

The second section, comprising two shorter and three full-length essays, takes us into the international dimension of the Ukraine conflict. Hiski Haukkala charts the evolution of the EU's policy towards its eastern neighbourhood and the causes of the rupture in relations between the EU and Russia. Marco Siddi highlights the importance of the Germany–Russia relationship and the former's continuing efforts to engage the latter in a constructive political and trade relationship. Rilka Dragneva and Kataryna Wolczuk interrogate Ukraine's policy towards Russia, with a particular focus on Ukraine's reluctant yet continual participation in integration projects. They explain why and how Ukraine reacted to, and engaged with, Russia-led projects in terms of balancing economic dependence and legal commitment. Derek Averre investigates the motivation behind Russia's intervention in Ukraine and the West's response to it, considering the implications in terms of security governance of Russia's apparent defection from the post-Cold War European security order. Lance Davies offers a close analysis of Russia's role in the Donbas conflict in the context of Moscow's broader approach to conflict management and the complex security logic underpinning Russian thinking.

The third and final section contains two essays in political economy. Richard Connolly assesses the costs imposed by the West's economic statecraft, in the form of sanctions and trade restrictions, on Russia, and the impact of Russia's response on its domestic political economy in the context of other economic factors. Tatiana Romanova examines the qualitative changes in the EU–Russia trade relationship resulting from the sanctions regime, highlighting the increasing poverty of governmental and transnational relations and the negative impact in terms of EU–Russia trade cooperation.

The collection of essays benefits from a time lapse of over two years since the Euromaidan.[3] In that period, we suggest, certain trends have become clear, notably the shift in Ukrainian national identity analysed by Kulyk and (in the context of the Euromaidan dynamic) Onuch and Sasse; the limits of the EU's transformative project in its eastern neighbourhood, as highlighted by Haukkala; the incompatible rationales of the EU and Russia-led integration projects, examined by Dragneva and Wolczuk; and the drift towards de-modernisation in Russia arising from the breakdown of governmental and economic relations with Europe described by Connolly and Romanova. In contrast, other aspects of domestic politics and foreign policies remain fraught with unpredictability and ambiguity. Fedorenko, Rybiy and Umland show that Ukraine's domestic political environment remains fragile; Siddi reflects on the unresolved dilemmas in Germany's traditional *Ostpolitik* towards Russia; and Averre and Davies both focus on the vacuum in security governance in the eastern neighbourhood

---

[3]We refer here to the protests which took place from November 2013 to February 2014 in Ukraine as the Euromaidan, as this is the most common term used in the English-language academic work, whereas in Ukraine they are increasingly referred to as the Revolution of Dignity.

stemming from Russia's highly ambivalent approach to the European rules-based order and the failure to institutionalise pan-European security. And finally, Wilson brings our attention back to the crucible of the Ukraine conflict, the resolution of which may be a long time in coming. We hope that by providing in-depth analysis on their respective subjects, all of the essays in this collection raise theoretical and empirical questions which will stimulate further scholarly enquiry.

References

Allison, R. (2009) 'The Russian Case for Military Intervention in Georgia: International Law, Norms, and Political Calculation', *European Security*, 18, 2.

Allison, R. (2014) 'Russian "Deniable" Intervention in Ukraine: How and Why Russia Broke the Rules', *International Affairs*, 90, 6.

Arel, D. (1996) 'A Lurking Cascade of Assimilation in Kiev?', *Post-Soviet Affairs*, 12, 1.

Åslund, A. & McFaul, M. (eds) (2005) *Revolution in Orange: The Origins of Ukraine's Democratic Breakthrough* (Washington, DC, Carnegie Endowment for International Peace).

Averre, D. (2009) 'Competing Rationalities: Russia, the EU and the "Shared Neighbourhood"', *Europe-Asia Studies*, 61, 10.

Bukkvoll, T. (1997) *Ukraine and European Security* (London, Royal Institute of International Affairs).

Bukkvoll, T. (2001) 'Off the Cuff Politics: Explaining Russia's Lack of a Ukraine Strategy', *Europe-Asia Studies*, 53, 8.

Burke-White, W. W. (2014) 'Crimea and the International Legal Order', *Survival*, 56, 4.

D'Anieri, P. (1995) 'Interdependence and Sovereignty in the Ukrainian–Russian Relationship', *European Security*, 4, 4, Winter.

D'Anieri, P. (1997) 'Dilemmas of Interdependence: Autonomy, Prosperity, and Sovereignty in Ukraine's Russia Policy', *Problems of Post-Communism*, 44, 1.

D'Anieri, P. (2006) *Understanding Ukrainian Politics: Power, Politics, and Institutional Design* (Armonk, NY, M.E. Sharpe).

Dragneva, R. & de Kort, J. (2007) 'Legal Regime for Free Trade in the CIS', *International and Comparative Law Quarterly*, 56, 2.

Dragneva, R. & Wolczuk, K. (2012) *Russia, the Eurasian Customs Union and the EU: Cooperation, Stagnation or Rivalry?*, Chatham House Briefing Paper REP BP 2012/01, August, available at: https://www.chathamhouse.org/sites/files/chathamhouse/public/Research/Russia%20and%20Eurasia/0812bp_dragnevawolczuk.pdf, accessed 4 April 2016.

Dragneva, R. & Wolczuk, K. (2013) *Eurasian Economic Integration: Law, Policy, and Politics* (Cheltenham, Edward Elgar).

Dusseault, D. (ed.) (2007) *The CIS: Form or Substance?* (Helsinki, Aleksanteri Institute).

Forsberg, T. (2016) 'From *Ostpolitik* to "Frostpolitik"? Merkel, Putin and German Foreign Policy towards Russia', *International Affairs*, 92, 1.

Freedman, L. (2014a) 'Ukraine and the Art of Limited War', *Survival*, 56, 6.

Freedman, L. (2014b) 'Ukraine and the Art of Crisis Management', *Survival*, 56, 3.

Freedman, L. (2015) 'Ukraine and the Art of Exhaustion', *Survival*, 57, 5.

Garnett, S. (1997) *Keystone in the Arch: Ukraine in the New Political Geography of Central and Eastern Europe* (Washington, DC, Carnegie Endowment for International Peace).

Gnedina, E. & Sleptsova, E. (2012) *Eschewing Choice: Ukraine's Strategy on Russia and the EU*, CEPS Working Document, No. 360, January.

Haukkala, H. (2009) 'From Zero-Sum to Win–Win? The Russian Challenge to the EU's Eastern Neighbourhood Policies', *SIEPS European Policy Analysis* 12–2009 (SIEPS, Stockholm).

Haukkala, H. (2011) 'The European Union as a Regional Normative Hegemon: The Case of European Neighbourhood Policy', in Whitman, R. (ed.) *Power Europe: Empirical and Theoretical Perspectives* (Basingstoke & New York, NY, Palgrave Macmillan).

Janmaat, J. (1999) 'Language Politics in Education and the Responses of the Russians in Ukraine', *Nationalities Papers*, 27, 3.

Kuzio, T. (ed.) (1998) *Contemporary Ukraine. Dynamics of Post-Soviet Transformation* (Armonk, NY & London, M.E. Sharpe).

Kuzio, T. (2012) 'Russianization of Ukrainian National Security Policy under Viktor Yanukovych', *Journal of Slavic Military Studies*, 25, 4.

Kuzio, T. & Wilson, A. (1994) *Ukraine: Perestroika to Independence* (London, Macmillan).

Laba, R. (1995) 'The Russian–Ukrainian Conflict: State, Nation and Identity', *European Security*, 4, 3.

Larrabee, S. (1996) 'Ukraine's Balancing Act', *Survival*, 38, 2.

Lester, J. (1994) 'Russian Political Attitudes to Ukrainian Independence', *Journal of Communist Studies and Transition Politics*, 10, 2.

Lieven, A. (1999) *Ukraine and Russia: A Fraternal Rivalry* (Washington, DC, US Institute of Peace Press).

Malfliet, K., Verpoest, L. & Vinokurov, E. (eds) (2007) *The CIS, the EU and Russia: The Challenges of Integration* (Basingstoke, Palgrave Macmillan).

Moroney, D., Kuzio, T. & Molchanov, M. (eds) (2002) *Ukrainian Foreign and Security Policy* (Westport, CT, Praeger).

Moshes, A. (2013) 'The Eurasian Customs Union and The Future of Russian–Ukrainian Relations', Paper presented at the 5th East Asia Conference for Slavic Eurasian Studies, Osaka, 9 August.

Pirie, P. (1996) 'National Identity and Politics in Southern and Eastern Ukraine', *Europe-Asia Studies*, 48, 7.

Puglisi, R. (2008) 'A Window to the World? Oligarchs and Foreign Policy in Ukraine', in Fischer, S. (ed.) *Ukraine. Quo vadis?*, Chaillot Paper No. 108 (Paris, EU Institute for Security Studies).

Sakwa, R. (2015a) 'The Death of Europe? Continental Fates after Ukraine', *International Affairs*, 91, 3.

Sakwa, R. (2015b) *Frontline Ukraine: Crisis in the Borderlands* (London, I.B. Tauris).

Sasse, G. (1996) 'The Crimean Issue', *Journal of Communist Studies and Transition Politics*, 12, 1.

Sherr, J. (2002) 'Ukraine and Russia: A Geopolitical Turn?', in Lewis, A. (ed.) *The EU and Ukraine: Neighbours, Friends, Partners?* (London, The Federal Trust).

Shulman, S. (1998) 'Competing versus Complementary Identities: Ukrainian–Russian Relations and the Loyalties of Russians in Ukraine', *Nationalities Papers*, 26, 4.

Smith, M. (2013) 'Beyond the Comfort Zone: Internal Crisis and External Challenge in the European Union's Response to Rising Powers', *International Affairs*, 89, 3.

Solchanyk, R. (1994) 'The Politics of State-Building: Centre-Periphery Relations in Post-Soviet Ukraine', *Europe-Asia Studies*, 46, 1.

Tsygankov, A. (2001) *Pathways after Empire: National Identities and Foreign Economic Policies in the Post-Soviet World* (Oxford, Rowman & Littlefield).

Tsygankov, A. (2015) 'Vladimir Putin's Last Stand: The Sources of Russia's Ukraine Policy', *Post-Soviet Affairs*, 31, 4.

Vinokurov, E. & Libman, A. (2012) *Eurasian Integration: Challenges of Transcontinental Regionalism* (Basingstoke, Palgrave Macmillan).

Wanner, C. (1998) *Burden of Dreams: History and Identity in Post-Soviet Ukraine* (University Park, PA, Pennsylvania State University Press).

Wilson, A. (1996) *Ukrainian Nationalism in the 1990s. A Minority Faith* (Cambridge, Cambridge University Press).

Wilson, A. (2005) *Ukraine's Orange Revolution* (Yale, CT, Yale University Press).

Wilson, A. (2014) *Ukraine Crisis. What it Means for the West* (New Haven, CT & London, Yale University Press).

Wolczuk, K. (2000) 'History, Europe and the "National Idea": The Official Narrative of National Identity in Ukraine', *Nationalities Papers*, 28, 4.

Wolczuk, K. (2009), 'Implementation without Coordination: The Impact of the EU Conditionality on Ukraine under the European Neighbourhood Policy', *Europe-Asia Studies*, 61, 2.

Wolczuk, R. (2003) *Ukraine's Foreign and Security Policy, 1991–2000* (London & New York, NY, Routledge Curzon).

Yost, D. S. (2015) 'The Budapest Memorandum and Russia's Intervention in Ukraine', *International Affairs*, 91, 3.

Zagorsky, A. (2011) 'Eastern Partnership from the Russian Perspective', *International Politics and Society*, 3 (Berlin, Friedrich Ebert Stiftung).

Zhurzhenko, T. (2002) 'Language and Nation-Building. Dilemmas of Language Politics in Contemporary Ukraine', *Transit*, 21.

The Maidan in Movement: Diversity and the Cycles of Protest

OLGA ONUCH & GWENDOLYN SASSE

Abstract

The Maidan protests provide us with insights into Ukrainian society and the dynamics of mobilisation more generally. Based on the *EuroMaidan Protest Participant Survey*, on-site rapid interviews with protesters, interviews with politicians, activists and journalists, and focus groups with ordinary citizens and activists, this essay maps the actors, claims and frames of each phase in the protest cycle. It highlights the diversity of actors and the inability of activists and party leaders to coordinate as the central features of the protests. Our analysis reveals the fluid and contingent nature of cleavages commonly portrayed as fixed and politically salient.

THE 2013–2014 MAIDAN1 IN UKRAINE MARKED THE BEGINNING of a dramatic cycle of political mobilisation and escalation. What started out as a peaceful mass protest of mostly 'ordinary citizens'2 turned into violent clashes, followed by the ouster of President Viktor Yanukovych and an interim government; it precipitated the annexation of Crimea by Russia, Russia-backed separatist mobilisation and war in the Donbas,3 and the most serious political standoff between Russia and the West since the end of the Cold War. The latter events in this chain tend to divert attention away from the Maidan itself. This essay offers two correctives: first, it returns to the beginning and offers a detailed analysis of the Maidan as a defining moment and lens onto Ukrainian politics and society. Second, it breaks with the initial focus on the Maidan as an exceptionally violent case of protest driven by narrow ethno-linguistic, nationalist or regional demands. This essay contributes to the growing literature on different aspects of the Maidan protest mobilisation (Bohdanova 2014; Etling 2014; Ryabchuk 2014; Onuch 2015a, 2015b; Onuch & Martsenyuk 2013), and research focusing more generally on the 'Ukrainian crisis' (Sakwa 2014; Wilson 2014; Hale *et al.* 2015; Judah 2015; Larrabee *et al.* 2015; Menon & Rumer 2015).

1Commonly referred to as the Euromaidan in its early stages.

2The terms 'ordinary Ukrainians' and 'ordinary citizens' are used by the authors to denote the non-activist, non-politicised citizens of the polity who tend to be generally disengaged from politics (though they might vote in elections), have not been active members of a Social Movement Organisation, and have not consistently participated in previous protests. Included are individuals of all socio-economic, employment and education backgrounds. The term 'ordinary citizens' (adapted from Onuch (2014a, 2015a)) draws on Bermeo's use of the term 'ordinary people' (Bermeo 2003).

3The Donbas includes Luhans'k and Donets'k *oblasti* in Ukraine.

Following the announcement of the anti-protest laws on 16 January 2014, millions of 'ordinary' Ukrainians watched live transmissions of the unfolding protests in disbelief, as their historic capital was set ablaze in order to prevent the regime militia (*Berkut*) from clearing the Maidan protest site.[4] The presence of violent repertoires marked a significant departure in the contemporary history of social mobilisation in Ukraine since the 1960s and certainly since 1991 (Onuch & Sasse 2014; Onuch 2014a, 2015b). Images of violence and rightwing radicalism are now a central element of the collective memory of the Maidan among both protesters and non-participants. Similarly, media coverage and scholarly analysis have focused on extreme flashpoints and the 'wall of fire', emblematic of the last stages of the protests.

Focusing predominantly on violent moments, however, overlooks important dimensions of the protests that are significant for explaining the violent turn. As this essay demonstrates, the violent denouement of the Maidan overshadows two key characteristics of this protest, namely its inherent diversity, which includes a range of different actors with varied claims and grievances, and the spatial and temporal diffusion of protest events and repertoires.

Tracing this multi-layered diversity distinctive of the protests breaks through the perceived linearity of the build-up to violence, while providing us with the necessary building blocks to explain why a violent repertoire became an option and a reality. The contentious politics literature helps us to identify several variables central to the mobilisation process: the triggers, resources and political opportunity structures (Kitschelt 1986; Goldstone & Tilly 2001), the composition of the protesters (Gould 1993; Diani & McAdam 2003), protesters' grievances, claims, frames and repertoires (Snow & Benford 1992; Della Porta 2013) and the location of the protests (Bohstedt 1994; Andrews & Biggs 2006).

We argue that only detailed process-tracing can unlock the causal dynamics within and across the stages of the protest cycle. Protest waves are in constant movement and evolve: one phase in the process critically shapes the next. The issues and events that trigger the initial protest may not be the same as the ones that expand and sustain a protest movement over time, or tip it into violence. Similarly, the actors identified as pivotal during one stage of the protests can alter throughout the protest cycle.

We employ existing theories of protest mobilisation, complemented by the scholarship on political preferences and behaviour in Ukraine, in order to provide a detailed exploration of the Maidan. Our analysis is based on original primary survey and rapid interview data of protest participant perceptions collected during the protest events (Onuch & Martsenyuk 2013), and is triangulated with focus groups with 'ordinary' citizens and activists as well as elite interviews conducted after the end of the mobilisation.

In this essay we first contextualise the Maidan. Second, we draw hypotheses for our analysis from the contentious politics literature, in particular the idea of protest cycles and its emphasis on structural variables enabling protest on the one hand (resources and political opportunity structures) and motivations and the discourse and means of mobilisation (grievances, claims, rights frames and repertoires) on the other. Third, the literature on political behaviour in Ukraine, with its emphasis on ethno-linguistic and regional identities, encourages us to probe the salience of these identities during a period of mass mobilisation. Fourth, our original multi-source data offer a fine-grained empirical picture of the composition, motivations and locations of the protesters throughout the stages of the protest cycle and a basis to test our hypotheses.

---

[4]Civic Sector activists focus group 2, Kyiv, 28 August 2014.

Our central finding concerns the multi-dimensional and shifting diversity characterising the Maidan. While diversity is inherent in most protests, including in previous mass mobilisation in Ukraine,[5] the degree of diversity and its effects on each stage in the protest cycle, make this case distinctive. A diverse set of actors, claims and levels of self-organisation during each stage of the protest cycle was augmented by the diffusion of small and medium-size protest events across the country. Crucially we find that neither the regime nor the party-based political opposition and activists were able to fully comprehend or manage this inherent diversity. Their misjudgements, in turn, created opportunities for the rise of radical voices and violent repertoires. Finally, we find that contrary to a widespread perception, the Maidan calls into question the salience and stability of ethno-linguistic and regional identities.

The Maidan in context

Mass mobilisation by 'ordinary' citizens is a rare event, especially if it lasts for a prolonged period of time. The protests, first called the Euromaidan, began on 21 November 2013. The mass protests held in the *Maidan Nezalezhnosty* (Independence Square) in Kyiv city centre (from 1 December 2013 onwards referred to as the Maidan), drew to a close around 21 and 22 February. Indirectly, the Maidan lives on: it has been frequently invoked as both a base of support for the current government and a potential veto player monitoring its action.[6]

Mass protests signal the breakdown of normal politics constrained by the institutional rules of the game. They put political regimes to the test and highlight not only socio-political fault-lines but also cross-cutting cleavages that may be less visible in 'normal' times. From a comparative politics perspective the Maidan makes for a particularly interesting case study. It moves the conceptual and empirical discussion of protest in Eastern Europe beyond the 'Colour Revolutions', a model that centred on electoral fraud and the diffusion of activist technologies in competitive authoritarian regimes (Levitsky & Way 2006; Beissinger 2007; Bunce & Wolchik 2011). Thus, the Maidan is both an episode with specific features—in particular compared to previous peaceful Ukrainian protests—and a case that fits into the wider comparative literature on protest beyond Eastern Europe.

The trigger of the Maidan protests—the decision by President Yanukovych not to sign the EU Association Agreement in November 2013—was an unusual one. Unlike in the cases of electoral fraud, as in the Orange Revolution, for which there was an obvious political response—the re-run of the elections—there was no immediate institutional or policy response to hopes of better living standards and living in 'a normal European country'.[7]

The Maidan also unfolded against the backdrop of the 2004 Orange Revolution and its aftermath: societal disenchantment about a stalled reform process, caused in part by personal rivalries between the leaders of the Orange Revolution, Viktor Yushchenko and Yulia Tymoshenko, the 2010 comeback of Viktor Yanukovych, and country-wide dissatisfaction

---

[5]See Beissinger (2013) on the Orange Revolution.

[6]As exhibited in protests by *Hromadskyi Sektor* (Civic Sector) and *Pravyi Sektor* (Right Sector)—in front of the Parliament and Presidential Administration respectively in July 2015—demanding the launch of a commission looking into the violence of the Maidan, and further action by the President in the east of the country. Both Social Movement Organisations used the language of 'the Maidan holding politicians accountable' (author's participant observation and informal discussion with Civic Sector activists who participated in protest events on 8, 10, 12 and 13 July 2015).

[7]Often mentioned in initial rapid interviews and discussions with activists, 26 November–1 December 2013.

about corruption prepared the ground for protest mobilisation in 2014. However, even the combination of an acute economic crisis and the memory of 2004 did not prove sufficient to generate a new wave of mass mobilisation for nearly a decade, thereby illustrating that mass protests require an environment that projects a political alternative (Beissinger & Sasse 2013). In interviews, activists explained that following the 2010 election of President Yanukovych, Social Movement Organisations began organising frequent small protest events in reaction to constitutional reforms, language law changes and the imprisonment of opposition politicians. At the same time, there was little coordination among activists who were also struggling to motivate the general population to join in.[8] Moreover, at the outset of the Maidan, Yanukovych was unpopular across the country, and there was also a country-wide rise in dissatisfaction with growing levels of corruption.[9] Thus, the roots of the 2013–2014 grievances were not partisan, ideological or even regional *per se*.

Framework for analysis

The study of protest in Eastern Europe

Mass protest is perhaps particularly perplexing in Central and Eastern Europe where citizens have demonstrated low levels of engagement (Pop-Eleches & Tucker 2014) and what has been described as 'patience' (Greskovits 1998). However, there has been a gradual increase in scholarly work on post-communist protests (Mueller 1997; Ekiert & Kubik 2001; Beissinger 2002; Osa 2003; Robertson 2010; Greene 2014). Our essay contributes to this growing literature by providing a nuanced understanding of the Maidan as a significant case of protest mobilisation.

Although research focusing specifically on activism and protest in Ukraine has also included studies of the Ukrainian labour movement (Marples 1991; Crowley 1997), women's movements (Martsenyuk 2005; Hrycak 2006; Phillips 2008; Zychowicz 2011) and dissident activism (Zakharov 2004), it has been overshadowed by analyses of the 2004 Orange Revolution. For the most part, this research has focused on the role of regional diffusion as well as elite level explanations of the 2004 protest (Wilson 2006; Bunce & Wolchik 2007; McFaul 2007; Nikolayenko 2007; Way 2008; Beissinger 2011). More recently, scholars have emphasised the micro-foundations of protest, analysing protester perceptions, preferences and behaviour (Tucker 2007; Beissinger 2013; Meirowitz & Tucker 2013; Onuch 2014a). Our study aims to make an empirical contribution to this developing literature as we employ survey data of individual protest participants' views and behaviour collected on-site as the protests unfolded. To our knowledge, it is the first study of its kind in the case of Ukraine.

The contentious politics literature

To date the discussion about the Maidan has concentrated on specific moments, in particular the violent ones. Employing the contentious politics literature with its longer time horizon allows us to put the Maidan in comparative perspective. Specifically, Tarrow's work on protest cycles—also known as 'cycles of contention'—provides a useful framework for tracing the

[8] Authors' interview with anonymous Civic Sector activist 6, Kyiv, 26 August 2014.
[9] See, Razumkov Sociological Polls 2009, 2011–2013, Razumkov Centre, available at: http://www.uceps.org/eng/poll.php?poll_id=90, accessed 29 July 2015.

political dynamics surrounding the Maidan (Tarrow 1993, 2011). According to Tarrow, the cycle of contention begins with a rapid diffusion of mobilisation as existing Social Movement Organisations create political opportunities for citizens to join in. This is followed by an innovation and expansion in the forms of contention as well as shifts in the collective action frames and protest discourse. The next phase is characterised by a coexistence of organised and unorganised civic engagement leading up to a period of heightened interaction between the party in power and the party in opposition. At each stage, the use of violent repertoires by activists or violent repression by the regime can shift the rules of the game, namely the forms of contention, collective action frames and protest discourse. This idea of the protest cycle provides us with our first hypothesis:

> H1. The Maidan follows a typical cycle of contention, and at each stage the use of violence on behalf of the regime or the protesters shifts the 'rules of the protest game'.

Structuralist accounts of mobilisation by McAdam *et al.* (2001) and Melucci (1996), among others, have discerned a difference between the role of established networks and social ties (organisations, associations, clubs) and opportunity structures (crises, divisions within the regime or the political elite more broadly, particular types of institutional arrangements), which can foster or inhibit collective identity and action. Tilly and Tarrow (2007) stress the need for pre-existing activist networks to be operational prior to any mass participation. They further explain that collaboration between these activist networks and the politico-economic elite can increase opportunities for successful mobilisation. Our second hypothesis draws on this role of protest legacies:

> H2. The experiences of recent mass mobilisation (2004) and continued smaller protest events, in particular pre-existing activist networks, facilitate and sustain mass mobilisation in 2013 and 2014.

Scholars have identified the strength and density of social ties among individuals (and organisations) as a mechanism that can help bridge different networks and cleavages in society and thereby support the mobilisation process (Gould 1991, 1993). Goldstone and Tilly (2001) and Koopmans (1999) explain that while the opposition elite (politicians and their financiers) can provide security and resources to activists and Social Movement Organisations, thereby strengthening their position *vis-à-vis* the regime, activists tend to be better equipped to connect and communicate with, and mobilise 'ordinary' citizens by bridging networks and legitimising protest events. However, when Social Movement Organisations or the political opposition are not well coordinated and are instead characterised by internal divisions, they can be perceived as weak in the eyes of the regime, making it more likely for the regime to use repression (Goldstone & Tilly 2001; Carey 2006). This leads us to our third hypothesis:

> H3. Internal divisions within Social Movement Organisations or the political opposition and their inability to coordinate their activity create a space for regime repression.

The literature on contentious politics also highlights the significance of different sets of actors in shaping the trajectory and 'success' of mass mobilisation (Bohstedt 1994; Andrews & Biggs 2006). Arguably, the broader the protest coalition, the more likely protest participants are to be observed in the streets (Gould 1993; Beissinger 2013). In order to differentiate among protest participants, and among different protest events, the literature points to the need to identify grievances (Opp 1988), claims (McAdam *et al*. 2001), the use of rights frames (Benford & Snow 2000), and protest tactics or repertoires (Della Porta 2013) throughout the different stages of the mobilisation process. While some authors have highlighted a divergence in grievances and claims in connection with the Maidan, most notably socio-economic (Onuch 2015a), foreign policy (Katchanovski 2014) and ethno-linguistic grievances (Ishchenko 2014), continuity and shifts throughout the process have not been analysed systematically. Our fourth hypothesis focuses on this diversity of actors and claims:

> H4. A diversity of actors or societal cleavages involved in the protests translates into a divergence of claims that can impede a collective identity and coordination during mobilisation.

The literature on protest points to two factors that can bring diverse actors or cleavages together in one protest mobilisation and help develop a common collective identity: key actors with bridging capacity (Gould 1991, 1993), as noted above; and unifying 'mobilisational frames' that combine diverse grievances (Snow & Benford 1992). Snow and Benford argue that mass mobilisation is more likely to occur when there is 'frame alignment' between the frames projected by Social Movement Organisations as 'carriers' and 'transmitters' of frames and the pre-existing frames of the majority of the potential participants (Benford & Snow 2000). Moreover, a crisis context can clarify and enhance an interpretive frame and facilitate a coalition of divergent participants (Snow *et al*. 1986). 'Rights' frames are seen as most successful in mobilising diverse groups when they can focus on universally accepted norms such as fundamental civic or human rights (Snow *et al*. 1986). Our fifth hypothesis thus, focuses on frame alignment:

> H5. Regime repression creates an opportunity for activists and opposition leaders to frame mobilisation as a defence of basic civic and human rights and build a coalition of different constituencies and claims.

The literature on political preferences and behaviour in Ukraine

Several of our hypotheses engage with the likelihood of building a coalition or collective identity that channels and sustains protest (Polletta & Jasper 2001). The search for the micro-foundations of preferences and behaviour in Ukraine has resulted in a tendency to resort to types of assumed identities rather than considering their existence and stability over time as open-ended questions. Over the last two decades, there has been much debate about whether and how political identities and behaviour in Ukraine are shaped by regional and ethno-linguistic cleavages (O'Loughlin 2001; Sasse 2010; Frye 2014). At least four intersecting divisions have been discussed: a regional divide (between 'east' and 'west' or distinctions between four macro-regions: centre, east, west, south) often illustrated by electoral maps (Birch 2000; Kubicek 2000; Barrington & Herron 2004; D'Anieri 2011; Osipian & Osipian 2012); a linguistic divide between Ukrainophones and Russophones (Arel 1995; Wolczuk 2006; Colton 2011; Kulyk 2011); an ethnic divide between Ukrainians and Russians (Arel 1993; Bremmer 1994; Beissinger 1998; Hale 2008; Shkolnikov 2012; Rampton 2014); and regional identities based on distinct historical legacies of the Austro–Hungarian, Russian and Ottoman empires (Darden & Grzymala-Busse 2006). Identity cleavages are generally portrayed as the best predictors of political preferences and behaviour (Hesli *et al.* 1998; Haran 2001; Riabchuk 2002; D'Anieri 2006). However, we still do not know much about how such identities are formed and whether and how they shape political patterns, including protest behaviour. Our data present a first step towards understanding the salience and formation of different identities as expressed during a period of intense mobilisation. We consciously avoid studying the Maidan through a conventional regional or ethno-linguistic lens in order to establish which cleavages and identities prove salient to the protesters themselves, thus resulting in the sixth hypothesis:

> H6. An episode of mass mobilisation demonstrates the salience of societal cleavages and political identities.

Methodology

We address our six hypotheses by employing Tarrow's (1993) theory and break down the Maidan protest cycle into distinct phases of mobilisation. For each phase we identify the key actors, political opportunity structures, actors, grievances and claims, and mechanisms of coordination (or the lack thereof). Our empirical analysis is based on original data.[10] The first wave of data collection consisted of an on-site survey of, and rapid on-site interviews with, protesters between 26 November 2013 and 16 January 2014 in Kyiv. During this period, researchers also took digital photos of slogans and posters held by protesters.

Survey sample

The *EuroMaidan Protest Participant Survey* (EPPS) was conducted among protesters on the *Maidan Nezalezhnosty* over several days between 26 November 2013 and 10 January 2014.[11] In total 1,475 protesters were surveyed by canvassers. The data presented in this essay refer to the final and updated dataset that includes 1,263 imputed questionnaires (covering the period of 28 November–27 December 2013).[12] To our knowledge, this is the only multi-day and the most representative survey of protesters before and after the regime repression on 30 November. Other surveys only capture data following the turn to violence and were collected on weekends (see Appendix 1 for a short description of the questionnaire).

---

[10]Collected by Onuch and her team of 20 research assistants from the National University of Kyiv Mohyla Academy and Taras Shevchenko University in Kyiv.

[11]While the EPPS team attempted to collect data at scheduled and regular intervals, canvassers had the right to leave the protest site when feeling unsafe or uncomfortable. Supervisors could also call off or suspend surveying if they saw any dangers or if the quality of the survey was compromised in any way.

[12]Due to the nature of conducting surveys during times of mass protest and crisis, there were several issues with imputation of the survey and with its delivery by courier or post. Thus, we only report data imputed by our research team for which we have questionnaires. Despite all due diligence, the context in which the survey was conducted made it impossible to guard against missing data and the possibility of preference falsification associated with repressive regimes (Kuran 1997). Other types of data were collected in order to triangulate the survey findings.

Rapid interviews

Rapid interviews were conducted by two members of the research team between 27 November 2013 and 16 January 2014. The protesters were asked up to five questions the answers to which were digitally or manually recorded on-site (see Appendix 2 for the questions). These rapid interviews allowed protesters to describe their participation in their own words, and provide a comparative reference point for later in the survey interview and focus group data.

Elite interviews and focus groups

During a second wave of data collection from January 2014 to August 2015, 68 interviews were conducted with activists, journalists and politicians (including both opposition members and regime insiders, see Table A2 in the Appendix) as well as three focus groups with activists and six focus groups with 'ordinary' citizens.[13] These original data have been further triangulated with activists' and journalists' archives, documents and video footage (see Table A3 in the Appendix). Due to the on-going sensitive nature of the crisis in Ukraine, interviewees have been anonymised.

The Maidan protest cycle

Following Tarrow (1993) and our first hypothesis, our process-tracing has led us to identify six distinct phases of the Maidan protest cycle. In our analysis of these phases below, we highlight the changing patterns of the mobilisation process in terms of the participants, their motivations and actions. Most importantly, we elucidate the diversity of protesters throughout the entire Maidan protest cycle. This diversity, we argue, is the key characteristic of the Maidan that explains both its scope and longevity, but also the inherent difficulties to channel and control it.

Phase 1 (21–30 November): creating political opportunities for citizens

The Maidan mobilisation began in the evening of 21 November. According to Tarrow (1993), in the first phase of the protest cycle, we expect to observe the development of political opportunities for engagement. Furthermore, in line with hypothesis 2 drawn from social mobilisation theory we expect pre-existing Social Movement Organisation networks and past protesters to become activated and activists and opposition to coordinate their activity to mobilise 'ordinary citizens'. Our data reveal four aspects that influenced the first phase and the subsequent trajectory of the Maidan mobilisation process: first, the political opportunity structure of President Yanukovych's policy shift on the EU Association Agreement was one to which even experienced activists and political opposition leaders were not prepared to react to; second, Yanukovych's violation of an electoral promise that centred around a foreign policy claim was difficult to frame as a coherent collective protest identity; third, both activist and political opposition networks proved to be not as organised and capable of coordinating or collaborating as in 2004; and fourth, the key elite players—from experienced activists, leaders

[13]Two activist focus groups were conducted with Civic Sector activists (mixed gender and age) and one was conducted with *Samo Oborona* activists (men only). The 'ordinary citizen' focus groups were composed of a random group of individuals who listed themselves at the Civic Sector coordination and information booth (as potential volunteers/helpers or just to receive information), during the Euromaidan (and thus, can be considered Euromaidan participants but not activists); the researchers aimed for a mix of age groups and genders.

of the formal political opposition, to regime representatives—seriously underestimated the broader societal discontent with Yanukovych's regime across many constituencies and thus, were misguided in their reaction to and framing of the protest events.

The initial protest began within hours of the announcement that Yanukovych would not sign the Association Agreement with the EU.[14] Most accounts describe activists and journalists taking to Facebook, personal blogs and online news sites simultaneously in response to this event. A long-time activist explained that these Social Movement Organisation 'leaders ... have a lot to say, writing mini-essays on the internet, but ... no clear agenda for action'.[15] In interviews, activists frequently described their frustration about their coordination problems. One activist voiced his concerns that 'although everyone was "posting", "sharing" and "liking", we saw no real action', explaining that the activists were faced with a collective action problem.[16] Social media provided a portal for rapid information exchange between divergent Social Movement Organisation networks and individual activists on 21 November, but, as explained by Civic Sector activists, the sudden opportunity for revolution 'caught ... [them] by surprise ... [they] had been preparing for the next election'.[17] Initial online posts, corroborated by activist interviews, point to the fact that activists and journalists were struggling to frame the grievances so that they would resonate with a broader public. Their posts focused on the European trajectory of Ukraine and the increasingly corrupt and authoritarian nature of the Yanukovych regime. Some public figures like Mustafa Nayem were able to bridge the two issues by linking them to a civic 'responsibility to act' (Nayem 2014), but the general discourse focused on Ukraine–EU relations. The most typical phrases used by the activists and journalists in their posts and in speeches were 'We want a European Ukraine', 'Yanukovych must sign the Association Agreement' and 'Ukraine is Europe' (*Ukraiina tse Evropa*).

The gradually growing calls for action included posts on the *Korespondent* website by Yuriy Andreyev and on Facebook by Ihor Lutsenko, Mustafa Nayem,[18] among other well-known figures, all urging their friends and followers not to simply 'like' their posts but to assemble on the Maidan between 9 and 10.30pm that evening (Nayem 2014).[19] As explained by activists, Nayem's personalised message benefitted from using a paid service offered by Facebook to 'promote' or 'boost' a post, and thus was disseminated to a broader network. It is possible to trace a few hundred such calls to protest, but all were limited in their success, as few people showed up to the Maidan.

[14]'Yevromaydan-2013. Ukraintsi Samoorhanizuvalysya, Shchob Pidtrymaty Kurs Na Yevropu', *Ukrains'ka Pravda*, 22 November 2013, available at: http://www.pravda.com.ua/photo-video/2013/11/22/7002696/, accessed 27 November 2014.

[15]Author's informal telephone interview with an anonymous journalist and politician, 17 December 2013.

[16]Author's interview with anonymous leftwing activist 2, Kyiv, 29 August 2014.

[17]For example, author's interview with anonymous Civic Sector activist 7, Kyiv, 27 August 2014.

[18]'UVAHA! Zbir s'ohodni na Maydani Nezalezhnosti o 22:30 !!! (+video)', Yuriy Andreyev's blog post, 21 November 2013, available at: http://blogs.korrespondent.net/blog/pro_users/3289622-uvaha-zbir-sohodni-na-maidani-nezalezhnosti-o-2230-video, accessed 12 February 2016; Ihor Lutsenko's posts, 21 November 2013, available at: https://www.facebook.com/igor.lutsenko/posts/670281052995887, and https://www.facebook.com/igor.lutsenko/posts/670206513003341, both accessed 12 February 2016; Mustafa Nayem's posts, 21 November 2013, available at: https://www.facebook.com/Mustafanayyem/posts/10201177280260151, and https://www.facebook.com/Mustafanayyem/posts/10201178184682761, both accessed 12 February 2016.

[19]Also noted in a telephone interview with anonymous Civic Sector activist 1, 30 November 2013.

In line with hypothesis 2, past mobilisation and pre-existing activist networks were central in the initial mobilisation process. As explained by early participants, those who joined the protests on the first night were predominantly well-known activists, activists-turned-politicians and journalists rather than 'ordinary' citizens.[20] From Kyiv to Donets'k, the first participants employed existing Social Movement Organisation networks to communicate and coordinate actions: they 'called each other's mobile phones, … [they] knew each other … [they] had past experience of protest'.[21] Activists repeatedly explained that their 'past experience allowed … [them] to quickly organise'.[22] They also expressed their dismay that initially 'only about a few dozen' protesters came out onto the Maidan. They remained uncertain about the mass appeal of the protest trigger but explained that their fears were lessened when the numbers rose to an estimated 1,000–2,000 participants.[23] Nevertheless, few activists thought that they could mobilise enough 'ordinary' citizens to start a 'revolution'.[24] Since 2010 there had been many such small protest events—'mainly coordinated and attended by the same individuals'.[25]

From its inception, the Maidan mobilisation was characterised by a degree of diversity that distinguished it from past moments of mass mobilisation.[26] As described by several activists, during the first night something surprising happened: although protests took place in the typical sites such as Kyiv and Lviv, activists sent around tweets, Instagram pictures, messages and posts from all over Ukraine, including Donets'k, which activists argue should have been a sign that there were more of them then they initially thought.[27]

A further departure from past protest events is the multi-regional scope of smaller protest events connected to the bigger Maidan mobilisation wave. In the east of the country five experienced activists and journalists began their own Maidan in Donets'k on 21 November and stayed out all night just like their counterparts in Kyiv. Although there was a sense of solidarity, there was little coordination with Kyiv.[28] Due to the unusual trigger of the protest and the lack of coordination even among experienced activists, as admitted by one long time Social Movement Organisation leader, activists were slow to realise the country-wide diffusion potential of the protests.[29]

Lack of coordination: the battle of the two Maidans

Between 21 and 23 November local journalists, activists and students continued to organise several small protest events on the *Maidan Nezalezhnosty* and in other cities. They continued to employ online social media to inform and motivate citizens *via* the #Euromaidan chain.[30]

---

[20]Author's telephone interview with anonymous Civic Sector activist 1, 30 November 2013.

[21]Author's interview with anonymous Kyiv/Donets'k activist, Kyiv, 12 May 2015.

[22]For example, author's telephone interview with anonymous Civic Sector activist 1, 30 November 2013.

[23]For example, author's interview with anonymous *Samo Oborona* activist 2, Kyiv, 25 August 2014.

[24]For example, author's interview with anonymous Civic Sector activist 6, Kyiv, 26 August 2014.

[25]Author's interview with anonymous Civic Sector activist 6, Kyiv, 26 August 2014.

[26]Such as, The Revolution on the Granite in 1990, Ukraine Without Kuchma in 2001, and the Orange Revolution in 2004, see Onuch (2014a).

[27]For example, author's interview with anonymous *Samo Oborona* activist 2, Kyiv, 25 August 2014.

[28]Author's interview with anonymous Donets'k-based activist/journalist 2, Kyiv, 14 May 2015.

[29]Author's interview with anonymous *Samo Oborona* activist 1, Kyiv, 25 August 2014.

[30]Euromaidan participants and supporters both in Ukraine and around the world employed the hashtags #EuroMaidan, #euromaidan, and the Cyrillic #євромайдан to communicate information about protest events in Kyiv, across Ukraine and internationally. For a deeper analysis, see Tucker *et al.* (2014).

Yet, it was not until political opposition leaders Vitaliy Klitschko, Arseniy Yatsenyuk and Oleh Tiahnybok jointly coordinated a pro-EU march on 24 November in Kyiv (on the anniversaries of both the *Holodomor*[31] and the Orange Revolution) that 'ordinary' citizens joined in larger numbers. The protests then quickly grew to an estimated 50,000 (according to a police estimate) or to 80,000–100,000 people (according to an estimate by the political opposition and reported by foreign media).[32]

In line with our third hypothesis, the simultaneous calls to action on 24 November by politicians and activists did not result in any meaningful cooperation or coordination, creating 'a sense of uncertainty' among participants and observers.[33] As reported by interviewees, each political party and Social Movement Organisation distributed their own paraphernalia and posted their own calls to protest on their separate organisational websites, message boards and Facebook events pages. In Kyiv, the various groups directed their members and supporters to congregate in different meeting places and even set up two different end points for their marches. Based on interviews and focus group discussions we know that the protesters split into at least two different groups. One group was led by non-partisan Social Movement Organisations, activists and student organisations convening their march in the *Maidan Nezalezhnosty*, and the other was led by political opposition groups to the *Yevropeis'ka Ploshcha* (European Square). They became known colloquially as the 'Student Maidan' and the 'Political Maidan' respectively, competing for both participants and control.[34] As described by several informants, parties wanted to compete for the role of the next 'hero' of the revolution, or the next 'saviour', thereby demonstrating that they had 'not learned from Yushchenko's mistakes'.[35] This was particularly surprising since, as suggested by hypothesis 2, most of the activists and political opposition leadership had recent experience in successful protest coordination in 2004. The lack of leadership made activists and political opposition appear weak in the eyes of both the regime and 'ordinary citizens'.

Several non-activist protest participants interviewed said they were put off by 'the absence of political will … [to] put egos aside and coordinate together'. They explained that the politicians 'misread the situation', that the protesters 'were not out there because of [the politicians], or the Association Agreement … [they] wanted something bigger … a change in the system of … corruption and lies'.[36] The claims voiced by the political opposition and activist leaders focused on the signing of the EU Association Agreement. They appeared out of touch with broader societal concerns, and both missed an opportunity to tap into a larger potential 'protestorate'. However, it is impossible to disentangle how many protesters came out on 24 November because of the EU agreement and what it symbolised—the *Holodomor* commemorations, support for particular partisan groups or general opposition to the Yanukovych regime.

[31]*Holodomor* means 'extermination by hunger' and refers to the man-made famine in the Ukrainian SSR in 1932–1933 that killed an estimated 2.5–7.5 million Ukrainians.

[32]See, 'Huge Ukraine Rally over EU Agreement Delay', *BBC News*, 24 November 2013, available at: http://www.bbc.co.uk/news/world-europe-25078952, accessed 29 July 2015.

[33]Author's interview with anonymous director of an NGO and long-time Civic Sector activist, Kyiv, 28 August 2014.

[34]Author's interview with anonymous political scientist 1, Member of the Rada, negotiator during Regime–Opposition Roundtables, Kyiv, 15 May 2015.

[35]For example, author's informal telephone interview with anonymous journalist and politician, 17 December 2013.

[36]Focus group 1, 'ordinary' citizens, Kyiv, 26 August 2014.

Missed opportunity: a potential all-Ukrainian protest coalition?

From this first weekend of contention the protests were, unlike ever before, an all-Ukraine, cross-regional phenomena. Yet, despite the instant diffusion of substantial protests to regional cities across central and western Ukraine (Lviv, Ivano Frankivsk, Lutsk, Rivne, Ternopil) and small protest events in southern and eastern centres, such as Donets'k, Sumy, Poltava, Kharkiv, Odesa and even Simferopil and Sevastopol, the potential protest capacity across the country was overlooked by most activists and politicians.

According to one political insider, the big parties' main strategy was to bring people from central Ukrainian villages and outskirts of the capital to the *Yevropeis'ka Ploshcha*. He lamented that the opposition parties, should have done more to 'support the protest events … in the east and south … in Donets'k' and could have done more to challenge the myth of the east–west division.[37] Just like the regime, the political opposition misread the level of broader societal discontent.

Although protest participants, their posters and their online posts hinted at an opportunity to unite protesters across the country with a universal claim against the regime, the student, activist and opposition organisers retained their singular focus on the EU Association Agreement.[38] As noted by Tarrow (1993), political opportunity structures, such as the non-signing of the Association Agreement, not only set the mobilisation process in motion but also guide (and even restrict) its subsequent development. According to interviewed protest participants, by the first weekend the central demands had shifted to 'a better way of life' and even though 'Ukraine is Europe' remained a key slogan, the broader protest discourse already focused on the expansion of political liberties, rights, state accountability and socio-economic security.[39]

The lack of coordination among Social Movement Organisations, their leaders and the political opposition resulted in an exaggeration of the centrality of the 'pro-EU' claim, the non-recognition of the diverse nature of the (potential) 'protestorate', and the oversight of the scope for diffusion across Ukraine. The (temporarily) shrinking protests were predominantly maintained by experienced activists and university students (organised into strike committees, most notably in Lviv, Kyiv and Sumy), with limited participation by other groups (such as middle-aged or young professionals). The peaceful protests included live concerts, and activists continued to reject partisan attempts at 'co-optation'.

Phase 2 (30 November–16 January): shift in collective action frames

Political opportunities for coordination and mobilisation can also arise in the form of miscalculations by the regime in power (McAdam *et al.* 1996). The non-signing of the EU Association Agreement was the first miscalculation; the second was misjudging the participants as 'a small group of disaffected activists and students'.[40] An even more serious miscalculation followed on 29 and 30 November when a small group of peaceful protesters—mostly students and journalists—were brutally beaten in the first *Berkut* raid. The miscalculation was twofold: first, by all accounts the activists were planning to disband following the lack of success at the

---

[37]Author's interview with anonymous government insider, Kyiv, 26 August 2014.

[38]For example, author's interview with anonymous Civic Sector activist 3, Kyiv, 22 July 2014.

[39]Focus group 'ordinary' citizens 1, Kyiv, 12 May 2015.

[40]Author's informal telephone interview with anonymous former Yanukovych administration insider, 28 January 2014.

Vilnius Summit earlier that day.[41] Second, the unprovoked violence pushed the activists and political opposition to unite into one Maidan and reframe mobilisation claims consistent with a broader civic and human rights discourse (in line with hypotheses 3 and 5). When foreign journalists and CCTV cameras caught the assault on unarmed peaceful protesters, including women and foreign journalists, the images 'went viral' on social media outlets—not only in Ukraine but globally (Tucker *et al.* 2014; Metzger *et al.* 2015). The instantaneous information diffused throughout the country galvanised an unexpected coalition of protesters. In rapid interviews and focus groups protest participants explained that from this moment onwards the protests were about 'saving Ukrainian democracy'. The protests were no longer referred to as the Euromaidan, but simply the *Maidan* or the *Revolution of Dignity*.[42]

On 1 December, after a coordinated effort by opposition parties and the Civic Sector, between 400,000 and 800,000 people joined the protests in Kyiv.[43] This was the biggest protest event of the Maidan protest wave. Moreover, large protests were held in all western and central regional city centres, and medium to small protest events (of up to 2,000 participants each) took place in Crimea, Odesa, Kharkiv, Sumy, Donets'k, Zaporizhzhya, Dnipropetrovs'k and Poltava.

Who was the Maidan?

One reason why the political opposition and the activists misread the scope for protest was the apparent lack of a common collective identity they could mobilise around. The protesters were not easily distinguishable in terms of traditional east–west cleavages or a division between Russian and Ukrainian speakers. The level of protest diffusion across Ukraine and specifically to regions beyond the centre–west was a novelty in post-communist Ukraine. Employing the Kyiv International Institute of Sociology (KIIS) macro regions schema for coding, the majority of protesters came from central Ukraine, in particular Kyiv and its surrounding areas (approximately 59%).[44] The largest proportion came from Kyiv city and Kyiv *oblast'* (approximately 57%). The second largest group of protesters (approximately 14%) came from western Ukraine, mostly from Lviv and Ternopil *oblasti* (see Figure 1).

While the broad majority of our survey respondents (83%) listed Ukrainian as their 'mother tongue', and self-identified as 'ethnically' Ukrainian, over two thirds of the respondents who reported their language use said that they used the Ukrainian language at work and/or in their private lives and approximately 20% of respondents were predominantly Russophones at home and/or at work. Approximately between 5% and 6% of those respondents who chose 'other' for language detailed using both languages equally at home or at work. We find that the self-reported rates of 'mother tongue' and ethnicity are directly consistent with data from the 2001 census and representative of central Ukraine (and specifically Kyiv *oblast'* and Kyiv

---

[41]Author's informal telephone interview with anonymous Civic Sector activist 1, 30 November 2013.

[42]Focus group 'ordinary' citizens 1, Kyiv, 12 May 2015; focus group 'ordinary' citizens 4, Kyiv, 8 July 2015.

[43]'Ukraine's Anti-Government Protesters Stage First Mass Rally of 2014', *Reuters*, 1 December 2013, available at: http://uk.reuters.com/article/2014/01/12/uk-ukraine-idUKBREA0B09820140112, accessed 29 July 2015.

[44]Kyiv International Institute of Sociology (KIIS) macro regions include: West (Chernivests'ka, Ivano-Frankivs'ka, Kmelnyts'ka, Lvivs'ka, Rivens'ka, Ternopils'ka, Volyns'ka and Zakarpats'ka); Center (Cherkas'ka, Chernihivs'ka, Kirovohrads'ka, Kyivs'ka, Poltavs'ka, Sums'ka, Vynnyts'ka and Zhytomyrs'ka); East (Dontes'ka, Kharkivs'ka and Luhans'ka); and South (Dnipropetrovs'ka, Khersons'ka, Kryms'ka, Mykolaivs'ka, Odes'ka and Zaporizhs'ka).

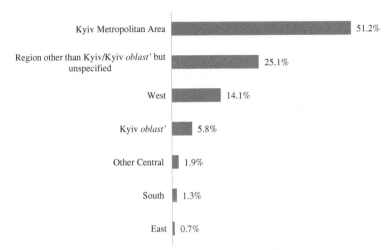

FIGURE 1. SURVEY RESPONDENTS BY REGION.
Note: n=1225.
Source: EuroMaidan Protest Participant Survey 2013.

city).[45] We also find that just under 20% of survey respondents who reported their language use identified using different languages at home and at work, suggesting more widespread bilingualism.[46]

The research team's field observations were in line with the focus group discussion, most of which pointed out that—somewhat surprisingly—language was not an issue for the protesters. The '*lingua franca*' of the average Maidan participant was Russian, or *Surzhyk*,[47] as noted by focus group participants. While protesters may self-identify as Ukrainian 'mother tongue' speakers they use Russian regularly, in particular in Kyiv.[48]

One of the theoretical expectations in (hypothesis 2) is that the participants of mass mobilisation have past protest and political engagement experience, possibly a similar or shared level of experience (Meyer 2004). The public discourse around the Maidan assumes that the protesters were made up of fairly homogenous 'types' of voters with similar protest experience (Ishchenko 2014; Shekhovtsov & Umland 2014). About two thirds of the survey respondents had participated in a protest event in the past (63% of the respondents reported some participation in the Orange Revolution). Thus, a significant number of Maidan protesters

---

[45]According to the 2001 census 92.3% and 72.1% of the Kyiv *oblast'* and Kyiv city populations respectively are Ukrainian 'mother tongue' speakers. Moreover, 92.5% and 82.2% of the Kyiv *oblast'* and Kyiv city populations respectively are ethnic Ukrainians. Whilst the census is outdated it is the best available source of information on both language and ethnicity in Ukraine (State Statistics Committee of Ukraine 2001).

[46]About 15% of the respondents stated that they used both languages equally (not an option in the survey; thus, it is possible that this number would have been larger).

[47]*Surzhyk* is a blend of the two languages most often used in casual conversation in Ukraine. It employs mostly Russian words and Ukrainian grammar as well as some slang words.

[48]Focus group 'ordinary' citizens 1, Kyiv, 12 May 2015; focus group 'ordinary' citizens 2, Kyiv, 6 July 2015; focus group 'ordinary citizens' 4, Kyiv, 8 July 2015.

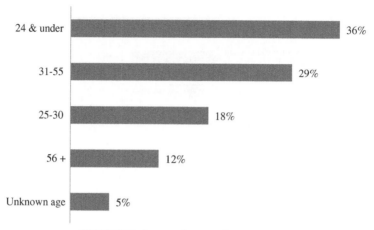

FIGURE 2. AGE OF SURVEY RESPONDENTS.
Note: n=1263.
Source: EuroMaidan Protest Participant Survey 2013.

were 'novices'. Coupled with the diffusion of protests across the country, these figures suggest an expanding or changing protest base in Ukraine.

The majority of protesters cannot be classified as highly politically engaged individuals: less than 30% of our survey respondents stated that they belonged to any civic movements (approximately 14%) or community organisations (approximately 10%), unions (approximately 11%) or political parties (approximately 9%). As most respondents did not declare a past vote choice openly, we should interpret these results carefully, but we definitely do not detect complete homogeneity. Although a broad majority of the Maidan protesters we surveyed reported having voted for opposition candidates/parties (Yushchenko, Our Ukraine—*Nasha Ukraiina*; Tymoshenko, Fatherland—*Batkivshchyna*; Klitschko, UDAR!; Yatsenyuk, Front of Change—*Front Zmin*; Tiahnybok, Freedom—*Svoboda*) they were not supporters of any one party or politician over time. Nor were they all conscientious voters: we estimate that in 2009 and 2010 approximately 18% of those who could vote (by age and citizenship) chose not to do so. As noted by focus group participants, protesters were 'normal people' and 'not really political'.[49] This is also in line with both interviews and focus group discussions conducted after the Maidan, when most protest participants expressed high levels of distrust of politicians and parties more generally.

Approximately 8% of survey respondents reported voting 'against all' in at least one of either the 2004, 2010 or 2012 elections.[50] Similarly, nearly one tenth of those who could vote reported not voting for Yanukovych's main opponent, Yulia Tymoshenko, but for other candidates, in the presidential elections in 2009 and 2010. And over all election cycles approximately between 2% and 3% of the survey respondents who reported their vote choice voted for Yanukovych, Tihipko or a party associated with the Yanukovych regime. Even if this number is small, it further underlines the lack of homogeneity. If a minority of protesters felt

[49]Focus group 'ordinary' citizens 1, Kyiv, 12 May 2015; focus group 'ordinary' citizens 3, Kyiv, 7 July 2015.
[50]Ukrainian election ballots include the option 'against all' and this option was among those reported by survey respondents.

safe enough to voice a potentially 'controversial' past vote choice in the middle of a protest, the protesters were indeed more diverse than initially assumed. Our multi-source process tracing also suggests that this diversity, at least initially, increased after the 29–30 November repressions.

According to the EPPS data, as early as 28 November, the average age of the protesters was 36. There were slightly more men (59%) than women involved in direct action, marches and meetings, but as reported in interview and focus group discussions women contributed to the protest activity in other ways that helped sustain the protests. The protesters were generally well informed, employed, and most had professional or higher or other tertiary education (see Table A4 in the Appendix). The protesters surveyed were primarily young or middle-aged professionals (see Figure 2). As explained in more detail elsewhere (Onuch 2014b, 2015a), rapid interviews and focus groups reveal a demographic distinction between three generational cohorts of protest participants: students (24 and under) and young professionals (25–30), many of whom were born after the fall of communism and had never voted in a presidential election; the working middle-aged with families (31–55 years old), whose formative years were heavily influenced by a difficult transition period since independence during which most had voted in at least two presidential elections; and finally, the pensioners or 'grandparents' (56 years old and over), many of whom had spent at least half of their lives under communist rule. Since they had the chance to vote in all post-Soviet elections, they also felt most 'responsible' for the political system of 2013.

In this initial period students and youth generally focused their claims and slogans on European integration. The middle-aged professionals' claims included typical median voter demands, such as economic security, less corruption—in particular the ability to conduct business without paying bribes—and unrestricted travel abroad. The oldest cohort of participants frequently mentioned that it was their 'responsibility to stand in the Maidan' out of a sense of 'civic duty'. In rapid interviews they stated that they wanted the 'corrupt bandits out', that they joined the protests 'for the children' for the 'future', but only few mentioned EU accession as a motivating factor.

The claims as presented to us by the different age cohorts align with the existing literature of generational voting preferences and practices of diverse constituencies in elections across Europe (Bartels & Jackman 2014; Dinas & Stoker 2014; Neundorf & Niemi 2014; Pop-Eleches & Tucker 2014). When protest participants were asked in interviews or focus groups what they wanted from the state, or what they hoped the 'democratic' or 'European' future had in store for them, the three different age groups of protesters described the following demands: the youngest group focused on the quality of higher education and better labour market prospects; the middle-aged group on socio-economic security, the liberalisation of EU–Ukraine travel and less corruption; and the oldest group on pensions and social redistribution. Thus, while the trigger that brought the majority of these diverse protesters out onto the streets was what they described as 'the breaking of a social contract' on 21 November and the 'violation of basic civic and human rights' on 29 and 30 November, the protesters joined the protests with a range of different claims motivating their behaviour. Neither the activists nor the political opposition were aware of the extent of the competing claims and grievances and thus, struggled to unite the demands under one umbrella.

It should be noted that our respondents and focus group participants did not by themselves bring up issues of language or ethno-nationalist demands, not even those who reported voting for *Svoboda* (with the exception of the *Samo Oborona* focus group). Moreover, most of the interviewees and focus group participants used a mixture of Ukrainian and Russian to answer the questions, and many spoke in Russian even though interviews, surveys and focus groups always begun in Ukrainian for the sake of consistency.

Shaping a collective identity through rights frames

The slogans of the protests are not necessarily the same as the actual motivations of the protesters. However, tracing the content of posters and related material can help us track shifts over time in the mobilisational discourse (Noakes & Johnston 2005; Githens-Mazer 2012). This discourse is generally believed to be framed by elite actors such as key journalists, Social Movement Organisations, activists and the political opposition leaders (Benford & Snow 2000). A unified rights frame is hypothesised (hypothesis 4) to help bring together a variety of diverse actors and shape a 'new' collective aim and identity (Noakes & Johnston 2005). In the case of the 2013–2014 mass mobilisation in Ukraine, protester slogans, posters, viral social media content and speeches from the stage in the square show several key shifts in the way the protest events were framed. This is best highlighted by the insistence of protesters (in interviews and focus group discussions) on separating the period 21–29 November, labelled Euromaidan, and the period from 30 November onwards, referred to simply as Maidan. In our own analysis of protestor poster and slogan content, we found that the initial focus was on how 'Ukraine is Europe' and on Ukrainians wanting 'to live in a "normal" European country'. This discourse quickly became more variegated following the repression of 29–30 November to include demands for the protection of civic and human rights more generally. This was exemplified by catch-all slogans of outrage against the regime, including '*Banda Het*' (Bandits Get Lost) and references to the regime having 'blood on its hands'.

EPPS data confirm that the protesters were more likely to be motivated by claims framed in a democratic rights discourse than EU accession. For instance, respondents who answered the question 'Why did you decide to join in the Euromaidan?' declared 'my rights were infringed upon by the government' (20%) and 'for a better future for Ukraine' (22.7%) as their top two motivations. Furthermore, when answering the question 'Why are you protesting today?' (in rapid interviews) or 'What motivated you to join the protests?' (in interviews and focus groups), most explained that they felt they had to join the protests out of 'civic duty', 'human dignity' and to 'defend their civic rights'.

When comparing focus group exchanges to interviews with politicians and activists, it becomes clear that the 'leaders' remained focused on the EU Association Agreement and on negotiating a new deal and fresh elections with the Yanukovych regime. They even complained about 'the *hromadskist*' [(civil society, citizenry)] [being] … out of touch' with the realities of politics, noting that the multi-dimensionality of the demands and voices made it difficult to coordinate and approach the Yanukovych regime from a position of strength.[51]

It is clear that there was a serious lack of connection between the people's Maidan and the Euromaidan of the political opposition and the activists. The political opposition, the activists and Social Movement Organisations, and their economic financiers remained divided as to

---

[51]For example, author's interview with anonymous political scientist 1, Member of the Rada, negotiator during Regime–Opposition Roundtables, Kyiv, 15 May 2015.

what messages to popularise.[52] Activists and the political elite were eventually forced to unite in 'a coalition of inconvenience'.

Although there is ample evidence of attempts at coordination and frame alignment (Snow *et al.* 1986) following the 29–30 November repressions, the lack of cohesion and organisational weakness of the activists and political opposition groups meant that they quickly lost control not only over the dominant messages but also the repertoires of protest. An organised protest response to the 29–30 November repressions proved difficult in view of the miscalculation on the part of the activists and political opposition of the diversity of the 'protestorate'; their underestimation of the scope for regional diffusion; and an underestimation of the protesters' capacity of self-organisation through social media. These three misunderstandings—reminiscent of the regime's misjudgement—created openings and opportunities for radical voices and action.[53]

Activists and opposition unable to control the protests

Activists have explained in interviews that from 1 December onwards they were increasingly struggling to control small groups of (predominantly young male) protesters from escalating an aggressive discourse and promoting or turning to direct action (occupations and road blockades, for example) and violent protest repertoires (such as the use of pepper spray, rocks and metal chains).[54] Although they tried to manage and constrain radical voices, the activists and politicians directly involved in the *Rada Maidanu* (Council of the Maidan),[55] explained that with each provocation, including attempts to clear the Maidan between 10 and 12 December, the beating of activists and journalists (including Tatyana Chornovil and Ihor Lutsenko, among others) '… it was more and more difficult to control the *hromads'kist'*'.[56] Off the record, several key leaders of Civic Sector and other liberal Social Movement Organisations expressed that from January 2014 onwards, they felt they had to compete and even collaborate with the extremist groups in the Maidan zone when vying for the attention of possible recruits.[57]

In December radically minded protesters (not necessarily members of rightwing organisations) established coordinating teams of 100–200 (*Sotni*) lightly armed individuals called *Samo Oborona* (Self-Defence) battalions.[58] These groups walked around the city centre wearing hard hats, holding bats, and some have been reported as chanting nationalist

---

[52]For example, author's interview with anonymous businessman and NGO director who paid for and coordinated medical supplies, Kyiv, 13 May 2015.

[53]Author's interview with anonymous leftwing activist 1, Kyiv, 29 August 2014.

[54]Focus group Civic Sector activists 2, Kyiv, 28 August 2014.

[55]*Rada HO «Vseukrayins'ke obyednannya Maydanu»* (The Council of the NGO 'All-Ukrainian Union Maidan') or Council of the Maidan, founded on 22 December 2013, was a council where leaders of civic organisations, political parties, experts and academics came together to discuss events, needs, and coordinate activities or responses. For a list of participants see Appendix 3.

[56]Author's interview with anonymous political scientist 1, Member of the Rada, negotiator during Regime–Opposition Roundtables, Kyiv, 15 May 2015.

[57]Author's interviews with anonymous Civic Sector activist 2, Kyiv, 21 July 2014; anonymous Civic Sector activist 5, Kyiv, 25 August 2014; anonymous Civic Sector activist 6, Kyiv, 26 August 2014; anonymous Civic Sector activist 7, Kyiv, 27 August 2014; anonymous long-time academic expert, activist and Minister, Kyiv, 21 July 2014; anonymous political scientist 1, Member of the Rada, negotiator during Regime–Opposition Roundtables, Kyiv, 15 May 2015.

[58]Focus group *Samo Oborona* activists, Kyiv, 15 May 2015.

and patriotic slogans.[59] The frequency of encounters between police forces and protesters significantly increased in the month and a half that followed (Popova 2014). Alongside this escalation in protest discourses and repertoires peaceful protests continued with nightly (or, in the regions, weekly) gatherings (also called *Viches*)[60] in city centres across the country.[61] Each violent encounter between protesters and militia lowered protest participation, with women dropping out at a faster rate than men. Protesters described a sense of growing desperation among participants of the Maidan. It was this despair, coupled with a feeling that the politicians and activists had neither a 'clear understanding of the protesters … [nor] any control over the events' that appears to have pushed a larger proportion of protesters to engage in or support ensuing episodes of violence.[62]

These findings confirm the expectations from the literature and our hypotheses (hypotheses 1, 3 and 5). A diversity of actors involved in the protests translated into a range of different demands, which were difficult to capture in one protest claim. The first use of regime repression created an opportunity for activists and opposition leaders to unite and frame the protest events employing a rights-based discourse. Due to internal divisions within the Social Movement Organisations and the political opposition, however, they were still unable to coordinate activities effectively. This, in turn, made it possible for radical voices to gain in strength and created the space for further regime repression.

Phase 3 (16–27 January): innovation and expansion of contention

On 16 January the regime and Party of Regions parliamentarians misjudged their own strength and the weakness of the protests a second time when they voted in the anti-protest laws. These laws, quickly dubbed the *Diktatorski Zakony* (Dictator's Laws), not only outlawed peaceful protest, but made any action related to protests a terrorist offence. For example, one could not wear a helmet in public (not even when riding a bicycle), carry an extra tyre in the car or wear a scarf covering the face.[63] These laws quickly became a rallying point for the protests, as they again affected a much wider group than those gathered in the Maidan. Similar to the 29–30 November repressions, the regime severely underestimated the diversity of the protesters, their willingness to continue their mobilisation, and the level of support for these protesters from the general population. Following the anti-protest laws, we observe what Tarrow would call an 'innovation' and 'expansion' in the forms of contention: more self-organisation (soup kitchens, volunteer medical clinics and donation drives) across the country and an increasing willingness among 'ordinary citizens' to turn to violent repertoires.

At first, the Maidan protesters reacted to the new laws with barricades on the perimeter of the square and extended the barricades to *Hrushevs'koho Street* and the top of *Instituts'ka Street*. They called this an 'occupation of public space' that was now to be 'defended by all

---

[59]Focus group *Samo Oborona* activists, Kyiv, 15 May 2015.

[60]A *Viche* was originally a meeting of the citizens of a Kyivan Rus' town to discuss matters of local import. Throughout Ukrainian history this term has been often used by dissidents and activists for nightly or weekly protest meetings.

[61]Author's interviews with anonymous Donets'k-based activist/journalist 1, Kyiv, 12 May 2015; anonymous long-time activist and Minister, Kyiv, 21 July 2014.

[62]Focus group 'ordinary' citizens 4, Kyiv, 8 July 2015; focus group *Samo Oborona* activists, Kyiv, 15 May 2015.

[63]Author's interview with anonymous leftwing activist 2, Kyiv, 29 August 2014; focus group Civic Sector activists 1, Kyiv, 28 August 2014.

citizens of the city'.[64] This move to direct action tactics resulted in a greater reaction from the regime. On 17 and 18 January several violent interactions occurred between the police and protesters. Activists from several NGOs explained how they tried but ultimately failed to prevent violent action in the name of the protests.[65]

Protesters and people in the vicinity of the Maidan reported receiving threatening text messages informing them that they were located in a banned protest zone and identified as engaging in an anti-social activity, noting that they could be imprisoned or become involved in an anti-terrorist operation.[66] Activists interpreted these threats as a direct provocation by the regime aimed at triggering 'an emotional irrational reaction'.[67] This finding was reiterated in all focus group discussions with 'ordinary citizens', only some of whom were involved in protests at that time: this was a 'clear provocation (*chysta provokatsiya*)' and explained that at least in Kyiv, 'it was obvious … you would get this threat [*via* SMS] even if you were far away from the Maidan'.[68] Interestingly, the focus group participants who took part in the events on *Hrushevs'koho Street* and *Instytuts'ka,* or worked in kitchens and medical clinics, saw themselves as 'only supporter[s] of the Maidan' and not protesters *per se.* In January and February they 'came to relieve the [real] protesters for a bit' or 'provide them with some food'.[69] Thus, the protest was being redefined by those supporting it, who—not unlike the regime and the activists—ultimately underestimated the overall capacity for protest.

On 19 January, *Berkut* attacked the protesters at night, and between 19 and 22 January at least three people died as a direct result of police action, and many more were injured.[70] Process-tracing and participant observation by members of our research team, and interviews highlight that this second wave of repressions changed the composition of protesters (but not necessarily the broader group of supporters): they now included a strong majority of young and middle-aged males,[71] and rightwing groups gained a foothold.[72]

[64]Focus group 'ordinary' citizens 1, Kyiv, 12 May 2015; focus group 'ordinary' citizens 4, Kyiv, 8 July 2015; focus group 'ordinary citizens' 5, Kyiv, 9 July 2015.

[65]For example, author's interviews with anonymous *Samo Oborona* activist 2, Kyiv, 25 August 2014; anonymous Civic Sector activist 2, Kyiv, 21 July 2014; anonymous leftwing activist 1, Kyiv, 28 August 2014.

[66]Focus group Civic Sector activists 1, Kyiv, 28 August 2014.

[67]For example, author's interview with anonymous long-time academic expert, activist and Minister, Kyiv, 21 July 2014.

[68]Focus group 'ordinary' citizens 1, Kyiv, 12 May 2015; and also discussed in focus group 'ordinary' citizens 4, Kyiv, 8 July 2015; focus group 'ordinary' citizens 5, Kyiv, 9 July 2015; focus group Civic Sector activists 2, Kyiv, 28 August 2014.

[69]Focus group 'ordinary' citizens 5, Kyiv, 9 July 2015; focus group 'ordinary' citizens 6, Kyiv, 10 July 2015.

[70]The first official death was already recorded on 22 December: Pavlo Mazurenko died after being beaten by police on 18 December 2013, although this incident was not well known at the time. The three who died on the 21/22 January were Yuriy Verbitsky, Serhiy Nihoyan (Ukrainian born Armenian) and Mikhailo Zhyznevskyy (a Belarusian). These were followed by the deaths of Roman Senik, Viktor Homyak, Bogdan Kalynyak, Alexander Badera and Sergiy Sinenko between 25 January and 15 February. See, Official government list of Nebesnya Sotinya (Heavenly Hundred) and Order of the Nebesnya Sotya, available at: http://iportal.rada.gov.ua/en/news/News/News/page/en/news/News/News/95089.html, accessed 13 February.

[71]It should be noted that several Sotnya's were made up of entirely women and one such young graduate student M. B. carries the nickname 'Molotov Princess', as she helped 'professionalise' the Molotov stations. Author's interviews with anonymous leftwing activist 1, Kyiv, 28 August 2014; anonymous Civic Sector activist 5, Kyiv, 25 August 2014; anonymous businessman and NGO director who paid for and coordinated medical supplies, Kyiv, 13 May 2015; anonymous female radical activist, Kyiv, 7 July 2015.

[72]Focus group *Samo Oborona* activists, Kyiv, 15 May 2015.

The expansion to extreme violent repertoires, such as Molotov cocktails, marked a sharp break in Ukraine's protest history. First-hand accounts also note an increase in the use of patriotic symbols.[73] These 'new' forms of contention risked polarising Ukrainian citizens, allowed opponents of the Maidan to present a caricature of the protests as narrowly rightwing and focused on western Ukraine, and encouraged the regime to employ so-called 'anti-terrorist measures'. Agitated protesters engaged in further occupations of government and administrative buildings in Kyiv and other cities, including in some eastern regions like Kharkiv, Dniropretrovsk and Poltava.

Facing increasing internal pressures from Party of Regions (*Partiia Rehioniv*) financiers and in an attempt to quell the escalation of violence, Prime Minister Mykola Azarov stepped down and offered the post to opposition leader Arseniy Yatsenyuk. The deal was taken to the *Rada Maidanu*, where the political opposition and activists of the Maidan, including Andriy Parubiy, Ihor Lutsenko and Volodymyr Viatrovych, declined the offer and demanded Yanukovych's resignation.[74] In an attempt to stop the diffusion of protests, the wave of repression subsided. But in line with our hypotheses, the multiple miscalculations of the support base of the protests and the willingness of some to 'defend the Maidan to the last man standing' created more uncertainty.[75] By this time *Pravyi Sektor* (Right Sector), *Samo Oborona* battalions and retired Afghanistan war veterans controlled most of the frontlines, leading to a further radicalisation in the protest repertoires. Claims and grievances of the broader protest population were still focused on the illegitimate rule of the Yanukovych regime and democratic and basic human rights, but those living on the Maidan saw themselves as engaged in a war to defend the existence of democracy, liberal rights and freedoms as well as 'of Ukraine itself'.[76]

Phase 4 (27 January–20 February): coexistence of organised and unorganised engagement

Dissatisfied with what protesters described as the 'opposition leaders' inability, ineffectiveness [and fear] to achieve the Maidan's aims', the official opposition protest events in the Maidan and the activities of the *Rada Maidanu* were supplemented by autonomous self-organised citizen initiatives.[77] Throughout the country (mostly in the centre–west, but also in some parts of the east and south including Sumy, Poltava, Donets'k, Luhans'k, Dnipropetrovs'k, Odesa and Kharkiv), citizens coordinated their own peaceful protest events. Activists continued to complain in interviews that neither they nor the opposition were able to control the protest movement even 'after blood had been shed'.[78] Protesters willing to engage in violence

---

[73]The so-called 'Banderite' black and red (or *kalyna*) coloured flag was one such symbol. It was most prominently used by the Ukrainian Insurgent Army (*Ukraiins'ka Povstans'ka Armiia*—UPA), led by Stepan Bandera. The flag was adapted from previous flags and symbols used by Ukrainian Cossacks (such as the Ukrainian Sich Riflemen in 1916) and thus predates the Organization of Ukrainian Nationalists (created in 1929 in Vienna), the UPA or Bandera (Moroz 2013). It is by many in Ukraine considered a flag symbolising the Ukrainian struggle for statehood and independence and was already used in anti-Soviet, dissident actions. In parts of Ukraine and outside of Ukraine, in particular in Poland and Russia, the flag is seen as a hostile symbol of west Ukrainian ethno-nationalism.

[74]Author's interview with anonymous political scientist 1, Member of the Rada, negotiator during Regime–Opposition Roundtables, Kyiv, 15 May 2015.

[75]Author's interview with anonymous *Samo Oborona* activist 3, Kyiv, 25 August 2014.

[76]Focus group *Samo Oborona* activists, Kyiv, 15 May 2015.

[77]Focus group *Samo Oborona* activists, Kyiv, 15 May 2015.

[78]Focus group Civic Sector activists 2, Kyiv, 28 August 2014.

explained that they had 'nothing to lose' and members of the *Pravyi Sektor* stated that they were 'prepared to die as heroes for their country'.[79] The lack of connection between the political 'leaders' (Yatsenyuk, Klitschko and Tiahnybok) and the 'people' had grown further: 'The *hromadskist'* did not understand the need for negotiations … the politicians did not understand the readiness of the *hromadskist''*.[80] The baseline claim uniting the protesters was the removal of Yanukovych from power, but some were now willing to go to extremes to reach this goal.

In February the Maidan spiralled out of control and some protest sites descended into extreme violence. From 18 February *Berkut* embarked on what would be the last wave of repressions of the Maidan. The Maidan HQ, the location of a press office, where most negotiations of the *Rada Maidanu* and the *Hromadskyi Sektor Maidanu* (Civic Sector of the Maidan) took place, was burnt down. *Berkut* and other special operations militia employed severe modes of repression against protesters, including the use of live ammunition, grenades and snipers. The violent storming of the Maidan in Kyiv left about 90 dead (a majority under the age of 25) and over 600 injured (from both sides of the barricades, but mostly from the protesters). At this point the worst-case scenario of a large-scale 'civil war' pitting the regime against the protesters seemed highly likely to the activists and protesters interviewed. These protesters felt that now they were 'fighting for the fate of their country'.[81]

Most analyses of the Maidan to date have looked at these final phases of the protests and focused on the *Svoboda* party and what scholars have called 'neo-Nazi' organisations and a 'nationalist right' preoccupied with ethno-linguistic-nationalist claims (Ishchenko 2014; Darden & Way 2014). What they have missed, however, is the remaining diversity among the protesters and the continuing diffusion of protest (including into the *spalni reiony*, the suburbs of Kyiv) throughout this phase in the protest cycle.

Diversity among the radicals

Perhaps surprisingly, throughout the Maidan even the rightwing party *Svoboda* and its leader Oleh Tiahnybok tamed their language and discouraged disruptive language or actions. According to different sources, including video documentation, on several occasions Tiahnybok demanded that protesters tone down their rhetoric and de-escalate their tactics.[82] Although, there is evidence that a portion of protesters who disclosed their vote choice were former *Svoboda* voters, the prominence of *Svoboda* on the Maidan is called into question by focus group participants struggling to remember Tiahnybok's name, referring to him on several occasions as 'the other one' while being able to name other political leaders such as Yatsenyuk, Klitschko, Lutsenko and Poroshenko.[83]

[79]For example, author's interview with anonymous *Samo Oborona* activist 2, Kyiv, 25 August 2014; telephone interview with anonymous Right Sector (*Pravyi Sektor*) activist, 10 February 2014; focus group *Samo Oborona* activists, Kyiv, 15 May 2015.

[80]Author's interview with anonymous political scientist 1, Member of the Rada, negotiator during Regime–Opposition Roundtables, Kyiv, 15 May 2015.

[81]Focus group *Samo Oborona* activists, Kyiv, 15 May 2015.

[82]See video of Tiahnybok trying to calm down violent protesters in 'All Things Ablaze: A Documentary' by Oleksander Techynskyi, Dmitry Stoykow and Aleksey Solodunov (a compilation of live stream content), available at: http://ablaze.honestfish.com.ua/All_Things_Ablaze/All_Things_Ablaze.html, accessed 13 February 2016. Also referenced in interviews with anonymous *Samo Oborona* activist 3, Kyiv, 25 August 2014; anonymous Civic Sector activist 7, Kyiv, 27 August 2014; anonymous leftwing activist 1, Kyiv, 28 August 2014.

[83]Focus group 'ordinary' citizens 4, Kyiv, 8 July 2015; focus group 'ordinary' citizens 5, Kyiv, 9 July 2015; focus group 'ordinary' citizens 6, Kyiv, 10 July 2015.

Focus group participants saw radical organisations and their members as a slim minority of about 5% of the protesters in the Maidan during the violent phases.[84] According to our various data sources, these groups may have represented a maximum of between 10% and 20% of protesters at the time of the violence.[85] Moreover, as explained by one Jewish Russian-speaking protester from Dnipropetrovs'k, slogans, such as '*Slava Ukraiini*' (Glory to Ukraine), are used by many different types of Ukrainians across the country, and can thus be misinterpreted by foreign media or analysts when taken out of context.

Attention has also focused on the role of *Pravyi Sektor* (Right Sector) during the final phases of the Maidan. The Yanukovych regime, some international news outlets and Russian political discourse branded the *Pravyi Sektor* as central to the mobilisation process. Analyses adopting a similar perspective fail to mention that until December *Pravyi Sektor* was simply a location in the right-hand corner of the Maidan protest zone where a variety of Social Movement Organisations, rightwing political parties and networks, as well as non-affiliated individuals gathered. By February *Pravyi Sektor* had become an actor and a brand in itself. In domestic and foreign reports *Pravyi Sektor* was often confused with a general 'western' Ukrainian identity and narrow ethno-linguistic claims. By now *Pravyi Sektor* has been institutionalised as a rightwing political party but during the Maidan it was a loose coalition of several rightwing groups.[86] While some participants, including *Pravyi Sektor* leaders like Dmytro Yarosh, Andriy Tarasenko and Borislav Bereza, were long-time members of pre-existing radical organisations, others had no organisational affiliation.[87] Darden and Way (2014) highlighted these organisations' western Ukrainian origins and ethno-nationalist anti-Semitic nature, but Dmytro Yarosh, the leader of *Pravyi Sektor*, and many of his coordinators are originally from Dnipropetrovs'k, in the east of the country, and several of its members are Jewish, including leaders of the organisation (such as Borislav Bereza) (Davidzon 2014).[88] Thus, there was even diversity within the rightwing groups themselves.

Activists and political opposition groups on the ground also struggled to grasp the nature of this mobilisation. When it became clear that the activists were unable to control the protest, they became an unreliable coalition partner for the political opposition. In February, as noted by participants of the *Hromadskyi Sektor Maidanu* and the *Rada Maidanu,* 'real' cooperation between these two groups ground almost to a halt. As noted by one interviewee, much of what the *Hromadskyi Sektor Maidanu* decided was overruled by the political leadership.[89] In turn, both the political opposition and the activist leadership were not seen as offering viable alternatives to the regime. Instead, they were regarded as failures by the protesters.[90]

---

[84]Focus group Civic Sector activists 2, Kyiv, 28 August 2014; focus group *Samo Oborona* activists, Kyiv, 15 May 2015.

[85]Focus group 'ordinary' citizens 3, Kyiv, 7 July 2015; focus group 'ordinary' citizens 4, Kyiv, 8 July 2015; focus group *Samo Oborona* activists, Kyiv, 15 May 2015.

[86]Author's interview with anonymous HromadskeTV journalist 1, Kyiv, 22 July 2014; interview with anonymous HromadskeTV journalist 2, Kyiv, 26 August 2014.

[87]Author's interview with anonymous *Samo Oborona* activist 2, Kyiv, 25 August 2014.

[88]Focus group *Samo Oborona* activists, Kyiv, 15 May 2015.

[89]Author's interview with anonymous political scientist 1, member of the Rada, negotiator during Regime–Opposition Roundtables, Kyiv, 15 May 2015.

[90]Focus group 'ordinary' citizens 1, Kyiv, 12 May 2015; focus group 'ordinary' citizens 3, Kyiv, 7 July 2015; focus group 'ordinary' citizens 4, Kyiv, 8 July 2015.

Phase 5 (20–22 February): interaction between the regime and opposition

The extreme violence triggered several significant developments: the imposition of sanctions by the US and EU on individuals tied to the Yanukovych regime, an EU-brokered political agreement, and an increasing number of defections from the regime by oligarchs, Party of Regions parliamentarians and ministers, and army and policy chiefs across the country. Insiders explained that the intense and often conflictual period of negotiations was overseen by EU representatives, such as Polish Foreign Minister Radoslaw Sikorski, who did not always calm the situation.[91] The externally brokered agreement of 21 February aimed to pave the way towards a transitional government and early presidential elections by the end of 2014. The agreement's immediate rejection by those on the Maidan was symptomatic of the failure of the regime, the political opposition and the activist leaders to understand the nature of the protests and their wider social context. The release from prison of Yulia Tymoshenko and her speech in the Maidan on 22 February, which was met with a lukewarm reception, illustrated how the political leaders of the Orange Revolution had lost touch with society and its demands.[92]

Those who were present during the final days of the Maidan have underlined that at this point the protesters could not accept anything short of the president's resignation.[93] The protesters were not accountable to any Social Movement Organisations or political leaders and made up their own rules of engagement. As the protesters jeered the opposition party leaders speaking on the Maidan, a rogue protest participant and member of a self-organised battalion took to the stage to announce that the protesters were giving Yanukovych an ultimatum to resign by 10 am on Saturday, 22 February.[94] A video of his declaration depicts the complete lack of control of opposition leaders like Klitschko, Tiahnybok or Yarosh over the crowd. It is likely that the realisation that the political opposition would not be able to control the situation—or ensure his safety—sealed Yanukovych's decision to flee the capital. Insiders point to the fact that Yanukovych's house was being packed up already during the negotiations with the opposition.[95] The day after Yanukovych had left protesters took over his private residence and the Presidential Administration. The Maidan had become almost entirely self-coordinating and thereby also by and large unmanageable.

Phase 6 (22 February onwards): rule by an uneasy alliance of opposition and protesters

When Yanukovych fled, the 'coalition of inconvenience', which barely survived through the protests, had to form an uneasy coalition in parliament. The army and police forces declared that they would not go against the protesters. The parliament took hasty decisions in an attempt to appease the most violent protesters. Parliament declared that the President had fled the country and called presidential elections for 25 May. It also released former Prime Minister Yulia Tymoshenko from prison and made the new Parliamentary Speaker

[91] For example, author's interview with anonymous political scientist 1, member of the Rada, negotiator during Regime–Opposition Roundtables, Kyiv, 15 May 2015.

[92] 'Ukraine Protests—Yulia Tymoshenko Returns To Kyiv; Speech at Maidan—22 February 2014', YouTube, available at: https://www.youtube.com/watch?v=Zg2SaTV-mIg, accessed 15 January 2016.

[93] For example, author's interview with anonymous *Samo Oborona* activist 2, Kyiv, 25 August 2014; focus group *Samo Oborona* activists, Kyiv, 15 May 2015.

[94] 'Lyudy Postavyly Ul'tymatum: Vidstavka Yanukovycha Do Ranku', *Ukrains'ka Pravda*, 21 February 2014, available at: http://www.pravda.com.ua/news/2014/02/21/7015590/, accessed 21 March 2015.

[95] For example, author's interview with anonymous political scientist 1, member of the Rada, negotiator during Regime–Opposition Roundtables, Kyiv, 15 May 2015.

Oleksandr Turchynov acting President. Although it seemed that the momentum was firmly with the diverse group of protesters and political opposition groups, even 'insiders' perceived a power vacuum at the heart of Ukrainian politics. Likewise, there was a real fear that the most violent protesters could turn on parliament at a given moment.[96] Discussions with activists also expressed a sense of dissatisfaction and a concern that the new parliament would fail to represent them.[97] Similarly, 'ordinary citizens' taking part in the focus groups summed up that the politicians were unable to represent the Maidan.[98]

Conclusions

Through detailed process-tracing based on original on-site data, this essay has demonstrated that while the Maidan protests mark a significant shift from previous protest repertoires in Ukraine, in particular with regard to the use of violence, the protest cycle followed the general pattern outlined by Tarrow (1993, 2001). In particular, each use of violence by either the regime or the protesters shifted the rules of engagement (hypothesis 1). Hypothesis 2, drawn from the social mobilisation literature on the critical role of pre-existing activist networks facilitating and sustaining protest, only partly held in the case of the Maidan. Activists' networks proved important for the initial protest mobilisation but they were quickly disempowered by the inherent diversity of the 'protestorate' whose broader grievances and scope they underestimated. Hypothesis 3 on the divisions among and between the activists and the political opposition creating the space for regime repression was confirmed, as was hypothesis 4 on the diversity of actors and claims that made it hard to mobilise a collective identity until regime repression provided an obvious frame centred on general human and civic rights (hypothesis 5).

Our analysis has revealed a continuously changing diversity of actors and claims within and across the stages in the protest cycle as the key feature of the Maidan protests. Diversity is not uncommon during protests in Ukraine or elsewhere, but its extent and the inability of activists, party leaders and the regime to understand and control it, is a novel phenomenon in Ukraine. Previously, diversity proved difficult or impossible to manage in the aftermath of victorious protests rather than in the midst of an ongoing protest. In turn, this diversity is also an important element of the causal mechanism behind the turn to violence in the latter stages of the protest cycle. Each of the four pivotal sets of actors—the Yanukovych regime; the political opposition; the activists; and self-organising 'ordinary' citizens—proved incapable of understanding and controlling the mobilisation's underlying diversity. This central finding distinguishes the Maidan from previous protests in Ukraine and is a timely corrective to a number of erroneous narratives about the Maidan that focus exclusively on the violent stages of the protest or use it to confirm widespread assumptions about a simple ethno-linguistic or east–west divide of Ukraine. By contrast, our fine-grained analysis of the protest cycle calls into question the salience and stability of ethno-linguistic and regional identities (hypothesis 6). While the majority of protesters were from central Ukraine, cross-cleavage coalitions

[96]For example, author's interview with anonymous political scientist 1, member of the Rada, negotiator during Regime–Opposition Roundtables, Kyiv, 15 May 2015.

[97]Group interview, mixed Social Movement Organisation activists, Kyiv, 18 July 2014.

[98]Focus group 'ordinary' citizens 1, Kyiv, 12 May 2015; focus group 'ordinary' citizens 2, Kyiv, 6 July 2015; focus group 'ordinary' citizens 3, Kyiv, 7 July 2015; focus group 'ordinary' citizens 4, Kyiv, 8 July 2015; focus group 'ordinary' citizens 5, Kyiv, 9 July 2015; focus group 'ordinary' citizens 6, Kyiv, 10 July 2015.

and the diffusion of protest events across the country, albeit to varying degrees, underline the fluid and contingent nature of cleavages commonly portrayed as fixed and the existence of alternative salient political identities. Our analysis of the nature and scope of the Maidan demonstrates that a conceptualisation of Ukrainian politics as being driven by ethno-linguistic or regional demands is too simplistic. If an extreme moment of mass mobilisation is not clearly aligned with ethno-linguistic or regional identities and rather focuses on country-wide concerns, such as a corrupt regime, and if it diffuses to the least likely arenas, namely, to the eastern regions, political identities in Ukraine are less deterministic than is often assumed.

Conceptually, our analysis points to three important dynamics that are not sufficiently captured by Tarrow's model and the comparative literature on contentious politics more generally: first, the extent to which sustained mass protest can be characterised by diversity (and a diversity that itself changes over time); second, the causal importance of this diversity which the regime, the political opposition and activists alike find impossible to grasp, thereby precipitating miscalculations on all sides; and third, the geographical diffusion of the protests beyond the protest centre. Last but not least, our analysis has also highlighted the methodological need for the collection of on-site data on protesters in order to gain a better understanding of the mobilisation dynamics as they unfold. Future research should aim to develop better tools for capturing and measuring protester diversity throughout the protest cycle and identifying the mechanisms connecting this diversity to the rise of violence and other protest outcomes. Moreover, the role of ethno-linguistic and regional identities in shaping political preferences and behaviour in Ukraine requires more nuanced analyses. A clearer distinction is needed between demographic descriptors and the salience of these characteristics as identities driving political behaviour.

References

Andrews, K. T. & Biggs, M. (2006) 'The Dynamics of Protest Diffusion: Movement Organizations, Social Networks, and News Media in the 1960 Sit-Ins', *American Sociological Review*, 71, 5.

Arel, D. (1993) *Language and the Politics of Ethnicity: The Case of Ukraine*, PhD thesis, University of Illinois at Urbana-Champaign, available at: http://www.ideals.illinois.edu/handle/2142/23297, accessed 11 January 2015.

Arel, D. (1995) 'Language Politics in Independent Ukraine: Towards One or Two State Languages?' *Nationalities Papers*, 23, 3.

Barrington, L. W. & Herron, E. S. (2004) 'One Ukraine or Many? Regionalism in Ukraine and its Political Consequences', *Nationalities Papers*, 32, 1.

Bartels, L. M. & Jackman, S. (2014) 'A Generational Model of Political Learning', *Electoral Studies*, 33, March.

Beissinger, M. (1998) 'Event Analysis in Transitional Societies: Protest Mobilization in the Former Soviet Union', in Rucht, D., Koopmans, R. & Neidhardt, F. (eds) *Acts of Dissent: The Study of Protest in Contemporary Democracies* (Berlin, Sigma).

Beissinger, M. (2002) *Nationalist Mobilization and the Collapse of the Soviet State* (Cambridge, Cambridge University Press).

Beissinger, M. (2007) 'Structure and Example in Modular Political Phenomena: The Diffusion of Bulldozer/ Rose/Orange/Tulip Revolutions', *Perspectives on Politics*, 5, 2.

Beissinger, M. (2011) 'Mechanisms of Maidan: The Structure of Contingency in the Making of the Orange Revolution', *Mobilization: An International Quarterly*, 16, 1.

Beissinger, M. (2013) 'The Semblance of Democratic Revolution: Coalitions in Ukraine's Orange Revolution', *American Political Science Review*, 107, 3.

Beissinger, M. R. & Sasse, G. (2014) 'An End to "Patience"?', in Bartels, L. & Bermeo, N. (eds) *Mass Politics in Tough Times: Opinions, Votes and Protest in the Great Recession* (Oxford, Oxford University Press).

Benford, R. D. & Snow, D. A. (2000) 'Framing Processes and Social Movements: An Overview and Assessment', *Annual Review of Sociology*, 26, August.

Bermeo, N. (2003) *Ordinary People in Extraordinary Times: The Citizenry and the Breakdown of Democracy* (Princeton, NJ, Princeton University Press).

Birch, S. (2000) 'Interpreting the Regional Effect in Ukrainian Politics', *Europe-Asia Studies*, 52, 6.

Bohdanova, T. (2014) 'Unexpected Revolution: The Role of Social Media in Ukraine's Euromaidan Uprising', *European View*, 13, 1.

Bohstedt, J. (1994) 'The Dynamics of Riots: Escalation and Diffusion/Contagion', in Potegal, M. & Knutson, J. F. (eds) *The Dynamics of Aggression: Biological and Social Processes in Dyads and Groups* (Hillsdale, NJ, Lawrence Erlbaum).

Bremmer, I. (1994) 'The Politics of Ethnicity: Russians in the New Ukraine', *Europe-Asia Studies*, 46, 2.

Bunce, V. & Wolchik, S. L. (2007) 'Transnational Networks, Diffusion Dynamics, and Electoral Revolutions in the Postcommunist World', *Physica A: Statistical Mechanics and its Applications*, 378, 1.

Bunce, V. J. & Wolchik, S. L. (2011) *Defeating Authoritarian Leaders in Postcommunist Countries* (Cambridge, Cambridge University Press).

Carey, S. C. (2006) 'The Dynamic Relationship between Protest and Repression', *Political Research Quarterly*, 59, 1.

Colton, T. J. (2011) 'An Aligning Election and the Ukrainian Political Community', *East European Politics & Societies*, 25, 1.

Crowley, S. (1997) *Hot Coal, Cold Steel: Russian and Ukrainian Workers from the End of the Soviet Union to the Post-Communist Transformations* (Ann Arbor, MI, University of Michigan Press).

D'Anieri, P. (2006) *Understanding Ukrainian Politics: Power, Politics, and Institutional Design* (New York, NY, M.E. Sharpe).

D'Anieri, P. (2011) 'Structural Constraints in Ukrainian Politics', *East European Politics & Societies*, 25, 1.

Darden, K. & Grzymala-Busse, A. (2006) 'The Great Divide: Literacy, Nationalism, and the Communist Collapse', *World Politics*, 59, 1.

Darden, K. & Way, L. (2014) 'Who Are the Protesters in Ukraine?', *The Washington Post*, 12 February, available at: http://www.washingtonpost.com/blogs/monkey-cage/wp/2014/02/12/who-are-the-protesters-in-ukraine/, accessed 21 March 2015.

Davidzon, V. (2014) 'Ukrainian Right Sector Parliamentarian Borislav Bereza is Proud to be Jewish', *Tablet Magazine*, available at: http://www.tabletmag.com/jewish-news-and-politics/187217/borislav-bereza, accessed 7 January 2016.

Della Porta, D. (2013) 'Repertoires of Contention', *The Wiley-Blackwell Encyclopedia of Social and Political Movements*, available at: http://onlinelibrary.wiley.com/doi/10.1002/9780470674871.wbespm178/full, accessed 16 September 2014.

Diani, M. & McAdam, D. (2003) *Social Movements and Networks: Relational Approaches to Collective Action* (Oxford, Oxford University Press).

Dinas, E. & Stoker, L. (2014) 'Age–Period–Cohort Analysis: A Design-Based Approach', *Electoral Studies*, 33, March.

Ekiert, G. & Kubik, J. (2001) *Rebellious Civil Society: Popular Protest and Democratic Consolidation in Poland, 1989–1993* (Ann Arbor, MI, University of Michigan Press).

Etling, B. (2014) 'Russia, Ukraine, and the West: Social Media Sentiment in the Euromaidan Protests', Berkman Center Research Publication, 13.

Frye, T. (2014) 'What Do Voters in Ukraine Want? A Survey Experiment on Candidate Ethnicity, Language, and Policy Orientation', *Problems of Post-Communism*, 62, 5.

Githens-Mazer, J. (2012) 'The Rhetoric and Reality: Radicalization and Political Discourse', *International Political Science Review*, 33, 5.

Goldstone, J. A. & Tilly, C. (2001) 'Threat (and Opportunity): Popular Action and State Response in the Dynamics of Contentious Action', in Aminzade, R., Goldstone, J. A. & McAdam, D. (eds) *Silence and Voice in the Study of Contentious Politics* (Cambridge, Cambridge University Press).

Gould, R. V. (1991) 'Multiple Networks and Mobilization in the Paris Commune, 1871', *American Sociological Review*, 56, 6.

Gould, R. V. (1993) 'Collective Action and Network Structure', *American Sociological Review*, 58, 2.

Greene, S. (2014) *Moscow in Movement: Power and Opposition in Putin's Russia* (Pal Alto, CA, Stanford University Press).

Greskovits, B. (1998) *The Political Economy of Protest and Patience: East European and Latin American Transformation Compared* (Budapest, Central European University Press).

Hale, H. E. (2008) *The Foundations of Ethnic Politics: Separatism of States and Nations in Eurasia and the World* (New York, NY, Cambridge University Press).

Hale, H., Kravets, N. & Onuch, O. (2015) 'Can Federalism Unite Ukraine in a Peace Deal?', PONARS Eurasia Policy Memo, 379, August, available at: http://www.ponarseurasia.org/sites/default/files/policy-memos-pdf/Pepm379_Hale-Kravets-Onuch_Aug2015.pdf, accessed 18 March 2016.

Haran, O. (2001) 'Can Ukrainian Communists and Socialists Evolve to Social Democracy?' *Demokratizatsiya*, 9, 4.

Hesli, V. L., Reisinger, W. M. & Miller, A. H. (1998) 'Political Party Development in Divided Societies: The Case of Ukraine', *Electoral Studies*, 17, 2.

Hrycak, A. (2006) 'Foundation Feminism and the Articulation of Hybrid Feminisms in Post-Socialist Ukraine', *East European Politics & Societies*, 20, 1.

Ishchenko, V. (2014) 'Volodymyr Ishchenko on Ukraine: Maidan, the Far Right and Civil War', *LINKS International Journal of Socialist Renewal*, 4 November, available at: http://links.org.au/node/4155, accessed 21 March 2015.

Judah, T. (2015) *In Wartime: Stories from Ukraine* (London, Penguin).

Katchanovski, I. (2014) 'East or West? Regional Political Divisions in Ukraine since the "Orange Revolution" and the "Euromaidan"', Paper presented at the APSA 2014 Annual Meeting, 28–31 August, available at: http://papers.ssrn.com/sol3/Papers.cfm?abstract_id=2454203, accessed 21 March 2015.

King, G., Keohane, R. & Verba, S. (1994) *Designing Social Inquiry: Scientific Inference in Qualitative Research* (Princeton, NJ, Princeton University Press).

Kitschelt, H. P. (1986) 'Political Opportunity Structures and Political Protest: Anti-Nuclear Movements in Four Democracies', *British Journal of Political Science*, 16, 1.

Koopmans, R. (1999) 'Political. Opportunity. Structure. Some Splitting to Balance the Lumping', *Sociological Forum*, 14, 1.

Kubicek, P. (2000) 'Regional Polarisation in Ukraine: Public Opinion, Voting and Legislative Behaviour', *Europe-Asia Studies*, 52, 2.

Kulyk, V. (2011) 'Language Identity, Linguistic Diversity and Political Cleavages: Evidence from Ukraine', *Nations and Nationalism*, 17, 3.

Kulyk, V. (2014) 'Ukrainian Nationalism since the Outbreak of Euromaidan', *Ab Imperio*, 3.

Kuran, T. (1997) *Private Truths, Public Lies: The Social Consequences of Preference Falsification* (Cambridge, MA, Harvard University Press).

Larrabee, F. S., Wilson, P. A. & Gordon, J. (2015) *The Ukrainian Crisis and European Security: Implications for the United States and US Army* (Washington, DC, Rand Corporation).

Levitsky, S. & Way, L. (2006) 'Linkage versus Leverage. Rethinking the International Dimension of Regime Change', *Comparative Politics*, 38, 4.

Marples, D. R. (1991) *Ukraine under Perestroika: Ecology, Economics and the Workers' Revolt* (Edmonton, University of Alberta Press).

Martsenyuk, T. (2005) *What is the Maidan Talking About?*, NaUKMA Working Paper, available at: http://www.ekmair.ukma.kiev.ua/handle/123456789/1395, accessed 18 March 2016.

McAdam, D., Tarrow, S. & Tilly, C. (2001) *Dynamics of Contention* (Cambridge, Cambridge University Press).

McAdam, D., Zald, M. & McCarthy, J. D. (1996) *Comparative Perspectives on Social Movements: Political Opportunities, Mobilizing Structures, and Cultural Framings* (Cambridge, Cambridge University Press).

McFaul, M. (2007) 'Ukraine Imports Democracy: External Influences on the Orange Revolution', *International Security*, 32, 2.

Meirowitz, A. & Tucker, J. A. (2013) 'People Power or a One-Shot Deal? A Dynamic Model of Protest', *American Journal of Political Science*, 57, 2.

Melucci, A. (1996) *Challenging Codes: Collective Action in the Information Age* (Cambridge, Cambridge University Press).

Menon, R. & Rumer, E. B. (2015) *Conflict in Ukraine: The Unwinding of the Post-Cold War Order* (Boston, MA, MIT Press).

Metzger, M., Nagler, J. & Tucker, J. A. (2015) 'Tweeting Identity? Ukrainian, Russian, and #Euromaidan', *Journal of Comparative Economics*, online first 21 December, available at: http://www.sciencedirect.com/science/article/pii/S0147596715001237, accessed 7 January 2016.

Meyer, D. S. (2004) 'Protest and Political Opportunities', *Annual Review of Sociology*, 30.

Moroz, V. (2013) '"Prapor Chervono-Chornyy—Tse Nashe Znameno…". Yakym Buv Styah UPA?', *Istorychna Pravda*, 18 October, available at: http://www.istpravda.com.ua/articles/2013/10/18/138044/, accessed 18 March 2016.

Mueller, C. (1997) 'International Press Coverage of East German Protest Events, 1989', *American Sociological Review*, 62, 5.

Nayem, M. (2014) 'Protests in Ukraine: It Started with a Facebook Message', *Open Society Foundation*, available at: https://www.opensocietyfoundations.org/voices/uprising-ukraine-how-it-all-began, accessed 18 November 2014.

Neundorf, A. & Niemi, R. G. (2014) 'Beyond Political Socialization: New Approaches to Age, Period, Cohort Analysis', *Electoral Studies*, 33, March.

Nikolayenko, O. (2007) 'The Revolt of the Post-Soviet Generation: Youth Movements in Serbia, Georgia, and Ukraine', *Comparative Politics*, 39, 2.

Noakes, J. A. & Johnston, H. (2005) 'Frames of Protest: A Road Map to a Perspective', in Noakes, J. A. & Johnston, H. (eds) *Frames of Protest: Social Movements and the Framing Perspective* (Boulder, CO & Lanham, MD, Rowman & Littlefield).

O'Loughlin, J. (2001) 'The Regional Factor in Contemporary Ukrainian Politics: Scale, Place, Space, or Bogus Effect?', *Post-Soviet Geography and Economics*, 42, 1.

Onuch, O. (2014a) *Mapping Mass Mobilizations: Understanding Revolutionary Moments in Ukraine and Argentina* (London, Palgrave Macmillan).

Onuch, O. (2014b) 'Who Were the Protesters?', *Journal of Democracy*, 25, 3.

Onuch, O. (2015a) 'Euromaidan Protests in Ukraine: Social Media versus Social Networks', *Problems of Post-Communism*, 62, 4.

Onuch, O. (2015b) 'Maidans Past and Present: Comparing the Orange Revolution and the EuroMaidan', in Marples, D. (ed.) *Euromaidan* (London, Columbia University Press).

Onuch, O. & Martsenyuk, T. (2013) 'EuroMaidan Protest Participant Survey', Ukrainian Protest Project, funded by British Academy Newton Fellowship and John Fell Fund.

Onuch, O. & Sasse, G. (2014) 'What Does Ukraine's #Euromaidan Teach Us about Protest?', *Washington Post*, 27 February, available at: http://www.washingtonpost.com/blogs/monkey-cage/wp/2014/02/27/what-does-ukraines-euromaidan-teach-us-about-protest/, accessed 16 May 2014.

Opp, K. D. (1988) 'Grievances and Participation in Social Movements', *American Sociological Review*, 53.

Osa, M. (2003) *Solidarity and Contention: Networks of Polish Oppositions* (Minneapolis, MN, University of Minnesota Press).

Osipian, A. L. & Osipian, A. L. (2012) 'Regional Diversity and Divided Memories in Ukraine: Contested Past as Electoral Resource, 2004–2010', *East European Politics & Societies*, 26, 3.

Phillips, S. D. (2008) *Women's Social Activism in the New Ukraine: Development and the Politics of Differentiation* (Bloomington, IN, Indiana University Press).

Polletta, F. & Jasper, J. M. (2001) 'Collective Identity and Social Movements', *Annual Review of Sociology*, 27.

Polyakova, A. (2014) 'From the Provinces to the Parliament: How the Ukrainian Radical Right Mobilized in Galicia', *Communist and Post-Communist Studies*, 47, 2.

Pop-Eleches, G. & Tucker, J. A. (2014) 'Communist Socialization and Post-Communist Economic and Political Attitudes', *Electoral Studies*, 33, March.

Popova, M. (2014) 'Why the Orange Revolution was Short and Peaceful and Euromaidan Long and Violent', *Problems of Post-Communism*, 61, 6.

Rampton, B. (2014) *Crossings: Language and Ethnicity among Adolescents* (London, Routledge).

Riabchuk, M. (2002) 'Ukraine: One State, Two Countries', *Transit Online*, 23, available at: http://www.eurozine.com/pdf/2002-09-16-riabchuk-en.pdf, accessed 12 January 2015.

Robertson, G. B. (2010) *The Politics of Protest in Hybrid Regimes: Managing Dissent in Post-Communist Russia* (Cambridge, Cambridge University Press).

Ryabchuk, A. (2014) 'Right Revolution? Hopes and Perils of the Euromaidan Protests in Ukraine', *Debatte: Journal of Contemporary Central and Eastern Europe*, 22, 1.

Sakwa, R. (2014) *Frontline Ukraine: Crisis in the Borderlands* (London, I.B. Tauris).

Sasse, G. (2010) 'The Role of Regionalism', *Journal of Democracy*, 21, 3.

Shekhovtsov, A. & Umland, A. (2014) 'Ukraine's Radical Right', *Journal of Democracy*, 25, 3.

Shkolnikov, V. (2012) 'Ukrainians and Russians in Ukraine and in Russia', in Meslé, F. & Vallin, J. (eds) *Mortality and Causes of Death in 20th-Century Ukraine* (Berlin, Springer), available at: http://www.demogr.mpg.de/books/drm/009/6.pdf, accessed 29 July 2015.

Snow, D. A. & Benford, R. D. (1992) 'Master Frames and Cycles of Protest', in Morris, A. D. & Mueller, C. M. (eds) *Frontiers in Social Movement Theory* (New Haven, CT, Yale University Press).

Snow, D. A., Rochford Jr, E. B., Worden, S. K., & Benford, R. D. (1986) 'Frame Alignment Processes, Micromobilization, and Movement Participation', *American Sociological Review*, 51, 4.

Snow, D. A., Soule, S. A. & Kriesi, H. (2008) *The Blackwell Companion to Social Movements* (Hoboken, NJ, John Wiley & Sons).

State Statistics Committee of Ukraine (2001) *All-Ukrainian Population Census*, available at: http://2001.ukrcensus.gov.ua/eng/results/, accessed 10 September 2015.

Tarrow, S. (1993) 'Cycles of Collective Action: Between Moments of Madness and the Repertoire of Contention', *Social Science History*, 17, 2.

Tarrow, S. (2011) *Power in Movement: Social Movements and Contentious Politics* (Cambridge, Cambridge University Press).

Tilly, C. & Tarrow, S. G. (2007) *Contentious Politics* (Boulder, CO, Paradigm Publishers).

Tucker, J. A. (2007) 'Enough! Electoral Fraud, Collective Action Problems, and Post-Communist Coloured Revolutions', *Perspectives on Politics*, 5, 3.

Tucker, J. A., Metzger, M. & Barberá, P. (2014) 'SMaPP Lab Data Report: Ukraine Protests 2013–2014', Preliminary Results 28 February, Social Media and Political Participation Lab, New York University, available at: http://smapp.nyu.edu/reports/Ukraine_Data_Report.pdf, accessed 10 September 2014.

Way, L. (2008) 'The Real Causes of the Color Revolutions', *Journal of Democracy*, 19, 3.

Wilson, A. (2006) 'Ukraine's Orange Revolution, NGOs and the Role of the West', *Cambridge Review of International Affairs*, 19, 1.

Wilson, A. (2014) *Ukraine Crisis: What It Means for the West* (New Haven, CT, Yale University Press).

Wolczuk, K. (2006) 'Whose Ukraine?: Language and Regional Factors in the 2004 and 2006 Elections in Ukraine', *European Yearbook of Minority Issues*, 5.

Zakharov, Y. (2004) 'History of Dissent in Ukraine', *Virtual Museum of the Dissident Movement in Ukraine*, available at: http://archive.khpg.org/en/index.php?id=1127288239, accessed 29 July 2015.

Zychowicz, J. (2011) 'Two Bad Words: FEMEN & Feminism in Independent Ukraine', *Anthropology of East Europe Review*, 29, 2.

Appendix 1. Description of survey questionnaire

The questionnaire was divided into five sections: date, frequency and type of participation; mobilisation factors (who, if anyone, did the protesters come with, how did they find out where to go to protest, and what sources of information did they use more broadly?); key claims and demands of the protesters; past political engagement in elections, protests, and membership in organisations and parties; and demographic and biographical information about the respondents (gender, ethnicity, language use and religion). The questions about a respondent's mother tongue in conjunction with questions about language use at work and in private mark a departure from the simplifications of linguistic issues in existing surveys of the Ukrainian population at large. For more see, www.ukrainianprotesproject.com, accessed 13 February 2016.

Appendix 2. Description of rapid interview questions asked

Three primary questions were asked: 'Why are you here today?'; 'Why did you decide to protest?'; and 'Why is your participation in the protests important?'. Two secondary questions were asked, time permitting: 'Who did you come with?'; and 'What source of information did you use to find out about the protest?'

Appendix 3. List of Rada HO «Vseukrayins'ke obyednannya Maydanu» (The Council of the NGO 'All-Ukrainian Union Maidan') Participants

Taras Boykiv; Oleksiy Haran'; Vasyl' Hats'ko; Ihor Zhdanov; Andriy Illyenko; Irena Karpa; Serhiy Kvit; V'yacheslav Kyrylenko; Ihor Koliushko; Vitaliy Klychko; Ruslan Koshulyns'kyy; Ivan Krul'ko; Ruslana Lyzhychko; Ihor Lutsenko; Yuriy Lutsenko; Mariya Matios; Andriy Mokhnyk; Valeriy Patskan; Oleh Osokhovs'kyy; Sashko Polozhyns'kyy; Petro Poroshenko; Vitaliy Portnykov; Serhiy Rakhmanin; Yehor Sobolyev; Serhiy Sobolyev; Oleksandr Sushko; Viktoriya Syumar; Borys Tarasyuk; Yulia Tymoshenko; Oleksandr Turchynov; Oleh Tiahnybok; Valeriy Chalyy; Refat Chubarov; Viktor Chumak; Zoryan Shkiryak; Yelyzaveta Shchepetil'nykova; Arseniy Yatsenyuk.

TABLE A1
PROTEST EVENTS IN THE RUN-UP TO THE MAIDAN

Protest event name	Protest event claim/ grievance	Estimated size for largest protest event	Political parties/ SMOs/ leaders involved
Anti-NATO protests 2009 & 2006, 2008, 2009, 2010	Against NATO accession	1,000–6,000 Repeatedly in Feodosiva, Kyiv, Kharkiv	Party of Regions; Communist Party of Ukraine
Podatkovyi Maidan protests December 2010 and January 2011 http://www.chesni-podatky.org/http://mistovoli.org/	*Demands*: Veto of the tax code; Protection of small businesses; the resignation of the Azarov government; new elections to the Verkhovna Rada for March 2011	6,000–10,000 Kyiv	Vladimir Dorosh, Mykhailo Volynets, Michael Svystovych, Oksana Prodan, Rima Bilotserkivska, small and medium businesses, B'YuT, NGOs, SMOs
AutoMaidan protests 2012 2013, 2014 http://www.automaidan.org.ua/	*Demands*: Termination of 'fictitious business activities' in Ukraine; against the refusal of registration of 2,500 election candidates	50 up to 2,000 Across central and western Ukraine, also in Sumy, Dnipropetrovsk and Odesa; mostly in Kyiv	Assembly of NGOs small and medium business Ukraine; NGO 'All-Ukrainian Union' Avtomaidan; Avtomaidan Community
Free Yulia protests 2011–2013	*Demands*: Release of Yulia Tymoshenko	6,000–10,000 Mostly in Kyiv	B'YuT; Opposition parties; NGOs; SMOs
Language Law protests 2012 and 2013	*Demands*: Overturn of Law №5029-VI (8 August 2012) 'On principles of state language policy'	2,000–10,000 Mostly in Kyiv, and Kharkiv	B'YuT; Opposition parties; UDAR; Svoboda; NGOs; SMOs

Source: Data compiled by authors, based on local online news media sources.

TABLE A2
NUMBERS OF TYPES OF INFORMANTS

Type	Number
Activist liberal	15
Activist leftwing	4
Activist rightwing	14
Activist/journalists/streamers	8
Diplomat/NGO/expert/foreign	4
NGO/expert/Ukrainian	10
Political insider—party in opposition	9
Political insider—party in power	4

Note: Streamers are people who recorded live footage of the protests to be posted on the internet.

TABLE A3
TRIANGULATED DATA SOURCES 2013–2014

Type of data	Approximate number
Digital Social Movement Organisation documents	478
Activist private notes/recordings	27
Personal correspondences	39
Video footage/streams	263

Source: Author's own data collection.

TABLE A4
THE MAIDAN PROTESTERS SURVEY SAMPLE DEMOGRAPHICS

Survey sample characteristics	
Mean age	36
Median age	32
Gender	Women 41%; Men 59%
Language (mother tongue)	83% Ukrainian; 12% Russian; 4% (both); 1% other
Language use (work)	68% Ukrainian; 22% Russian; 6% (both); 4% other
Language use (private life)	69% Ukrainian; 23% Russian; 6% (both); 2% other
Ethnicity	92% Ukrainian; 4% Russian; 4% other
Religion	33% (Orthodox, Kyiv Patriarchate); 25% (Ukrainian Greek Catholic); 16% (not practising/non-believer); 8% (Orthodox, Moscow Patriarchate); 2% (Ukrainian Autocephalous Orthodox Church); 2% (Roman Catholic); 2% (Ukrainian Protestant Church); 12% Other

Notes: Median employment status: employed full time. Mean and median education level: higher education (at least some tertiary education). Percentage present on first day of protest: 14%.

National Identity in Ukraine: Impact of Euromaidan and the War

VOLODYMYR KULYK

Abstract

The essay examines the impact of the Euromaidan protests and the subsequent Russian aggression on Ukrainian national identity. It demonstrates that national identity has become more salient *vis-à-vis* other territorial and non-territorial identities. At the same time, the very meaning of belonging to the Ukrainian nation has changed, as manifested first and foremost in increased alienation from Russia and the greater embrace of Ukrainian nationalism. Although popular perceptions are by no means uniform across the country, the main dividing line has shifted eastwards and now lies between the Donbas and the adjacent east-southern regions.

ONE OF THE MOST NOTEWORTHY CONSEQUENCES OF THE RECENT events in Ukraine is a dramatic change in Ukrainian national identity. In various media one can regularly encounter assertions of individuals' increased self-identification as Ukrainian, greater pride in being a citizen of the Ukrainian state, stronger attachment to symbols of nationhood, enhanced solidarity with compatriots, increased readiness to defend Ukraine or work for Ukraine, and increased confidence in the people's power to change the country for the better. Most speak of their own experiences or those of people around them, while some generalise individual changes and assert a greater consolidation of the Ukrainian nation or even the 'birth' of a nation out of people supposedly lacking in national consciousness. The reverse side of this consolidation of Ukrainianness is a sense of alienation from or even enmity towards Russia, which is targeted primarily at the state but sometimes also at the people, who, it is believed, overwhelmingly support the state's aggressive policy towards Ukraine.

These changes are attributed to the Euromaidan protests and subsequent Russian aggression against Ukraine which started with the annexation of Crimea and continues with the war in the Donbas. Some argue that the consolidation of national identity is primarily the result of the war, while the readiness to contribute to democratic change originated in the social mobilisation against the authoritarian regime. For example, journalist-turned-politician

The research on which this essay is based was supported by different sources: the 2014 survey and 2015 focus group discussions were funded by a research grant from the Canadian Institute of Ukrainian Studies, University of Alberta from the Stasiuk Family Endowment Fund; the 2012 survey was made possible by a grant from the Shevchenko ScientiSociety in the US from the Natalia Danylchenko Fund. Part of the research for this essay was conducted within the framework of the Research Initiative on Democratic Reforms in Ukraine. Thanks are also due to Andrew Wilson, Kataryna Wolczuk, Derek Averre and the two anonymous referees for their comments on earlier drafts of the essay.

Mustafa Nayyem argued that 'the most important, if not the only result of the Maidan has become the political class' fear of society', while 'an unprecedented rise of patriotic feelings, a conscious national identification' and other positive changes of the post-Maidan year result primarily from the war.[1] Others believe that the national transformation and consolidation started on the Maidan itself, in a readiness to defend the common cause and support other people fighting for it; people who came to be perceived as Ukrainians rather than merely fellow protesters. Thus, journalist Fedir Sivtsov has described how he became a nationalist after a riot police attack on the Maidan in December 2013: 'When I looked around and instead of the empty place saw an endless stream of people—Ukrainians who were not indifferent to the fate of their compatriots'.[2] As with many other such revelations, this post was written by a Russian speaker who proudly asserted his Ukrainian identity which he viewed not as linked to ethnic origin or language use but rather as based on free choice, a predominant view among participants in the Maidan and in the subsequent defence of the country.

How representative are these views? Although differing in their preferred language, place of residence and social status, most of the authors of such assertions belong to the same group of activists and elites (politicians, journalists, Maidan participants, volunteer combatants or aid organisers) whose views are not necessarily typical of the entire population.[3] This study is intended to verify activist perceptions on the mass level, that is, to check whether changes in mass views correspond to those asserted by the activists and elites. By comparing the data of two nationwide surveys that were conducted in September 2014 and February 2012, respectively, I examine changes in popular views for the period encompassing the Euromaidan protests and an early stage of the war. In addition, focus group discussions conducted in February and March 2015 in different regions of Ukraine reveal nuances in and motivations behind certain preferences.

My main task is to analyse recent changes in two main dimensions of Ukrainian national identity, namely its salience *vis-à-vis* other identities people have and its content, or the meaning people attach to their perceived belonging to the Ukrainian nation. On each dimension, I will examine contestation within the nation, or the degree of disagreement between its putative members (Abdelal *et al.* 2007; Kulyk 2011).[4] Salience will be measured in relation not only to territorially anchored identities (both subnational and supranational) but also to other social identities such as those defined by gender, religion, occupation and political views. As far as content is concerned, I will not limit my investigation to those aspects pertaining to the Ukrainians' perceived ethnocultural distinctions but also to include views of their main sociopolitical characteristics. Finally, contestation will be primarily assessed by

---

[1]Mustafa Nayyem's Facebook page (in Russian), 20 February 2015, available at: https://www.facebook.com/Mustafanayyem/posts/10203987979405873, accessed 24 March 2016.

[2]Fedir Sivtsov's Facebook page (in Russian), 11 December 2013, available at: https://www.facebook.com/photo.php?fbid=787526201273292&set=a.686668548025725.1073741826.100000477598029&type=3&theater, accessed 24 March 2016.

[3]For an analysis of activist assertions of their own and the nation's identity changes, see Kulyk (2014a).

[4]Abdelal *et al.* (2007) conceptualise identity as a variable with two dimensions, content and contestation, which they consider more productive as characteristics of a collective self-perception than salience, a concept supposedly limited to the individual level. I argue, however, that what methods such as surveys and focus group discussions reveal are not characteristics of a collectivity *per se* but rather individuals' perceptions of their belonging to certain collectivities and of these collectivities themselves. Therefore, variation of a certain individual identity across the collectivity can be best conceptualised in terms of salience and content, for which we can also measure the degree of contestation within the collectivity (Kulyk 2011).

the distribution of responses to survey questions having to do with the salience and content of identity. Prior to dealing with recent changes, however, I would like to discuss scholarly analyses of Ukrainian identity in the two first decades of national independence.

Ukrainian identity before Euromaidan

Similarly to other perceptions of people as members of certain collectivities, national identity has been conceptualised on both individual and collective levels, that is, both as individuals' attachment to their perceived nation and as the nation's supposedly distinct organisation. Moreover, national identity can pertain to either an ethnic (cultural) or civic (political) community, both of which are routinely referred to as nations, particularly in the West (Smith 1991; Parekh 1995). Many scholars bemoan the widespread confusion in elite and popular discourse of what they view as conceptually different aspects of nationhood. On the one hand, Bhikhu Parekh has argued that while a political community is a 'territorially concentrated group of people bound together by their acceptance of a common mode of conducting their affairs', many discussions 'look for the identity of a political community … in the cultural or ethnocultural characteristics that are supposed to be common to all its members' (Parekh 1994, pp. 501–2). That is, such discussions confuse the features of the nation that are collectively enacted by its members and individual features that the members have in common. On the other hand, Alfonso Alfonsi has emphasised that 'citizenship (belonging to a political collectivity) and nationality (inclusion in a cultural community) are not co-terminous', although they 'have always been seen as synonymous in the empirical reality of the European countries' (Alfonsi 1997, pp. 53–4). However, such attempts at conceptual disentanglement do not prevent those discussing national identity from bringing together different elements which they believe contribute to the specific character of the nation under discussion. This is all the more so because people's acceptance of a common mode of behaviour is facilitated by and, at the same time, contributes to the commonality of their cultural characteristics, so that the supposedly political community has a certain ethnocultural basis (Kuzio 2002). Rather than trying to change the way people think about the nation, scholars should aim at discerning different aspects in that thinking and explaining their interaction.

The confusion of ethnic and civic dimensions of nationhood is particularly characteristic of thinking and speaking about the titular nations of certain states or autonomous units, that is, cultural communities constituting a core of eponymous political collectivities. As long as (would-be) Ukrainians did not have their 'own' independent state, they perceived their national distinction solely in cultural terms, with references to a particular religion, language, place of residence (which distinguished them from outsiders speaking or believing differently) or, with the spread of organic concepts of ethnicity, biological origin. During the Soviet decades, nationhood was institutionalised on both personal and territorial levels, that is, through the ascription of ethnonational identity ('nationality') to every person and the establishment of autonomous political units as national homelands of nations whose members were defined by this supposedly unchangeable identity (Brubaker 1994). Although this double institutionalisation made Ukrainian identity national rather than merely ethnic (Hrytsenko 1998, p. 153), membership of the nation seemed to be perceived primarily in ethnocultural rather than civic terms, due to both the social salience of personal 'nationality' and a lack of clear political distinctiveness of the Ukrainian republic from other constituent units of the USSR. Unfortunately, the scarcity of sociological studies of this sensitive topic in the USSR does not allow us persuasively to demonstrate the relative strength of these competing identifications.

With the establishment of an independent state, Ukrainian identity started gaining in salience and shifting toward civic content, while its ethnocultural basis was gradually acquiring elements that had been suppressed by the Soviet regime as 'nationalistic'. However, the salience and especially the content of this identity were strongly contested, reflecting not only inherited dissimilarities between particular groups of the population but also new disagreements inculcated by political and cultural elites, some of which promoted the formerly suppressed version and others adhered to the one inherited from Soviet times (Pirie 1996; Kuzio 2001). People disagreed even on how the national collectivity is to be defined, that is, whether it should comprise the entire population or only its ethnically Ukrainian part. Not only was it hard for many to switch from an ethnic to a civic definition of nationhood but also heated debate on how members of the Ukrainian nation should think and behave contributed to disagreement on who could be full-fledged members of the nation. The two aspects of identity content—the criterion of membership and the view of members' appropriate behaviour—were often confused even in scholarly works, all the more so because the authors referred to surveys using different terms with dissimilar connotations. Certainly, these aspects are closely connected as the predominant view of the appropriate behaviour determines the chances of belonging for certain 'peripheral' groups (ethnic, linguistic, religious and other minorities). Nevertheless, it is important to distinguish analytically between them since it may be easier for putative members of a nation to agree on common membership than on common beliefs and policies.

For example, when asked in a 1998 survey, 'What makes someone a Ukrainian?', a plurality of respondents preferred a purely subjective understanding, 'consciousness of oneself as a Ukrainian', while two smaller groups indicated the apparently objective but very different criteria, namely ethnic ('Ukrainian ancestors') and civic (Ukrainian citizenship). At the same time, in response to the question whether Ukraine should be 'a state of the Ukrainian nation' or 'a state without ethnic designation', just about a half of respondents indicated one of these polar options, with a considerable preference for the latter, while more than a third chose something in between (Wilson 2002). Another survey (conducted in 2001) seemed to demonstrate a clear preference for a civic definition of the Ukrainian community as the majority of respondents chose 'coexistence and equal rights in the framework of one state' as the main factor that 'unites or could unite the people of Ukraine into a single community', leaving far behind various ethnocultural designations. Moreover, civic characteristics such as respect for the Ukrainian state's institutions and laws, its citizenship and the perception of Ukraine as one's homeland scored much higher than language, ethnic origin or religion on the list of qualities that are 'most important for considering a person to be a real member of Ukrainian society' (Shulman 2004). Based on these responses, Stephen Shulman concluded that 'civic national identity in Ukraine seems to be substantially stronger than ethnic national identity', whatever the specific content of the latter (Shulman 2004, p. 53). However, the apparent preference for civic identity may have to do with the researcher's use of terms such as 'the people of Ukraine' and 'Ukrainian society' which have a clearly civic connotation, unlike 'a Ukrainian' and 'the Ukrainian nation' that were used in the 1998 survey. While members of different groups mostly agreed that equal rights and obligations were the main factor uniting all the people of Ukraine, given obvious ethnocultural differences between them, they did not necessarily accept all of these people into their nation or considered such an exclusive 'nation' a less important community than the inclusive 'people'. Actually, Shulman's own comparative study of elite perceptions in two big Ukrainian cities, L'viv in the west and Donets'k in the southeast, revealed that elites in each city view people in the other (or rather the region it belongs to) less than positively. Moreover, Donets'kites felt much better about Russians in Russia than about Ukrainians in western Ukraine, a clear indication of a weakness of civic national identity as a country-wide 'sense of togetherness and belonging' (Shulman 1999, p. 1015), which the new state's institutions had yet to engender.

While Shulman examined the strength of national identity which he related to the perceived cultural distance between constituent ethnic groups and the manner of inter-group interaction, several other studies sought to assess its salience *vis-à-vis* other identities that putative members of the Ukrainian nation may have. Despite using different designations of national identity, these studies revealed a gradual, but by no means uniform increase in salience. Scholars asking the respondents to indicate their primary self-designation among those related to territorial entities of different scale, from local to global, found that 'a citizen of Ukraine' had become the most salient of such designations. A 1997 survey indicated roughly equal preferences for the national and the subnational level, the latter combining identifications with the locality and region of residence (Stehnii & Churylov 1998, p. 45).[5] By 2006, national identity clearly overshadowed subnational identities (Besters-Dilger 2009, p. 389). At the same time, differences between regional groups in their identity preferences became even more pronounced, with the salience of national identity decreasing rather consistently from west to southeast.[6] In contrast, a longitudinal study of the post-Soviet identification processes in L'viv and Donets'k examined the salience of not only territorial identities but also those defined by other characteristics such as gender, religion, occupation and ideology. It revealed that the (rather ambiguous) identity as 'a Ukrainian' was one of the most salient in both cities but it mattered much more in the former than in the latter. While L'vivites consistently manifested it as much more salient than any other identity except for the local one, in Donets'k Ukrainian identity was much less pronounced than local identity and roughly equal in salience to those defined by gender and social status (Hrytsak 2007).

The above and other studies demonstrated that ethnocultural elements of the national identity content were more strongly contested than civic ones, that is, particular regional and ethnolinguistic groups differed more in their views of the former than of the latter. For example, L'viv respondents in the L'viv–Donets'k study tended to evaluate positively those historical events and personalities associated with the nationalist narrative of Ukraine's history which emphasises its orientation towards independence, while Donets'k residents supported primarily those phenomena featured in the East Slavic narrative which views Ukrainians as closely linked to Russians (Sereda 2007).[7] Shulman (2002) made a similar distinction between what he called Ethnic Ukrainian and East Slavic versions of national identity, the former based on the titular language and culture and the latter on the supposedly common culture

[5]In view of their strong attachment to the locality and region, it is remarkable that in that study the Donbas respondents predominantly identified as citizens of Ukraine (Stehnii & Churylov 1998, p. 45).

[6]This conclusion is based on my processing of raw data of a nationwide representative survey (2,015 respondents) conducted by the sociological centre Hromadska Dumka in December 2006 within the framework of an international project in which I participated (Besters-Dilger 2009).

[7]For a discussion of the nationalist and East Slavic historical narratives, see Kulyk (2011, 2014b).

of Ukrainians and Russians. He argued that the sharply dissimilar views of the ethnocultural basis of national identity in the western and south-eastern parts of Ukraine could explain their different preferences for other elements of the identity content, such as the state's foreign policy. That is, adherents of ethnic Ukrainian identity stood for breaking political ties with Russia which they viewed as undermining Ukraine's distinctiveness, while supporters of the East Slavic version insisted on close relations with Russia as a means of preserving the two people's commonality. Although they did not relate them to national identity, Arel and Khmelko (1996) indicated regionally polarised preferences regarding Ukrainian–Russian relations and the status of the Russian language in Ukraine as the most divisive issue in Ukrainian politics.

Such profound disagreement on the content of national identity stemmed from dissimilar ethnolinguistic profiles and historical trajectories of different regions, but its persistence in independent Ukraine had much to do with political elites' effort to mobilise the respective constituencies for the defence of their alleged interests. This effort considerably increased during and after the Orange Revolution when the anti-Orange parties sought to defeat their rivals by portraying them as representing the west of Ukraine and hostile to the east and south (Wolczuk 2007). The Orange government's attempt to strengthen the ethnocultural foundation of national identity which manifested itself in more resolute promotion of the Ukrainian language and the nationalist narrative of Ukraine's history was met with strong resistance of the anti-Orange opposition. In addition to close ties with Russia and attachment to the Russian language, it sought to distinguish the east-southern regions by a pantheon of heroes from the East Slavic narrative, the worship of whom was to be accompanied by hostility towards Ukrainian nationalist heroes honoured in the west (Kulyk 2009; Zhurzhenko 2013). While the political confrontation drove apart the preferences of the two 'halves' of Ukraine regarding these salient issues, the experience of independence and institutional discourses such as education instilled in all regions rather similar views of many less conspicuous ethnocultural aspects of national identity (Kulyk 2014b). Shekhovtsov has argued that although the Orange Revolution claimed to unite all Ukrainian citizens, its allegedly inclusive identity 'had pronounced exclusionary traits based on the ethno-cultural understanding of membership in this "imagined community"' (Shekhovtsov 2013, p. 740). However, it seems more appropriate to say that the Orange elites sought to build an inclusive civic identity but put it on a strong Ukrainian ethnocultural basis, which made it problematic for many members of other ethnolinguistic groups to join. At the same time, the Orange government's promotion of Ukrainian nationalist content that was a taboo under the Soviet regime and was viewed with suspicion by many post-Soviet people shifted the mainstream view of national identity, a shift that Euromaidan could build on.[8]

Euromaidan, like the Orange Revolution, was perceived by its participants and sympathisers as a unifying popular protest against the corrupt authoritarian regime, but the regime sought to weaken the protest by presenting it as led by the westerners and hostile to the easterners. Similarly, while Russia justified its intervention in the Crimea and Donbas by its concern for

---

[8]A vivid illustration of this shift is a change in popular perceptions of the Great Famine of 1932–1933, or *Holodomor*, which the Orange elites presented as the communist regime's genocide of the Ukrainian people. After the anti-Orange triumph in the 2010 election this interpretation was questioned and the scale of commemoration of the victims curtailed but this political backlash could 'hardly negate the new public awareness about the scale of the Great Famine, or devalue the moral aspects of the Holodomor memory' (Zhurzhenko 2013, p. 634).

the Russian speakers of those and adjacent regions, many members of different linguistic and regional groups viewed it as aggression against the entire Ukrainian people who, accordingly, must unite, resist and make an alliance with the West (Kulyk 2014a; Onuch 2015). The two processes can thus be expected to have caused significant changes both in the salience of national identity and in some aspects of its content, changes that can vary by the region and language of preference. It is these changes that the present study seeks to examine.

The salience of national identity after the Maidan and Russian aggression

To analyse recent changes in Ukrainian identity, I employ two complementary sets of data. On the one hand, the data of a nationwide representative survey conducted by the Kyiv International Institute of Sociology (KIIS) in September 2014 (2,035 respondents) indicate the relative strength of support for certain attitudes and policy preferences. Whenever possible, the results of this survey will be compared with the responses to identical questions in a survey conducted by the same institute in February 2012 (2,029 respondents) in order to examine changes for the period encompassing the Euromaidan protests and an early stage of the war. Since the 2014 survey did not include Crimea, in the 2012 data Crimean respondents had to be excluded as well in order to make the responses comparable. In order to examine different dynamics in different parts of the country, figures are presented not only for Ukraine as a whole but also for four particular macro-regions. Apart from the traditionally defined West and Centre, I separate the Donbas and include the remaining eastern and southern *oblasti* in what I call East/South for want of a better name. Although by September 2014 the Donbas was affected by an intense military conflict in which Ukrainian troops fought separatist and Russian forces, the survey encompassed both Ukrainian-controlled and separatist-controlled territories. In addition to discussing significant differences between the four macro-regions, I examine distinctions between the two parts of the Donbas which might have to do with their disposition on the opposite sides of the frontline.[9]

In addition, eight focus group discussions were conducted by the KIIS in February and March 2015 in different parts of Ukraine: in the capital of Kyiv and eastern metropolis of Kharkiv, as well as in two medium sized provincial capitals, Kirovohrad in the centre of the country and Chernivtsi in the south-west.[10] In each city, one group included people of 20–35 years who participated in the Maidan or supported it, and the other people of 35–50 years who reported a negative or rather negative attitude toward the Maidan.

These discussions reveal the nuances of and motivations behind certain preferences, in particular the respondents' attribution of certain changes in their own or other people's views and identities to the Maidan and/or the war. Separate groups for people with opposing positions on the Maidan, one for people supportive of the Maidan, and one for those viewing it critically, were created to avoid overt confrontation and promote openness; the division by age was used to allow young people to speak freely and not feel uneasy in contradicting

---

[9]The accuracy on the survey in the Donbas may be questioned due to both substantial migration out of the war-torn and separatist-controlled localities and the social climate in which some people may have been afraid to express views that ran counter to those of the authorities. In any case, the detected differences are too large to be attributed to survey errors.

[10]Since the focus group discussions took place several months after the survey, the attitudes revealed by two instruments might differ somewhat, all the more so because the situation in the country was rapidly changing at that time. However, this difference does not seem to significantly affect my findings as I use focus groups to elicit different explanations of changing attitudes rather than assess the change itself.

TABLE 1
FREQUENCIES OF ANSWERS TO THE SURVEY QUESTION, 'WHOM DO YOU CONSIDER
YOURSELF TO BE PRIMARILY? INDICATE ONE MOST IMPORTANT ANSWER', BY THE REGION
(%)

	Ukraine		West		Centre		East/South		Donbas	
	2012	2014	2012	2014	2012	2014	2012	2014	2012	2014
Resident of my city/town/village	28.1	20.7	28.2	14.8	23.5	9.9	30.0	34.2	32.9	27.7
Citizen of Ukraine	51.7	61.4	55.7	78.0	64.9	80.7	48.7	47.7	32.0	24.7
European	2.5	1.1	4.3	0.7	2.9	0.9	1.1	1.9	2.5	0.3
Resident of my region	10.4	8.8	7.8	4.1	3.5	3.6	11.1	6.2	19.0	30.1
Citizen of the earth	2.9	4.2	1.5	2.2	2.9	1.7	3.5	4.6	4.4	10.8
Resident of the post-Soviet space	3.1	3.0	1.3	0	1.1	1.6	4.4	5.1	7.0	5.7
Hard to say	1.3	0.8	1.3	0.2	1.2	1.6	1.2	0.3	2.2	0.6

Sources: Kyiv International Institute of Sociology, February 2012 and September 2014.

their older compatriots. This design seemed to work well as many participants expressed views contradicting those apparently shared by the majority of the group and such dissenting views, although sometimes retorted, were never attacked as aggressively as to intimidate their holders. However, as with all focus groups, one cannot exclude that some participants' limited contribution to the discussion at least partly resulted from a fear of expressing views with which others were likely to disagree.

Starting with salience, I sought to check whether popular sentiment followed activists' feelings in attaching more importance to national identity and whether this change is characteristic of all regions or only those western and central ones where the majority of the population supported the Maidan.[11] Both the 2012 and 2014 surveys included a question on the primary territorial identification of the respondents, replicating the one in the above-mentioned studies of 1997 and 2006. In both recent surveys, national identification clearly prevailed over the local, regional, post-Soviet, European and global ones (see Table 1). In 2014, 61% of respondents in the nationwide sample preferred the identity as 'a citizen of Ukraine', in contrast to 21% who identified with their city or village and 9% with their region. Other options scored lower than 5% but it is worth noting that the global identity turned out to be no less popular than the post-Soviet one. Moreover, in comparison with the 2012 survey national identification increased by a full 10% while the local one decreased by 7%, and the regional remained virtually unchanged. That is, the gap between national identity and its sub- and supranational competitors has widened considerably. As the most popular identity is now prioritised by a clear majority of Ukraine's population, the nationwide contestation of the hierarchy of salience seems to be weakening.

However, the preference for national identity is not evenly distributed across the country. Being clearly predominant in the West and Centre, it is somewhat less prevalent (although still the most salient of all territorial identifications) in the east-southern *oblasti,* but in the Donbas it is only the third most salient identity, after regional and local ones. Moreover, while in the West and Centre its salience increased between the two surveys, in the Donbas it significantly decreased, with a simultaneous gain in the salience of regional identification. This means that

[11]On the regional distribution of attitudes toward Euromaidan, see 'IRI Public Opinion Survey in Ukraine: March 2014', 6 April 2014, available at: http://www.slideshare.net/Ratinggroup/2014-april-5-iri-public-opinion-survey-of-ukraine-march-14-26-2014, accessed 24 July 2015.

TABLE 2
FREQUENCIES OF ANSWERS TO THE SURVEY QUESTION, 'WHICH OF THE WORDS LISTED
BELOW BEST CHARACTERISES YOU? IF IT IS HARD FOR YOU TO CHOOSE ONE, INDICATE A
FEW BUT NOT MORE THAN THREE MAIN CHARACTERISTICS', BY THE REGION AND SELF-
DECLARED NATIONALITY (%)

	Ukraine	West	Centre	East/South	Donbas	Ukrainian nationality	Russian nationality
Orthodox	26.2	26.1	20.5	30.8	29.4	26.2	26.5
Man/woman	44.7	32.7	43.5	49.4	52.6	43.7	52.6
Worker	4.8	2.4	3.9	7.7	4.8	4.6	5.7
Soviet person	2.0	0	1.0	4.3	2.4	1.4	7.1
Student	1.7	2.9	1.3	1.2	1.8	1.9	0.9
Resident of my city/village	28.2	30.1	21.8	30.2	34.9	25.8	22.3
Peasant	1.7	1.0	3.2	1.0	0.6	2.0	0.5
Greek Catholic	2.4	11.5	0.1	0	0	3.0	0
Ukrainian	47.1	71.6	57.4	36.5	12.0	56.3	8.5
Intelligentsia	3.2	4.8	1.1	2.2	6.9	2.6	5.7
Entrepreneur	0.6	0.7	0	0.9	0.9	0.4	1.4
Nationalist	1.1	2.2	0.9	0.5	1.2	1.1	1.4
Russian	3.4	0.5	1.1	4.1	10.8	0.1	28.4
Resident of my region	16.1	20.3	6.9	13.1	35.4	13.3	20.4
Pensioner	11.4	7.2	11.9	13.1	12.0	11.4	14.2
European	1.6	2.6	0.9	2.0	0.9	1.5	2.4
Patriot	7.3	12.9	6.2	5.6	5.7	7.8	2.8
Unemployed	1.3	1.0	1.1	1.7	1.5	1.3	0.9
Russian-speaker	3.9	0	2.9	2.9	12.6	1.7	15.6
Non-believer	0.5	0.5	0.6	0.5	0.6	0.4	0.9
Other	1.1	0.7	0.4	1.9	1.5	0.7	3.8
Hard to say	1.1	0.2	2.2	0.7	0.9	1.1	1.9

Source: Kyiv International Institute of Sociology, September 2014.

the Donbas residents increasingly distinguished themselves from the rest of Ukraine, which is hardly surprising in view of the fact that about a half of them lived in September 2014 in the separatist-proclaimed 'republics', even if they did not necessarily support them. (It is on the separatist-controlled territories that the identification with the Ukrainian state was particularly low.) At the same time, the relative salience of national and subnational identities remains much more contested in the Donbas and the East/South than in the West and Centre, which are strongly consolidated around the primary attachment to the nation.[12]

Remarkably, national identity is the most salient not only of all territorially anchored identifications but also of any social identities, its only match being identity defined by gender. When asked in the 2014 survey which of 20 listed words best characterise them, and allowed to choose no more than three, 47% of respondents nationwide indicated 'Ukrainian' and 45% 'man or woman' (see Table 2). At the same time, 28% opted for 'resident of my city or village',

---

[12]A curious manifestation of widespread confusion about identity is an unusually high share of the respondents from the separatist-controlled territories who identified as 'citizens of the Earth' (17% as compared with less than 5% in any other part of Ukraine), which seems to indicate their reluctance to choose between the national, regional and local attachments.

26% for 'Orthodox', 16% for 'resident of my region', 11% for 'pensioner' and 7% for 'patriot'. (Other characteristics were mentioned by less than 5%.) Although the specific meaning of the word 'Ukrainian' for a particular respondent is unclear, whether national or civic, ethnic or some combination thereof, the fact is that this self-perception is extremely salient in today's Ukraine. Here again, the salience of Ukrainian identity decreases as one moves eastward and southward; it is the most salient in the West and Centre, second after the gender identity in the East/South, and much weaker than the gender, regional, local and religious identifications in the Donbas. Even in the Donbas, however, Ukrainian identity is much stronger than Russian or Russian-speaking identities in the Ukraine-controlled territories, and it is only in the separatist enclaves that the hierarchy is reversed, another indication of a negative impact of these enclaves on people's identification with Ukraine.[13] It is unsurprising that people indicating their nationality as Russian were much less inclined to think of themselves as Ukrainians than those reporting Ukrainian nationality. More surprisingly, one in 12 of self-designated Russians also considered it important to identify as Ukrainian, meaning that the latter identity was for them primarily civic and the former primarily ethnic. In such an ambiguous situation, each of these supposedly complementary identities turned out to be much less salient than for those people who identified as Ukrainian in both ethnic and civic terms.

The focus group discussions provide explanations of both why the salience of national identity has increased and why this identification remains, or has become problematic for some people. As national identity can be related to both the nation and the state, those people who are discontented with the current policies of the state are less likely to develop or declare such identification than those who support the authorities. As a Kharkiv participant put it: 'Unfortunately, now I understand that my country treats me, a citizen of Ukraine, like a brute, excuse my expression. … Love should be mutual. If I am hated, why should I love?'.[14] Moreover, while the feeling of empowerment contributes to stronger national identity, the opposite feeling of powerlessness and helplessness makes it more problematic. The following discussion vividly illustrates this point:

Respondent 1:	I think that citizens' attitude towards the Ukrainian state has changed significantly [for the better] in the last years. Towards the flag, the anthem.
Respondent 4:	*I don't know, for me it's the contrary. Helplessness.*
Respondent 6:	*Same with me.*
Respondent 4:	*You cannot do anything. Helplessness.*
Respondent 1:	This is just one side of the coin, and the other is, yes, people cannot do anything. They are sent … some sent to the war, others are just unemployed.
Moderator:	So, on the one hand, there is some consolidation of the nation?

[13]While it is possible that some people in the separatist-controlled territories were afraid to reveal their attachment to Ukraine to the interviewer, the difference between two parts of the Donbas on this matter is much bigger than on most other ones, which indicates that there has been genuine re-identification from Ukrainians to Russians.

[14]Respondent 2, in Russian, focus group Kharkiv 2, with participants of 35–50 years who viewed the Maidan critically, 22 February 2015. When quoting from a focus group discussion, I will indicate the language of the quoted expression. If a quote comprises pieces (from full replication to single words) in both languages, I will list them in the decreasing order of contribution and italicise pieces in that which was used less. For example, if the quote contains 70% Russian and 30% Ukrainian I present it as 'in Russian and Ukrainian', and italicise that which is in Ukrainian. Moreover, in order to indicate which member of the focus group is being quoted, I give the numbers assigned to the participants in the transcripts provided by the Kyiv International Institute of Sociology.

Respondent 1:   There are some positive moments, but on the other …
Respondent 8:   Yes, there are some positive [moments], of course.
Moderator: And on the other, there is helplessness?
Respondent 8:   It's just that people are different. Some are stronger morally, in spirit, others
                are weaker, and much depends on that too.[15]

At the same time, the effect of recent changes in one's attachment to the nation and state is modified by one's pre-existing feelings about them. In Kyiv, Kirovohrad and Chernivtsi, most people in both the 'pro-Maidan' and 'anti-Maidan' groups shared at least to some extent the general feeling of national consolidation, a commonality that largely blurred the contrast between the two sets of groups. Even some of those who bemoaned the severe economic crisis in war-stricken Ukraine argued that 'there is more patriotism, so one [should] respect one's country more, more strongly believe in changes for the better, [believe] that it will win, that is, the war will end and the crisis will end'.[16] Many participants tried to reconcile their dissatisfaction with current policies and their national sentiment by declaring their preference for their identity as Ukrainians to be designated as 'Ukraine's citizen'. Another participant from Kirovohrad contrasted her fully fledged patriotic feeling of being a Ukrainian with a deficient feeling as a citizen of Ukraine tainted with the realisation that one is not protected by one's state as a citizen should be.[17]

In contrast, some people in the 'anti-Maidan' group in Kharkiv disapproved of the state's policies so much as to question their identity as Ukrainians, a stance exemplified by the following statement:

Well, my attitude has become worse. Because while earlier I came to Russia and was called a *khokhol* [Ukrainian] and for me it was a badge of pride and I was really proud of this [being Ukrainian], I embroidered [traditional Ukrainian] shirts, we were happy to sing Ukrainian songs. … Today I love my country no less than earlier but I am ashamed of participating in this, well, unpleasant process that is going on today. In effect, Ukraine today looks like a fascist state that, roughly speaking, may be [controlled] by some [external] forces, and we here are like puppets provoking and fanning a third world war.[18]

For this and some other participants in the same group, a strong attachment to Russia and support for Russia-friendly policies of Ukraine virtually predetermined a negative attitude toward what they perceived as anti-Russian protests on the Maidan and the policies of the post-Maidan authorities, which, in turn, led them to side with the Russian state in its confrontation with the Ukrainian one. Such an attitude was clearly exceptional for participants in the focus group discussions. Even in that Kharkiv group where most people were rather critical of the current situation in Ukraine, it was challenged by another participant who considered it unacceptable for a Ukrainian citizen: 'Why live here and scold this country while you can

---

[15]Focus group Kyiv 2, in Ukrainian and Russian, with participants of 35–50 years who viewed the Maidan critically, 19 February 2015.

[16]Respondent 7, in Ukrainian, focus group Kirovohrad 2, with participants of 35–50 years who viewed the Maidan critically, 12 March 2015.

[17]Respondent 1, in Ukrainian, focus group Kirovohrad 2, with participants of 35–50 years who viewed the Maidan critically, 12 March 2015.

[18]Respondent 3, in Russian, focus group Kharkiv 2, with participants of 35–50 years who viewed the Maidan critically, 22 February 2015.

TABLE 3

FREQUENCIES OF ANSWERS TO THE SURVEY QUESTIONS 'HOW HAS YOUR ATTITUDE
TOWARD THE FOLLOWING CHANGED FOR THE LAST YEAR?' (%)

	Improved a lot	Improved somewhat	No change	Worsened somewhat	Worsened a lot	Hard to say
National anthem of Ukraine	25.3	14.8	53.5	3.0	2.4	1.0
National flag of Ukraine	23.8	15.9	53.6	3.4	2.5	0.8
Ukraine's independence	21.4	13.8	54.0	5.9	3.2	1.6
Ukrainian language	21.7	13.6	58.3	3.2	2.5	0.8
Russian language	1.9	2.7	75.6	12.0	6.6	1.2
Russian state	1.5	3.6	40.5	24.5	27.9	2.0
Ukrainian nationalists	10.3	10.0	47.7	11.2	13.8	6.9
NATO	13.4	20.2	36.1	10.3	11.8	8.1

Source: Kyiv International Institute of Sociology, September 2014.

[leave it]. You love Russia so much? It is close. Pack your bags and leave. That is, citizens of Ukraine consciously stay here, they consciously want to … they may be mistaken but they consciously want to build, create, change something'.[19]

Another manifestation of the increased salience of national identity can be seen in changed attitudes towards the attributes or values of the nation and state such as the national anthem, flag, independence and language. Numerous participants in various focus groups mentioned such an improvement as one aspect of their changed self-perception as Ukrainians and Ukraine's citizens. A young man in Chernivtsi made the following response to a more general question on the most important changes in Ukrainian society in the last year: 'At last, everybody knows [how to sing] the Ukrainian anthem'.[20] Based on earlier statements to that effect in various media, the 2014 survey specifically inquired about respondents' perception of how their attitude towards these attributes had changed 'in the last year', measured on a five-point scale including more or less radical changes in both directions and the preservation of the *status quo*. As the upper part of Table 3 makes clear, there has been a similar shift in all these attitudes: between 35% and 40% of respondents reported some change for the better, while less than 10% said that their attitude had become worse. Although the table only includes nationwide figures, the regional breakdown reveals that the balance of change is positive in all macro-regions except for the Donbas whose alienation from Ukraine manifests itself, among other things, in worsening attitudes towards its symbols, particularly in the separatist-controlled territories. With the changes in the Donbas going in the opposite direction to those in the other regions, the inter-regional contestation of national identity seems to increase, although on the bulk of the Ukrainian territory there is a growing consensus on its primary importance. Remarkably, the attitude toward the titular language has improved roughly as

[19]Respondent 8, in Ukrainian, focus group Kharkiv 2, with participants of 35–50 years who viewed the Maidan critically, 22 February 2015.

[20]Respondent 8, in Ukrainian, focus group Chernivtsi 1, with participants of 20–35 years and supportive of the Maidan, 10 March 2015.

much as toward the anthem and flag, which indicates that Ukrainian citizens perceive the state language not only in legal terms, as the language of the state apparatus, but also in symbolic terms, as the national language. This perception is confirmed by focus group statements that present the apparently increased use of Ukrainian as a manifestation of national consolidation: 'Perhaps we have come to feel ourselves stronger as a nation, as Ukrainians. At least, most people have recalled that we have a nation, that we are Ukrainians. It even seems to me that we have come to speak Ukrainian more due to this'.[21]

At the same time, attitudes toward the nation's attributes can be conceptualised as elements of the content of national identity since they indicate perceived components of the meaning of national belonging: a Ukrainian is one who loves the Ukrainian anthem, flag, independence and language. These attitudes thus provide a conceptual link between the salience and content of identity.

Changes in the content: Russian as opposed to Ukrainian, Russia as opposed to the West

If, contrary to the expectations of the former president Yanukovych and his allies in Moscow, the Maidan and Russian intervention made most Ukrainians more, not less, strongly attached to their state or nation, then it can be surmised that their views of the values and interests of the state and nation have moved away from Russia and towards the West. Indeed, the survey and focus group data demonstrate that an alienation from Russia constitutes an important part of recent changes in the content of Ukrainian identity.

The lower part of Table 3, also relating to perceived changes in attitudes, clearly pertains to the content of identity, as the attitudes in question characterise some of the many attachments that membership of the Ukrainian nation may or may not involve. In contrast to the Ukrainian language, attitudes to which have improved as much as to other obvious attributes of nationhood, the Russian language came to be viewed somewhat more negatively, particularly in the predominantly Ukrainian-speaking western and central regions. At the same time, the bulk of the population did not change their attitude towards Russian, however good or bad it might have been. This means that for most people a stronger Ukrainian identity does not mean a worse attitude toward the Russian language; in other words, speaking or liking Russian was not perceived as incompatible with being Ukrainian, even among those who speak mainly Ukrainian themselves. Such an attitude indicates the ethnocultural inclusiveness of the new Ukrainian identity (which does not mean ethnocultural neutrality as the titular language and culture occupy a special place, at least outside of the Donbas).

This perception of the Russian language is very different from that of the Russian state, attitudes toward which, according to the respondents' declarations, drastically worsened during 2014, particularly among those who primarily consider themselves to be citizens of Ukraine, an identity which the Russian state currently seems to question and in various ways undermine. Once again, a change for the worse is to be found in all macro-regions apart from the Donbas, the latter differing sharply from the East/South whose residents retained their (presumably positive) attitude toward their own main language but came to view Russia much more negatively. At the same time, this negative attitude did not usually extend to

---

[21]Respondent 5, in Ukrainian, focus group Kirovohrad 2, with participants of 35–50 years who viewed the Maidan critically, 12 March 2015.

the Russian people. While the survey did not specifically inquire about a change in attitude towards Russians, another question sought to elicit respondents' opinion about the following statement: 'Whatever the authorities do, the Russian people [*narod*] will always be close to the Ukrainian one'. Some 24% fully agreed with this view and a further 40% 'rather agreed', while only 11% more or less firmly objected. Even among those who viewed themselves primarily as citizens of Ukraine, 59% resolutely or hesitantly supported this Russians-friendly statement. Moreover, the agreement with the statement was much stronger than disagreement in all macro-regions, with the latter being in single digits everywhere but the West. These figures imply that proximity between the Ukrainian and Russian peoples remains one of the least contested aspects of Ukrainian identity, even if Ukrainians disagree on the exact nature of this proximity.

The focus group participants explained the nuances of their attitudes towards the Russian state, people and language. Both the 'pro-Maidan' and 'anti-Maidan' groups were predominantly critical of the Russian authorities, although in Kharkiv some participants in the latter group were reluctant to give up their fondness for Russia, all the more so because they did not consider it primarily guilty for the current predicament in Ukraine. Most participants in all groups stressed that their negative attitude towards the state did not extend to the Russian people who were not to blame for the authorities' wrongdoings. However, some respondents saw the people's guilt in that 'they follow their leader obediently, like sheep';[22] that is, not only are they afraid to protest but also prefer to believe the state propaganda. In the words of a Kirovohrad woman: 'In our information age, one can take information not only from television. Now there are internet resources. Through the internet one can filter it, select. That is, they do not want to do this. I don't know, they simply swallow like a sponge everything that they are [fed]'.[23] At the same time, many more respondents in all groups doubted that the Russian people could still be considered 'brotherly' to the Ukrainians, as Soviet propaganda had taught them to believe, and some argued that other peoples such as Polish, Georgians or Lithuanians were now worthier of the title of brothers to the Ukrainians.[24] Apart from an attempt to distinguish between the 'bad' authorities and 'good' people, such ambivalence seems to reflect a contradiction between established beliefs and new developments.

As for the language, while many respondents mentioned their greater attachment to and/or more frequent use of Ukrainian due to the Maidan and war, nobody viewed these developments as a reason to change their attitude toward Russian, let alone abandon their accustomed practice of relying on it (primarily or in addition to Ukrainian) in their everyday life. The following exchange in the predominantly Russian-speaking Kharkiv revealed various arguments used to justify this position:

[22]Respondent 8, in Ukrainian, focus group Kharkiv 1, with participants of 20–35 years and supportive of the Maidan, 22 February 2015.

[23]Respondent 7, in Ukrainian, focus group Kirovohrad 2, with participants of 35–50 years who viewed the Maidan critically, 12 March 2015.

[24]In May 2014, after the annexation of Crimea and the first military clashes in the Donbas, a nationwide survey by the Razumkov Center found that 62% of respondents still considered the Ukrainians and the Russians to be 'brotherly' peoples and 68% 'friendly' ones. The latter designation was supported by a majority of respondents in all macro-regions (defined somewhat differently than in this essay), and the former in all but the West. See 'Rezul'taty sotsiolohichnoho doslidzhennia "Zovnishniopolitychni orientatsii hromadian Ukraïny"', Razumkov Center, 13 May 2014, available at: http://www.razumkov.org.ua/ukr/news.php?news_id=477, accessed 30 May 2015.

Moderator:	Some people believe that this is now the enemy's language and, therefore, they cannot perceive it the same way as earlier. What do you think about this?
Respondent 2:	Well, we have communicated in Russian since childhood.
Respondent 6:	*Have grown accustomed since* childhood, *yes.*
Respondent 4:	*We do not associate it with Russia.*
Respondent 5:	*It is not the language we are at war with.*
Respondent 4:	*Yes.*
Respondent 1:	In any case, both our Ukrainian language and the Russian language is primarily a means of communication.
Respondent 4:	Yes.
Respondent 1:	And whether we like it, love it, scold it, it's [not that important].
Respondent 4:	It is convenient for us to speak [Russian], is all.
Respondent 8:	We cannot all instantly switch to Ukrainian.[25]

At the same time, some of the respondents who critically viewed the post-Maidan developments in Ukraine reported a change for the worse in their attitude toward the *Ukrainian* language. As a woman in Kharkiv said: 'Too many killings took place in that language. Too much is related to that language'.[26]

Changes in attitudes towards Russia were of course influenced by the respondents' views of the primary responsibility for the current bloodshed, a matter specifically inquired about in the survey. While 43% of respondents placed such responsibility on 'the Russian authorities which provide armed support to the separatists', a surprisingly large part of the nationwide sample, 19%, saw the main villain in 'the participants in the Maidan protests who have overthrown the legitimate president of Ukraine', both suggested options being based on arguments articulated in public discourse. Other popular attributions, each favoured by 8% of respondents, were directed at 'Donbas residents that support the separatists' and 'the Western powers provoking enmity between the brotherly Slavic peoples'. Only 2% were ready to place the primary responsibility on 'the population of Russia supporting its authorities' actions with regard to Ukraine', the only common feature of the otherwise sharply different views of the various macro-regions. It is only in the Donbas that virtually nobody blamed the Russian authorities, the overwhelming majority seeing the main cause of the deterioration in the Maidan protests or the West's interference. The West and Centre almost unanimously blamed Russia, while the residents of the East/South turned out to be rather evenly divided in their attribution of guilt to Russia and the Maidan. It is hardly surprising that those with a salient Ukrainian identity were particularly inclined to blame Russia (56%), while those primarily attached to their region—a choice most popular in the Donbas—tended to attribute the responsibility to the Maidan protesters or the West (41% and 23%, respectively).

The perceived responsibility of external powers and their allies within Ukraine for the current crisis also informed people's preferences with regard to foreign policy in the future, as evidenced in both the survey and focus group discussions. Pro-Maidan participants mostly rejected the idea of a union or close cooperation with Russia, which they viewed through the prism of a perceived attempt by the 'big brother' to subordinate Ukraine in the past and thus did not deem it possible to have equal relations in the future. As a young Kyivan put it:

[25]Focus group Kharkiv 1, in Ukrainian and Russian, with participants of 20–35 years and supportive of the Maidan, 22 February 2015.

[26]Respondent 6, in Russian, focus group Kharkiv 2, with participants of 35–50 years who viewed the Maidan critically, 22 February 2015.

'When being friends with Russia, you will always be there, at the bottom'.[27] Accordingly, their foreign policy choice was clear: 'To stay away from Russia. And be friends with *various countries: Europe, America*'.[28] In contrast, those who viewed the Maidan as a Western plot saw no viable alternative to continued cooperation with Russia and did not support integration into the EU or NATO: 'We have no friends except for Russia, none'.[29]

Quantitatively, the statement that 'Ukraine's future lies within the European Union' was fully supported by 32% and 'rather supported' by a further 20% of the survey respondents. However, the level of firm or hesitant support constituted 91% among those who declared their positive attitude toward Euromaidan and only 10% among those viewing it negatively. The latter group predominantly, albeit less resolutely, supported the opposite choice in favour of Ukraine's future 'in a union with Russia and Belarus', with 34% fully agreeing and a further 32% rather agreeing (the respective figures in the sample as a whole were much lower, namely 10% and 17%). The link between respondents' foreign policy choice and their most salient identity proved to be equally strong: 64% of those viewing themselves primarily as citizens of Ukraine firmly or hesitantly supported the integration in the EU, in contrast to 28% of people prioritising their identity as residents of a certain region, while the choice for an East Slavic union was favoured by 55% of 'regionals' and only 13% of 'nationals'.

A similar relation to identity preferences can be found in reported changes in attitudes toward NATO (see Table 3). Among the respondents prioritising national identity, changes for the better greatly exceed changes for the worse (44% compared with 12%). In contrast, those people primarily attached to their region came to view NATO more critically (49% compared with 12% for a change in the opposite direction), although one can assume that their attitude was rather negative all along. In the sample as a whole, although more people reported a change for the better than a change for the worse (35% compared with 22%), both parts were considerable, which means that this aspect of the identity content remains highly contested. At the same time, the orientation towards the EU clearly prevails now over the striving for a post-Soviet union, whereas in 2012 the latter option was still more popular than the former. This indicates a decreased nationwide disagreement over Ukraine's foreign policy orientation or at least its economic dimension (as distinct from the military one where the western vector is still widely associated with NATO).

Changes in the content: nationalism, national past and national heroes

Another major aspect of the content of national identity pertains to the perceptions of Ukrainian nationalism in the past and present. Since the early years of independence, this has been one of the most contentious issues in Ukrainian politics and society, as people considering nationalism a driving force of national liberation clashed with those adhering to the Soviet postulate relating nationalism to Nazism. The survey and focus group discussions vividly demonstrate that post-Soviet changes in the perception of this phenomenon continue to be constrained by lingering Soviet stereotypes, but the ongoing Russian aggression facilitates the

[27]Respondent 6, in Ukrainian, focus group Kyiv 1, with participants of 20–35 years and supportive of the Maidan, 17 February 2015.
[28]Respondent 7, in Ukrainian and Russian, focus group Kharkiv 1, with participants of 20–35 years and supportive of the Maidan, 17 February 2015.
[29]Respondent 3, in Russian, focus group Kharkiv 2, with participants of 35–50 years who viewed the Maidan critically, 22 February 2015.

embrace of nationalist beliefs in general and anti-Russian attitudes in particular. This embrace is a vivid illustration of how an external threat, even if primarily perceived in civic terms, can result in the reinforcement of the ethnocultural basis of national identity.

Starting with the recent changes in attitudes presented in Table 3, the attitude toward the unspecified 'Ukrainian nationalists' remained almost the same, with the changes for the better and for the worse largely balancing each other. In this case, the dividing line between the mostly positive and mostly negative change lay between the West and Centre on the one hand and East/South and the Donbas on the other, although in the Donbas changes for the worse were much more pronounced than in other eastern and southern regions. While a salient national identity did not necessarily entail a positive change in attitude toward nationalists, the preference for its regional, local or post-Soviet alternatives tended to be coupled with a change in the opposite direction. This means that far from all people prioritising their attachment to the Ukrainian nation many perceive this priority as nationalism, that is, their view of nationalism is likely to be affected by a negative connotation which was established in the USSR and sustained after its demise by various domestic and international discourses.

As focus group discussions revealed, however, these discourses are by no means uncontested. Although many participants still held the view of nationalism as national exclusivity or even Nazism, most argued that nationalism means nothing more than love for one's people and desire to see one's country free. Several people clearly embraced the term as their own ideological self-designation, a stance exemplified by the following statement of a young Kyivan: '*I am a Russian-speaking Ukrainian nationalist.* This is because I believe that the state should develop based on national interests. And it is this emphasis that I view as my nationalism'.[30] Remarkably, many more respondents were ready to perceive nationalism as the just struggle for national liberation than to call themselves nationalists, yet another illustration of an ambivalent post-Soviet combination of old and new beliefs. At the same time, this positive perception was more often related to World War II Ukrainian nationalism, which many people considered more genuine and heroic than the current actions of those who call themselves nationalists.[31] Some participants explicitly criticised the actions of today's nationalists as driven by fashion or even self-interest. This is how the same Kyivan responded to the moderator's question whether there were now more nationalists in the city and entire Ukraine than before: 'Maybe there aren't more nationalists but there are many more people who can say, "I am a nationalist" because this is trendy'.[32] Such distinction between the past and the present implies that the impact of the Maidan and post-Maidan developments may have been less important for the change in attitudes toward nationalism than long-term institutional practices such as education or media. No wonder that this distinction appeared to be particularly widespread among younger people who had been more exposed to post-Soviet education and less to family narratives of fear and/or hatred of 'nationalists'. Moreover, many people argued that this is not a specifically Ukrainian phenomenon and that nationalism

[30]Respondent 6, in Ukrainian and Russian, focus group Kyiv 1, with participants of 20–35 years and supportive of the Maidan, 17 February 2015.

[31]This seems to confirm Alexander Motyl's pre-Maidan argument that not only do World War II nationalists represent 'a rejection of all things Soviet, a repudiation of anti-Ukrainian slurs, and unconditional devotion to Ukrainian independence' but they 'are also seen as the polar opposites of the corrupt, incompetent, and venal Ukrainian elites who have misruled Ukraine for the last twenty years' (Motyl 2010, p. 9).

[32]Respondent 6, in Ukrainian, focus group Kyiv 1, with participants of 20–35 years and supportive of the Maidan, 17 February 2015.

TABLE 4

FREQUENCIES OF ANSWER TO THE SURVEY QUESTIONS, 'WHAT IS YOUR ATTITUDE TOWARD STEPAN BANDERA/JOSEPH STALIN', BY THE REGION (%)

		Positive		Rather positive		Rather negative		Negative		Don't know such a figure		Hard to say	
		2012	2014	2012	2014	2012	2014	2012	2014	2012	2014	2012	2014
Attitude towards Bandera	Ukraine	11.3	16.4	13.2	16.2	16.4	15.5	36.4	26.3	3.7	3.2	19.0	22.3
	West	35.5	52.4	27.2	22.5	11.8	4.3	11.2	3.3	0.5	1.2	13.8	16.3
	Centre	8.2	11.8	15.7	22.1	16.6	14.1	25.3	2.4	3.4	2.0	30.8	37.6
	East/ South	2.6	4.4	6.2	12.6	18.5	22.8	50.6	39.1	5.8	6.6	16.2	14.5
	Donbas	5.1	2.4	6.7	2.4	20.9	19.9	57.1	61.4	3.8	2.1	7.3	11.7
Attitude towards Stalin	Ukraine	7.3	6.5	20.7	16.9	22.6	23.2	33.1	38.4	0.6	0.5	15.6	14.4
	West	2.5	0.2	9.3	2.9	20.6	11.0	58.0	79.0	0.5	1.7	9.0	5.2
	Centre	5.6	2.7	17.5	8.2	25.6	31.4	32.9	37.4	0.8	0.4	17.5	19.8
	East/ South	5.8	8.2	29.1	30.5	19.8	22.3	25.7	26.1	1.1	0.2	18.5	12.8
	Donbas	18.0	19.6	28.2	29.2	23.1	22.9	16.1	10.5	0	0	14.6	17.8

Sources: Kyiv International Institute of Sociology, February 2012 and September 2014.

plays an important positive role in many societies, including those they view as examples for Ukraine: 'If you come to America, to any European country, you will see how [strong] their patriotism and nationalism is. Flags are everywhere there. This is normal'.[33]

An increasingly positive view of Ukrainian nationalism was confirmed by responses to survey questions pertaining to its prominent figures and fundamental tenets. On the one hand, the attitude towards Stepan Bandera, a prominent nationalist leader of the inter-war period and a symbol of the Ukrainian nationalist resistance to the Soviet and German rule during and after World War II, markedly improved between the 2012 and 2014 surveys, even though somewhat more people still view him negatively than positively (see Table 4). At the same time, the attitude towards his perceived antagonist, the Soviet dictator Joseph Stalin who ultimately crushed the nationalist resistance of the Ukrainian and other peoples of the Soviet empire, further deteriorated. Accordingly, while in 2012 the attitude towards Bandera was roughly as negative as towards Stalin (53% of those with negative or rather negative attitudes for the former figure versus 56% for the latter), now it is much less negative (42% compared with 62%).

Once again, it is only in the Donbas that the perception of Bandera has become more critical than it was two years ago, and it is only in that region that attitudes towards Stalin have become less critical. Remarkably, the attitude towards Bandera has not only greatly improved among Ukrainian speakers but it has also become somewhat less negative among people speaking primarily Russian, the change in the latter group running contrary to the markedly negative shift in its attitude toward the 'Ukrainian nationalists' in general. At the same time, many of the Ukrainian-speaking and central residents have abandoned (or no longer feel comfortable expressing in the semi-official setting of a survey) their negative views of the nationalist leader but are not yet ready to embrace positive ones, which is reflected in an unusually high percentage of undecided responses. The widespread uncertainty and roughly

[33]Respondent 7, in Russian, focus group Kharkiv 1, with participants of 20–35 years and supportive of the Maidan, 22 February 2015.

equal shares of positive and negative attitudes point to persistent contestation of this aspect of Ukrainian identity.

However, the explicit embrace of Ukrainian nationalism does not encompass all manifestations of its acceptance in today's Ukraine. No less important is the acceptance of its ideological postulates that are not necessarily perceived as nationalist. Even those focus group participants who declared a rather negative view of nationalism tended to argue that the current unfair treatment of Ukraine by Russia is typical of the history of relations between the two countries. Similarly, when asked if they agreed that 'from ancient times to these days, Ukrainians have been fighting for their freedom from Russia's oppression', 47% of the survey respondents resolutely or hesitantly agreed, while 29% expressed more or less strong disagreement and 14% remained ambivalent. Once again, the only region predominantly rejecting this view was the Donbas. However, in other regions this nationalist view of the past coexists with the above-mentioned view of the close relations between the Ukrainian and Russian peoples in the present and future. This ambivalence implies that the content of Ukrainian national identity will not necessarily be anti-Russian in the years to come.

The widespread acceptance of Ukrainian nationalism was also demonstrated in focus group responses to the question about who can be called Ukrainian national heroes. Among many figures from the past and present that were mentioned in various groups, figures featured in the nationalist narrative of Ukrainian history clearly predominated (except for the 'anti-Maidan' group in Kharkiv where most people referred to those seen as champions of Ukraine's friendship with Russia). Although some of these figures such as poet Taras Shevchenko and Cossack leader Bohdan Khmelnytskyi were also praised by the Soviet regime, others were only rehabilitated after the proclamation of independence for which, as the new interpretation read, they had been devotedly fighting. In various cities, people mentioned perceived independence fighters of various periods of the past, including Bandera who, in one participant's words, 'fought for liberation, for Ukraine'.[34] The nationalist pantheon of the past was usually supplemented by contemporary heroes, particularly those who had died on the Maidan or were fighting the Russian aggressors in the Donbas. For example, a list suggested by a Kirovohrad student included Mykhailo Hrushevskyi, one of the leaders of the short-lived Ukrainian state after World War I, Roman Shukhevych, a commander of the nationalist resistance during and after World War II, and 'the warriors who are now [fighting] in the Anti-Terrorist Operation' in the Donbas.[35] Such a combination of old and new heroes demonstrates that the nationalist view of history implanted by the post-Soviet discourses informs the popular interpretation of current political developments which, in turn, facilitate the appropriation of that view.

Conclusion

The above analysis has demonstrated that recent changes in the salience and content of Ukrainian national identity on the mass level confirm the assertions made by activists and elites. On the one hand, national identity has become more salient *vis-à-vis* other territorial and non-territorial identities than it was before the Maidan and the war, so now its only match

[34]Respondent 7, in Ukrainian, focus group Kirovohrad 2, with participants of 35–50 years who viewed the Maidan critically, 12 March 2015.

[35]Respondent 4, in Russian, focus group Kirovohrad 1, with participants of 20–35 years and supportive of the Maidan, 12 March 2015.

is the self-designation in terms of gender. On the other hand, the very meaning of belonging to the Ukrainian nation has changed, a change most vividly manifested in the increased alienation from Russia and the greater embrace of Ukrainian nationalism as a worldview and, accordingly, as a historical narrative. At the same time, most Ukrainians remain ambivalent about distancing themselves from the Russian people who they seek to distinguish from the state pursuing a hostile policy towards Ukraine. Similarly ambivalent is the popular perception of Ukrainian nationalism, which seems to be more acceptable as an historical phenomenon than a contemporary ideological current. This ambivalence reflects the uneasy coexistence of Soviet-era beliefs and post-Soviet developments, particularly Russia's current aggression against Ukraine. Moreover, people in various parts of Ukraine are reluctant to give up their accustomed reliance on the Russian language, although they recognise the special role of the titular language as a national attribute. While the continued legitimacy of Russian contributes to the inclusive perception of Ukrainian identity as primarily based on accepted bonds rather than inherited traits, the dominant identity project actually combines a civic criterion of membership and a strong ethnocultural basis.

Although popular perceptions are by no means uniform across the country, the main dividing line has shifted eastwards and now lies between the Donbas and the adjacent east-southern regions. Residents of the latter have acquired a stronger and more anti-Russian Ukrainian identity, while in the former people increasingly prioritise the attachment to their region or particular localities, coupled with a political and/or cultural orientation towards Russia. For a decade after the Orange Revolution, Ukrainian society was characterised by the uneasy coexistence of two roughly equal territorial 'halves' with their respective divergent identities and policy preferences. Now the bulk of the population seems to agree on the salience of national identity and main elements of its content, including a pro-Western foreign policy, the nationalist historical narrative and the legitimacy of both languages with the symbolic primacy of Ukrainian. Those who resolutely disagree differ not so much in their striving for a different, Russian-friendly Ukraine as in their wish to distance themselves from Ukraine as such. Given that much of the Donbas is currently under Russian control, with uncertain prospects of reintegration into Ukraine, the Ukrainian nation is likely to be somewhat smaller but more consolidated.

At the same time, my research has revealed an important distinction between those who consider the Maidan and post-Maidan developments as empowering Ukrainian people and those who view it as another stage of their deprivation. The former tend to be proud of their belonging to the Ukrainian nation and the latter frustrated by the state which has allegedly abandoned them, even if not necessarily less fond of the country or its culture. This distinction demonstrates that the cultural dimension of national identity should be examined in relation to its democratic dimension, in accordance with the double nature of this identity as pertaining to both the cultural and political nation. In terms of prospects for Ukrainian society, this means that further consolidation of national identity will depend on the success of political and economic reforms. Not only will perceptible improvement in justice and wellbeing contribute to a greater embrace of civic elements such as respect for state institutions and laws, but also Ukrainian ethnocultural traditions and European values promoted by the post-Euromaidan government will resonate much more strongly if people perceive the government as taking care of their needs.

References

Abdelal, R., Herrera, Y. M., Johnston, A. I. & McDermott, R. (2007) 'Identity as a Variable', *Perspectives on Politics*, 4, 4.

Alfonsi, A. (1997) 'Citizenship and National Identity: The Emergent Stirring in Western Europe', in Oommen, T. K. (ed.) *Citizenship and National Identity: From Colonialism to Globalism* (New Delhi & Thousand Oaks, CA, Sage).

Arel, D. & Khmelko (1996) 'The Russian Factor and Territorial Polarization in Ukraine', *The Harriman Review*, 9, 1–2.

Besters-Dilger, J. (ed.) (2009) *Language Policy and Language Situation in Ukraine: Analysis and Recommendations* (Frankfurt am Main, Peter Lang).

Brubaker, R. (1994) 'Nationhood and the National Question in the Soviet Union and Post-Soviet Eurasia: An Institutional Account', *Theory and Society*, 23, 1.

Hrytsak, Y. (2007) 'Istoriia dvokh mist: L'viv i Donets'k u porivnaial'nii perspektyvi', in Hrytsak, Y., Portnov, A. & Susak, V. (eds) *L'viv–Donets'k: sotsiial'ni identychnosti v suchasnii Ukraïni* (special issue of *Ukraïna Moderna*) (Kyiv & L'viv, Krytyka).

Hrytsenko, O. (1998) *'Svoia mudrist': Natsional'ni mifolohii ta 'hromadians'ka relihiia' v Ukraïni* (Kyiv, Ukraïns'kyi tsentr kul'turnykh doslidzhen').

Kulyk, V. (2009) 'Language Policies and Language Attitudes in Post-Orange Ukraine', in Besters-Dilger, J. (ed.).

Kulyk, V. (2011) 'The Media, History and Identity: Competing Narratives of the Past in the Ukrainian Popular Press', *National Identities*, 13, 3.

Kulyk, V. (2013) 'Language and Identity in Post-Soviet Ukraine: Transformation of an Unbroken Bond', *Australian and New Zealand Journal of European Studies*, 5, 2.

Kulyk, V. (2014a) 'Ukrainian Nationalism since the Outbreak of Euromaidan', *Ab Imperio*, 3.

Kulyk, V. (2014b) 'Narodowościowe przeciwko radzieckiemu: pamięć historyczna na niepodległej Ukraine', in Nikžentaitis, A. & Kopczyński, M. (eds) *Dialog kultur pamięci w regionie ULB* (Warsaw, Museum of Polish History).

Kuzio, T. (2001) 'Identity and Nation-building in Ukraine: Defining the "Other"', *Ethnicities*, 1, 3.

Kuzio, T. (2002) 'The Myth of the Civic State: A Critical Survey of Hans Kohn's Framework for Understanding Nationalism', *Ethnic and Racial Studies*, 25, 1.

Motyl, A. (2010) 'Ukraine, Europe, and Bandera', Cicero Foundation Great Debate Paper No. 10/05, March, available at: http://www.cicerofoundation.org/lectures/Alexander_J_Motyl_UKRAINE_EUROPE_AND_BANDERA.pdf, accessed 20 January 2016.

Onuch, O. (2015) 'EuroMaidan Protests in Ukraine: Social Media versus Social Networks', *Problems of Post-Communism*, 62, 4.

Parekh, B. (1994) 'Discourses on National Identity', *Political Studies*, 42, 3.

Parekh, B. (1995) 'The Concept of National Identity', *New Community*, 21, 2.

Pirie, P. S. (1996) 'National Identity and Politics in Southern and Eastern Ukraine', *Europe-Asia Studies*, 48, 7.

Sereda, V. (2007) 'Regional Historical Identities and Memory', in Hrytsak, Y., Portnov, A. & Susak, V. (eds) *L'viv–Donets'k: sotsiial'ni identychnosti v suchasnii Ukraïni* (special issue of *Ukraïna Moderna*) (Kyiv & L'viv, Krytyka).

Shekhovtsov, A. (2013) 'The "Orange Revolution" and the "Sacred" Birth of a Civic-republican Ukrainian Nation', *Nationalities Papers*, 41, 5.

Shulman, S. (1999) 'The Cultural Foundations of Ukrainian National Identity', *Ethnic and Racial Studies*, 22, 6.

Shulman, S. (2002) 'The Internal-External Nexus in the Formation of Ukrainian National Identity: The Case for Slavic Integration', in Kuzio, T. & D'Anieri, P. (eds) *Dilemmas of State-Led Nation Building in Ukraine* (Westport, CT, Praeger).

Shulman, S. (2004) 'The Contours of Civic and Ethnic National Identification in Ukraine', *Europe-Asia Studies*, 56, 1.

Smith, A. D. (1991) *National Identity* (London, Penguin).

Stehnii, O. & Churylov, M. (1998) *Rehionalizm v Ukraïni iak ob'ekt sotsiolohichnoho doslidzennia* (Kyiv, no publisher).

Wilson, A. (2002) 'Elements of a Theory of Ukrainian Ethno-national Identities', *Nations and Nationalism*, 8, 1.

Wolczuk, K. (2007) 'Whose Ukraine? Language and Regional Factors in the 2004 and 2006 Elections in Ukraine', *European Yearbook of Minority Issues*, 5.

Zhurzhenko, T. (2013) '"Capital of Despair": Holodomor Memory and Political Conflicts in Kharkiv after the Orange Revolution', *East European Politics and Societies*, 25, 3.

The Ukrainian Party System before and after the 2013–2014 Euromaidan

KOSTYANTYN FEDORENKO, OLENA RYBIY &
ANDREAS UMLAND

Abstract

The formation of a party system is widely regarded as a key to successful and sustainable patterns of democratisation. In this essay we examine the evolution of the party system in Ukraine, focusing on the extent to which the Euromaidan has addressed previous problems and weaknesses. So far the post-Soviet Ukrainian party system has been exceptionally unstable as electoral legislation, the factional composition of Ukraine's parliament, and the dominant parties in Ukraine underwent frequent changes. We argue that, despite advances in democratisation as a result of the revolutionary events of 2013–2014, the essential features of Ukraine's party system have not changed. The legislative, ideological and organisational foundations of the Ukrainian party-political landscape and parliamentary politics have remained fragile.

ONE OF THE MOST NOTEWORTHY POLITICAL DEVELOPMENTS during the last years of Soviet Ukraine was the rapid re-emergence of political parties, even before they received the right to officially register in 1990.[1] Over the following two decades, Ukraine's party system underwent almost constant change: new parties quickly rose to temporary prominence and then declined; some established parties completely disappeared; election legislation changed with equal rapidity, as did the general 'rules of the game' of Ukraine's political system. After the so-called Euromaidan of 2013–2014, the Ukrainian party system has continued to change.

In this essay, we sketch a history of Ukraine's post-Soviet party system focusing on its functionality for structuring state–society relations, rather than on the fate of individual parties. We compare developments in Ukraine's electoral regulations, party landscape and parts of its socio-economic system before and after the dramatic political events of 2013–2014, and conclude with a tentative assessment of the quality of Ukraine's party system, as of mid-2015.[2] Our analysis indicates much continuity and hence leads to pessimistic conclusions: while political competition has become stronger in post-Euromaidan Ukraine, a 'normalisation' of

The authors would like to thank Kataryna Wolczuk, Derek Averre, Khrystyna Parandii as well as the two anonymous reviewers of *Europe-Asia Studies* for their kind help in improving this essay. Responsibility for remaining imprecision lies with us.

[1]When the USSR collapsed in 1991, Ukraine already had 12 officially registered parties (Karmazina 2012a, p. 587).

[2]Ukraine's October 2015 local elections are not included in the scope of this essay.

the Ukrainian party system—that is its institutionalisation, rationalisation and stabilisation—is far from complete.

This essay aims to provide a comprehensive survey rather than to investigate some narrow specifics of Ukraine's party system or individual political parties. It aims to locate the novelty of the socio-political situation after the Euromaidan in the broader context of developments since independence and thereby contribute to political research on Ukraine, which is still underdeveloped (Shevel 2015). The Ukrainian party system has been studied by a number of scholars over the last 20 years (Wilson & Bilous 1993; Hesli *et al.* 1998; Ishiyama & Kennedy 2001; Zimmer 2005; Bader 2010; Meleshevych 2010; Karmazina 2012b; Rybiy 2013; Kudelia & Kuzio 2014; Kuzio 2014). Yet the picture painted by these studies of the re-emergence of a multi-party landscape in Ukraine is incomplete. This concerns especially the most recent and dramatic developments in the Ukrainian party system, including the issue of continuity and change before and after the 2013–2014 Euromaidan. The essay attempts to fill this gap by providing a comprehensive survey of the development of the political party system in Ukraine in order to identify the patterns of continuity and change. However, it needs to be emphasised that at the time of writing, the developments in Ukraine are undergoing rapid change.

The essay attempts to indicate why and how Ukrainian parties have been largely unable to fulfil their social function properly, as aggregators and transmission belts of social interests as well as mediators between state and society. Among the many determinants of the relatively unsuccessful socio-economic development of Ukraine over the past 25 years, the dysfunctionality of its party system may be one of the major ones. The utilisation, misuse or even capture of organisations calling themselves and posing as political parties by private interests has been made possible, as well as aggravated, by other post-Soviet pathologies in a variety of areas ranging from political culture to economic development.

The roots and nature of under-institutionalisation of the party system in Ukraine

Since the 1990s, political competition in Ukraine has faced peculiar challenges that persist to date. Election after election, Ukrainian parties failed to adequately represent social interests, and lacked transparency in party financing. Oligarchs frequently bought and sold parties, were involved in machine politics rather than party politics, and created numerous 'technical parties'.[3] Political organisations of dubious authenticity were founded or revived *ad hoc* before an upcoming election. These and other tactics hindered the stabilisation of the party system of Ukraine, caused significant fluctuation in voters' electoral preferences, disoriented society, and hindered the development of trust in Ukraine's political system as a whole. The persisting under-institutionalisation and general weakness of the Ukrainian party system have undermined the development of Ukrainian democracy. They have limited parties' accountability, prevented long-term commitments between parties and potential supporters, and eased the rise of populist anti-party politicians (Birch 2001; Mainwaring & Torcal 2005).

One determinant of the party system's under-institutionalisation and instability has been the unusually frequent changes in electoral legislation during the last 25 years. Since independence, Ukraine has tried all major forms of electoral system for parliamentary votes—majoritarian, mixed and proportional. New electoral rules have continually been introduced. While the elections of

---

[3]'Technical parties' is a specifically post-Soviet term used to designate pseudo-organisations created *ad hoc* for manipulative purposes in order, for example, to take away votes from real parties with similar sounding names and public profiles. See Wilson (2005).

1990 and 1994 took place according to the majoritarian system, those of 1998 and 2002 were held under mixed-voting rules, whereas those of 2006 and 2007 used proportional representation. Those of 2012 and 2014, again, took place under the mixed system.

The majoritarian system, according to which the deputies to Ukraine's unicameral parliament, the *Verkhovna Rada* (Supreme Council), of 1990 and 1994 were elected, reflected fatigue after decades of one-party rule. Thus, campaigning by 'independent' candidates who explicitly did not align themselves with any party was widespread (Klyuchkovs'kyi 2006, p. 12). The transition to a mixed electoral system in 1997 was caused mainly by endogenous factors, in particular, a search for ways to improve the legislative productivity and political responsibility of MPs and their factions. Politically unaffiliated deputies who were predominant in the parliament of 1994 often were unable to reach a consensus on different issues and this was hindering Ukraine from determining fundamental priorities of its post-Soviet development. A lack of commitment to official, sustainable political organisations, it has been argued, may have also been a result of some parliamentarians' strategies to avoid publicly taking easily identifiable responsibility for the catastrophic social situation during the 1990s (Klyuchkovs'kyi 2006, p. 13).

The switch from the mixed to the proportional electoral system in 2006 can be interpreted as a way of maximising the number of seats that could be won by the parliamentary forces that were dominant at that time.[4] The proportional representation system was adopted even though opinion poll results had shown that it was the least popular then among respondents.[5] The fact that popular opinion was ignored in the introduction of the proportional representation system illustrated a continuing misfit between the Ukrainian electorate's preferences and Ukraine's political system.

Similar motives drove the change from proportional representation back to a mixed system on the eve of the 2012 elections. As a result of the reintroduction of a partially majoritarian electoral system, the *Rada* faction of the ruling Party of Regions (*Partiya rehioniv*), which had been losing popularity, with 2 million fewer votes during the 2012 elections than in the 2007 elections, managed to maintain its hegemony in parliament. The revised system ensured the election of numerous candidates who were either officially or unofficially linked to the Party of Regions in single-member constituencies. Since the 2014 parliamentary elections, civic activists and representatives of non-governmental organisations have started to lobby actively for a return to a proportional system—though with open lists now. Although the motive for this proposal is the strengthening of the connection between parties and voters, yet another change in the electoral rules will also further postpone the institutionalisation and stabilisation of Ukraine's party-political landscape.

In weakly institutionalised party systems, political parties regularly appear and disappear. In addition, the level of support for institutionalised parties substantially varies from election to election (Thames 2007, p. 458). There are a number or reasons why Ukraine's party system continues to be unstable. These include the appearance in each election of a wide range of well-funded and publicly conspicuous new parties; a high level of electoral volatility; the low level of party organisation of many, including the most influential, political parties; the weak roots in society of Ukrainian political parties; and insufficient communication of parties with their voters between elections.

[4]This conforms to the maximising model of electoral system change as discussed by Benoit (2004, p. 373).

[5]'Which System of Parliamentary Elections do You Believe is Best for Ukraine? (Dynamics 2001–2007)', Oleksandr Razumkov Ukrainian Center for Economic and Political Research, available at: http://www.razumkov.org.ua/ukr/poll.php?poll_id=99, accessed 1 June 2015.

Half of today's registered parties in Ukraine still do not have their own websites, and are thus unable or unwilling to provide citizens with even a minimum of information about themselves. Those parties which are represented on the internet are usually not or not fully transparent regarding their history, member numbers, membership fees, financial situation, changes in their leadership and ideology, key decisions at congresses, and contact information of regional offices (see Table 1). Almost a quarter of all Ukrainian political parties have changed their names at least once, usually in order to pose as a 'new party' in an upcoming election.

Personalities instead of ideologies; quantity instead of quality

The lack of ideological clarity of Ukrainian parties, especially concerning socio-economic issues, also affects the stability of the party system. Many programmes of political parties and individual candidates are populist and devoid of a coherently formulated ideological framework. A peculiar Ukrainian post-Soviet predicament has been the low salience of parties' socio-economic agendas, both in programmes, and for voters. In 2012, sociologists found that of greatest importance to a Ukrainian voter is not a party's rightwing or leftwing orientation, but differences concerning a party's geopolitical orientation (namely rapprochement either with NATO and the EU, or with Russia) and its stance on language issues (namely support for or opposition to the granting of official status to the Russian language).[6]

Against the background of unstable programmatic connections between parties and voters, individual party leaders play an important, if not decisive role in Ukrainian elections. These are usually prominent public figures, who are often also among the financial donors of their parties. Sometimes this personalisation is directly reflected in the names of the parties when they include the leader's name, such as Petro Poroshenko's Bloc 'Solidarity' Party (*Partiya Blok Petra Poroshenka 'Solidarnist'*); Vitalii Klychko's UDAR Party (*Partiya UDAR Vitaliya Klychka*); Oleh Lyashko's Radical Party (*Radykalna partiya Oleha Lyashka*). Among others, the absence of traditions and procedures of internal party democracy does not allow for overcoming the continuous 'personification' of numerous Ukrainian parties. In order to ensure stable voter support, independent from prominent front-runners, parties need a core team of leaders, functionaries and activists who develop their organisations over the years and build up trust among citizens. However, in circumstances where Ukrainian politicians often change the registration data and names of their parties, not investing much in developing parties as self-sufficient organisational structures, voters have little opportunity to establish stable and long-term ties with them.

Among other crucial characteristics of the Ukrainian party system are the high number of parties and the significant fluctuation in the electoral preferences of Ukrainians. There existed 242 active political parties, as of July 2015. Between 1990 and 2012, 260 parties were registered, many of which have now disappeared (Karmazina 2012a, p. 587). Between 2013 and mid-2015 alone, 45 new parties were registered. Only a small number of them have taken part in parliamentary elections, and only a handful of the non-parliamentary parties were active in politics between elections. Half of all Ukraine's groupings once registered as 'parties' have never participated in national elections while 150 Ukrainian parties have participated in parliamentary elections, at least once.

---

[6]'Vyznachalnym dlya vybortsiv e heopolitychnyi vybir partii ta movne pytannya', The Ilko Kucheriv Democratic Initiatives Foundation (DIF), available at: http://dif.org.ua/ua/commentaries/sociologist_view/-viznacha.htm, accessed 1 June 2015.

TABLE 1
INFORMATION PROVIDED BY THE WEBSITES OF UKRAINIAN PARLIAMENTARY PARTIES BEFORE THE 2014 ELECTIONS

	Statutory documents		Party leadership	Regional offices/party branches		News sections on the party's activities:		Instructions on how to become a party member
	Party programme	*Party regulations*		*Contacts*	*Websites*	*in the parliament*	*outside the parliament*	
Popular Front	1	0	0	1	0	1	0	1
Petro Poroshenko's Bloc	1	1	1	1	1	1	1	0
'Self-Reliance' Union	1	0	0	1	0	1	0	1
Opposition Bloc	1	0	0	0	0	1	0	0
Oleh Lyashko's Radical Party	1	0	0	1	0	1	0	0.5
All-Ukrainian Union 'Fatherland'	1	1	1	1	1	1	1	1

Notes: 0=information was not available; 1=information was available; 0.5=information was partially available.
Source: Parandii (2015).

TABLE 2

SUMMARY OF THE 2014 PARLIAMENTARY ELECTIONS IN COMPARISON TO THOSE OF 2012

Party	Vote %	Difference between 2012 and 2014 elections	Seats (proportional representation)	Seats (single member districts)	Total seats	Difference between 2012 and 2014 elections
People's Front	22.14	n/a	64	18	82	n/a
Poroshenko's Bloc	21.82	n/a	63	69	132	n/a
'Self-Reliance'	10.97	n/a	32	1	33	n/a
Opposition Bloc	9.43	−20.57*	27	2	29	−156*
Oleh Lyashko's Radical Party	7.44	+6.36	22	0	22	+21
'Fatherland'	5.68	−19.86	17	2	19	−82
'Freedom'	4.71	−5.73	0	6	6	−31
Communist Party of Ukraine	3.88	−9.3	0	0	0	−32
'Strong Ukraine'	3.11	n/a	0	1	1	n/a
'Civic Position'	3.1	n/a	0	0	0	n/a
'Zastup'	2.65	n/a	0	0	0	n/a
Right Sector	1.8	+1.75**	0	1	1	n/a

Notes:*Compared to the 2012 Party of Regions results.**Compared to the 2012 results of the Ukrainian National Assembly (re-registered in 2014 as the Right Sector).

Only 38 parties (13% of all Ukrainian political parties) have ever been in parliament. Only 16 were able to enter the *Verkhovna Rada* independently, that is, not within a bloc or alliance with other parties. Among those parties that had entered parliament on their own are the Communist Party of Ukraine (*Komunistychna partiya Ukrainy*—CPU) (five times), the Party of Regions (three times), the All-Ukrainian Union 'Fatherland' (*Vseukrainske ob'ednannya 'Bat'kivshchyna'*) (twice), the Social-Democratic Party of Ukraine (United) (*Sotsial-demokratychna partiya Ukrainy (ob'ednana)*—SDPU(o)) (twice) and the Socialist Party of Ukraine (*Sotsialistychna partiya Ukrainy*) (twice). Only one of them, 'Fatherland', was elected to parliament at the 2014 elections (see Table 2). Ukrainian parties have been either surprisingly inactive or seriously under-performing during elections. Only relatively few powerful parties have managed to perform well in several elections.

An indicator of the party system's low institutionalisation and stability is that few, if any, of the most popular parties have performed consistently. For example, in a poll conducted in 2001, the CPU led with 19% of support among those surveyed. It was followed by the Popular Movement of Ukraine ('Movement') (*Narodnyi rukh Ukrainy ('Rukh')*) (5%), the Green Party of Ukraine (*Zelena partiya Ukrainy*) (4%), SDPU(o) (4%) and the Socialist Party of Ukraine (4%).[7] However, only two of these five parties took part in the parliamentary elections of 2014, and none of them entered parliament. Parties such as the Party of Regions, which (within a bloc or independently) was represented in parliament four times, or the CPU, which entered parliament five times, are not present in Ukraine's 8th parliament elected in 2014. Such changeability does not contribute to stable voting preferences.

The significant fluctuation in the level of electoral support for Ukrainian parties is reflected in the high values Ukraine scores in the Pedersen Index of Electoral Volatility which tracks

[7]'Hromads'ka dumka pro politychnykh lideriv i partii: cherven' 2001', The Ilko Kucheriv Democratic Initiatives Foundation (DIF), June 2001, available at: http://dif.org.ua/ua/polls/2001_polls/gromadska-dumka-pro-politichnih-lideriv-i-partii-cherven-2001-r_.htm, accessed 1 June 2015.

party strength from one election to the next, between losing and winning parties (Pedersen 1979). The data show high electoral volatility in the Ukrainian party system for the period between 1998 and 2014 (see Table 3). The average score of electoral volatility for Ukraine during this 16-year period is very high at 48.15% (and is similar to Nicaragua's value for the period 1980–1997 (Roberts & Wibbels 1999). For developed democratic countries, the Pedersen Index is usually below 10. For the US, for instance, it was 3.3 between 1946 and 2002 (Mainwaring & Zoco 2007, p. 159). In addition to extremely high electoral volatility in Ukraine, the volatility of Ukrainian party preference from election to election decreased only gradually, rising again significantly in the last elections of 2014.

Other indicators also show deterioration in party system institutionalisation. In the 2012 elections to the *Verkhovna Rada*, there were five 'novice' parties of which two, the All-Ukrainian Union 'Freedom' (*Vseukrains'ke ob'ednannya 'Svoboda'*) and Vitalii Klychko's UDAR Party, entered parliament. In contrast, 17 out of 29 parties that took part in the 2014 parliamentary elections were taking part in elections for the first time. As a result of the 2014 parliamentary elections, five newcomer parties, namely Petro Poroshenko's Bloc, the Popular Front (*Narodyi front*), Opposition Bloc (*Opozytsiynyi blok*), Union 'Self-Reliance' (*Ob'ednannya 'Samopomich'*) and Oleh Lyashko's Radical Party, succeeded in entering parliament. Only one party, the All-Ukrainian Union 'Fatherland' led by Yulia Tymoshenko, is an experienced parliamentary player.

Another indication of instability was an increase in the number of votes given to parties that did not pass the 5%-barrier. While in the 2012 parliamentary elections, 6.82% of the votes had been lost because they went to parties that did not reach the threshold, this rose to 22.52% in 2014. Yet another worsening trend concerned Ukrainians' trust in their country's political organisations. According to polling data gathered in March 2014, only 0.6% of the respondents had full confidence in political parties while 34.8% said they had no confidence in political parties.[8] This indicator is twice as low as the lowest analogous indicators during the period 2001–2013.[9] Such a high level of distrust prevents parties and elections from functioning as legitimate and effective channels of articulating social interests—a basic feature of the institutionalisation of a party system.

In sum, various indicators suggest that Ukraine's party system is still unstable and fluid, with several factors concurrently preventing the institutionalisation of a stable party system, which in turn hinders voters in developing longer-term political attachments. The high level of personalisation of parties, their unclear ideological platforms, as well as their poor electoral activity are continuing to undermine the creation of a sustainable party system.

Deficiencies in legislation

The low institutionalisation and low quality of political parties as social interests' aggregators can be explained in part by incomplete or deficient legal regulation. The 2001 Law 'On Political Parties' did not provide for effective party system development in Ukraine.[10] The procedure for establishing a party, as formulated in this law, is too simple. It allows for easy

[8]'Do You Trust Political Parties?', Razumkov Centre, March 2015, available at: http://www.uceps.org/ukr/poll.php?poll_id=1030, accessed 1 June 2015.

[9]'Do You Trust Political Parties?', Razumkov Centre, 2001–2011, available at: http://www.razumkov.org.ua/ukr/poll.php?poll_id=82, accessed 1 June 2015.

[10]'Pro politychni partii', Law No. 2365-14, adopted in 2001, last edited in February 2016, available at: http://zakon4.rada.gov.ua/laws/show/2365-14, accessed 24 March 2016.

TABLE 3
INDICATORS OF THE DYNAMICS OF ELECTORAL PREFERENCES IN UKRAINE

Parliamentary elections (year/ type of electoral system)	1998 (mixed system)	2002 (mixed system)	2006 (proportional system)	2007 (proportional system)	2012 (mixed system)	2014 (mixed system)
Number of parties that compete for elections (in blocs or independently)	40	63	79	40	21	29
Number of new parties which entered into parliament in blocs or independently (total number of parties in the parliament in brackets)	n/a (9)	17 (22)	1 (11)	8 (16)	2 (5)	5 (6)
Party Replacement Index	n/a	29.47	14.39	1.39	16.72	77.4
Electoral Volatility Index*	n/a	40.46	64.83	17.5	35.63	82.35

Notes: *The application of the Pedersen formula to analysis of the level of electoral volatility in Ukraine has a number of methodological particularities outlined in detail in Rybiy (2013, pp. 408–10). In particular, (1) while elections in 1998, 2002 and 2012 were run according to the mixed system, the calculations do not take into account the results of voting of the second part of the ballot, that is, the votes for majoritarian candidates; (2) the parties which changed their names, but did not change their registration information, were considered to have maintained continuity; (3) regardless of the fact that Pedersen's Index was designed for the analysis of the dynamics of electoral support only among parties, we included in the analysis all of the parties which made up the winning blocs, and the percentage of votes which a particular party received within the bloc using the following formula:

$$\%_i = \frac{\%_b * n_i}{n_b - n_a}$$

where $\%_i$ is the percentage of votes for the party i; n_i is the number of members from the party i within the bloc; n_b is the total number of a bloc's members; n_a is the number of members with no party affiliation within the bloc; $\%_b$ is the percentage of votes for the bloc.

creation of fictitious organisations or the registration of non-existent regional party branches. It also did not establish clear rules of control and responsibility for rule violations by parties, for example, providing false information at their registration. In addition, the enforcement of existing sanctions was inadequate. For example, parties often violated the Law 'On Political Parties' with impunity, demanding that, within a ten-year period, they should participate at least once in the election of the President or the *Verkhovna Rada*. Only once, in 2003, did the Ministry of Justice conduct an extensive review of parties, and, within one year, cancelled the registration of 31 political forces that had violated this legislation. Yet, on average, between 2003 and 2013, registration certificates were cancelled for one party per year only.

The information about political parties of Ukraine provided by the State Registration Service has so far been limited. As a result, civil society groups were unable to monitor the activities of parties adequately. Public access to the Registry of Political Parties was made possible only in October 2009. Until that time, one could only guess about the diversity of parties in Ukraine, since a significant number of them, during the entire time of their existence, had not figured in electoral lists nor displayed any activity in the mass media. As of 2015, the Register of Political Parties still does not provide information on the contact details of party offices, the party programmes and statutes, the history of changes to their names and changes in leadership.

After the 2013–2014 Euromaidan, discussion on the introduction of state financing of parties as a method of providing for the more effective and democratic development of Ukraine's party system commenced. Within the framework of anti-corruption measures, in October 2016 the Rada adopted the law 'On Introducing Certain Changes to Legislative Acts of Ukraine in Connection with the Prevention of and Counter-Action Against Political Corruption', which introduced state financing for parties that have received more than 3% in the previous election.[11] The civic activists who were pushing for such a law argued that this allows for greater transparency of parties and overcomes their dependence on a limited number of private donors. Yet, oddly, as far back as 2003, this issue had been already addressed in a bill, passed by parliament, called the Law 'On Introducing Changes to Certain Legislative Acts of Ukraine in Connection with Introducing State Financing of Political Parties in Ukraine' (27 November 2003). However, this bill never came into force.[12]

Among further deficiencies of Ukraine's regulation of party activities that prevent responsible behaviour by parties, and which new legislation needs to address, are that parties are currently not obliged to detail their statutes when registering with the Ministry of Justice; there is no examination of the authenticity of the documents submitted by parties; there are no timelines for party reports to be submitted; and there is a lack of publicly available information about political parties.

The Ukrainian legislation does not sufficiently encourage transparency of registered political organisations, and has not been able to prevent the rise of numerous fictional, 'technical' and pseudo-parties. Deficient laws and their partial implementation have allowed shrewd 'political technologists' to manipulate Ukraine's party landscape, to confuse the electorate and to subvert real political competition (Wilson 2005). Pragmatic exploitation of

---

[11]'*Pro vnesennya deyakykh zmin do zakonodavchykh aktiv Ukrainy shchodo zapobihannya i protydii politychnii koruptsii*', Law No. 731-19, adopted on 8 October 2015, available at: http://zakon4.rada.gov.ua/laws/show/731-19/page, accessed 24 March 2016.

[12]'*Pro vnesennya deyakykh zmin do deyakykh zakonodavchykh aktiv Ukrainy u zv'yazku z zaprovadzhenniam derzhavnoho finansuvannya politychnykh partii v Ukraini*', Law No. 1349-15, adopted on 27 November 2006, available at: http://zakon5.rada.gov.ua/laws/show/1349-15, accessed 24 March 2016.

legal loopholes by cynical party entrepreneurs has contributed to the under-institutionalisation, dysfunctionality and instability of the Ukrainian multi-party system, and the inability of parties to fulfil their socio-political function as aggregators of society's interests.

New actors in Ukraine's post-Euromaidan parliament

The parliamentary elections of 2014 resulted in an overhaul of the Ukrainian party system which stood out even within the context of Ukraine's highly volatile previous election cycles. Out of the six parties that entered parliament in total,[13] only one—'Fatherland' headed by Yulia Tymoshenko— had participated in the 2012 elections (see Table 2). Moreover, this party had a drastically reduced share of the vote: from 25.54% in 2012, when the party finished second in the nationwide multi-member constituency (CVK 2012), to 5.68% in 2014. Politicians that had been members of UDAR and the Party of Regions, and entered the electoral lists of Poroshenko's Bloc and the Opposition Bloc respectively, left their parties before the new electoral season. They were marked as 'nonpartisan' in the electoral lists of their new parties. 'Fatherland' is thus today the only main party to win seats in at least two parliamentary elections (Meleshevych 2010), and it has gained seats in the proportional representation vote in 2014. Moreover, four out of five parties entering the parliament *via* proportional representation had only been registered within the previous four years.[14] The high support that these new parties received in 2014 contradicted an earlier pattern of Ukrainian elections according to which Ukrainians tended to prefer voting for parties which had been registered back in the 1990s (Rybiy 2013, p. 407).

The party system's overhaul also brought many new faces to the *Verkhovna Rada*—yet another manifestation of the Ukrainian party system's under-institutionalisation. To be sure, there was also a positive dimension to this fact—in particular, an influx of civil society representatives to politics. More than half of the deputies (56%, 236 out of 422) elected in 2014 had never sat in national parliament before (Razumkov Centre 2015a). This percentage could—and, some Ukrainian experts believe, should—have been higher had the electoral system been changed, as was planned, from a mixed to a proportional one (keeping the 5% threshold), with open lists. Despite the first post-Euromaidan ruling coalition's promise to change the existing electoral system in spring 2014 (Kovalchuk 2015), the outgoing parliament failed to make this change happen. Thus, many pre-Euromaidan incumbent single-member district deputies returned to their seats, even though Ukrainian politics had gone through deep changes during 2014.

Paradoxically, 141 out of 225 (63%) of the MPs elected *via* proportional representation in 2014 did not have any official party affiliation although they entered parliament *via* a party list. This included 70% of the MPs of Poroshenko's Bloc, 94% of those of 'Self-Reliance', and all MPs from the Opposition Bloc. Overall, as many as 310 out of the 423 MPs of the current Ukrainian parliament lacked in 2014 an official party affiliation (Parandii 2015).

Majoritarian elections in Ukraine 'provide disincentives for the development of political parties' because candidates are relying on personal clientelistic networks instead of party platforms, as noted by IDEA experts.[15] Similarly, Zimmer and Haran argue that majoritarian

---

[13]Despite their names, both Poroshenko's Bloc and the Opposition Bloc are not party alliances, but proper parties themselves, since blocs are forbidden under current electoral law.

[14]'The List of Political Parties', State Registration Service, available at: http://www.drsu.gov.ua/party, accessed 1 June 2015.

[15]'Ukraine: Extract from "Programmatic Parties"', IDEA, 2011, available at: http://www.idea.int/ development/upload/ukraine.pdf, accessed 1 June 2015.

electoral rules in Ukraine 'encourage clientelistic behavior', and that they were initially adopted because they served the interests of the Communist *nomenklatura* (Zimmer & Haran 2008, p. 546). As the networks necessary to secure electoral support within a small district are usually easier to maintain than to build, local politicians are often re-elected repeatedly. Thus, out of the 198 single-member districts where elections were held in 2014, 83 were won by the same candidates as in 2012.[16] The strong localism in Ukraine's majoritarian elections is yet another determinant of the lack of programmatic differentiation in Ukrainian party politics and low institutionalisation of the party system. Single-member district candidates often win due to some specific social, cultural and economic benefits they have (or are seen as having) secured or are assumed to be able and willing to secure for their local constituencies, rather than due to their past parliamentary performance or future plans of action on the national level.

Even more surprising is the fact that victory in single-member district elections was not the only and most significant path for pre-revolutionary deputies to re-enter parliament after the Euromaidan. The majority of them have done so by virtue of being placed high enough on their parties' electoral lists. In fact, as a Governance and Social Development Resource Centre report on Ukrainian parliamentarianism states: 'The key players remain established politicians who are attempting to prove their "revitalisation"' (Whitmore 2014). Some answers to the question of why most parties in the parliament are new, yet many older politicians have remained in the *Verkhovna Rada*, may be found in the background of the new parties.

Prominent parties participating in the 2014 parliamentary elections

Three out of the six parties that passed the electoral threshold in October 2014 were only created shortly before, and because of the 2014 elections. The Popular Front was set up by Prime Minister Arseniy Yatseniuk and former interim President Oleksandr Turchynov because they were, as once leading politicians of 'Fatherland', reportedly unable to convince Tymoshenko to allow them to nominate more of their *protégés* for 'Fatherland's' electoral list (Nikolaenko 2014). Poroshenko's Bloc was built on the popularity and in support of Ukraine's newly elected President. The Bloc brought together prominent representatives of Vitalii Klychko's UDAR, former politicians and businesspeople associated with Viktor Yushchenko, some journalists as well as military commanders, and several figures from the previous regime (Whitmore 2014, p. 9). The Opposition Bloc was created by former leading members of the Party of Regions and their close allies. Being the *ancien regime*'s successor party, the Opposition Bloc was funded by, among other oligarchs, the industrial magnate Dmytro Firtash.

The two other parties that managed to pass the 5% barrier, Oleh Lyashko's Radical Party and 'Self-Reliance', had been created several years before, but had been only marginal players in Ukrainian politics before 2014. The Radical Party had participated in the 2012 previous national parliamentary elections, yet had won only 1.08% of the vote (see Table 2). 'Self-Reliance' had previously been an NGO created by the L'viv mayor Andrii Sadovyi. In 2012, it transformed into a party and in 2014, gained nationwide attention by winning 6.87% in the Kyiv City Council elections, in spite of its West Ukrainian roots.

---

[16]'Mazhorytarna dynamika mizh vyboramy 2012 ta 2014. Infohrafika', *PRportal*, 2014, available at: http://prportal.com.ua/Peredovitsa/mazhoritarna-dinamika-mizh-viborami-2012-ta-2014-infografika, accessed 1 June 2015.

A party that did not pass the 5% barrier but is worth mentioning is the Right Sector, created in late 2013. This ultra-nationalist organisation was initially an umbrella organisation comprising a number of extra-parliamentary radical rightwing 'groupuscules' which took part in the Euromaidan (Likhachev 2014). Although it then had a membership of only a few hundred, largely young men, the Right Sector's insignia were highly visible on Kyiv's Independence Square. The relatively unimportant activities and presence of the Right Sector during the events of the Euromaidan were heavily reported by Russian state-controlled mass media, and thus were part of the creation of a skewed foreign image of the uprising (Likhachev 2014; Shekhovtsov & Umland 2014).[17] Building on the disproportionately high international attention for the originally miniscule fringe organisation, the Right Sector formed its own party in 2014, participated in the October 2014 parliamentary elections, and expectedly failed to pass the electoral threshold, by a wide margin (see Table 2).

As in previous elections, the ideological positions of many of the parties that successfully entered the parliament as a result of the 2014 elections were unclear. Most of them openly supported Ukraine's European and Atlantic integration. Only the Opposition Bloc stood for international neutrality and had a relatively pro-Russian, yet still generally pro-European, foreign policy agenda (Whitmore 2014, p. 10). In terms of their socio-economic agendas, all of these parties adopted positions in a range between liberal-conservative and social-democratic, and did not further clarify their exact ideological and philosophical position in Ukraine's and Europe's political spectrum. Oleh Lyashko's Radical Party supported the creation of a welfare state while also using a heavily nationalist rhetoric.

Three key parties, with clear ideologies—the ultra-nationalist All-Ukrainian Union 'Freedom', the Right Sector and the leftwing, Soviet-nostalgic CPU—all failed to pass the 5% barrier. In the previous 2012 elections, 'Freedom' had received 10.44% and was surprisingly widely supported by educated, urban and pro-EU voters as the most radical opposition to the Yanukovych regime (Fedorenko 2013; Shekhovtsov 2013; Vasylchenko 2013; Belitser 2014). Once this threat had disappeared, however, the votes of the core supporters of the party, mostly based in Western Ukraine (Polyakova 2014, 2015), were insufficient to allow the party to pass the electoral barrier (Shekhovtsov 2014). Radical nationalism is therefore represented, in the 423-member parliament elected in 2014, by no more than 13 MPs, mostly elected in majoritarian constituencies.

A major change in post-Soviet Ukrainian parliamentarianism was the disappearance of the Communists from parliament in 2014, and from politics altogether in 2015. The CPU had commanded the largest fraction in the Ukrainian parliament before 2002, and continued to be a notable presence in all elections up to 2012, as well as in daily political and media discourse. A major reason for its spectacular failure in 2014 was that most voters from Crimea and many in the Donets Basin, that is, in its core electoral strongholds, could not vote, and that the turnout in Ukraine's Eastern and Southern Russophone regions was exceptionally low.[18] This spectacular electoral failure was the beginning of the end of the once mighty CPU. In December 2015, the Kyiv District Administrative Court issued a decision to ban the CPU,

[17]The first violent escalation during the protests, in front of Ukraine's Presidential Administration, on 1 December 2013 involved rightwing extremists. Yet the clash happened under dubious circumstances and may not have been a genuine confrontation, but a staged escalation in order to discredit the protests (Likhachev 2014).

[18]'Natsionalnyi ekzyt-poll'2012', DIF, 2014, available at: http://dif-exitpoll.org.ua/ua/golovna.htm, accessed 10 July 2015.

which was confirmed by the High Administrative Court a month later.[19] This was carried out in accordance with a previously adopted law condemning the Communist regime, on a par with that of the Nazis, and actions as well as symbols aimed at propagating them. A normally plausible suspicion of the new Ukrainian authorities' motive behind this move was that it was aimed at removing a competitor from the opposition camp. Yet, this is unlikely since the CPU's support had been fading already before the regime change and before the 2014 elections. At best, one could claim that the anti-Communist laws, leading to the CPU's ban, were politically motivated in so far as they constituted a populist action aimed at pleasing the electorate of the ruling parties, in times of deep socio-economic crisis. The majority of MPs from the five coalition parties voted in favour of the anti-Communist laws.

There were two further noteworthy parties that failed to pass the 5% barrier. Serhii Tihipko's 'Strong Ukraine' (*Syl'na Ukraina*) aimed to attract voters in the Southeast by using pacifist and moderately pro-Russian rhetoric, akin to that of the Opposition Bloc. In contrast, Anatolii Hrytsenko's 'Civic Position' (*Hromadyans'ka pozytsiya*) attempted to attract the pro-Western, reform-oriented middle class also courted by 'Self-Reliance' (Kravchenko 2014), with the latter attracting the bulk of this shared support base.

Most of the main competitors in the 2014 elections were relatively new parties either specifically created for this electoral campaign, or without any significant electoral support before. Two of the latter ('Self-Reliance' and 'Civic Position') specifically targeted pro-Western middle-class voters. Yet neither of these two, nor most of the new participants— except for the unsuccessful ultra-nationalist Right Sector—promoted any particular ideology. Despite a major overhaul in the composition of its leading actors, there was no substantive structural change in the Ukrainian party system, which remains dominated by ideologically vague and rhetorically populist competitors. The two older most clearly ideological parties— the rightwing 'Freedom' and Soviet-nostalgic CPU—failed to enter parliament. In terms of general democratisation, this was a positive development as it marginalised two, in different ways, distinctly illiberal forces, and demonstrated the voters' preference for moderate political positions. Yet, a notable and lasting programmatic differentiation of the more or less liberal and pro-democratic Ukrainian political party-spectrum has yet to occur.

Old and new features of Ukraine's party system in 2015

How far did the events of the winter of 2013–2014 affect the socio-organisational foundations of Ukraine's political regime? In this section, we discuss issues in relation to the institutionalisation of Ukraine's party system, namely the predominance of party leaders in the political contest, the role of ideologies in political parties, the underrepresentation of women in parliament, the dubious sources of party financing, the declining salience of ethno-linguistic cleavages, the enduring use of administrative resources, the continuities in Ukraine's political elite's behavioural patterns and the impact of corruption on the party system. We argue that some changes in Ukraine's political landscape in 2014–2015, such as the diminishing impact of ethnicity and language on the Ukrainian polity, have been noticeable and are clearly beneficial to the consolidation of Ukraine's polity. Nevertheless, most of the old pathological patterns have not disappeared in spite of the regime change, and remain, as of mid-2015, yet to be overcome.

---

[19]'Vyschyi adminsud pidtverdyv zakonnist' zaborony KPU', *Zaxid.net*, 25 January 2016, available at: http://zaxid.net/news/showNews.do?vishhiy_adminsud_pidtverdiv_zakonnist_zaboroni_ kpu&objectId=1380324, accessed 5 February 2016.

In spite of the fundamental changes after the regime change, so far the dependence of Ukrainian parties on the personal popularity of their leaders continues. Whitmore has observed after the elections that '[t]here would be no "Fatherland" without Tymoshenko', its charismatic leader (Whitmore 2014, p. 5). A 2009 poll had indicated that 58% of Ukrainians base their vote in parliamentary elections on the personality of a party's leader (Razumkov Centre 2009). It was no surprise therefore that, in the 2014 elections, Poroshenko's Bloc and Lyashko's Radical Party did well, while the Popular Front also relied on Yatsenyuk's and Turchynov's relatively high popularity, at that point. The emergence of significant electoral support for 'Self-Reliance' was a corollary of the success and charisma of Andrii Sadovyi as mayor of L'viv (Stadnyk 2014).[20] The public image of 'Strong Ukraine' and 'Civic Position', two parties that came close to, but did not pass the threshold, too were principally shaped by their leaders—Serhii Tihipko and Anatolii Hrytsenko respectively. In contrast, parties with strong ideologies, namely the CPU and the nationalistic 'Freedom' and Right Sector, were not as closely identified with their leaders Petro Symonenko, Oleh Tyahnybok and Dmytro Yarosh respectively.[21]

After the leaders of the Party of Regions, Viktor Yanukovych and Mykola Azarov, had left the country and the party was dissolved, its successor organisation, the Opposition Bloc, became a peculiar phenomenon in the 2014 elections. Not only were its listed candidates not actually members of this successor organisation, but the Bloc was also the only contender that did not have a clearly identifiable and popular charismatic leader figure. Instead, the Opposition Bloc relied on the Party of Regions' strong traditional voter-base in Ukraine's south-eastern *oblasti*, and sought to benefit from remnants of the once salient ethno-linguistic, memory-political and geopolitical division in the Ukrainian electorate, and the residual sympathies for Ukraine's *ancien regime*. In today's Ukraine, this division seems less pronounced, but still exists. For instance, asked about accession to the EU and the Russia-led customs union, 87% of the respondents in Western Ukraine said in 2015 they would rather join the EU, while only 51% in the South and 20% in the East would rather do so.[22] The Opposition Bloc's reliance on political, cultural and other social cleavages rather than charismatic leader figures made it, oddly, in a certain way more 'modern' than most other Ukrainian parties heavily relying on their more or less popular party leaders.

Another sign of the continuing dysfunctionality of the party system for society was its inability to properly aggregate the interests of the population. While the 2014 *Verkhovna Rada* elections brought more female politicians into parliament than ever before in post-Soviet Ukraine, women remain heavily underrepresented. The 47 elected female deputies constitute merely 11% of the 423 elected MPs.[23] Out of 29 parties participating in the proportional representation elections, only ten fulfilled the new legal norm to include over 30% of women in their party lists. Interestingly, the competitors violating this norm included not only such contenders as 'Freedom', the Right Sector and the Communists, namely anti-Western and/or

---

[20]Sadovyi however, was only 50th in his party's list, thereby signalling that he preferred to remain L'viv's mayor, rather than become a national politician, for the time being.

[21]'Fatherland' was, moreover, one of only two parties which did not include a single nonpartisan candidate on their electoral list, while only two non-members were included in the Communist Party's list.

[22]'Public Opinion Survey: Residents of Ukraine', Rating Group Ukraine & International Republican Institute, 2015, available at: http://www.iri.org/sites/default/files/wysiwyg/2015_11_national_oversample_en_combined_natl_and_donbas_v3.pdf, accessed 5 February 2016.

[23]'U novii Verkhovnii Radi naibil'she zhinok za vsyu istoriyu—KVU', *Ukrains'ka Pravda*, 12 November 2014, available at: http://www.pravda.com.ua/news/2014/11/12/7044034/, accessed 1 June 2015.

TABLE 4
RELATIVE OFFICIAL CAMPAIGN EXPENDITURE PER VOTE FOR PARTIES THAT OVERCAME THE
5% BARRIER*

Party	% of party votes	Party campaign spending (official data) (in hryvna)	Cost of a vote (in hryvna)
Popular Front	22.14	93,645,384	26.85
Petro Poroshenko Bloc	21.82	97,347,782	28.32
'Self-Reliance' Union	10.97	27,342,011	15.81
Opposition Bloc	9.43	106,396,169	71.59
Oleh Lyashko Radical Party	7.44	73,228,723	62.45
All-Ukrainian Union 'Fatherland'	5.68	109,483,429	122.35

Note: *In the proportional part of the Ukraine's October 2014 parliamentary elections. The cost of a vote—official expenditures of political parties in the election campaign.
Sources: Parandii (2015); Informational Analytical Center Info-Light, available at: http://infolight.org.ua/about, accessed 1 June 2015.

nationalist parties, but also Poroshenko's Bloc and 'Self-Reliance'—that is, explicitly pro-European parties. An officially pro-Western ideological and geopolitical orientation of a party does not yet necessarily translate into its giving priority to gender equality.

Whether seen as a pathological or a normal phenomenon, the amounts of funds spent on campaigning by Ukrainian parties in 2014 were, in most cases, roughly proportional to their electoral results. A partial exception was Tymoshenko's 'Fatherland', which was the second best funded party in the elections, yet barely made it over the 5% threshold. 'Self-Reliance', on the other hand, was third in terms of electoral support in the proportional representative system voting, yet came only 9th in the campaign spending ranking (see Table 4). Nevertheless, the top ten highest spending parties were also the top ten most successful parties in the elections. The only clear exception was the Communists who spent little cash, and relied instead on Soviet-era networks and the nostalgia of the electorate. As a result, Ukraine continues to be ruled by those able to collect large donations for their campaigns from the oligarchs.

The most negative interpretation of this relationship is that Ukraine's parliament is still dominated by MPs ready to sell their parties' future loyalty to self-serving sponsors. Kuzio alleges, moreover, that the oligarchic funding often comes from the shadow economy (Kuzio 2014, p. 316). So far, sources of funding other than private donations have played only a minor role. Instead, big business continues to use financing as a tool to lobby economic interests. In the absence of state funding, a party without oligarchic support is unable to conduct a nationally competitive campaign against those parties backed by Ukraine's economic heavyweights.

The heavy dependence of electorally successful parties on ultra-rich donors and their narrow interests then shapes the agendas pursued by these parties once they are in parliament or government. This is, a phenomenon also observable in many developed democracies, yet it is far more salient within Ukraine's (and other post-Soviet countries') parliamentary affairs. The notorious manipulations of voting procedures and curiosities in the formation of coalitions in the Ukrainian legislative process (Bredies 2007), the frequent incoherence in Kyiv's executive decision-making and public policies, as well as the many contradictions in Ukraine's legal documents are, against this background, no big surprise.

As mentioned, geopolitical rather than socio-economic orientations expressed by the parties have played a key role in Ukrainian electoral campaigns and voting since 1991. Most parties that entered parliament or came close to doing so—except for the Opposition Bloc and the Communists—were loudly pro-Western (UCIPR 2014). While they tried to emphasise programmatic differences, their programmes have been seen as 'unclear' and partly unrealistic.[24] A USAID-commissioned analysis concludes: 'In their programs, the parties focused attention on elaborating their positions regarding the most problematic issues of these days: territorial integrity, peace and defence capacity of the country. The other questions … were secondary'.[25]

While the geopolitical orientation articulated by a party used to be traditionally one of the most defining factors for the structuring of Ukrainian politics, the increase, before the 2014 parliamentary elections, of pro-Western attitudes across the Ukrainian electorate resulted in a sea-change in Ukraine's electoral landscape. The broadly pro-Western stance of the active electorate reduced the salience of one of Ukrainian politics' most enduring and prevalent challenges—the sharp and seemingly irreconcilable regional cleavages in the electoral support for different parties prior to 2014 (Katchanovski 2006a, 2006b, 2007). The marked decline of this cleavage's salience is not only consequential for the future of Ukraine's party system, but can, more broadly, be seen as a sign of the emergence of a consolidated political nation in Ukraine. However, this consolidation process leaves out Crimea and the occupied territories of the Donets Basin, and, as pro-Russian attitudes are strong in these regions, increases the mental distance between them and the majority of Ukraine. Moreover, as large numbers of Ukraine's current internally displaced persons were unable to vote in the 2014 elections, it remains to be seen how far they will become part of this consolidation process. Finally, the ban on the CPU, and thus the alienation of its voters, leaves them outside of this process as well.

As the country was fighting against, and threatened by further, Russia-induced separatism, the parties in 2014 did not revert to their traditional appeal to polarising issues such as the status of the Russian language and the interpretation of World War II (Whitmore 2014, p. 5). Instead, most parties emphasised the idea of cross-regional cross-ethnic unity and all-Ukrainian political patriotism in their campaigns. The growing prevalence of this theme in Ukrainian electoral campaigning was demonstrated by the unexpected rise of a militant Russophone Ukrainian nationalism in Southern and Eastern Ukraine—regions that provide a large share of Ukraine's volunteer troops employed in the Donbas.[26] Against this background, the public use of the Russian language in political discourse has become perceived by many Western and Central Ukrainian nationalists in a more positive light than hitherto.

This shift in the perception of the Russian language, and the inability to conduct elections in Crimea and parts of the Donbas, that is, in densely populated and relatively 'pro-Russian' territories, contributed to a marked decrease of the 'Russia factor' in Ukrainian party politics. In contrast to

[24]'Porivnyannya prohram politychnykh partii', *Ukrains'ka Pravda*, 21 October 2014, available at: http://www.pravda.com.ua/articles/2014/10/21/7041350/, accessed 1 June 2015.

[25]'Politychni partii prydilyayut pomitno menshu uvahu rozvytku pidpryemnytstva ta maloho i seredn'oho biznesu—analiz program', CIPE, 2014, available at: http://cipe-eurasia.org/%D0%BF%D0%BE%D0%BB%D1%96%D1%82%D0%B8%D1%87%D0%BD%D1%96-%D0%BF%D0%B0%D1%80%D1%82%D1%96%D1%97-%D0%BF%D1%80%D0%B8%D0%B4%D1%96%D0%BB%D1%8F%D1%8E%D1%82%D1%8C-%D0%BF%D0%BE%D0%BC%D1%96%D1%82%D0%BD%D0%BE/, accessed 1 June 2015.

[26]'Poroshenko: Bol'shynstvo voyuyushchikh za Ukrainu na Donbasse—russkoyazychnye', *Korrespondent. net*, 31 March 2015, available at: http://korrespondent.net/ukraine/3497931-poroshenko-bolshynstvo-vouiuischykh-za-ukraynu-na-donbasse-russkoiazychnye, accessed 1 June 2015.

earlier elections, in 2014, the Ukrainian voters, according to opinion polls,[27] were more uniformly pro-Western than ever before. Even the Opposition Bloc, 'Strong Ukraine' and the Communists, having most of their electoral support in the Russophone South and East, did not accentuate regional and linguistic differences. This growing consolidation of Ukrainian national identity was furthered by an increasingly trans-regional consensus on the issue of Ukraine's European integration. Already before the 2012 parliamentary elections, Melnykovska *et al.* had speculated that 'a European civic supra-national identity may potentially provide a way to unite a majority of Ukrainian citizens, regardless of their ethnic identity' (Melnykovska *et al.* 2011, p. 1062).

The Soviet legacy in post-Soviet Ukraine

In order to fully assess the quality of the party systems of post-authoritarian states, it is important to explore how winning parties use and organise their democratically gained power: how far is their post-electoral approach to general political development distinct from patterns characteristic of the behaviour of the previous, authoritarian regime? As we can only partly outline here, there is evidence to suggest that Ukrainian governments, in the new century, are still abusing power through the use of informal networks and methods developed by their predecessors in the 1990s. The latter, in turn, obtained their positions in government or state-related structures due to resources they had acquired in the Soviet system. In other words, while official institutions have changed fundamentally since 1990, many unofficial patterns of political elite behaviour still remain today, in somewhat transmuted forms (Bredies 2007).

For instance, Zimmer and Haran (2008) have classified the Party of Regions, among other 'centrist' parties in Ukraine, as a *de facto* successor party to the Soviet regime. They employ the definition of John T. Ishiyama of successor parties as those parties 'which inherited the preponderance of the former ruling parties' resource and personnel' (Ishiyama 1998, p. 62). Zimmer and Haran (2008) trace the 'line of succession' from the ruling communist party of Soviet Ukraine, through the 'red director' elites, the People's Democratic Party (*Narodno-demokratychna partiya*—NDP) and the coalition 'For a United Ukraine' (*Za edynu Ukrainu*—ZaEDU), to one of the former members of this coalition—the Party of Regions (now continued by the Opposition Bloc). Their argument parallels Bredies' (2007) identification of striking continuities in the habitus and behaviour of the political elite before and after the Orange Revolution of 2004 as a major problem for post-Soviet Ukraine.

These earlier continuities could also mean that the recent removal of the Party of Regions from power may not yet result in a full discontinuation of the behavioural patterns of the old political elite. Above all, despite the replacement of Yanukovych and his acolytes, many of the corruption networks in post-Soviet Ukraine apparently continue to exist, or have reinvented themselves. Some can be traced as far back as the early 1990s, with money flows controlled by 'red directors', who had been represented by the Party of Regions until 2014. Under the rule of Yanukovych, certain figures from the Donbas, often personally loyal to the president, were placed in control of the most attractive corruption mechanisms in key ministries.[28] In spite of the changes of 2014, some of these mechanisms—like rent extracting

---

[27]'Use bil'she ukraintsiv khochut' v NATO ta ES—opytuvannya', *Ukrains'ka Pravda*, 20 November 2014, available at: http://www.pravda.com.ua/news/2014/11/20/7044855/, accessed 1 June 2015.

[28]'U klyuchovykh ministerstvakh do 75% kerivnykh posad zaimayut' vykhidtsi z Donbasu', *Dzerkalo Tyzhnya*, 21 September 2013, available at: http://dt.ua/POLITICS/u-klyuchovih-ministerstvah-do-75-kerivnih-posad-zaymayut-vihidci-z-donbasu-128837_.html, accessed 1 June 2015.

hierarchies—are still in place and adapting to the new circumstances. The reconstitution of informal exchange mechanisms in present-day Ukraine has the potential to fundamentally undermine its seemingly reshaped polity, including the party system.

Sustainable improvement in the functioning of Ukraine's party system is thus an integral part of the reform of the entire Ukrainian socio-political system, and will depend on appropriate changes in electoral and other party-related legislation. Even if formal rules are upgraded significantly, such reforms could remain ineffective as long as covert financial flows continue to subvert Ukraine's rule of law in general. For instance, in an April 2015 poll, 57.2% of the surveyed heads of Ukrainian enterprises stated that the situation regarding corruption in Ukraine had not changed during the preceding year, while 27.7% replied that it had even become worse.[29] In a public opinion poll, held in December 2014, 47.3% of Ukrainians replied that there had been no change in the level of corruption in the country during the year, and 31.8% thought that it had actually increased.[30] Apparently, the previously existing 'kickback' ('*otkaty*') mechanisms, and other criminal ways of earning money through exploitation of state power have, at least until summer 2015, been left intact, even if some of the beneficiaries have changed (Leshchenko 2014).[31] Unless these more profound dysfunctionalities of Ukraine's political and socio-economic system lose their salience, the party system is also likely to remain dysfunctional, unstable and under-institutionalised—whatever improvement there may be in electoral and party-related legislation.

The same argument applies to the pathology of 'administrative resources', namely illegal methods of pressure by the authorities on political opponents, mainly during the electoral campaign periods—a feature particularly prominent in the weeks preceding the 2012 parliamentary elections.[32] In 2014, this instrument was also used, to various extents, in support of all the major parties, but, most frequently, by Poroshenko's Bloc and the Popular Front due to the executive positions of their leaders at the time of the elections, as President and Prime Minister respectively (OPORA 2014).

After the elections of October 2014, no single ruling party emerged—a result markedly different from the parliamentary elections during Yanukovych's presidency. Yet, the post-2014 situation is not entirely new and, in some regards, is reminiscent of the 'coalition of rival centrist parties' (Zimmer & Haran 2008, p. 553) under President Kuchma in the late 1990s and early 2000s. At least, by mid-2015, despite the proclaimed anti-corruption and pro-European goals of Ukraine's new leadership, Ukraine's mode of party government continues, in many ways, a line of succession reaching back to patterns of political behaviour during the late Soviet and early post-Soviet periods.

Ukraine's problem after the elections of 2014 is that, as Sarah Birch (2001) notes, within poorly institutionalised party systems, election winners are unlikely to support a democratisation

[29] 'Bil'she nizh polovyna kerivnykiv ukrains'kykh pidpryemstv vvazhayut', scho sytuatsiya z koruptsiieyu za pivroku ne zminylasya, kozhen chetvertyi vidznachae pohirshennya—opytuvannya', *Interfax-Ukraine*, 15 April 2015, available at: http://ua.interfax.com.ua/news/general/260559.html, accessed 1 June 2015.

[30] 'Maizhe 80% ukraintsiv perekonani, shcho z koruptsieyu u kraini nichoho ne zminylosya', *Ukrains'ka Pravda*, 27 December 2014, available at: http://www.pravda.com.ua/news/2014/12/27/7053476/, accessed 1 June 2015.

[31] 'Eks-nardep: smotryashchi vid Yanukovycha lyshylysya, im navit' lyustratsiya ne zahrozhue', *Ekonomichna Pravda*, 13 October 2014, available at: http://www.epravda.com.ua/news/2014/10/13/497791/, accessed 1 June 2015.

[32] 'Ukraine—Parliamentary Elections, 28 October 2012: Final Report', OSCE ODIHR, available at: http://www.osce.org/odihr/elections/98578, accessed 9 August 2015.

process as they fear defeat in a later electoral cycle. A poll by the Kyiv International Institute of Sociology in March 2015 showed that the Popular Front, the surprise winner of the October 2014 elections, was supported by only 6.6% of those Ukrainians who already had a party preference for the next vote. Some 19.7% of the voters did not know whom to support (KIIS 2015). It is thus not surprising that, despite many campaign promises, Ukraine's ruling parties had, by mid-2015, still not adopted laws that would secure more democratic elections, such as an open-list proportional representation system or public financing of electoral campaigns.

This specific failure to adopt timely changes to the legislation on political competition reflects a trend identified by VoxUkraine research group whose researchers analysed possible correlations between voting patterns of individual MPs.[33] Their goal was to find which MPs vote together, and thus determine who, in fact, participates or does not participate in, what could be called, the 'real' ruling coalition: those who actually support or reject the bills passed by the governmental majority. All parties of the formal ruling coalition (Poroshenko's Bloc, the Popular Front, the Radical Party,[34] 'Self-Reliance' and 'Fatherland') belong to this 'core', as well as 'Economic Development' (*'Ekonomichnyi rozvytok'*), a centrist fraction encompassing deputies elected by single-member districts. Yet, some civic activists in factions that are part of the governmental coalition appear as dissenting voters with regard to certain pro-governmental initiatives. Some of these dissenters belong to a group of, in mid-2015, 27 Euromaidan activists. Their inter-factional network is tellingly called 'Euro-optimists' and consists of MPs who—through various party lists—entered parliament in order to continue the cause of the Euromaidan protests inside the legislature (Worschech 2014).

The presence of former extra-parliamentary activists in Ukraine's 8th parliament is one of the factors suggesting that eventually new legislation may be adopted which would create the preconditions for a more predictable, rational and transparent functioning of Ukrainian political parties. The activists' political capital is based on their image of being a new force willing to change the way politics is done in Ukraine. The group of MPs include prominent journalists like Mustafa Nayyem and Serhiy Leshchenko, and seasoned anti-corruption campaigners like Hanna Hopko and Svitlana Zalishchuk. In late 2015, after the initial text of this essay had been completed, the Euro-Optimists managed to push through parliament a law that introduces, starting in 2017, state funding for parties which have received over 3% of the national vote during the last electoral cycle. The law also prescribes penalties for parties hiding additional funding sources and actual spending. However, the law does not extend to the issue of electoral campaign funding.[35] As mentioned above, parties are often funded in a non-transparent manner—the sources and sums are not revealed. So far, there has been no case of a law-enforcement body preventing or even detecting dubious campaign funding. While the adoption of this new law will make Ukrainian party politics more transparent, as of early 2016, it remains to be seen whether and what legal action against abusers will be taken.

[33] 'VoxUkraine Report on Voting Patterns in Rada: The Real Coalition and is Samopomich a Dissenter?', VoxUkraine, 2015, available at: http://voxukraine.org/2015/04/16/voxukraine-report-on-voting-patterns-in-rada-the-real-coalition-and-is-samopomich-a-dissenter/, accessed 1 June 2015.

[34] On 1 September 2015, after the draft of this essay was completed, the Radical Party formally left the coalition (see, 'Lyashko zayavyv, shcho Radykal'na partiya vykhodyt z koalitsii', *Novoe Vremia*, 1 September 2015, available at: http://nv.ua/ukr/ukraine/politics/ljashko-zajaviv-shcho-radikalna-partija-vihodit-z-koalitsiji-66616.html, accessed 17 January 2016). Afterwards, its MPs voted according to circumstances, and often with the governmental majority.

[35] 'Rada Formalizes Budget Funding of Political Parties', *UNIAN*, 8 October 2015, available at: http://www.unian.info/politics/1147297-rada-formalizes-budget-funding-of-political-parties.html, accessed 17 January 2016.

Conclusions

Although the regime change of 2013–2014 produced a significant impetus for the deeper democratisation of Ukrainian politics, the level of institutionalisation of its leading parties, as well as of the party system as a whole, remains low. Some repercussions of the Euromaidan and the Russo–Ukrainian war have led to a more stable, functional and institutionalised party system. For instance, Ukraine's historic 2014 events marginalised, at least temporarily, extremist parties and lessened the regional divide among electorally active voters. Yet, many dysfunctionalities of the pre-2014 period remain in place; a number of them have intensified. Moreover, this has happened against the background of, as of early 2016, largely intact mechanisms of bribes and 'kickbacks' subverting Ukraine's entire social—including its party—system.

Within the context of the successor states of the founding republics of the USSR, Ukraine's electoral process has become relatively free and fair, as a result of the Orange Revolution of 2004 and Euromaidan of 2013–2014. Moreover, the high level of mobilisation of Ukrainian civil society, and the presence of some of its most admired leaders in Ukraine's national legislature and executive raise expectations for substantive improvement in both the *modus operandi* and quality of output of these institutions. Yet, even after Ukraine's two large post-Soviet upheavals, state–society relations continue to be hampered by a comparatively low level of organisational development, political accountability, social rootedness, demographic representativeness (especially, in terms of gender equality) and the public transparency of Ukrainian parties, as well as by the perseverance of corruption in society, at large. Ukraine still lacks both proper legislative regulation of electoral campaigns, as well as an institutionalised party system. Its parties are not yet fulfilling their function as aggregators of social interests—a grave defect whose direct and indirect repercussions continue to hamper Ukrainian political, economic and social development.

References

Bader, M. (2010) 'Party Politics in Georgia and Ukraine and the Failure of Western Assistance', *Democratization*, 17, 6.

Belitser, N. (2014) 'Vseukrainskoe ob"edinenie "Svoboda" i ego elektorat, 2012–2013', *Ideologiya i politika*, 1.

Benoit, K. (2004) 'Models of Electoral System Change', *Electoral Studies*, 23, 3.

Birch, S. (2001) *Electoral Systems and Party System Stability in Post-Communist Europe*, Working Paper (Colchester, University of Essex), available at: http://www2.essex.ac.uk/elect/database/papers/sbvolatility.pdf, accessed 1 June 2015.

Bredies, I. (2007) *Institutionenwandel ohne Elitenwechsel: Das ukrainische Parlament im Kontext des politischen Systemwechsels 1990–2006* (Münster, LIT).

CVK (2012) '*Tsentral'na vyborcha komisiya Ukrainy—WWW vidobrazhennya IAC "Vybory narodnykh deputativ 2012"*', available at: http://www.cvk.gov.ua/pls/vnd2012/wp300?PT001F01=900, accessed 1 June 2015.

CVK (2014a) '*Tsentral'na vyborcha komisiia Ukrainy—WWW vidobrazhennia IAC "Vybory narodnykh deputativ 2014"*', available at: http://www.cvk.gov.ua/pls/vnd2014/wp300?PT001F01=910, accessed 1 June 2015.

CVK (2014b) '*Tsentral'na vyborcha komisiya Ukrainy—IAC "Vybory Prezydenta Ukrainy"'*, available at: http://www.cvk.gov.ua/pls/vp2014/wp001, accessed 1 June 2015.

CVK (2014c) '*Vyborchyi spysok: politychna partiya Vseukrains'ke ob''ednannya "Bat'kivschyna"'*, available at: http://www.cvk.gov.ua/pls/vnd2014/WP406?PT001F01=910&pf7171=149, accessed 1 June 2015.

Desnitsky, A.(2014) 'Tserkovnyi orden kommunista', *Gazeta.ru*, 30 June, available at: http://www.gazeta.ru/comments/column/desnitsky/6090513.shtml, accessed 10 July 2015.

DIF (2001) *Opytuvannya: Hromads'ka dumka pro politychnykh lideriv i partii* (Kyiv, The Ilko Kucheriv Democratic Initiatives Foundation), available at: http://dif.org.ua/ua/polls/2001_polls/gromadska-dumka-pro-politichnih-lideriv-i-partii-cherven-2001-r_.htm, accessed 1 June 2015.

DIF (2012) *Vyznachal'nym dlya vybortsiv e heopolitychnyi vybir partii ta movne pytannya* (Kyiv, The Ilko Kucheriv Democratic Initiatives Foundation), available at: http://dif.org.ua/ua/commentaries/sociologist_view/-viznacha.htm, accessed 1 June 2015.

Fedorenko, K. (2013) 'Protestnaya aktivnost' krainikh pravykh v Ukraine v 2010–2012 gg.: Vseukrainskoe ob''edinenie "Svoboda" v sravnitel'noi perspektive', *Forum noveishei vostochnoevropeiskoi istorii i kul'tury*, 9, 1, available at: http://www1.ku-eichstaett.de/ZIMOS/forum/docs/forumruss19/04Fedorenko.pdf, accessed 1 June 2015.

Hesli, V., Reisinger, W., & Miller, A. (1998) 'Political Party Development in Divided Societies: The Case of Ukraine', *Electoral Studies*, 17, 2.

Ishiyama, J. T. (1998) 'Strange Bedfellows: Explaining Political Cooperation between Communist Successor Parties and Nationalists in Eastern Europe', *Nations and Nationalism*, 4, 1.

Ishiyama, J. & Kennedy, R. (2001) 'Superpresidentialism and Political Party Development in Russia, Ukraine, Armenia and Kyrgyzstan', *Europe-Asia Studies*, 53, 8.

Karmazina, M. (2012a) 'Ukrains'ka bahatopartiinist': stanovlennya i rozvytok', in Karmazina, M. (ed.) (2012b).

Karmazina, M. (ed.) (2012b) *Ukrains'ka bahatopartiinist': politychni partiyi, vyborchi bloky, lidery (kinets 1980-kh—pochatok 2012)* (Kyiv, IPiEND).

Katchanovski, I. (2006a) *Cleft Countries: Regional Political Divisions and Cultures in Post-Soviet Ukraine and Moldova* (Stuttgart, ibidem Verlag).

Katchanovski, I. (2006) 'Regional Political Divisions in Ukraine in 1991–2006', *Nationalities Papers*, 34, 5.

Katchanovski, I. (2007) 'Regional Political Cleavages, Electoral Behavior, and Historical Legacies in Ukraine', in Bredies, I., Umland, A. & Yakushik, V. (eds) *Aspects of the Orange Revolution III: The Context and Dynamics of the 2004 Ukrainian Presidential Elections* (Stuttgart, ibidem-Verlag).

KIIS (2015) '*Opytuvannya: Sotsialno-politychna sytuatsiya v Ukraini: berezen' 2015 roku*', available at: http://kiis.com.ua/?lang=ukr&cat=reports&id=511&page=1, accessed 1 June 2015.

Klyuchkovs'kyi, Yu. (2006) 'Proportsiini vybory ta rozvytok partiinoi systemy Ukrainy', *Vybory i Demokratiya*, 3, 9.

Kovalchuk, Yu. (2015) 'Bytva za vyborchu systemu', *Den'*, 29 May.

Kravchenko, D. (2014) 'Khto pryyde na zminu parlaments'kym starozhylam', *Forbes Ukraine*, 12 June, available at: http://forbes.ua/ua/nation/1372864-hto-prijde-na-zminu-parlamentskim-starozhilam, accessed 1 June 2015.

Kudelia, S. & Kuzio, T. (2014) 'Nothing Personal: Explaining the Rise and Decline of Political Machines in Ukraine', *Post-Soviet Affairs*, 31, 3.

Kuzio, T. (2014) 'Impediments to the Emergence of Political Parties in Ukraine', *Politics*, 34, 4.

Leshchenko, V. (2014) 'Koruptsiini skhemy pislya Maidanu lyshylysia, zminylysia sumy khabariv—ekspert', *Radio Svoboda*, 20 August, available at: http://www.radiosvoboda.org/content/article/26541376.html, accessed 1 June 2015.

Likhachev, V. (2014) '"Pravyi sektor" i drugie: natsional-radikaly i ukrainskii krizis kontsa 2013 g.—nachala 2014 g.', *Forum noveishei vostochnoevropeiskoi istorii i kul'tury*, 10, 2, available at: http://www1.ku-eichstaett.de/ZIMOS/forum/docs/forumruss22/09LikhachevPravysektor.pdf, accessed 1 June 2015.

Mainwaring, S. & Torcal, M. (2005) 'Party System Institutionalization and Party System Theory after the Third Wave of Democratization', Kellogg Institute for International Studies, available at: http://kellogg.nd.edu/publications/workingpapers/WPS/319.pdf, accessed 1 June 2015.

Mainwaring, S. & Zoco, E. (2007) 'Political Sequences and the Stabilization of Interparty Competition: Electoral Volatility in Old and New Democracies', *Party Politics*, 13, 2.

Meleshevych, A. (2010) 'Political Parties in Ukraine: Learning Democratic Accountability?', in Lawson, K. & Kulik, A. (eds) *Political Parties and Democracy, Volume III: Post-Soviet and Asian Political Parties* (Santa Barbara, CA, Praeger).

Melnykovska, I., Schweikert, R. & Kostiuchenko, T. (2011) 'Balancing National Uncertainty and Foreign Orientation: Identity Building and the Role of Political Parties in Post-Orange Ukraine', *Europe-Asia Studies*, 63, 6.

Nikolaenko, T. (2014) 'Tymoshenko i Turchynov ne podilyly "Bat'kivshchynu"', *The Insider*, 26 August, available at: http://www.theinsider.ua/politics/53fcbadbb204f/, accessed 1 June 2015.

OPORA (2014) '*Pidkup vybortsiv i administratyvnyi resurs: osoblyvosti parlaments'kykh vyboriv 2014 (utochneno)*', available at: http://oporaua.org/news/6694-pidkup-vyborciv-i-administratyvnyj-resurs-osoblyvosti-parlamentskyh-vyboriv-2014, accessed 1 June 2015.

Parandii, Kh. (2015) *Aktualizatsiya problem ukrains'koi partiinoi systemy v konteksti parlaments'kykh vyboriv-2014*, unpublished BA thesis (Kyiv, NaUKMA).

Pedersen, M. (1979) 'Electoral Volatility in Western Europe, 1948–1977', *European Journal of Political Research*, 7, 1, available at: http://janda.org/c24/Readings/Pedersen/Pedersen.htm, accessed 1 June 2015.

Polyakova, A. (2014) 'From the Provinces to the Parliament: How the Ukrainian Radical Right Mobilized in Galicia', *Communist and Post-Communist Studies*, 47, 2.

Polyakova, A. (2015) 'Parties and Subcultures in the Process of Mobilization: The Internal Dynamics of the Radical Right in Ukraine', in Minkenberg, M. (ed.) *Transforming the Transformation? The East European Radical Right in the Political Process* (London, Routledge).

Razumkov Centre (2007) *Opytuvannya: Yaku system vyboriv vy vvazhaete naikrashchoyu dlya Ukrainy? (Dynamika 2001–2007)*, available at: http://www.razumkov.org.ua/ukr/poll.php?poll_id=99, accessed 1 June 2015.

Razumkov Centre (2009) *Opytuvannya: Yake znachennia dlya vas pid chas holosuvannya za politychnu partiyu mae te, khto same ocholyue tsyu partiyu?*, available at: http://www.uceps.org/ukr/poll.php?poll_id=557, accessed 1 June 2015.

Razumkov Centre (2011) *Opytuvannya: Chy doviryaete vy politychnym partiyam? (Dynamika 2001–2011)*, available at: http://www.razumkov.org.ua/ukr/poll.php?poll_id=82, accessed 1 June 2015.

Razumkov Centre (2015a) 'Ukraine 2014–2015: Overcoming Challenges (Assessments)', available at: http://www.razumkov.org.ua/upload/Pidsumky_2014_2015_A4_fnl.pdf, accessed 1 June 2015.

Razumkov Centre (2015b) 'Opytuvannya: Chy doviryaete vy politychnym partiyam?', available at: http://www.uceps.org/ukr/poll.php?poll_id=1030, accessed 1 June 2015.

Roberts, K. M. & Wibbels, E. (1999) 'Party Systems and Electoral Volatility in Latin America: A Test of Economic, Institutional, and Structural Explanations', *American Political Science Review*, 93, 3.

Rybiy, O. (2013) 'Party System Institutionalization in Ukraine', *Demokratizatsiya: The Journal of Post-Soviet Democratization*, 21, 3.

Samofalov, A. (2015) 'Partiia Kolomoiskogo', *Hubs.ua*, 2 April, available at: http://hubs.ua/authority/partiya-kolomojskogo-34222.html, accessed 1 June 2015.

Shekhovtsov, A. (2013) 'Vseukrainskoe ob''edinenie "Svoboda": problema legitimnosti bor'by za vlast'', *Forum noveishei vostochnoevropeiskoi istorii i kul'tury*, 9, 1.

Shekhovtsov, A. (2014) 'From Electoral Success to Revolutionary Failure: The Ukrainian Svoboda Party', *Eurozine*, 5 March, available at: http://www.eurozine.com/articles/2014-03-05-shekhovtsov-en.html, accessed 1 June 2015.

Shekhovtsov, A. & Umland, A. (2014) 'Ukraine's Radical Right', *Journal of Democracy*, 25, 3.

Shevel, O. (2015) 'Ukrainian Political Science and the Study of Ukraine within American Political Science: How Similar, How Different?', *Journal of Ukrainian Politics and Society*, 1, 1.

Stadnyk, H. (2014) 'Skil'ky Sadovoho u zleti "Samopomochi"?', *Deutsche Welle*, 28 October, available at: http://www.dw.de/%D1%81%D0%BA%D1%96%D0%BB%D1%8C%D0%BA%D0%B8-%D1%81%D0%B0%D0%B4%D0%BE%D0%B2%D0%BE%D0%B3%D0%BE-%D1%83-%D0%B7%D0%BB%D0%B5%D1%82%D1%96-%D1%81%D0%B0%D0%BC%D0%BE%D0%BF%D0%BE%D0%BC%D0%BE%D1%87%D1%96/a-18025512, accessed 1 June 2015

Thames, F. (2007) 'Discipline and Party Institutionalization in Post-Soviet Legislatures', *Party Politics*, 13, 4.

UCIPR (2014) *Visnyk 'Tvi vybir-2014. Parlaments'ki vybory*', 6 (Kyiv, UCIPR).

Umland, A. (2008) 'Die andere Anomalie der Ukraine: ein Parlament ohne rechtsradikale Fraktionen', *Ukraine-Analysen*, 41.

Umland, A. (2013) 'A Typical Variety of European Right-Wing Radicalism?', *Russian Politics and Law*, 51, 5.

Vasylchenko, S. (2013) '"Svoboda" protiv vsekh: kratkii obzor rezul'tatov krainikh pravykh 1994–2012', *Forum noveishei vostochnoevropeiskoi istorii i kul'tury*, 9, 1.

Vasylchenko, S. (2015) *Ukraine's New Political Landscape: 2014 Elections Maps* (Kyiv, UCSD).

Whitmore, S. (2014) *Political Party Development in Ukraine* (London, GSDRC), available at: http://www.gsdrc.org/docs/open/HDQ1146.pdfz, accessed 1 June 2015.

Wilson, A. (2005) *Virtual Politics: Faking Democracy in the Post-Soviet World* (New Haven, CT, Yale University Press).

Wilson, A. & Bilous, A. (1993) 'Political Parties in Ukraine', *Europe-Asia Studies*, 45, 4.

Worschech, S. (2014) 'Vom Maidan ins Parlament, vom Maidan in die Provinz: Neue Wege der ukrainischen Zivilgesellschaft', *Ukraine-Analysen*, 142.

Zimmer, K. (2005) 'The Comparative Failure of Machine Politics, Administrative Resources and Fraud', *Canadian Slavonic Papers*, 47, 1–2.

Zimmer, K. & Haran, O. (2008) 'Unfriendly Takeover: Successor Parties in Ukraine', *Communist and Post-Communist Studies*, 41, 4.

The Donbas in 2014: Explaining Civil Conflict Perhaps, but not Civil War

ANDREW WILSON

Abstract

This essay argues that historical and identity factors, economic fears and alienation from the new government in Kyiv were only part of the reason for the rise of the separatist movement in the Donbas, Ukraine, in the spring of 2014. They set a baseline, but one not high enough to account for the creation of two mini-'Republics' and a prolonged war, without considering the effect of Russian sponsorship and the role of local elites, mainly from the literal and metaphorical 'Family' of former President Viktor Yanukovych.

THE WAR IN EAST UKRAINE THAT BEGAN IN THE SPRING OF 2014 has produced many contrasting analyses. Some commentators have chosen to read the origins of the separatist movement in the Donbas region not just as mainly domestic, but as a 'grassroots' phenomenon with genuine 'popular support' (Sakwa 2015, p. 149). Others have largely blamed Russia for provoking the conflict from the outside. This essay argues that there was sufficient alienation from Kyiv to provide a baseline for a local civil conflict, and that alienation fed off a long-standing tradition of social distance in Donbas identity, but that all the key triggers that produced all-out war were provided by Russia and by local elites in the Donbas. Baseline factors were precisely that. They set a higher level of support for a pro-Russian movement in the Donbas than in other parts of eastern and southern Ukraine, but not at a level high enough to lead to armed rebellion and sustain a drawn-out war. Moreover, the baseline factors have themselves been subject to manipulation from above, by both Ukrainian and Russian elites. That said, civil conflicts and, ultimately, 'civil wars are highly "endogenous" processes', so the war itself has now had deep and long-lasting effects of its own, changing both 'preexisting popular allegiances' and narratives (Kalyvas 2006, pp. 3, 389); but that is not why the conflict escalated in the first place.

Existing explanations

One interpretation of the outbreak of the conflict is that the Donbas was the most serious of many fault-lines in internal Ukrainian identity politics. According to Nicolai Petro, 'the peremptory removal of President Yanukovych violated the delicate balance of interests forged between

Galicia and Donbas. It was thus seen as a direct threat to the core interest of Russophone Ukrainians' (Petro 2015, p. 31). Allied to the grievances of the high concentration of local Russophones, the unique 'regional identity' of the Donbas and its 'inherent contradictions, which worked in an unexpected ruinous way' (Klinova 2014), then provided the spark for the separatist movement.

Others have looked not to pre-existing popular allegiances, but to material interests which led locals to want to preserve economic ties with Russia, which they saw as threatened by the new government in Kyiv after the Maidan protests of 2013–2014, and a growing sense of alienation from 'orange' and west Ukrainian politics since the first abortive 'Orange Revolution' of 2004 (Giuliano 2015). Zhukov (2016) also argues for the predominance of economic over identity factors, and argues that of the three main types of local economic activity, metallurgy, coal mining and machine-building, anti-Kyiv resistance was strongest in areas dominated by machine-building, which was most at risk from any disruption of trade with Russia—and from Russian sanctions.

Others have broadened the list to political factors, but kept them mainly internal. According to Serhii Kudelia, 'popular emotions specific to the region—*resentment and fear*' combined with 'political factors—*state fragmentation, violent regime change, and the government's low coercive capacity*' to 'launch the armed secessionist movement' (Kudelia 2014, emphasis in original). Arel and Driscoll argue that 'regime collapse' in Kyiv (that is, the rapid desertion of members of parliament from the ruling Party of Regions (*Partiia rehioniv*) after the killings in Kyiv on 21 February 2014, apart from diehards from the party's strongholds of Crimea and the Donbas) as well as initial 'state incapacitation' in the Donbas were the main factors in the local genesis of the conflict. They also suggest that this allowed for the penetration of Russian special forces, which they date to between four and six weeks later, and ultimately to conventional war.[1]

This essay argues that identity factors are an insufficient explanation. 'Preexisting popular allegiances' were not that different in the Donbas (see the two sections on identity below). Local political factors were hugely important, but 'state incapacitation', and even more so state collapse, is an exaggeration. Parts of the state did not operate. The new authorities in Kyiv were incompetent or distracted. But the story also involves the defection of key parts of the state and the penetration of others. And, as resource mobilisation theory would predict (Smith & Wilson 1997), more was needed in terms of resources and elite leadership for the separatist movement to develop. And also to point it in the direction it took—the initial mood in the Donbas was febrile and even contradictory, and compatible with several possible outcomes.

Other commentators see outside factors as key (Mitrokhin 2015a, 2015b): namely Russia, which played the key role in stitching together a coalition of local forces. Local actors would not have acted as they did without Russian support. Arel and Driscoll have cited the work of Regan (2000) that two thirds of seemingly intrastate civil wars in fact involve 'intervention' (more serious than mere influence) by third party foreign powers—and are still civil wars.[2] But there is a world of difference between joining in a civil conflict or civil war and either starting it or enabling its escalation. On its own, the Donbas rebellion was actually a triple

---

[1]See 'The Civil War in Ukraine', draft paper in preparation, presentation available at: www.youtube.com/watch?v=BfQ9IgTNu-M, accessed 18 February 2016.

[2]See 'The Civil War in Ukraine', draft paper in preparation, presentation available at: www.youtube.com/watch?v=BfQ9IgTNu-M, accessed 18 February 2016.

failure. Without sufficient Russian support, the first attempt at revolt was smouldering away in March and early April 2014, with several nasty 'flare-ups', but was deemed insufficiently incendiary to warrant the attempt by Igor Girkin's special forces to fan the flames from the middle of April. The attempts at revolt in Kharkiv and Odesa at the same time were less successful, and there was no broad rebellion in 'Novorossiia', a variable Russian term, but most often meaning the whole of eastern and southern Ukraine. And finally, the rebels were being pushed back by Ukrainian forces in the summer and were saved from further reverse by the massive Russian escalation in August 2014.

The remainder of this essay looks in turn at history and at identity, both before and after Ukrainian independence in 1991, as baseline factors but ambiguous resources for the Donbas separatist movement, and then looks at how both local elites and Russia combined to create a separatist movement from weak and patchy 'grassroots' material.

Baseline factors—history

Donbas history is a limited resource. It is almost all new, largely confined to a story of industrial development in the late Tsarist and Soviet eras. To the Russian side, this makes the concentration on the Soviet era only natural; to the Ukrainian side local 'historiography' therefore looks skin-deep. Attempts to go back further have little resonance for such a young society, especially on the Russophile side. And this history has led to ambiguous and shifting identities among the local population.

But all rebel movements need a story to tell. Russian nationalists in the Crimea have a resonant, if controversial story. Putin (2014) has escalated talk of the baptism of Volodymyr/ Vladimir, Prince of Kyiv/Kiev on the peninsula in 988, into comparing Crimea to the Temple Mount, even though Volodymyr went back to Kyiv after his baptism. The Golden Age of Russian Crimea can also be celebrated, although in truth it only stretched from the Crimean War in 1853–1856 until 1917, which is much shorter than the Crimean Tatar era, from the thirteenth century until 1783.

In the Donbas, in contrast, rebel leaders have jumped from one potential historical story to another. The region was never part of Volodymyr's kingdom of Rus', but was periodically under Crimean Tatar rule. The Russian view of medieval history rejects the Ukrainian idea that it was then mainly colonised from the west, by Zaporozhian Cossacks, that is, Ukrainians or proto-Ukrainians,[3] for the idea of colonisation from the north and the east, predominantly by Russians or proto-Russians. Large numbers of northern settlers supposedly crossed the river Siverskii Donets heading south from around 1600. But this does not create a Russian ethnic history of the region; traditionally this historiography fed the pluralist idea of a Russian-led, but still multi-ethnic population that used Russian as a *lingua franca* (Wilson 1995).

The Don Cossacks, meanwhile, pushed in from the east. But despite the use of Cossack symbols during the post-2014 war and the presence of a strong 'Don Cossack' militia, the idea of the Donbas as a Cossack heartland is problematical. The self-proclaimed Don Cossack 'Ataman' Nikolai Kozitsyn has declared that no one 'invited' Ukrainians to their territory.[4]

---

[3] 'Donetskaia i Luganskaia oblasti—eto istoricheskie zemli donskikh kazakov, a ne Ukrainy?', *Likbez*, 2015, available at: http://likbez.org.ua/donetsk-and-luhansk-region-a-historic-land-of-the-don-cossacks-not-ukraine. html, accessed 18 February 2016.

[4] 'ART Interview with Nikolai Kozitsyn', *YouTube*, 8 February 2015, available at: www.youtube.com/ watch?v=2A_XmeOfdog, accessed 16 February 2016.

But the historical territory of the Don Cossack ends at the river Kal'mius in the west and the Siverskii Donets in the north. This is precisely why the territory east of the Kal'mius was not part of the Novorossisk guberniya of 1764–1783 and 1796–1802. There was a separate 'Land of the Don Host' (*Oblast' Voyska Donskogo*) after 1786, renamed a guberniya in 1870. It is no coincidence that the Don Cossack fighters are now on this territory, which in modern terms is southern Luhans'k, and declare it to be Cossack territory, rather than the Donbas as a whole (Bredikin 2015). So-called Don Cossack historiography is actually mainly narrowly bound up with the struggle between the Ataman and the leadership of the LNR (the self-proclaimed 'Luhans'k People's Republic') over who controls the 'Don Host' militia.[5] Nevertheless, both sides have drawn on the mythology of the Cossack era, and of 'their' nationalised Ukrainian or Russian Cossacks, as well as their successors from the Civil War era in 1918–1921, the *otamany*, to try and bolster their legitimacy (Gilley 2015).

Ironically or not, as of spring 2015 the line from the river Kal'mius to the Siverskii Donets' was basically the border of the rebel republics (the LDR plus the 'Donets'k People's Republic' or, from the Russian, DNR), with the addition of small territories in the north and at the western edge around Donets'k. But it would be hard to argue that this was because military fortunes reflected deep-lying historical factors. The ebb and flow of the front line—initial rebel land seizure to the north-west around Slov''ians'k in 2014, followed by large Ukrainian gains, only reversed by conventional Russian invasion in August 2014—was much more dependent on the situation on the battlefield and the level of Russian commitment of money and arms (see below). The historical 'border' also partially matches a concentration of industry to its east, though far from exactly, and again this is not historically determined. Yuri Zhukov's research (2016) has located many strongholds of rebel resistance in areas dominated by certain industries, especially machine-building, but military matters decided the area of rebel occupation. Ukrainian reluctance to advance into urban areas was also part of the military calculation.

It should also be pointed out that administrative 'borders', this time the one between the Russian and Ukrainian Soviet Republics, were also adjusted several times in the 1920s (Yefimenko 2014).[6] Large amounts of the Don territory were first awarded to Ukraine on ethnographic grounds in April 1920 and then split in October 1925, with more easterly territories going to Russia. The area around Stanytsia Luhans'ka, at the time of writing in early 2016 still in Kyiv's hands, was shifted to Ukraine in August 1920.

The alternative and broader idea of Novorossia is also vague and open to multiple interpretations, as well as referring only to brief and discontinuous periods between Russian imperial absorption of the northern Black Sea littoral after 1774 through to 1917. The Ukrainian side has successfully deconstructed the myth of a united 'Novorossiya' (Brekhunenko 2014; Gava 2014) while limited support for rebellion beyond the Donbas made the Kremlin go cold on the idea, at least temporarily. By 2015, the official web page of the DNR on 'occupied territories' referred not to Kharkiv or Odesa but only to those parts of Donets'k and Luhans'k under Ukrainian army control.[7] The leaders of the DNR have increasingly fallen back on

---

[5]'Kazachyi soyuz "Oblast Voiska Donskogo"', *Ksovd.org*, 2015, available at: http://ksovd.org/, accessed 21 March 2016.

[6]'Dons'ke pytannia u derzhavnii politytsi ukraïns'koho Hetmanata i Dyrektorii', *Haidamaka* website, available at: http://haidamaka.org.ua/page_donpythetdyrdon.html, accessed 4 June 2015.

[7]See, Dnrespublika.info, available at: http://dnrespublika.info/category/novosti/novorussia-new/novosti-dnr/okkupirovannaya-territoriya/, accessed 8 August 2015.

references to the 'Donets'k nation' (*Donetskii narod*), most notably in a series of posters in 2015 under the slogan 'the Donets'k nation decides'.[8]

In 2015 the rebel leaders were also toying with the idea of the Donets'k–Kryvyi Rih Soviet Republic (DKR) of 1918 (the Russian spellings are Donets'k and Krivoi Rog) as a historical precedent for their project, starting with a rally in Donets'k on 12 February 2015 on the 97th anniversary of its proclamation in 1918 (Barabanov 2015).[9] On 6 February 2015 the DNR issued a Memorandum 'On the basis of state-building, political and historical continuity', proclaiming 'the continuation of traditions of the Donets'k–Krivoi Rog Republic and declar[ing] that the state of the Donets'k People's Republic is its successor'.[10] The DNR has also tried to revive the myth of the local Bolshevik leader 'Artem' (Fyodor Sergeyev, 1883–1921), hero of the local revolution and the founder of the DKR. Kyiv, on the other hand, took down his monuments in two Donbas cities that it re-occupied in the summer of 2014, Slov"ians'k and Artemivs'k, and a plaque to him in the capital Kyiv was vandalised, with other streets and places due to be renamed.[11]

The DKR can serve as a partial substitute for Novorossiya, as its imagined borders supposedly included what are now Kharkiv, Dnipropetrovs'k, Zaporizhzhia and Kherson—potentially the borders of an expanded DNR and LNR, the putative borders of which are not yet defined, other than by claiming the (post-1920s) *oblasti* of Donets'k and Luhans'k. Although rebel leader Andrei Purgin has made ritual denials of further territorial claims, stating that the 'DKR is an industrial region [whose] regions were united on economic principle ... we are talking about the Russian world'.[12]

But the DKR is still a problematic symbol, despite the best efforts of a tiny number of local propagandists, led by one local historian Vladimir Kornilov (2011).[13] It was not founded because of the threat of the Ukrainian National Government, which had just left Kiev. It was a ploy in Lenin's shifting calculations as Ukrainian, German and Bolshevik forces fought over Ukraine. The hope of a united Bolshevik Ukraine made the DKR irrelevant, and the arrival of German occupying forces made it redundant. Lenin then ordered the Republic to be suppressed on 20 March 1918 (Stefanko 2014). The DKR was then depicted negatively in Soviet historiography (Studenna-Skruvka 2014, p. 187). The DNR flies the black–blue–red

---

[8]'"Donetskii narod reshaet?" Bilbordy grupirovki "DNR" (fotogalereia)', *Kiev Pravda*, 29 June 2015, available at: www.kievpravda.com/news/7241, accessed 16 February 2016.

[9]'V Donetske proshel miting v chest' rozhdeniia Donetsko-Krivorozhskoi Respubliki', 12 February 2015, available at: http://novorossia.ws/video/62013-v-donecke-proshel-miting-posvyashennij-sozdaniyu-dkr.html, accessed 31 March 2016.

[10]'DNR ob'iavliaetsia preemnitsei Donetsko-Kryvorozhkoi Respubliki', *Zavtra.ru*, 5 February 2015, available at: http://zavtra.ru/content/view/dnr-obyavlyaetsya-preemnitsej-donetsko-krivorozhskoj-respubliki/, accessed 21 March 2016.

[11]'V Artemis'vku znesly pam"iatnik Artemu', *Dzerkalo tyzhnia*, 10 July 2015, available at: http://dt.ua/UKRAINE/v-artemivsku-znesli-pam-yatnik-artemu-178461_.html, accessed 16 February 2016.

[12]'DNR ne pretenduet na territorii Donetsko-Kryvorozhskoi respubliki—Purgin', *DAN news*, 6 February 2015, available at: http://dan-news.info/politics/dnr-ne-pretenduet-na-territorii-donecko-krivorozhskoj-respubliki-purgin.html, accessed 16 February 2016.

[13]'Pisatel' Vladimir Kornilov: Donbass idet k ideiam sovobody uzhe pochti stoletie', *LUG* (Lugansk Information Centre), 6 February 2015, available at: http://lug-info.com/comments/one/pisatel-vladimir-kornilov-donbass-idet-k-ideyam-svobody-uzhe-pochti-stoletie-251, accessed 16 February 2016.

tricolour flag that the previous 'Republic' supposedly used in the few weeks of its existence in 1918, but the evidence for its use is unclear (Edwards 2014). The DKR was a leftwing project, but most modern versions of the flag add a double-headed Russian imperial eagle.

The myth of the DKR therefore had little place in local consciousness. It may now have a better 'fit' for a Donbas mini-Republic or two, but it will largely have to be created *ex nihilo*. The rebel Republics are really reliant on an amalgam of Soviet historiography and its myths about the Donbas (see next section), with pan-Russian nationalism. For most locals World War II and their own experience in the practical habitus of Soviet industrialisation provide a more 'usable' past (Lipskii 2014). This history is even more recent than it seems, as the *Holodomor* (the death of millions in the famine that followed collectivisation in 1932–1933) in the region reset the clock, transforming the ethnic balance by depopulating huge areas of rural east Ukraine, as people were forced to flee to the towns to survive, where they were more subject to subsequent Russification, and by a general influx of Russian-speakers to replace the millions who were lost (Kramarenko 2006).[14] In the villages, more died because this was the steppe, simply because there was some minimal sustenance in the forest zones further north (Kuromiya 1998, pp. 167–68). The region's pre-Soviet Cossack-agricultural history died with the *Holodomor*.

Although the 'Stakhanovite' movement associated with the Donbas began in the 1930s and many historians have dated the emergence of the modern Donbas identity to the interwar period (Kuromiya 2015), 'in the Donbas people's memories don't really go past the Great Patriotic War'. Moreover, the consolidation of post-war Donbas society really dates from the Khrushchev years, after further post-war turbulence in Stalin's last years of rule. The key commemoration dates designed to cement the 'small homeland' local version of Soviet identity—the 'Day of liberation of the Donbas from German-fascist invaders' on 8 September, and the all-Soviet Victory Day on 9 May—only really date from 1965. The massive monument to the Donbas Liberators in Donets'k was only finally opened in 1984.

Baseline factors—identity

Soviet identity

Part of the reason for the separatist movement and war in the Donbas therefore lies with local identity politics, but only a part. The identity created in the Soviet Donbas is a persistent and hardy residual, which provides a baseline identity marker differentiating the region from the rest of Ukraine. But the line is not as sharp as between Crimea and the rest of Ukraine, and the sharpness of that differentiation has been variable. Nevertheless, such an identity does exist. As argued by Kostiantyn Skorkin, 'ignoring these processes will lead to the creation of a myth like the Ukrainophobe cliché about the "Habsburg General Staff", which in its time allegedly "invented" Ukraine' (Skorkin 2014, p. 27).

Soviet identity put down deep roots in the Donbas because nothing much came before it. The Soviet legacy is so determinant that separatist leaders have even claimed that 'Kiev's rejection of the legacy of the USSR [a reference to the de-Communisation laws passed by

---

[14]'Donbas Has Always Been Ukraine: The Holodomor and Russification Legacies', *Voices of Ukraine*, 5 June 2014, available at: http://maidantranslations.com/2014/06/05/donbas-has-always-been-ukraine-the-holodomor-and-russification-legacies/, accessed 16 February 2016.

Kyiv in April 2015] deprives it of any right to the territory of the Donbas'.[15] The 'parliament' of the DNR also claims that pre-Soviet history is irrelevant to the region, as it was never part of any previous 'Ukrainian' states (though this was only partially true of the easternmost Don territories): 'the DKR was never a part of the UNR [Ukrainian National Republic of 1917–1918], nor Skoropadsky's Hetmanate [1918], nor the revived "state" declared by supporters of Bandera in L'viv in June 1941'.[16]

Ironically, attachment to the Soviet legacy was also because of resistance to ethnic nationalism, which has never had much of a history or appeal in the Donbas (Osipian & Osipian 2006), and its myth of a labour culture in which ethnic origins are dissolved. There are also hardly any real 'indigenous' locals; almost everyone is new—there is no real local myth of the 'land of our fathers'. Ukrainian and Russian masses interacted without much of a local cultural intelligentsia. State authorities were only minimally present until the very late Tsarist era, which facilitated the persistence of a strong local anarchist tradition (ironically in part the reverse of the Ukrainian Cossack myth), tempered by readiness to submit to power from above if sufficiently strong—but little tradition of public politics or civic activism in between.

Hiroaki Kuromiya (2015) has argued that this also made the Donbas open to a surprising variety of ideologies, albeit instrumentally. Political parties, even the Bolsheviks, were weak; civil society was even weaker, including organised religion. An intense informal culture of 'looking after one's own' and of 'winner takes all' took the place of any politics of 'give-and-take'. The Donbas also never had a classic proletariat: settlements grew up piecemeal and were often semi-rural, the technical intelligentsia was not strong enough to provide an elite and the humanist intelligentsia was tiny (Kuromiya 1998, p. 116). The population was often transient; the Donbas had a reputation as a haven for criminals who organised gangs with exotic names like the Malakhovs and Sibriakovs (Kuromiya 1998, p. 32). As many as a fifth of the local population had experience of Soviet prisons, but the local culture forgave all past lives, as factory directors were always short of labour (Klinova 2014).

The Soviet authorities wanted to build the Donbas as a 'little homeland' within the USSR, with considerable success, but the Donbas remained a law onto itself. Much of the rest of urban southern and eastern Ukraine was a melting-pot, but where relatively strong identities were often combined, resulting in hybridity as the characteristic cultural mode. But the Donbas was characterised by a triple distance (separation would be too strong a word): horizontal distance from the Soviet authorities in Moscow and then from the new Ukrainian authorities in Kyiv after 1991; vertical distance from rulers, both local and national, due to both paternalism and the privatisation of life; and an ideological or axiological distance from other people's narratives, including the more ideological parts of Soviet socialism, if not the eulogisation of labour culture, as well as Ukrainian nationalism.

[15] 'Otkaz Kieva ot naslediia SSSR lishaet ego prava na territoriu Donbassa, schitaiut v Narodnom Sovete', *DAN news*, 21 May 2015, available at: http://dan-news.info/politics/otkaz-kieva-ot-naslediya-sssr-lishaet-ego-prava-na-territoriyu-donbassa-schitayut-v-narodnom-sovete.html, accessed 16 February 2016.

[16] 'Otkaz Kieva ot naslediia SSSR lishaet ego prava na territoriu Donbassa, schitaiut v Narodnom Sovete', *DAN news*, 21 May 2015, available at: http://dan-news.info/politics/otkaz-kieva-ot-naslediya-sssr-lishaet-ego-prava-na-territoriyu-donbassa-schitayut-v-narodnom-sovete.html, accessed 16 February 2016.

Identity since 1991

Much of this culture persists. A majority of 57% in the Donbas still regretted the fall of the USSR in 2013; and 69% supported a 'strong hand' in politics, 50% a planned economy and only 24% a free press.[17] The population is radically paternalist: only 17% thought they were responsible for their own fate and well-being, the rest thought the state should provide in varying degrees (Skorkin 2014, p. 28). There was a local strike movement in the late Soviet era and the very early 1990s, but it was soon replaced by the paternalism of the local 'red directors' backed by local mafias. Consequently, 'the idea of self-organisation was discredited' by the late 1990s (Skorkin 2014, p. 28).

However, the whole tenor of academic debate from 1991 to 2013 was not about (potential) separatism, or rivalry between Ukrainian ethnic nationalism and some kind of Donbas equivalent, but about the extent to which a social and regional Donbas identity was compatible with various forms of internal Ukrainian pluralism or civic identity (Hrytsak 1998, 2007). In the early 1990s Soviet and social identities (of workers and retired people) remained dominant. Then, 'during the next ten years, these identities faded away, and it was the regional identity of *Donets'kie* (Donets'kites) that has firmly asserted itself on the top' (Hrytsak 2009, p. 17). Regional identities can be nested, they can be overlapping, they can promote separatisms, but the consensus was that the Donbas had a 'borderland' identity, not an irredentist one (Vermenych 2015). From 1994 to 2004, the number in Donets'k city whose primary identity was 'Soviet' declined from 40.1% to 9.9%. The numbers stressing the social identities of 'worker' or 'pensioner' stayed reasonably high, only falling from 66.4% to 54.5%. The number identifying with the Donbas region was already the highest, at 55.7% in 1994, before rising further to 69.5% in 2004. The number of self-declared 'Ukrainians' went up a little, from 39.4% to 42.7%; while the number of 'Russians' fell from 30.1% to 21.1%. In between the last Soviet census in 1989 and the only one undertaken in post-Soviet Ukraine in 2001, the population of Donets'k region changed from 50.7% Ukrainian in 1989 to 56.9% in 2001, with the number of Russians falling from 43.6% to 38.2%. In Luhans'k, the number of Ukrainians grew from 51% to 58%, and the number of Russians fell from 44.8% to 39%.[18] This was interpreted as only partly due to migration, and mainly to ethnic re-identification. Though the Eastern Slavs of all three types (Ukrainians, Russians and Belarusians) have a tendency to identify with local state power, so these processes would have been easy to erode after 2014. The 'Orthodox' rose and fell, from 31.2% up to 35.4% and then back to 27.7% (Hrytsak 2007, p. 50). Donets'k city was the centre of a local Muslim revival. Local intellectuals like Yevgenii Yasenov (2008) celebrated the diversity of local identity, including its Scythian and 'Welsh' pasts (Donets'k was founded by a Welshman, John Hughes, in 1869), and its embryonic modernisation and sporting success.[19]

This type of regionalism did not seem fundamentally incompatible with Ukrainian unity. The same surveys that showed the rise of the regional identity showed 'Ukrainian' or the more civic idea of 'citizen of Ukraine' rising from second to third place (Hrytsak 2007, p. 50). In

[17]'Kil'ka tez pro tsinnisni oriientyry ukraïntsiv', Rating Group Ukraine, 5 June 2013, available at: http://ratinggroup.ua/research/ukraine/neskolko_tezisov_o_cennostnyh_orientirah_ukraincev.html, accessed 21 March 2016.

[18]'About Number and Composition Population of UKRAINE by Data All-Ukrainian Population Census'2001 Data' (sic), available at: http://2001.ukrcensus.gov.ua/eng/results/general/nationality/, accessed 13 January 2016.

[19]See also Yasenov's website, available at: donjetsk.com.

Donets'k the number agreeing with the statement, 'The unity of Ukraine is more important than the needs of separate regions' rose from 44.5% in 1994 to 73.1% in 2004. The number agreeing with the statement that 'My region has a common fate with the rest of Ukraine' rose from 70.9% to 74.2%. Though (contradictory) ambivalence was visible as usual; the number saying 'My region would be richer if it was not part of Ukraine' rose from 22.8% to 47.8% (Chernysh & Malanchuk 2007, p. 89).

The younger generation in the Donbas was shifting most quickly to a civic identity. Fewer younger people considered the Ukrainian language to be their native tongue (10.5% compared to the oldest generation's 21.7%), but Soviet identity was in sharp decline (9.2% for the youngest generation, 36.1% for the oldest, despite some rising nostalgia for the USSR in the 2000s amongst those young enough not to remember the worst of its privations). The number considering themselves to be a 'citizen of Ukraine' rose from 39.8% in the oldest generation to 61.8% in the youngest (Chernysh 2007, pp. 112–14), though this more inclusive, political or civic understanding of the nation was never as successful as it should have been in Ukraine as a whole.

More recently, Michael Gentile has argued that blurred identities were being replaced by slightly sharper Ukrainian and Russian/East Slavic identities. Ethnic minorities were emerging at both ends of the spectrum, but identities were also driven by geopolitical attitudes, rather than the other way around (Gentile 2015). Arguably, these were more susceptible to manipulation (see below). On the one hand, this provided a slightly stronger baseline for pro-Russian mobilisation, but also grew a pro-Ukrainian group who were isolated and intimated, and ultimately left the region after March 2014, reversing the tentative, and contradictory, signs of rapprochement before 2013. Moreover, such trends were still tentative. It was because local identities were still relatively blurred that they were so quickly instrumentalised from the spring of 2014 onwards.

During 23 years of Ukrainian independence from 1991 to 2014, observers were not blind to tensions between Kyiv and the Donbas, but they were rightly calibrated below the serious threat of mass support for separatism. Even at the height of the previous crisis in 1994, in a consultative vote organised by local elites, locals demanded not independence or even autonomy, but the use of Russian as a state language, both locally and nationally, the federalisation of Ukraine and Ukraine's membership in the Commonwealth of Independent States (Arel & Wilson 1994, p. 15).

Polarisation did increase after the Orange Revolution in 2004. Viktor Yanukovych's first attempt at the presidency crystallised a tendency towards 'Galician intellectual reductionism' and the negative stereotyping of the Donbas (Portnov 2014). This theme took on a new intensity once the war began, and Ukrainians from the west and Kyiv deepened their stereotyping of the Donbas with pejorative neologisms like 'Lugandon', 'Luganda', 'Ugandon' and 'Donbabve'—that is, Donets'k and Luhans'k as Uganda or Zimbabwe (Mokrushyna 2015). Increasingly, the theme, and its opposite—the demonisation of 'fascist' west Ukraine—was taken up by 'political technologists' in an eight year series of elections (2004, 2006, 2007, 2010 and 2012) as a means of territorialising the vote, securing power and hiding their clients' corruption. 'Anti-fascist' stereotyping of west Ukraine was therefore on the rise in the Donbas even before 2014 (see below). Analytically, it is hard to disentangle the effect of bottom-up stereotyping and top-down propaganda, but it can be said that the Donbas elite was more responsible for anti-west Ukrainian propaganda than its counterparts were for the anti-east Ukrainian equivalent, first in the campaigns of 2006 and 2007 and then under Yanukovych. The 'Orange' governments of 2005 and 2007–2010 were, however, responsible for the own failings, and both sides deployed extremely negative PR in the close-fought 2010 election. Under Yanukovych, the authorities played both sides; there is considerable evidence that they covertly supported the rise of the new Ukrainian nationalist party *Svoboda* to create an easily defeatable 'scarecrow' for their own supporters in the east (Shekhovtsov 2013). This propaganda was often organised by Russian citizens, but was also the main theme of the so-called 'Komsomol group' in the Party of Regions, such as the head of the Rada faction and self-styled 'boss' of Luhans'k, Oleksandr Yefremov (Skorkin 2014, p. 29). Research from the Ukrainian sociologists of KIIS, measuring alignment with the key tropes of Russian media coverage, has shown that the Donbas was the Ukrainian region most susceptible to Russian propaganda.[20] It would be fruitful to track changes in public opinion once rebels began switching off Ukrainian television from April 2014. Before then, one poll showed roughly equal but low faith in Ukrainian mass media (34%) and Russian (24%), but a third distrusting all media (Kipen' 2014).

The Komsomol group also overlapped with openly pro-Russian groups such as the Donets'k Republic established in 2005 (Shekhovtsov 2014), or the Luhans'k anti-Fascist Forum in May 2013, with links to Moscow political technologist Sergei Markov. But both promoted a new brand of Donbas identity, and this small minority of locals were not as local as they seemed. Many were trained at the annual Donuzlav camp of Russian-organised 'Eurasianists' in the Crimea—the 2013 event was the seventh.[21] But the kind of Russian-sponsored Russian nationalism represented by Nataliya Vitrenko and the Russian Block were still unsuccessful at elections: Vitrenko won 2.9% of the vote in Donets'k in the 2007 elections, the Russian Block 0.4% in 2012.

Separatist ideologues in the Donbas, such as they are, have therefore produced a strange melange since 2014. Of what Marlène Laruelle (2016) has called the 'three colours' of Russian nationalism designed for export—red (Soviet), white (Orthodox) and brown (fascist)—none is a natural fit for the Donbas. The myths and imagery of local Sovietness (Cadioli 2014; Edwards 2014) were originally embedded in a broader fraternity trope; the slogan that 'the Donbas feeds the USSR' was a claim to self-importance, but also of self-sacrifice. The successor slogan that 'the Donbas feeds Ukraine' became embedded in particular anti-western, 'anti-fascist' myths of economic exploitation by Kyiv and west Ukraine, west Ukrainian guest workers (*zarobitchany*) and international capital—the last being necessary cover for the fact that it was actually the Yanukovych 'Family' and allied oligarchs who were the real exploiters. The local myth of Soviet victory in the Great Patriotic War has been revisited with renewed vigour since 2014. The DNR celebrated the 71st anniversary of liberation from Nazi occupation on 8 September 2014,[22] and tried to link it to the Minsk Agreement, despite the fact that the

[20]'Indeks rezul'tatyvnosti rosiis'koï propahandy', *KIIS*, 25 March 2015, available at: http://kiis.com.ua/?lang=ukr&cat=reports&id=510&page=1, accessed 16 February 2016.

[21]'VII Mezhdunarodnyi lager' v Krymu "Donuslav-2013"', *Vkontakte*, August 2013, available at: http://vk.com/club56144396, accessed 22 March 2016.

[22]'Den' osvobozhdeniya Donbassa. Zhiteli Novorossii nesut tsvety na Saur-Mogilu (foto, video)', *Russkaya Vesna*, 8 September 2014, available at: http://rusvesna.su/news/1410205838, accessed 16 February 2016.

great tank battles of 1943 were fought against the Wehrmacht, not the 'phantom existential threat in the shape of "Ukrainian fascists"' (Pakhomenko & Podybaylo 2013; Osipian 2015) on which DNR–LNR propaganda has been primarily based.

The admixture of militant Orthodoxy can partly be explained by the presence of the same 'enemy'—fascist, Catholic, west Ukrainians (Flanagin 2015). But religion was never a big factor in Donbas society, though that is arguably what has allowed militant Russian Orthodoxy to displace and persecute other religions since 2014.[23] None of the prominent leaders of the DNR and LNR are real Orthodox activists. Lastly, on 'brown' nationalism, there are arguably more real fascists on the rebel side than the Ukraine side; and their presence will cause some cognitive dissonance in the longer term (Mitrokhin 2015a, 2015b).

The fact that some locals have adopted a morphed Russian–Orthodox–Soviet absolutist nationalism that Ukrainians have dubbed *Rashyzm*, itself an awkward amalgam of minority views, was due to outside factors and a minority group taking over. To some other Ukrainians, the locals are therefore 'victims of Stockholm Syndrome' or 'captive to an extremely dangerous quasi-religious psychosis, eschatological dream about "Heavenly New Russia"' (Skorkin 2014, p. 29). A more subtle explanation would be that the millennial elements are necessary to mask the ideological contradictions, and that ambiguous identities left many locals open to the kind of left–right eclecticism that is argued to be part of local culture (Skorkin 2014). It should be pointed out that this also means that Ukrainian intellectuals are wrong when they argue that the political culture of the Donbas has always been toxically anti-Ukrainian (Portnov 2014).

Redefining the 'master cleavage'

Russian sponsorship of separatism in 2014 and the day-to-day realities of conflict soon worked to harden opinion on the ground, but that is the opposite of the claim that such sentiments were widespread enough to create the separatist movement in the first place. The local population in rebel territories is likely to gravitate towards what Stathis Kalyvas calls a new and much more explicitly anti-Ukrainian 'master cleavage', but only after it had been redefined by local elites, ideologues and political entrepreneurs (Kalyvas 2006).

As argued above, the local population before the war contained some baseline separatism, but it was not a predominant sentiment and there was minimal evidence of support for armed uprising. The local elite ran the country. The Donbas was therefore subsidised at election time, though not at especially generous levels, while the Donbas elite continued its path to self-enrichment. Local incomes were 21% above the Ukrainian average, but there were plenty of hidden, or not-so-hidden, socio-economic problems. Almost a third, between 30% and 31%, of local income came from pensions. Life expectancy was one year less than the Ukrainian average. The population of Luhans'k had fallen by 21.6% and that of Donets'k by 18.3%. Official unemployment was low, but only 65% of 18–65 year-olds were economically active in Donets'k and 63.7% in Luhans'k. Donets'k had lost 332,000 jobs in the decade before 2013, Luhans'k had lost 554,000 (Libanova *et al.* 2015, pp. 9–11). When the local

---

[23]'Human Rights Activists Published Evidences of Religious Persecution in the Occupied Donbas', *Institute for Religious Freedom*, Kyiv, 13 May 2015, available at: www.irf.in.ua/eng/index.php?option=com_content&view=article&id=431:1&catid=34:ua&Itemid=61, accessed 18 February 2016.

elite were threatened by the Euromaidan events, locals initially reacted in characteristically ambivalent fashion: many feared the loss of even meagre subsidies, many looked to Russia for salvation, and many campaigned against local oligarchs. According to local sociologist Oksana Mikheieva:

> This specific ambivalence of Donbas residents was exploited ... the events of 2014 almost completely closed social elevators. People totally without rights or prospects (none of the security forces protected the average person), poverty, the denial of human dignity—all of this pushed people to the limit. And all this discontent, because of the same ambivalence of ordinary residents of the Donbas, was able to be directed against the Maidan, its values, mythical 'Banderites' and so on, because technologically it could have been channelled in any direction. This was a serious miscalculation by the Ukrainian state—at the time when Russian actors were working in full force in the Donbas, no one was working from the pro-Ukrainian territories with the Donbas. Moreover, there were no messages as to what the Donbas could expect next, what its status in the new Ukraine would be, what would change and how. All this caused fear of the future and a search for defence in strength (working with paternalistic attitudes that have always been strong in the Donbas).[24]

According to an extensive opinion poll conducted throughout eastern and southern Ukraine in April 2014, only 27.5% in Donets'k and 30.3% in Luhans'k backed the separatist cause, and only 11.9% and 13.2% definitely in each case.[25] Another poll in March 2014, this time in Donets'k alone, showed a similar picture. A total of 31.6% supported separatist options (8.7% favoured Ukraine joining Russia or a restored USSR, 18.2% backed Donets'k joining Russia, and 4.7% wanted it to be independent). But 50.2% favoured 'Ukrainian' options (18.6% the *status quo* of a unitary Ukraine, 31.6% opted for more decentralisation). In the middle, 15.5% backed a federal Ukraine, though almost half saw that as implying a right to separation (Kipen' 2014). Ambivalence and distance were also still prominent. Similar figures said they would support the Russian (21.5%) and Ukrainian armies (20.9%) if there was conflict, but 46.2% would remain neutral. Larger numbers were against anything that increased the threat of destabilisation: 26.5% thought pro-Russian meetings were fully legitimate, but the figure for meetings in support of 'Ukrainian unity' was 40.8%. Large majorities were against the occupation of government buildings (77%) and the raising of the Russian flag on such buildings (70%).

It obviously became more difficult to conduct meaningful surveys in territories once they were controlled by the Russians and the DNR and LNR. But a Democratic Initiatives poll in March–April 2015 in areas of Luhans'k under restored Ukrainian control, comparing the towns of Severodonets'k and Starobils'k, showed that 64% and 61% still saw their future as part of Ukraine. A mere 1% supported independence for the DNR and LNR; only 5% backed union with Russia in Severodonets'k and 2% in Starobils'k. Rather more in Starobils'k blamed the current leadership of Ukraine for the situation (58%), as opposed to the Yanukovych elite (49%) or Russia (41%). In Severodonets'k, 39% blamed Russia, 38% the Yanukovych elite and 16% the current Ukrainian leadership.[26]

[24]Author's email conversation with Oksana Mikheieva, local sociologist, 8 January 2016.

[25]'Mneniia i vzgliady zhitelei yugo-vostoka Ukrainy: aprel' 2014', *Zn.ua* (Dzerkalo tyzhnia), 18 April 2014, available at: http://zn.ua/UKRAINE/mneniya-i-vzglyady-zhiteley-yugo-vostoka-ukrainy-aprel-2014-143598_. html, accessed 16 February 2016.

[26]'Luhanshchyna: bil' i nadiia', *Democratic Initiatives*, 2015, available at: http://dif.org.ua/ua/mass_media/ygsyujmvzsrtjklkjbf.htm, accessed 18 February 2016.

In another poll in Kyiv-controlled areas of Donets'k region in late 2014, in the towns of Slov"ians'k and Kramators'k, 50% still wanted to be part of Ukraine, as against 20% who backed independence and 15% union with Russia (Coynash 2015). However, both towns voted heavily for the pro-Russian Opposition Block in the local elections in 2015. And in a broader poll in late 2014 only 15.6% in Donets'k saw the DNR as a legitimate power, 6.1% fully and 9.5% basically—not that much higher than the figure of 6.7% in Ukraine as a whole—though 23.3% of locals 'supported' the DNR. Only 18.5% supported union with Russia, 4.6% fully and 13.9% basically.[27] Another survey by KIIS in occupied Donets'k in March 2015 (with a poll of only 200) showed only 42% supporting secessionist options (16% for independence and 26% for annexation to Russia), but 51% for versions of Ukrainian unity (15% for the old *status quo* and 36% for autonomy within Ukraine).[28] An IRI poll of Kyiv-controlled Donbas in November 2015 (1,284 were over-sampled in Donets'k and Luhans'k) showed 75% supporting three options of Ukrainian unity, including the *status quo*, decentralisation and special regional autonomy, compared to 86% nationwide.[29]

This picture is once again mixed, both in the areas of the Donbas that ended up in rebel control and those that did not by 2015. In the liberated Donbas there was no militant pro-Ukrainian mood, but little sympathy for the rebel side either. Support for separatism in areas newly re-controlled by Kyiv had barely changed since the March 2014 baseline, which can be taken as evidence for the importance of local leadership by militias and others, who were clearly in advance of public opinion.

But at least one other opinion poll finding presented a starker picture. In late March 2014 locals were asked to identify the 'main threat to inhabitants of the Donbas' (Kipen' 2014). A large number, 60.5%, opted for 'radically-minded inhabitants of Western Ukraine—"Banderites"'. 'The central power in Kiev' was mentioned by 46.7%, and 'European and American politicians' by 37.9%. That meant that between 40% and 60% were convinced by the trope of threats emanating from the west. Characteristically, the threat from the east was also mentioned: 22.8% named 'citizens of Russia who take part in organising pro-Russian meetings' and 21% named 'Russian politicians and military'. But only a smaller number named local threats, with 16.8% citing 'criminal circles of the Donbas', 11.2% 'radically minded' locals, and 11% 'regional powers'. But the high number seeing the primary threat as coming from the west is notable, most likely because of the triple effect of Russian propaganda reinforcing the similar message from the Party of Regions, and the alienating effect of anti-Donbas discourse from Ukrainian nationalist circles since 2004.

The role of local elites in mobilisation and revolt

This essay has argued that history and identity were 'baseline' factors, and were not enough in themselves to explain the outbreak of war in 2014. Two other factors were required: elites enabled the protests and helped fuel their escalation, even if they did not directly lead them;

[27]'Takoi raznyi Yugo-Vostok', *Dzerkalo tyzhnia*, 26 December 2014, available at: http://opros2014.zn.ua/donbass, accessed 16 February 2016.
[28]*The Ukrainian People on the Current Crisis*, Kiev International Institute of Sociology and Program for Public Consultation, 9 March 2015, available at: www.public-consultation.org/studies/Ukraine_0315.pdf, accessed 16 February 2016.
[29]'Public Opinion Survey Residents of Ukraine, November 19–30, 2015', *IRI*, available at: www.iri.org/sites/default/files/wysiwyg/2015_11_national_oversample_en_combined_natl_and_donbas_v3.pdf, accessed 16 February 2016.

and Russian intervention was decisive in turning a civil conflict into an actual war. As Andrii Portnov argues: 'the annexation of Crimea and the war in Donbas are still more frequently described using the categories of "identity" and "historical rights" than through a careful analysis of the behaviour of key actors (above all, the local elites and the Russian intervention)' (Portnov 2015a). We concur with this view: elites and the resources they provided were the keys to converting a marginal movement into a mass phenomenon.

Serhiy Kudelia attempted to identify the political factors behind the separatist movement as 'state fragmentation, violent regime change, and the government's low coercive capacity' (Kudelia 2014). As previously stated, however, the extent of 'state fragmentation' at the time is exaggerated; violence in Kyiv was disproportionally on the side of the outgoing government, and largely self-limiting on the protestors' side, although the threat of violence spreading from Kyiv was an important element of local discourse in the Donbas. In Donets'k in April 2014, 22.5% were worried by the 'growth of radicalism and nationalism', and 40.6% by the 'threat of civil war', compared to 51.5% concerned about the 'rise of banditism in the country'; 24.5% worried about losing their job and 9.4% about the 'imposition of one language'.[30] By September 2014, 46.3% in the Donbas felt threatened by 'the growth of extremism', compared to 47.7% who felt threatened by 'external armed aggression'—which was the main factor named by 96.9% in west Ukraine.[31]

The government's coercive capacity in the Donbas was still high in early 2014—although it would soon change sides as it was taken over by pro-Russian forces. The Donbas militia was perfectly able to coerce protest, in the form of the pro-Maidan protestors in January and February—and brutally, often using local mafia as auxiliaries—but did the opposite when pro-Russian protests began in the spring. Conversely, the police failed to protect rival demonstrations in support of Ukrainian unity (Yeremenko 2015). The authorities also failed to control the border as crowds were artificially inflated by bussed in demonstrators and hooligans from Russia. Some officials were permissive, others organised crowds themselves. The new authorities in Kyiv disbanded the paramilitary Berkut (4,000 men) and released huge numbers of police for 'non-compliance with their oath' (17,000 locally), creating a huge poll of potential separatist recruits with nothing to lose (Malyarenko 2015).[32] Demonstrators followed political signalling by elites, particularly because demonstrations in the Donbas had a tradition of being organised and paid for. On the other hand, this was also the case in Kyiv before November 2013, and Euromaidan protestors managed to break with that tradition. There is no intrinsic reason why demonstrations in the Donbas could not also be spontaneous, so the extent to which elite money and organisation helped them to get off the ground remains controversial (Shynkarenko 2014), so is still a subject worthy of further research.

Kudelia's (2014) description of 'the diffusion of resistance tactics used by Euromaidan activists and later adopted by the emergent separatist movement' is a misnomer. Euromaidan tactics were crudely 'cloned' and distorted, not reflected back. Public meetings in the Donbas where a handful of activists of unknown origin noisily elected a 'mayor' were completely

---

[30]'Mneniia i vzgliady zhitelei yugo-vostoka Ukrainy: aprel' 2014', *Zn.ua* (Dzerkalo tyzhnia), 18 April 2014, available at: http://zn.ua/UKRAINE/mneniya-i-vzglyady-zhiteley-yugo-vostoka-ukrainy-aprel-2014-143598_.html, accessed 16 February 2016.

[31]'Hromadiany Ukraïny pro bezpeku: otsinky, zahrozy, shliakhy vyrishennia problem', Razumkov Centre, 2014, available at: www.uceps.org/upload/1412757450_file.pdf, accessed 18 February 2016.

[32]'Avakov uvolil 17 tysych mililtsionerov Donbassa za izmenu prisiage', *Khvylia*, 18 October 2014, available at: http://hvylya.net/news/digest/avakov-uvolil-17-tyisyach-militsionerov-donbassa-za-izmenu-prisyage.html, accessed 18 February 2016.

different from the mass protests seen in Kyiv which noisily criticised all politicians from afar rather than assuming to take their place. They were also different from the ill-advised 'Viche' (Ukrainian for 'popular assembly') when the new government in Kyiv was paraded before the Maidan on 26 February 2014. This was a populist exercise in booing or cheering new ministers already chosen—not electing or self-selecting them. DNR–LNR activists used a permissive argument—if they can do it in Kyiv, we can do it here—but they were not doing the same thing.

As Umland (2014) has pointed out, any properly political analysis should consider the organising role of elites. In reality, the Yanukovych 'Family' provided key resources for the separatist movement (Serbina 2014; Shybalov 2014). The first key resource was money, channelled in by Oleksandr Yanukovych and others. The 'Family' fled to Russia with plenty of cash, but Oleksandr's enterprises—like MAKO (his main holding company) and the All-Ukrainian Development Bank—carried on working in Donets'k and distributed money to the separatists. Money was also channelled through the steel (Donetskstal') and coke plants owned by oligarch Viktor Nusenkis, a Russian citizen, but born in the Donbas, and long-time associate of Viktor Yanukovych.[33] In October 2014 allegations were made in a Kyiv court that Oleksandr Yanukovych and the 'Family' curator Serhii Arbuzov had directly financed the initial separatist protests.[34]

The networks controlled by the 'Family' were just as important as its money. The local police and security services were appointed to guard the interests of the 'Family', not to uphold the law. Oleksandr Yanukovych was responsible for intimidating them to cooperate with the separatists. The 'Family' also had long experience with assembling crowds with cash payments and 'administrative resources' and with local mafia, who were important for providing physical force in early 'civic' demonstrations before the conflict reached a military phase (Wilson 2014, pp. 127–28). Rustam Temirgaliev, deputy prime minister of occupied Crimea, described such operations in dry technical terms; it was just a matter of being professional: 'There are organisational issues—printing flags, banners, the payment of foremen who collected people. It all required a certain cost' (Kozlov 2016).

Local oligarchs played a more complicated role. The richest of them, Rinat Akhmetov, had not fled like the 'Family'. Preserving his business empire under enormous pressure was his main priority, as well as maintaining his leverage in Kyiv (Kazanskyi 2015).[35] Akhmetov also had a large role in controlling the local police and city mayors in his factory towns. Initially, his supporters helped to assemble crowds. He then used his links to the local security services (SBU) and fight clubs like Oplot to try and protect his business interests as the situation on the ground deteriorated. Aleksandr Zakharchenko, self-styled 'Prime Minister' of the DNR, had

[33]'Yanukovych i Nusenkis finansuit' dial'nist' ohrupyvannia DNR—ZMI', *Dzerkalo tyzhnia*, 18 June 2015, available at: http://dt.ua/UKRAINE/yanukovich-i-nusenkis-finansuyut-diyalnist-ugrupovannya-dnr-zmi-176337_.html, accessed 18 February 2016.

[34]'Pechers'kyi sud zniav aresht iz rakhunkiv Arbuzova—ZMI', *Tyzhden.ua*, 29 November 2014, available at: http://tyzhden.ua/News/124710, accessed 18 February 2016.

[35]'Il Paperone dell'Ucraina offre una soluzione a Putin', *Il Giornale*, 9 April 2014, available at: www.ilgiornale.it/news/esteri/paperone-dellucraina-offre-soluzione-putin-1008950.html, accessed 18 February 2016.

originally led the local Oplot that helped to suppress local Euromaidan protests.[36] At the start of the protests, his role seemed to be more protecting local politicians linked to Akhmetov (Kalashnikov 2015).

Defections or demonstrative passivity were commonplace among local police and security forces when the separatists were taking over local police buildings (Shuster 2014). The central government arguably had the capacity to retake key buildings after rebel 'stormings', but key opportunities were missed. The security forces were not absent, they were paralysed (Portnov 2016). Some were bribed to 'turn a blind eye' (Tymchuk 2014). By late 2014 Akhmetov was allegedly supplying the DNR and LNR with food in return for keeping his remaining businesses open (Kazanskyi 2015).

But there were also some 'bottom-up' grievances. The Donbas rebellion was both manipulated by local elites and directed against them, thanks to a highly clientelistic local political culture, shaped just as much by post-independence clan politics as longer-term historical factors. According to Nikolai Mitrokhin, the initial separatist coalition was heavily biased towards middle and lower strata of society: the 'main strike forces were small criminal groups (and "*gopniki*" attracted by them as reinforcements), who hoped to get rid not only of the Ukrainian authorities, but also of the old Mafia giants' (Mitrokhin 2015b).[37] In Mitrokhin's words:

> The political and economic elite of the region, which is the core of the Party of Regions, obviously did not want to join the Donbas to Russia, which would mean the redistribution of property and other troubles. For small businessmen, criminal figures, officials (mostly associated with the most criminalised sectors of the economy), and district-level police officers such radical political changes, on the contrary, gave great hope. (Mitrokhin 2015b)

Mitrokhin, however, misreads the motives of the 'Family' at least. While elites in Kharkiv and Odesa were prepared to limit their support for separatism in return for Kyiv's acquiescence in their continued local power (Portnov 2016), in Dnipropetrovsk, local elites saw an opportunity to expand their power by parlaying their military support for Kyiv on the front line (Portnov 2015b). Mitrokhin may be right that the rational course for Donbas elites was not to risk dispossession under Russian or rebel rule, but they gambled. Moreover, playing both sides had been a political strategy that had worked for them in the past.

The role of Russia

It is not yet possible to judge whether the 'Family' would have fomented revolt anyway, without Russian support. Viktor Yanukovych backed away from declaring an alternative capital in the east in Kharkiv on 22 February 2014. But the origins of the separatist movement reflected the logic of 'Phantom States' laid out by Daniel Byman and Charles King (2012), where it is the relationship between 'peripheral elites' and 'external patrons' that matters. The

---

[36]'Zanesennyi vetrom. Kak elektromekhanik Zakharchenko vozglavil DNR', *Novoe vremia*, 4 March 2015, available at: http://nv.ua/publications/zanesennyy-vetrom-kak-elektromehanik-zaharchenko-vozglavil-dnr-37195.html, accessed 18 February 2016; 'Terrorist DNR rasskazal o sotrudnichesstve glavaria Zakharchenko s Akhmetovym i o razborkakh s "neogodnymi",—video', *IPress.Ua*, 19 March 2015, available at: http://ipress.ua/ru/news/terroryst_dnr_rasskazal_o_sotrudnychestve_glavarya_zaharchenko_s_akhmetovim_y_o_razborkah_s_neugodnimy__vydeo_115612.html, accessed 18 February 2016.

[37]'Gopnik' is a slang term for alienated post-Soviet urban youth.

external patron was of course Russia; peripheral elites in the Donbas were active in seeking out its assistance, but Russia was an active player, trying different sparks until one caught light. The first Donbas demonstrations in March 2014, even when violent, and even when reinforced by Russians bussed in from outside, and with the central Ukrainian state caught off guard, failed to achieve as much as was expected. As stated by the Atlantic Council: 'buying into its own propaganda, the Kremlin believed that providing leadership, money, and weapons would be enough to spark a local rebellion against Kyiv in the Donbas'. 'But the locals did not rise to the task: numerous intercepts from Girkin-Strelkov made clear that he asked Moscow to send more and more "volunteers" to sustain the rebellion' (Czuperski *et al*. 2015, pp. 4–5). The idea that Russian forces only arrived in August 2014 (Sakwa 2015, pp. 155, 175) contradicts abundant evidence. Nikolai Mitrokhin's study of 'infiltration, instruction [and] invasion' (Mitrokhin 2015a) identifies the August escalation as a third phase:

> The first phase began in April 2014, when special forces (*spetsnaz*) troops and secret service officials supported criminals from the Donbas region and Russian nationalists who had travelled in from Russia with the aim of seizing power in several cities in the Donbas region, as part of a Russian special operation aimed at destabilising Ukraine. (Mitrokhin 2015a, pp. 220–21)

One Ukrainian website, informnapalm.org, has tried to document the escalating Russian presence. 'Tourists', that is Russians bussed in from over the border, were always part of the early demonstrations. Another site, Information Defence (sprotyv.info), has looked at the role of GRU agents (Russian external intelligence) in organising early protests and then coordinating militias into rebel armed forces—though more research is clearly needed to clarify their role.[38] In May 2015 the Ukrainians claimed to have the names of 60 GRU agents active in the Donbas since March 2014.[39] The detailed 2015 RUSI report (Sutyagin 2015),[40] confirms that a few hundred special forces and GRU in command-and-control functions were ever-present in the Donbas from March 2014, along with volunteers from Russia and specialist crews for advanced weaponry. Simple proximity to Russia was a key factor in facilitating the flow of both 'tourists' and GRU, even compared to Kharkiv, which has fewer urban centres than the Russian side of the nearby border.

The rapid appearance of so much weaponry is the most obvious sign of Russian involvement, and of escalation from civil conflict to civil war. Genuine domestic Ukrainian rebels at best only had access to some small arms, obtained when local militia stations were over-run. But the rebels soon had hundreds of tanks at their command. One Russian source counted 200 armoured vehicles by early August 2014.[41]

Secular Russian activists, that is Russian citizens from various Russian nationalist and Eurasian organisations, were also already in the Donbas at the same time (Kostromina 2015).

---

[38]'O "turistakh" Putina ili voina malykh grupp', *Information Defence/Informatsionnoe soprotivlenie*, 30 July 2015, available at: http://sprotyv.info/ru/news/kiev/o-turistah-putina-ili-voyna-malyh-grupp, accessed 18 February 2016.

[39]'SBU predstavila novye dokazatel'stva uchastiia voennykh GRU RF v agressii protiv Ukrainy', *Dzerkalo tyzhnia*, 21 May 2015, available at: http://zn.ua/UKRAINE/sbu-predstavila-novye-dokazatelstva-uchastiya-voennyh-gru-rf-v-agressii-protiv-ukrainy-176822_.html, accessed 18 February 2016.

[40]See also Czuperski *et al*. (2015).

[41]'Dlya kontrnastupleniya pod Donetskom opolchentsy podgotovili 200 bronemashin', *Vesti.ru*, 12 August 2014, available at: www.vesti.ru/doc.html?id=1885210&tid=105474, accessed 18 February 2016.

Many key early separatist leaders were Russian passport-holders: including Girkin, Antifeev, Bezler, Mozhaev, Motorola, Bashirov, Koryakin and Borodai. The extent to which all the local DNR and LNR leadership was subject to orders from Russian 'curators' is described in an ICG report (Sutyagin 2015).[42]

This 'first phase' had two parts, with the distinction between the two providing further evidence of the amount of artifice in the process. There was no mass uprising in March 2014, and the storming of local SBU (security service) buildings that began on 6 April was inconclusive until Igor Girkin arrived with 52 fighters in Slov"ians'k in the north west of the Donbas on 12 April. Girkin (aka Strelkov) himself later stated that 'I was the one who pulled the trigger of the war. … If our unit hadn't crossed the border, everything would have fizzled out—like in Kharkiv, like in Odesa'. But even in Slov"ians'k he admitted, 'At first, nobody wanted to fight' (Dolgov 2014).[43]

The second phase began with Girkin's complaint on 18 May that he was already short of men and arms leading up to his departure from Slov"ians'k on 4–5 July.[44] He had already been supplied with small arms, ammunition, MANPADS (shoulder-fired missiles) and ATGMs (anti-tank missiles) (Mitrokhin 2015b), but this proved insufficient. Mitrokhin (2015b) defines the four key features of the second phase as, first, a huge increase in the number of 'volunteers' from Russia in response to Girkin's appeal; second, the supply by Russia of more and more modern arms, including tanks, modern artillery and rocket launchers, one of which, according to overwhelming evidence, shot down flight MH17; third, shelling from over the border; and finally the participation of regular Russian units in the fighting by the end of July.[45] The third phase began when Ukrainian forces continued their advance and threatened supply lines from Russia, which would have been less of a concern to a genuinely local fighting force (Mitrokhin 2015a, pp. 220–21).

The presence of large numbers of regular Russian troops had been a constant feature since July 2014, but the exact number varied, depending on the task in hand. The balance between Russians and locals has been estimated by researchers examining data from social media, photographic evidence and border crossings, and movement in and out of Russian garrison towns, although such methods are clearly inexact (Gilley 2015). The initial pattern avoided sending ready-made units into battle, which would have been too conspicuous. Instead they were assembled from all over Russia; but ultimately whole battalion-sized tactical groups were committed for the big battles, meaning 10,000 regular Russian troops in Ukraine by the end of 2014, and 42,000 men in total, rotated in and out across the border, to keep frontline troops fresh and Ukraine and the West confused (Sutyagin 2015, p. 4). There were

[42]'Eastern Ukraine: A Dangerous Winter', Crisis Group Europe, Report No. 235, 18 December 2014, available at: www.crisisgroup.org/en/regions/europe/ukraine/235-eastern-ukraine-a-dangerous-winter.aspx, accessed 18 February 2016.

[43]'Girkin: "Opolchenstsi" zhanialy kryms'kykh deputativ do zaly dlia holosuvannia', *Krym.Realiï*, 24 January 2015, available at: http://ua.krymr.com/content/article/26811497.html, accessed 18 February 2016.

[44]'Obrashchenie Igorya Strelkova', *YouTube*, 17 May 2014, available at: www.youtube.com/watch?v=KIHdrSm6jrU, accessed 18 February 2016.

[45]'MH17: Source of the Separatists' Buk: A Bellingcat Investigation', *Bellingcat*, November 2014, available at: www.bellingcat.com/wp-content/uploads/2014/11/Origin-of-the-Separatists-Buk-A-Bellingcat-Investigation1.pdf, accessed 18 February 2016; 'Bellingcat Report—Origin of Artillery Attacks on Ukrainian Military Positions in Eastern Ukraine Between 14 July 2014 and 8 August 2014', *Bellingcat*, 17 February 2015, available at: www.bellingcat.com/news/uk-and-europe/2015/02/17/origin-of-artillery-attacks/, accessed 18 February 2016; 'MH17—Potential Suspects and Witnesses from the 53rd Anti-Aircraft Missile Brigade', *Bellingcat*, 23 February 2016, available at: www.bellingcat.com/news/uk-and-europe/2016/02/23/53rd-report-en/, accessed 24 March 2016.

also between 26,000 and 28,000 Russian troops in a now heavily militarised Crimea. The number of Russian dead was 800 by early 2015, according to one source (Crowley 2015),[46] or 220 according to the Nemtsov Report (Nemtsov 2015, pp. 24–31). The number of Russian nationalist volunteers from Russia was several hundred (Yudina 2014). Local fighters were provided with Russian uniforms by June 2014; significantly, kit from the time of the Chechen and Georgian wars was used.

Mitrokhin (2015a, pp. 238–39) estimates that by mid-August 2014, before the decisive battle at Ilovais'k often cited as a one-off Russian intervention, there were between 20,000 and 25,000 troops fighting in the Donbas, and only between 40% and 45% were 'locals'. The Nemtsov Report questioned how many of the 30,000 Russians who had served in the Donbas at one time or another were 'volunteers or mercenaries?', as it claims monthly pay in the early stages of the fighting, before later inflation, was between 60,000 and 90,000 rubles, which produced a steady stream of fighters, but cast doubt on their motivations (Nemtsov 2015, pp. 24–31). In one sense, Russia's role was actually reduced after August 2014, because the Kremlin wanted to create an impression of 'indigenisation'. According to one commentator, 'rebel formations in essence have been used as cannon fodder' (Sutyagin 2015, p. 7). Mitrokhin (2015b) argues that 'the local pro-Russian political activists' were 'the most insignificant military and most important politically'; Russian troops from Russia did the hard fighting when necessary, but the local Donbas troops provided indispensable political cover.

Conclusions

Historical and identity factors have been extensively cited as key explanations of the separatist movement in the Donbas. However, neither the creation of the DNR and LNR nor the war would have happened without resources. These came from Russia and from the Yanukovych 'Family' and some allied oligarchs. The changes undergone by the local state apparatus also made it much easier for the Russians to intervene; but there was no total state collapse—more a combination of state weakness, neglect by Kyiv, defections and disloyalty, the hollowing out of the system by Yanukovych 'Family' elites both still in the Donbas and in Russia, and decisions that backfired, like disbanding the Berkut and dismissing so many from the local police. The local state was weak, but far from collapsed; it was also permissive and enabling.

Local opinion was malleable to an extent, allowing the leadership of the DNR and LNR to increase their initial support. But their leaders were never an autonomous force, and were repeatedly changed at Russian instigation. The war that began in 2014 was not a civil war with foreign intervention, but a process catalysed and escalated by local elites and by Russia, with local foot-soldiers. The last word could be given to President Lukashenka of Belarus, who declared in October 2014, 'let's be honest, the days of the DNR and LNR would have been numbered long ago without Russia'.[47]

---

[46]See also Urban (2015).

[47]'Lukashenko: Dni DPR i LPR bez Rossii davno bylo by sochteny', *Belaplan*, 17 October 2014, available at: http://belapan.com/archive/2014/10/17/734133/, accessed 18 February 2016.

References

Arel, D. & Wilson, A. (1994) 'The Ukrainian Parliamentary Elections', *RFE/RL Research Report*, 3, 26, 1 July.

Barabanov, I. (2015) 'Ni shakhty nazad', *Kommersant"*, 13 February, available at: www.kommersant.ru/doc/2666045, accessed 22 March 2016.

Bredikin, A. (2015) 'Luganshchina—kazach'ya zemlya!', *Novorus.info*, 5 January, available at: http://novorus.info/news/obshetvo/32119-luganschina-kazachya-zemlya.html, accessed 16 February 2016.

Brekhunenko, V. (2014) 'Ukraïns'kyi Pivden' i Skhid', *Tyzhden.ua*, 23 June, available at: http://tyzhden.ua/History/112654, accessed 16 February 2016.

Brekhunenko, V. (2015) 'Cossacks or Kozaks, no Russians We', *The Ukrainian Week*, no. 4, April.

Byman, D. & King, C. (2012) 'The Mystery of Phantom States', *The Washington Quarterly*, 35, 3, Summer.

Cadioli, G. (2014) 'Symbolism in Donetsk', *Vostok Cable*, 29 May, available at: https://vostokcable.wordpress.com/2014/05/29/symbolism-in-donetsk/, accessed 18 February 2016.

Chernysh, N. (2007) 'Pokolinnievi modeli hrupovikh identychnostei l'viv"ian ta donechchan (1994–2004 rr.)', *Ukraïna moderna*, 12, 2.

Chernysh, N. & Malanchuk, O. (2007) 'Dynamika identychnostei meshkantsiv L'vova i Donets'ka: komparatyvnyi analiz (1994–2004 rr.)', *Ukraïna moderna*, 12, 2.

Coynash, H. (2015) 'Liberated Donbas Fears Return of Kremlin-backed Militants more than Nationalists', *Kharkiv Human Rights Group*, 20 March, available at: http://khpg.org/index.php?id=1426517734, accessed 18 February 2016.

Crowley, S. (2015) '(Not) Behind Enemy Lines 1: Recruiting for Russia's War in Ukraine', *Leksika.org*, 25 June, available at: www.leksika.org/tacticalanalysis/2015/6/24/not-behind-enemy-lines-i-recruiting-for-russias-war-in-ukraine, accessed 18 February 2016.

Czuperski, M., Herbst, J., Higgins, E., Polyakova, A. & Wilson, D. (2015) *Hiding in Plain Sight: Putin's War in Ukraine*, Atlantic Council Report, 27 May, available at: www.atlanticcouncil.org/publications/reports/hiding-in-plain-sight-putin-s-war-in-ukraine-and-boris-nemtsov-s-putin-war, accessed 21 March 2016.

Dolgov, A. (2014) 'Russia's Igor Strelkov: I Am Responsible for War in Eastern Ukraine', *The Moscow Times*, 21 November, available at: www.themoscowtimes.com/news/article/russias-igor-strelkov-i-am-responsible-for-war-in-eastern-ukraine/511584.html, accessed 18 February 2016.

Edwards, M. (2014) 'Symbolism of the Donetsk People's Republic', *Open Democracy*, 9 June, available at: www.opendemocracy.net/od-russia/maxim-edwards/symbolism-of-donetsk-people%E2%80%99s-republic-flag-novorossiya, accessed 18 February 2016.

Flanagin, J. (2015) 'The People's Republic of Donetsk is Becoming a Theocracy', *Quartz*, 25 March, available at: http://qz.com/#369015/the-peoples-republic-of-donetsk-is-becoming-a-theocracy/, accessed 18 February 2016.

Gava, O. (2014) 'Istoriia "Novorosiï" ta ïï etnichnyi sklad u XIX storichchi', *Istorychna pravda*, 7 May, available at: www.istpravda.com.ua/articles/2014/05/7/142762/, accessed 18 February 2016.

Gentile, M. (2015) 'West Oriented in the East-oriented Donbas: A Political Stratigraphy of Geopolitical Identity in Luhansk, Ukraine', *Post-Soviet Affairs*, 31, 3.

Gilley, C. (2015) 'Otamanshchyna? The Self-Formation of Ukrainian and Russian Warlords at the Beginnings of the Twentieth and Twenty-First Centuries', *Ab Imperio*, 3.

Giuliano, E. (2015) 'The Social Bases of Support for Self-determination in East Ukraine', *Ethnopolitics*, 14, 5.

Hrytsak, Y. (1998) 'National Identities in Post-Soviet Ukraine: The Case of Lviv and Donetsk', *Harvard Ukrainian Studies*, 22.

Hrytsak, Y. (2007) 'Istoriia dvokh mist: L'viv i Donetsk u porivnial'nii perspektyvi', *Ukraïna moderna*, 12, 2.

Hrytsak, Y. (2009) 'One World is Not Enough, or my Adventures with National Paradigm', in *Scripta ucrainica europaea*, Greifswald conference, 15–26 August, available at: http://shron.chtyvo.org.ua/Hrytsak_Yaroslav/One_World_is_not_enough_or_my_Adventures_with_National_Paradigm_anhl.pdf, accessed 21 March 2016.

Kalashnikov, M. (2015) 'Vlast' titushek v Donetske', *Live Journal*, 25 August, available at: http://m-kalashnikov.livejournal.com/2391622.html, accessed 18 February 2016.

Kalyvas, S. (2006) *The Logic of Violence in Civil War* (Cambridge, Cambridge University Press).

Kazanskyi, D. (2015) 'Akhmetov's Losing Bet', *Ukrainian Week*, 18 May, available at: http://ukrainianweek.com/Politics/136673, accessed 18 February 2016.

Kipen, V. P. (2014) 'Travmovana svidomist' yak naslidok i faktor nestabil'nosti (doslidzhennia masovykh natroïv Donets'ka)', *Skhid*, 2, available at: http://skhid.com.ua/issue/view/1391/showToc, accessed 18 February 2016.

Klinova, O. (2014) '"Esli vmesto golovy snariad …". Yak formuvalas' identychnist' Donbasu', *Istorychna Pravda*, 11 December, available at: www.istpravda.com.ua/articles/2014/12/11/146063/, accessed 18 February 2016.

Kornilov, V. (2011) *Donetsko-Krivorozhskaya respublika. Rasstreliannaya mechta* (Donets'k, Folio).

Kostromina, D. (2015) 'Po vine naborshchika', *Grani.ru*, 12 March, available at: http://grani.ru/Politics/World/US/RF/m.238998.html, accessed 22 March 2016.

Kozlov, P. (2016) 'Rustam Temirgaliev o razvitii sobytii, privedshikh k referendumu v Krymu', *Vedomosti*, 16 March, available at: www.vedomosti.ru/politics/characters/2015/03/16/esli-eto-imelo-opredelennuyu-rezhissuru—rezhisseru-nuzhno-postavit-pyat-s-plyusom, accessed 24 March 2016.

Kramarenko, O. (2006) 'The "So-Called" Holodomor … Consequences for Ukraine', *Den'*, 21 November, available at: www.day.kiev.ua/en/article/close/so-called-holodomor, accessed 18 February 2016.

Kudelia, S. (2014) *Domestic Sources of the Donbas Insurgency*, PONARS Eurasia Policy Memo, no. 351, September, available at: www.ponarseurasia.org/memo/domestic-sources-donbas-insurgency, accessed 18 February 2016.

Kuromiya, H. (1998) *Freedom and Terror in the Donbas: A Ukrainian-Russian Borderland, 1870s–1990s* (Cambridge, Cambridge University Press).

Kuromiya, H. (2015) *Zrozumity Donbas*. (Kyiv, Dukh i Litera).

Laruelle, M. (2016) 'The Three Colors of Novorossiya, or the Russian Nationalist Mythmaking of the Ukrainian Crisis', *Post-Soviet Affairs*, 32, 1.

Libanova, E. M., Amosha, O. I., Vyshnevs'kyi, V. P., Heiets, V. M., Borodina, O. M., Makarova, O. V., Shynkaruk, L. V., Antoniuk, V. P., Briukhovets'ka, N. Yu., Bulieiev, I. P., Holian, V. A., Dieieva, N. M., Dzhumahel'diieva, H. D., Zapatrina, I. V., Zaiats', T. A., Zel'dina, O. R., Kaleniuk, I. S., Kuz'menko, L. M., Levchuk, N. M., Lepa, R. M., Lisohor, L. S., Liashenko, V. I., Miamlin, S. V., Novikov, V. M., Novikova, O. F., Palekha, Yu. M., Ploskyi, V. O., Popova, O. L., Prokopa, I. V., Pshin'ko, O. M., Rynhach, N. O., Tarash, L. I., Ustymenko, V. A., Khvesyk, M. A., Tsymbal, O. I., Shubravs'ka, O. V., Hvelesiani, A. H., Herasymenko, H. V., Diakonenko, O. I., Yeremieieva, N. V., Zbaraz'ka, L. O., Zemliankin, A. I., Kalashnikova, T. M., Korniichuk, O. P., Kraievs'ka, H. O., Krymova, M. O., Lohachova, L. M., Liakh, O. V., Malolitneva, V. K., Nikiforova, V. A., Nychyporenko, S. V., Novak, I. M., Okhten', O. O., Pan'kova, O. V., Pidorycheva, I. Yu., Pozniak, O. V., Prokopenko, K. O., Prokopenko, R. V., Russiian, O. A., Snihova, O. Yu., Soldak, M. O., Tkachenko, L. H., Tolmachova, H. F., Khmelevs'ka, O. M., Cherevats'kyi, D. Yu., Cheren'ko, L. M., Shvets', P. V., Shevtsova, H. Z., Yarosh, O. M., Kasperovych, O. Yu., Petrova, I. P., Okhremenko, S. V. (2015) *Vidrodzhennia Donbasu: otsinka sotsial'no-ekonomichnykh vtrat i priorytetni napriamy derzhavnoï polityky* (Kyiv, Academy of Sciences).

Lipskii, A. (2014) 'Rossiya i Ukraina: Moment istiny', *Novaya gazeta*, 16 April, available at: www.novayagazeta.ru/politics/63205.html, accessed 21 March 2016.

Malyarenko, T. (2015) 'Playing a Give-Away Game? The Undeclared Russian–Ukrainian War in Donbas', *Small Wars Journal*, 23 December, available at: http://smallwarsjournal.com/jrnl/art/playing-a-give-away-game-the-undeclared-russian-ukrainian-war-in-donbas, accessed 18 February 2016.

Mikheieva, O. (2014) 'Lektsiia Oksany Mikheievoï, "Liudyna z Donbasu: osnovni skladovi sotsial'noho konstruktu"', 20 December, available at: http://uamoderna.com/videoteka/mikheeva-lecture-donbas-ucu, accessed 18 February 2016.

Mitrokhin, N. (2015a) 'Infiltration, Instruction, Invasion: Russia's War in the Donbass', *Journal of Soviet and Post-Soviet Politics and Society*, 1, 1.

Mitrokhin, N. (2015b) 'Ukrainskii konflikt v 2014 godu: khronika krovavoi rekonstruktsii', *Neprkosnovennyi zapas*, 1, 99.

Mokrushyna, H. (2015) 'De-humanizing the Other: Retrograde, Soviet Donbas as an Anti-hero of Progressive Euromaidan Ukraine in the Discourse of Ukrainian Political Elites and Media', paper presented at the Geopolitical Economy Research Group (GERG) conference, 27 September, available at: http://gergconference.ca, accessed 24 March 2016.

Nemtsov, B. (2015) *Putin. War*, Nemtsov Report, available at: www.4freerussia.org/putin.war/, accessed 22 March 2016.

Osipian, A. (2015) 'Historical Myths, Enemy Images and Regional Identity in the Donbass Insurgency (Spring 2014)', *Journal of Soviet and Post-Soviet Politics and Society*, 1, 1.

Osipian, A. L. & Osipian, A. (2006) 'Why Donbas Votes for Yanukovych: Confronting the Ukrainian Orange Revolution', *Demokratizatsiya*, Fall.

Pakhomenko, S. & Podybaylo, M. (2013) '"Ukrainian Nationalism" vs "Patriotism of Donbas": The Withstand [sic] of the Media Images in the Contemporary Information Space of Donetsk District', *Almanach via Evrasia*, 2, available at: www.viaevrasia.com/en/22-ukrainian-nationalism-vs-patriotism-of-donbas-the-withstand-of-the-media-images-in-the-contemporary-information-space-of-donetsk-district-sergey-pakhomenko-maria-podybylo.html, accessed 18 February 2016.

Petro, N. N. (2015) 'Understanding the Other Ukraine: Identity and Allegiance in Russophone Ukraine', in Pikulicka-Wilczewska, A. & Sakwa, R. (eds) *Ukraine and Russia: People, Politics, Propaganda and Perspectives* (E-International), available at: http://www.e-ir.info/wp-content/uploads/2015/03/Ukraine-and-Russia-E-IR.pdf, accessed 18 February 2016.

Portnov, A. (2014) 'Ukraine's "Far East": On the Effects and Genealogy of Ukrainian Galician Reductionism', *NYU Jordan Center*, 15 August, available at: http://jordanrussiacenter.org/news/ukraines-far-east-effects-genealogy-ukrainian-galician-reductionism/, accessed 18 February 2016.

Portnov, A. (2015a) 'On Decommunization, Identity, and Legislating History, From a Slightly Different Angle', *Krytyka*, May, available at: http://krytyka.com/en/solutions/opinions/decommunization-identity-and-legislating-history-slightly-different-angle, accessed 18 February 2016.

Portnov, A. (2015b) '"The Heart of Ukraine"? Dnipropetrovsk and the Ukrainian Revolution', in Wilson, A. (ed.) *What Does Ukraine Think?* (London, European Council on Foreign Relations), available at: www.ecfr.eu/page/-/WHAT_DOES_UKRAINE_THINK_pdf.pdf, accessed 18 February 2016.

Portnov, A. (2016) 'How "Eastern Ukraine" was Lost', *Open Democracy*, 14 January, available at: www.opendemocracy.net/od-russia/andrii-portnov/how-eastern-ukraine-was-lost, accessed 18 February 2016.

Putin, V. (2014) 'Poslanie Prezidenta Federal'nomu Sobraniyu', The Kremlin, 4 December, available at: http://kremlin.ru/events/president/news/47173, accessed 16 February 2016.

Regan, P. M. (2000) *Civil Wars and Foreign Powers: Interventions and Intrastate Conflict* (Ann Arbor, MI, University of Michigan Press).

Sakwa, R. (2015) *Frontline Ukraine: Crisis in the Borderlands* (London, I.B. Tauris).

Serbina, S. (2014) 'DPR [i.e. DNR] Connections: The Lux Company and Yanukovych's "Family"', *The Insider*, 26 September.

Shekhovtsov, A. (2013) 'Vseukraïns'ke ob'iednannia "Svoboda": problema legitymnosty borot'by za vladu', *Ukraïna moderna*, 20.

Shekhovtsov, A. (2014) 'The "Ukraine Crisis" is a Long-planned Operation', 29 August, available at: http://anton-shekhovtsov.blogspot.co.uk/2014/08/the-ukraine-crisis-is-long-planned.html, accessed 18 February 2016.

Shuster, S. (2014) 'Ukrainian Policemen Stand By as Pro-Russian Separatists Seize Control', *Time*, 29 April, available at: http://time.com/81475/ukrainian-policemen-stand-by-as-pro-russian-separatists-seize-control/#81475/ukrainian-policemen-stand-by-as-pro-russian-separatists-seize-control/, accessed 18 February 2016.

Shybalov, Y. (2014) '"DNR" zseredyny. Korotkyi liknep', *Dzerkalo tyzhnia*, 26 September, available at: http://gazeta.dt.ua/internal/dnr-zseredini-korotkiy-liknep-_.html, accessed 18 February 2016.

Shynkarenko, O. (2014) 'Who's Funding East Ukraine Militancy?', *IWPR*, 16 May, available at: https://iwpr.net/global-voices/whos-funding-east-ukraine-militancy, accessed 18 February 2016.

Skorkin, K. (2014) 'Mit Novorosiï: krai reaktsiinykh utopii', *Krytyka*, 9–10.

Smith, G. & Wilson, A. (1997) 'Rethinking Russia's Post-Soviet Diaspora: The Potential for Political Mobilisation in Eastern Ukraine and North-East Estonia', *Europe-Asia Studies*, 49, 5.

Stefanko, S. L. (2014) 'Yak V. Lenin borovsia z Donets'kym separatyzmom', *Firtka.if.ua*, 17 June, available at: http://firtka.if.ua/?action=show&id=54016, accessed 18 February 2016.

Studenna-Skrukva, M. (2014) *Ukraïns'kyi donbas: oblychchia rehional'noï identychnosti* (Kyiv, Laboratory of Legislative Initiatives).

Sutyagin, I. (2015) *Russian Troops in Ukraine*, Royal United Services Institute, Briefing Paper, March, available at: https://rusi.org/sites/default/files/201503_bp_russian_forces_in_ukraine.pdf, accessed 18 February 2016.

Tymchuk, D. (2014) 'Militsieskoe nachal'stvo na Vostoke sdavalo svoi otdely separatistam za neplokhie summy', *Glavcom*, 6 May, available at: http://glavcom.ua/articles/19354.html, accessed 22 March 2016.

Umland, A. (2014) 'In Defense of Conspirology: A Rejoinder to Serhiy Kudelia's Anti-Political Analysis of the Hybrid War in Eastern Ukraine', *PONARS Eurasia*, 30 September, available at: www.ponarseurasia.org/article/defense-conspirology-rejoinder-serhiy-kudelias-anti-political-analysis-hybrid-war-eastern, accessed 18 February 2016.

Urban, M. (2015) 'How Many Russians are Fighting in Ukraine?', *BBC News*, 10 March, available at: www.bbc.co.uk/news/world-europe-31794523, accessed 18 February 2016.

Vermenych, Y. (2015) *Donbas yak porubizhnyi rehion: terytorial'nyi vymir.* (Kyiv, Academy of Sciences, Institute of History).

Wilson, A. (1995) 'The Donbas Between Ukraine and Russia: The Use of History in Political Disputes', *Journal of Contemporary History*, 30, 2, April, available at: www.ecfr.eu/blog/entry/ukraine_and_russia_the_use_of_history_in_political_dispute, accessed 18 February 2016.

Wilson, A. (2014) *Ukraine Crisis: What it Means for the West* (London & New Haven, CT, Yale University Press).

Yasenov, Ye. (2008) *Progulki po Donetsku* (Donets'k, Donetchina).

Yefimenko, H. (2014) 'Formuvannia kordony mizh USRR ta RSFRR v 1917–1928 rr.', *Historians.in.ua*, 16 November, available at: http://historians.in.ua/index.php/doslidzhennya/1342-hennadii-yefimenko-formuvannia-kordonu-mizh-usrr-ta-rsfrr-v-1917-1928-rr, accessed 18 February 2016.

Yeremenko, A. (2015) *Razmyshleniia o luganskoi Vandeiu* (Russia online publication, Just a Life).

Yudina, N. (2014) 'Ul'trapravye strasti po Ukraine', *SOVA Centre*, 15 September, available at: www.sova-center.ru/racism-xenophobia/publications/2014/09/d30505, accessed 18 February 2016.

Zhukov, Y. M. (2016) 'Trading Hard Hats for Combat Helmets: The Economics of Rebellion in Eastern Ukraine', *Journal of Comparative Economics*, 44, 1.

Zhurzhenko, T. (2014) 'From Borderlands to Bloodlands', *IWM*, 29 September, available at: www.iwm.at/read-listen-watch/transit-online/borderlands-bloodlands/, accessed 18 February 2016.

A Perfect Storm; Or What Went Wrong and What Went Right for the EU in Ukraine

HISKI HAUKKALA

Abstract

This essay analyses and discusses the background and the evolution of the conflict in Ukraine in light of the wider contestation between the European Union and Russia. The main argument is that the conflict in Ukraine is first and foremost a symptom and not the root cause of the wider conflict between Russia and the West. The essay puts particular emphasis on examining the problems in the EU's approach concerning the East. In particular the problems in policy and scenario planning are pointed out. The essay ends with conclusions, warning of the potential for a wider rupture and even conflict between the EU and the West and Russia.

THE SEVERE CRISIS IN UKRAINE, GENERATING CONFLICT AND even war, has resulted in key Western actors and institutions indulging in much soul-searching, the European Union (EU) included. This is hardly a surprise, as the collapse of the regime of President Viktor Yanukovych and the events that followed took the whole Western scholarly and diplomatic community largely by surprise. First, by annexing the Crimean peninsula and incorporating it swiftly into its federal structure and, second, engaging in continuing destabilisation of Ukraine through hybrid means, Russia has not only revealed its acute displeasure with the course of events in Ukraine and Eastern Europe but has also thrown down the gauntlet, essentially challenging the very foundations of the European security architecture and, indeed, international law.

Yet the crisis did not come out of the blue. On the contrary, it can be seen as one that has been in gestation for years and was bound to come to a head eventually (Haukkala 2015). In order to understand why this is the case, and why the eruption of the crisis nevertheless took the majority of Western actors by surprise, we must take an analytical look at how the European order, and consequently EU–Russia relations, have been developing during the post-Cold War era and how the EU's policies, however well-intentioned, have inadvertently contributed to the negative situation in which we find ourselves. This essay seeks to accomplish both aims. This is done, first, by briefly outlining the main contours of post-Cold War order in Europe and the role the EU has played in seeking to tie Russia into that very order; and secondly by a separate examination of the role the EU policies have played in the formation of the conflict dynamics between the EU, and to an extent the West more generally, and Russia.[1]

The main argument of this essay is that the conflict in Ukraine is first and foremost a symptom and not the root cause of the wider conflict between Russia and the West. In other words, Ukraine is the stage on which the main *dramatis personae* of the wider conflict act their roles and play out that conflict. This is not to suggest that either the EU or the wider West is the main culprit in the conflict. On the contrary, the conflict in Ukraine can be likened to a perfect storm created by the characteristics and policies of the EU, Russia and Ukraine and their consequent interaction. This is a conflict that no single party either wanted or necessarily promoted—although we now know that Russia has been gearing potentially to wage such a conflict since at least the Orange revolution of 2004 (Jonsson & Seely 2015). Laying blame is hardly ever a fruitful intellectual exercise—and in the world of international politics and diplomacy even less so—but one has to see fault in all the parties. In Ukraine, successive governments essentially ran the country into the ground, squandering opportunities for reform and meaningful economic and social development and aggravating latent tensions in its own body politic, as well as between the EU and Russia through its inept handling of relations in all directions (Dragneva-Levers & Wolczuk 2015). In Russia, the faults lay in deciding to frame the EU's increasing presence in the so-called 'common neighbourhood' (a term never accepted by Russia, by the way) in zero-sum terms and taking full advantage of the opportunities afforded by the fall of President Viktor Yanukovych in February 2014 (Forsberg & Haukkala 2016, chs 2, 8). As for the EU—although its sins are mainly those of omission—we shall argue that, contrary to what Russia has asserted, the defining feature of its policy has been the essential unwillingness of the EU to engage in a game of 'spheres of influence' in the East and its propensity to develop policies devoid of long-term thinking about the strategic ramifications these policies might have. It is this continuing 'sleep-walking' (House of Lords 2015, p. 6) that seems to be the defining characteristic of EU responses in the East that is both the main concern and the object of criticism in this essay.

The problems of incorporating Russia into an EU-centric order

When viewed from Brussels, the Grand Narrative of EU–Russia relations has been the EU's repeated attempts at 'constructive engagement' with a view to tying Russia into an EU-centric order. In this reading, 'Brussels' and its institutions have been the 'unipole' with Russia envisaged as a recipient of norms, values and a whole gamut of policy best practices promoted by the EU. It should be pointed out that although Russia has been granted several privileges by the EU—the role of special 'strategic partner', as well as a much more lenient application of political conditionality—Moscow has been subjected to the same treatment as the rest of the EU's Eastern neighbourhood. For all intents and purposes, they have been based on the EU's claim of normative hegemony in Europe, built on asymmetrical sovereignty-challenging approaches (Haukkala 2010).

The question of whether the EU is in fact a genuine actor needs briefly to be addressed. To cut a long story short, two aspects merit attention, particularly in the context of EU–Russia relations. The first deals with the extent the EU can be considered an actor to begin with.

[1]This essay brings together over 15 years of research concerning the topic and insights gained while acting as a policy planner at the Finnish Ministry for Foreign Affairs between 2009 and 2010 and again in 2014–2015. It goes without saying that none of what follows necessarily represents the official Finnish position.

Keukeleire and Delreux have captured the essence of what they call the EU's foreign policy by arguing that it is 'single in name, dual in policy-making method, [and] multiple in nature'; a foreign policy system defined precisely by the, at times, uneasy co-existence of two different and, at times, clashing policy-making modes of intergovernmentalism and community method (Keukeleire & Delreux 2014, p. 61). Following White (2001, pp. 24, 40–1), the EU can be envisaged as an interacting 'foreign policy system' that is constituted of three different layers of foreign policy making: the EU external relations (the former Community foreign policy, or foreign economic policy), the Union foreign policy (the CFSP and to a certain extent the CSDP), and the national (member state) foreign policies. The sometimes paradoxical entity called 'European foreign policy' is therefore an amalgamation forged in the interaction between these three layers of foreign policy making. To a certain extent, the different layers can be expected to have competing, or at least inconsistent, objectives and agendas. What is more, it should not be taken for granted that any of the layers in their own right would be internally consistent and coherent either. In fact it can be argued that, at least some of the time, European foreign policy can be envisaged as an internal crisis-management mechanism for the Union through which the competing agendas and (national) interests are managed (Keukeleire 2003, pp. 34–6).

Secondly, at the same time it cannot be denied that regardless of the level and quality of its actorness the EU has adopted and is implementing policies. Indeed, it can be argued that the adoption and development of the EU's Eastern Neighbourhood Policy (ENP) played a role (although not necessarily the key role) in paving the way to the current conflict with Russia. But even though the EU might be promoting policies, the true origins of its objectives and agenda have been questioned. For example, Richard Sakwa (2015) has suggested that the problem in the EU's approach has been its increasing immersion into the US-driven 'New Atlanticism' that has set it on a collision course with Russia, with dangerous implications for the future of European security. This seems to be an interpretation put forward by key Russian officials as well, including President Vladimir Putin himself. Yet, in our view, this is a vulgar interpretation of the EU's international role that does not do justice to 'Brussels' or the member states for that matter. Therefore in this essay we will proceed from the assumption that the EU indeed has indigenous actorness and it is precisely the various shortcomings it has portrayed in this department that makes the EU also at least partly culpable for the present situation.

This is not the occasion to discuss the problems in EU–Russia relations at length (Forsberg & Haukkala 2016; Maass 2016). At least initially, Russia also subscribed to the value-driven integrationist agenda: in the early 1990s, Moscow repeatedly voiced its ambition to join the 'community of civilised states', a process that was seen to entail the one-sided adoption of Western liberal standards of democracy and market economy (English 2000). Although during Vladimir Putin's leadership this rhetoric subsided, some of the calls for closer integration and cooperation with the EU put forward in the early 2000s were still based on at least a tacit acceptance of the rules of the game propagated by the EU.

That said, under Putin Russia has increasingly come to reject the notion of a unipolar Europe, an eventuality that has come about gradually in three stages (Haukkala 2013). In the first instance, already visible during the 1990s, Russia made little or no headway at all in terms of converging on EU standards, while nevertheless still paying official lip service to them and the ideals that underpin them. In the second period, from the early 2000s, Russia started to disassociate itself from most of the objectives and principles propagated by the

EU. The new narrative emerging from Moscow revolved around three main complaints: first, how 'the West'—usually understood to be represented by the US, but increasingly by the EU as well—took advantage of Russia's temporary weakness in the 1990s and imposed an alien set of policies and principles on Russia while side-lining the country politically in Europe (Averre 2007, p. 183); second, how Moscow was consequently unable to affect the EU's policies towards Russia, with 'Brussels' insisting instead on a rigid implementation of often ready-made packages without consulting Russia properly (Karaganov 2005, p. 27); and third, how the EU has used its increased presence in the so-called 'common neighbourhood' to force the countries to make a false choice either between the EU or Russia (Stewart 2009).

Although the rhetoric coming from Moscow during this phase was at times increasingly belligerent (Schiffers 2015), the essential gist of the Russian argument seems to have been defensive, to cordon off alien influences to enable the indigenous and somehow more organic and 'natural' development of Russia. This has changed in the third and most recent stage with Russia taking a much more assertive role in promoting its preferred vision of order beyond its borders. In the first instance, this took the form of the Eurasian Customs Union and Economic Union (EEU) through which Russia has started to invest in a more institutionalised bipolar setting in Europe, with Moscow as the leading power in the other half of the continent with the expectation of attracting the majority, if not all, of the post-Soviet states under Russia's leadership (Dragneva & Wolczuk 2013). Although the EEU has gained momentum in recent years, as exemplified by the expansion of its members from the original three to five, it is too early to declare the mission completed. The fact that Russia has been forced to resort to open blackmail and coercion to attract new members to the EEU speaks volumes about the power of attraction of the new regional bloc. Also the re-imposition of customs checks on the Russian–Belarusian border by Russia in summer 2015 was an indication of how fragile the new arrangements still were.

Indeed, Russia's inability to pull the largest piece of the sub-regional puzzle, Ukraine, into its orbit prefaced the latest phase of events, with Russia assuming an openly belligerent stance against the continued projection of EU and wider Western policies and values in the East (MacFarlane & Menon 2014). The most spectacular manifestation of this was the conflict which erupted in November 2013 due to then President Yanukovych's decision not to sign the Association Agreement with the EU at the Eastern Partnership Summit in Vilnius. The decision, actively spurred by both threats and promises of rewards from Moscow, resulted in a domestic uprising under the banner of Euromaidan that resulted in the collapse of Yanukovych's presidency in February 2014. Russia's response to these events was as swift as it was spectacular, first annexing Crimea in early March and then quickly moving on to the destabilisation of Eastern Ukraine to halt Ukraine's march towards closer European and wider Euro-Atlantic integration in its tracks (Wilson 2014; Menon & Rumer 2015).

The problems in the EU's approach towards its Eastern neighbourhood

This section will examine the role the EU has played in the gestation of the conflict between Ukraine and Russia. It also draws from my personal experiences as a policy planner but will be backed up with documentation and secondary literature to the extent that this is possible. The discussion will proceed in the form of five brief observations that, when taken together, paint a rather grim picture of the EU's role in the process.

The EU wanted neither an Eastern neighbourhood nor a European Neighbourhood Policy

One may argue that to a degree both were in fact unwanted by-products of a wider process that had also been essentially unwanted: the Eastern enlargement of the EU. Rhetoric about the enlargement being the biggest success story of EU foreign policy (Rehn 2006)—albeit true—masks the essential difficulties and unwillingness the EU faced in embracing the process during the 1990s (Smith 1999; Schimmelfennig 2003), a feat that was repeated when it came to the Eastern neighbourhood. Indeed, anyone who recalls the debates in the early 2000s should know that at the time the EU was not looking forward to assuming new responsibilities beyond the Eastern 'Big Bang' enlargement. On the contrary, the main concerns revolved around the question of the EU's own absorption capacity in terms of new members and the perceived need to take a break from the continuous rounds of enlargements that had started to resemble a perpetual motion engine (Haukkala 2008).

The adoption of the ENP must be analysed keeping this background in mind. As a consequence, originally the ENP was not an aspirational policy aimed at achieving a genuine gear change with the EU's relations with its new neighbours but an essentially defensive policy meant to stave off demands, expectations and obligations both from new members and prospective neighbours. It is hardly a coincidence that the essential blueprint for the new ENP was launched in 2003, prior to the emergence of both new members and neighbours: it was a deliberate move on the part of some key member states to take the initiative in the development of ties with the Eastern neighbours in order to control and contain the process that was soon forthcoming.

At the same time, the EU paradoxically adopted a policy template that was wildly ambitious both in its rhetoric and its voiced objectives. As part of a 'ring of friends' the new neighbours were offered 'everything but institutions' that would entail wide-ranging cooperation and eventual association with the EU (Prodi 2002). The aim was also to (re)invigorate the Union's normative agenda and apply conditionality more stringently to relations with non-candidate countries. Taken together, the ENP was an attempt at squaring the circle of relinquishing—or at least deferring indefinitely—enlargement, and retaining the Union's normative power in Eastern Europe, while controlling and perhaps even curtailing the internal dynamics concerning the issues within the post-enlargement EU itself (Dannreuther 2006; Kelley 2006; Sasse 2008). As a consequence, the policy template was loaded with internal contradictions ranging from the discrepancy between the voiced ambitions and the EU's actual willingness and ability to deliver to the existence of contradictory logics between security and cooperation in the implementation of the policy (Christou 2010).

The EU learned the wrong lessons from the Eastern enlargement

In the aftermath of the Big Bang enlargement the EU was convinced that its own transformative power had been the key in turning the fortunes of the Central and East European countries around. Although the accession process played an important role, the real factor was the essential willingness and, more importantly, the ability of the accession candidates themselves to engage in meaningful reforms (Vachudova 2005). What is more, the EU has been operating in a fairly presentist frame of mind, neglecting the influence of historical legacies on the prospects of successful Europeanisation, in particular when it comes to securing the gains made even in some of the Central and East European countries. Indeed, some of the democratic backsliding evident in Hungary and elsewhere has hinted at the possible limits of the EU's approach in making a lasting impact on the new members while suggesting that the impediments for the EU might be even greater in the Eastern neighbourhood (Cirtautas & Schimmelfennig 2010; Schimmelfennig & Scholtz 2010, p. 454).

On top of this the EU was also operating in a benign geopolitical environment with no third party seriously questioning, let alone challenging, its policies and strategic objectives. On the contrary, the EU was actively supported and encouraged in its tasks by the global hegemon, the US (Baun 2004). To a degree the rapid enlargement of the EU was a regional application of liberal principles that were in the final analysis backed up by US primacy. In this respect it is noteworthy than on several occasions the US played a crucial protecting, enabling and spurring role in Europe, initially by pacifying the Yugoslav wars and later supporting and encouraging the EU's Eastern enlargement, including opening accession negotiations with Turkey (McGuire & Smith 2008, pp. 222–25).

None of these crucial factors applied in the case of the 'common neighbourhood': the neighbours themselves were not reliable partners and agents of change; Russia increasingly acted as a regional challenger and even spoiler; and the US increasingly took a back seat in the East, increasingly concentrating on its own domestic problems and its pivot towards Asia. None of these lessons were, however, appreciated or anticipated by the EU at the time of devising and developing the ENP. On the contrary, the EU approached its Eastern neighbourhood as essentially uncontested, where it could seek a continuation of its accession model by other means. With its ENP the EU has been busy devising relations that, when taken together, would move Eastern Europe towards becoming part of a wider EU-centred order of prosperity, stability and integration. Although this approach has been rooted in geography, it has not been a geopolitical power projection project in the crude sense of the term. Indeed, the EU has been manifestly uninterested in pursuing spheres of influence and has declined to frame its role in the East in this manner, thereby highlighting its own strategic thinking that shuns zero-sum conceptions of international relations, and seeking to defuse tensions with Russia, which has been a much more 'traditional' actor in this respect. Despite all the rhetoric of partnership—now largely silent—the underlying reality has been that the EU's policies have flown in the face of Russia's insistence on framing the EU's role in the Eastern neighbourhood in largely negative and competitive terms. As a consequence, the EU has been locked into an integration competition with Russia, despite being unwilling and ill-equipped to play that game (Forsberg & Haukkala 2016, ch. 8).

Internal dynamics have dominated the EU's policy towards its neighbourhood

This was true at the inception of the policy, as was already mentioned, but the consequent development of the policy has been at the mercy of internal cleavages in the EU as well. The competition between the Eastern and Southern groupings has been real and enduring. The majority of member states have treated one direction as dominant while the other has been treated with indifference and/or suspicion. A good illustration of these dynamics is French President Nicolas Sarkozy's decision to propose the formation of a 'Union for the Mediterranean' to complement the Southern dimension of the ENP during the French EU Presidency in 2008. French unilateralism was one, although not the only, factor behind the adoption of the ill-fated Eastern Partnership a year later, as the Northern and Eastern caucuses in the EU tried to rectify the perceived imbalance between the East and the South. As a consequence, the EU has not at any time had a shared understanding concerning the stakes and prospects when it comes to the Eastern neighbourhood, or the Southern neighbourhood for that matter. This still applies.

Unforeseen events have been crucial in affecting both the parameters within which the EU's policy would unfold and in the policy itself

Four issues are worth briefly flagging up. Firstly, the Orange revolution—which took both the EU and Russia by surprise—changed Moscow's tack concerning the role the EU played in the region. Moscow's previous indifference ended and it began to view the EU's growing role and the Western orientation of CIS countries with increasing suspicion (Gretskiy *et al.* 2014). Although it was not appreciated at the time, the Orange revolution was the starting gun for the preparation of operations and practices witnessed first in Georgia in 2008 and then in Crimea and Eastern Ukraine since 2014 (Franke 2015).

Second, the war in Georgia in August 2008 was a dress rehearsal for the kind of hybrid—or full spectrum—conflict waged by Russia (Jonsson & Seely 2015). It effectively killed off the other leg of perceived Western encroachment on Russia's sphere of influence, namely the enlargement of NATO. It also spurred the EU to launch the Eastern Partnership (although as mentioned internal EU dynamics played a role as well), interpreted by Russia as an 'upping the ante' in terms of geopolitical competition over the neighbourhood countries. The subsequent US reset and the lessening of overall US interest towards Eastern Europe during Obama's first term sent to Russia the signal that it could act almost with impunity in its neighbourhood (Lo 2015, p. 172). These dangerous perceptions directly contributed to Russia's subsequent actions in Ukraine.

Third, domestic events in Russia were crucial in a turn for the worse in Moscow's perception of the EU's role in the East. The so-called White Revolution in Moscow, where the rigged *Duma* elections of December 2011 resulted in hundreds of thousands of people taking to the streets, was decisive in effectively halting Russia's modernisation drive and making Putin in particular more worried about perceived Western attempts at destabilising the country by effecting 'regime change' there. Thus the events in Ukraine in 2013–2014 were viewed in very sinister terms by Moscow (Hill & Gaddy 2015).

Fourth, the tenacity and effectiveness of the so-called Euromaidan in Ukraine took all the key actors by surprise. Yanukovych assumed that the decision to back down from signing the Association Agreement was solely his to make and would cement his position in Ukraine. Russia expected nothing short of a full change of direction in Ukraine's foreign policy while the EU, too, essentially capitulated and did not engage in bidding to win Ukraine over. Without the grassroots political movement in Ukraine Russia would have acquired at least a temporary victory in November 2013. The fact that this did not transpire was due to the dogged opposition on the Euromaidan which, while undoing the power of Yanukovych, also acted as the backdrop for the wider conflict between Ukraine and Russia.

The EU has been unable to examine both its own role and the role of Russia in the region through a strategic lens

The need for strategy in international politics is an overrated good and by no means a silver bullet. At the same time, the EU's utter inability to appreciate the strategic ramifications of its own policies and ongoing changes in its environment over the past decade is nothing short of astonishing. The reason for this partly resides at a profound discursive level. According to Kował (2015, p. 13) the reason why policy analysts' manifold warnings over the years about the problems in the EU's approach in the East fell on deaf ears were the politicians 'who were ready to listen only to the melodies that they themselves had created' (Kował 2015, p. 13). Indeed, the habits of thinking and speaking about 'Europe' had become so entrenched that any notion of a sphere of influence was beyond the pale for the West, the EU included. Russia, too, seemed to be aware of this as by and large its protestations against the EU policies were in fact disingenuous, making claims that did not withstand serious scrutiny and giving grounds for EU representatives to dismiss these concerns as unfounded.

One should note an interesting precedent which probably goes some way towards explaining why the EU had a hard time deciphering Russia's messages correctly. On the eve of the Big Bang enlargement in February 2004 Russia threatened to refuse to extend the Partnership and Cooperation Agreement (PCA) to the ten new EU member states, unless its specific concerns over the negative impact of the Union's enlargement on the Russian economy and society were taken into consideration. For its part, the Union refused to accept a linkage between the extension of the PCA and its enlargement, while stressing its willingness to discuss Russia's concerns in a separate context. The crisis was resolved in April with the adoption of a joint declaration that essentially dispelled most Russian concerns, especially in the realm of the economy, by showing that they had been largely erroneous to begin with, and soothed Moscow by promising that the outstanding issues would be resolved in a mutually acceptable way in the future (Van Elsuwege 2008, pp. 336–9). With the ENP the EU has continued this tradition, seeking to allay fears that the Union is somehow seeking to displace Russia in the post-Soviet space or is trying to undermine regional cooperation Russia has been developing with its neighbours, by simply insisting that the developments are, in fact, not directed against Russia and that they are compatible with Russia's own long-term interests (Haukkala 2010, p. 149).

Having established this, one should note that at the same time Russia repeatedly voiced its increasing displeasure at EU policies, so that the EU should have at least entertained the possibility that Moscow would not remain indifferent to a radical shake-up of the political setting in the region. The ENP and the Eastern Partnership drew Russia's repeated ire (Stewart 2009). For example, during the post-EU–Russia Summit press conference in Khabarovsk in May 2009 President Dmitry Medvedev commented on the EU's Eastern Partnership initiative, adopted earlier in the month: 'I'll put it succinctly. We tried to convince ourselves [that the EU project is harmless] but in the end we couldn't. … What worries us is that in some countries attempts are being made to exploit this structure as a partnership against Russia' (Rettman 2009). Although there is some evidence that many member states were aware of this tendency, the EU machinery clearly was not.

It is striking to note how little strategic foresight and reflection there has been when it comes to the making of EU foreign policy in general and perhaps its policies towards the East in particular. For example, the Commission's report concerning foresight activities in the EU fails to mention the External Action Service entirely, as if the institution or foresight activities there did not exist (European Commission 2015); one commentator admits that at least at the time they did not (Missiroli 2013). Although there might be bureaucratic reasons for this oversight, as the relations between these two institutions have not been the best, this impression that foreign policy has indeed been a blind spot in the Union's foresight activities is strengthened by the fact that the main tool for producing future-related insights for the EU—the European Strategy and Policy Analysis System (ESPAS), a loose network of actors from EU institutions and member states dealing with strategic foresight—has devoted its energies to the medium and long time frames while concentrating mainly on economic and societal trends and the future of governance and power globally (ESPAS 2016). Even in cases where issues pertaining to the Eastern neighbourhood were mentioned, such as in the *Empowering Europe's Future* report (Grevi *et al.* 2013), and although the discussion concerning the essential and dangerous dynamics is apt, the right conclusions were not drawn and dangerous scenarios were not pondered. Instead, the report merely stated that 'Russia is likely to remain essentially a status quo power, chiefly interested in preserving its status at all of the top tables of international politics' (Grevi *et al.* 2013, p. 55), in effect intellectually foreclosing the possibility of a course of events that nevertheless became a reality soon after the launch of the report. To make matters worse, to my knowledge no policy planning papers pondering the effects of the EU's policies were prepared or debated even internally, no scenarios seriously pondered. None of this is meant to say that the EU should have seen the violent conflict with Russia coming. Not a lot of people did at the time. But the point is that the EU should have at least entertained that possibility or thought about different negative scenarios in advance to be better prepared for that eventuality. Instead, the EU was in the business of achieving strategic effects with no strategic reflection, as it still is.

In lieu *of a conclusion: did the EU get anything right?*

The discussion above suggests a set of rather gloomy conclusions. Not only has the EU failed to tie Russia into its preferred order but it has failed in its attempts at stabilising its immediate neighbourhood in the East as well. To be fair the EU has been forced to operate in an exceptionally and even increasingly challenging environment while grappling with a host of other pressing issues both internally and externally. The main shortcoming in the EU's policies has been their non-strategic character. Essentially the EU has unwillingly, and in a rather haphazard manner, been sleepwalking into ever deeper strategic commitments with scant strategic thought. Although the intentions have been good, the outcome is anything but. Russia's repeated protestations against the EU's approach have fallen on deaf ears. For the EU, the response has been to argue the problem away, explaining time and time again to Russia why its approach should be in the interest of Russia as well. In essence, Russia's readings of the evolving situation have been incompatible with the policy discourses in the West and the EU. As a consequence, they have simply failed to register and have not been taken seriously. Hence the acute surprise when Putin finally put his foot down in February 2014.

Since the outbreak of the conflict, the EU has nevertheless fared better than expected in handling the conflict in Ukraine and the crisis with Russia. Tough sanctions have been adopted and the political line and internal EU solidarity have both held. Ukraine has received a good deal of political and economic support. The role of Germany in consolidating the EU line has been indispensable. Yet all this success has come with a bitter twist: none of this has prevented Russia from achieving its objectives in a piecemeal way or by proxy. Crimea is effectively 'done and dusted'. Sanctions have now been linked with the implementation of the Minsk II Agreement, which are much more favourable to Russian interests than the preceding one. Russia has in an unprecedented way been given consultation rights when it comes to the implementation of the EU–Ukraine Association Agreement, potentially compromising the integrity of both the Agreement and the underlying EU policy (Dragneva & Wolczuk 2014). Ukraine and Russia are also locked in a 'chicken and egg' dynamic when it comes to the implementation of the Minsk Agreements: Kyiv will only implement domestic reforms once the military parts of the Agreement have been implemented, while Russia and the separatist forces, fearing the loss of military leverage, will implement those parts only once the political reforms are securely in place.

Even in the best scenario we are looking at a long-lasting division of Ukraine, a permanently dysfunctional state and society unable to realise its European orientation and meet the strategic objectives negotiated with the EU. Although at the time of writing the fighting in Ukraine has largely subsided, the conflict is far from resolved, as is the case with the wider contestation concerning the shared neighbourhood and indeed wider European security. The 'new normal' in relations between the EU and Russia is far from stable. The continued sanctions are far from optimal for Russia, and the situation remains precarious. We have not seen the end of the conflict in Ukraine nor of Europe's wider conflict with Russia. Indeed, the danger this essay is trying to highlight is that Russia is most likely not simply going through a phase that will soon subside. On the contrary, there are plenty of indications that we are dealing with a more profound and long-lasting change in Russia. Yet the EU continues to insist on upholding principles without thinking strategically about the situation.

That said, rectifying the shortcomings discussed above would probably have gone against the grain of EU values and its nature as an international actor. None of this should be taken as an attempt to exonerate Russia either, whose actions in Ukraine have been destructive. Nor should it be construed as a call for the EU and the West simply to cave in under Russian pressure and let Putin have his way with the countries of Eastern neighbourhood. On the contrary, the EU has the right—perhaps even the obligation—to remain engaged in the region and to continue to promote its values and vision for the future of Europe.

But the path towards that destination is fraught with difficulties, even dangers for the EU. Two trends seem to be emerging in the EU's policy towards the East. On the one hand, the EU has assumed what could be called a 'more of the same' approach where it has simply sought to speed up and enhance the implementation of the policies contested by Russia. On the other hand, these attempts are at the same time increasingly marked by a certain degree of timidity, as exemplified by the EU's lacklustre performance at the Eastern Partnership Summit in Riga in May 2015 (Walker 2015). This continued mixture of ambition and timidity is not a happy one, as it sends mixed signals that may encourage further challenges and even aggression on the part of Russia.

If the EU is to play its game more successfully it must acknowledge that the challenge is strategic and that it will require some head-on collisions with Russia in certain issues while avoiding conflict in others. It also means strategic patience and the ability to assess and decide when the stakes are too high for overall European security. A 'game of chicken', which now seems to be in the offing in the East, is not a particularly safe sport, especially if in the vehicle there are 28 pairs of hands at the wheel. Indeed, the underlying concern is that the auto-pilot mode of EU and Western responses to the current crisis may result in further sleepwalking, into another and potentially much bigger clash with Russia. It is high time for the EU to acknowledge the radically altered nature of the game in the East and start to act accordingly, carefully weighing possibilities and risks, options and dangers. This is admittedly a tall order for an amorphous international actor such as the EU: too tall, perhaps?

References

Averre, D. (2007) '"Sovereign Democracy" and Russia's Relations with the European Union', *Demokratizatsiya*, 15, 2.

Baun, M. (2004) 'The Implications of EU Enlargement for the United States', *Perspectives*, 21, Winter.

Christou, G. (2010) 'European Union Security Logics to the East: The European Neighbourhood Policy and the Eastern Partnership', *European Security*, 19, 3.

Cirtautas, A. M. & Schimmelfennig, F. (2010) 'Europeanisation Before and After Accession: Conditionality, Legacies and Compliance', *Europe-Asia Studies*, 62, 3.

Dannreuther, R. (2006) 'Developing the Alternative to Enlargement: The European Neighbourhood Policy', *European Foreign Affairs Review*, 11, 2.

Dragneva, R. & Wolczuk, K. (eds) (2013) *Eurasian Economic Integration: Law, Policy and Politics* (Cheltenham, Edward Elgar).

Dragneva, R. & Wolczuk, K. (2014) 'The EU–Ukraine Association Agreement and the Challenges of Inter-Regionalism', *Review of Central and Eastern European Law*, 39, 3–4.

Dragneva-Levers, R. & Wolczuk, K. (2015) *Ukraine between the EU and Russia. The Integration Challenge* (London, Palgrave).

English, R. D. (2000) *Russia and the Idea of the West. Gorbachev, Intellectuals, and the End of the Cold War* (New York, NY, Columbia University Press).

ESPAS (2016) 'Work in Progress', European Strategy and Policy Analysis System website, available at: http://europa.eu/espas/work-in-progress/index_en.htm, accessed 10 January 2016.

European Commission (2015) 'Concurrent Design Foresight: Report to the European Commission of the Expert Group on Foresight Modelling', EUR 26865, 2015, available at: http://ec.europa.eu/research/swafs/pdf/pub_governance/concurrent_design_foresight_report.pdf, accessed 10 January 2016.

Forsberg, T. & Haukkala, H. (2016) *The European Union and Russia* (London, Palgrave).

Franke, U. (2015) *War by Non-military Means. Understanding Russian Information Warfare*, FOR-R-4065-SE, March 2015 (Stockholm, FOI).

Gretskiy, I., Treshchenkov, E. & Golubev, K. (2014) 'Russia's Perceptions and Misperceptions of the EU Eastern Partnership', *Communist and Post-Communist Studies*, 47, 3–4.

Grevi, G., Keohane, D., Lee, B. & Lewis, P. (2013) *Empowering Europe's Future: Governance, Power and Options for the EU in a Changing World* (Brussels, European Union), available at: http://europa.eu/espas/pdf/espas-report-governance-power.pdf, accessed 10 January 2016.

Haukkala, H. (2008) 'The European Union as a Regional Normative Hegemon: The Case of European Neighbourhood Policy', *Europe-Asia Studies*, 60, 9.

Haukkala, H. (2010) *The EU–Russia Strategic Partnership: The Limits of Post-Sovereignty in International Relations* (London & New York, NY, Routledge).

Haukkala, H. (2013) 'The Impact of the Eurasian Customs Union on EU–Russia Relations', in Dragneva, R. & Wolczuk, K. (eds).

Haukkala, H. (2015) 'From Cooperative to Contested Europe? The Conflict in Ukraine as a Culmination of a Long-Term Crisis in EU–Russia Relations', *Journal of Contemporary European Studies*, 22, 1.

Hill, F. & Gaddy, C. (2015) *Mr. Putin—Operative in Kremlin* (Washington, DC, Brookings Institution Press).

House of Lords (2015) 'The EU and Russia: Before and Beyond the Crisis in Ukraine', European Union Committee, 6th Report of Session 2014–15 (London, Stationary Office), available at: http://www.publications.parliament.uk/pa/ld201415/ldselect/ldeucom/115/115.pdf, accessed 2 February 2016.

Jonsson, O. & Seely, R. (2015) 'Russian Full-Spectrum Conflict: An Appraisal after Ukraine', *The Journal of Slavic Military Studies*, 28, 1.

Karaganov, S. (2005) 'Russia and the International Order', in Lynch, D. (ed.) *What Russia Sees*, Chaillot Paper No. 74, January (Paris, European Union Institute for Security Studies).

Kelley, J. (2006) 'New Wine in Old Wineskins: Promoting Political Reforms through the New European Neighbourhood Policy', *Journal of Common Market Studies*, 44, 1.

Keukeleire, S. (2003) 'The European Union as a Diplomatic Actor: Internal, Traditional, and Structural Diplomacy', *Diplomacy and Statecraft*, 14, 3.

Keukeleire, S. & Delreux, T. (2014) *The Foreign Policy of the European Union* (2nd edn) (Basingstoke, Palgrave Macmillan).

Kował, P. (2015) 'The Poverty of Analysts', *New Eastern Europe*, no. 1 (XV).

Lo, B. (2015) *Russia and the New World Disorder* (London & Washington, DC, Chatham House and Brookings Institution).

Maass, A.-S. (2016) *EU–Russia Relations (1999–2015): From Courtship to Confrontation* (London & New York, NY, Routledge).

MacFarlane, N. & Menon, A. (2014) 'The EU and Ukraine', *Survival*, 56, 3.

McGuire, S. & Smith, M. (2008) *The European Union and the United States. Competition and Convergence in the Global Arena* (Basingstoke, Palgrave Macmillan).

Menon, R. & Rumer, E. (2015) *Conflict in Ukraine. The Unwinding of the Post-Cold War Order* (Cambridge, MA, MIT Press).

Missiroli, A. (2013) *Strategic Foresight—and the EU*, Brief 13/2013 (Paris, EU Institute for Security Studies), available at: http://europa.eu/espas/pdf/euiss_brief_13.pdf, accessed 10 January 2016.

Prodi, R. (2002) 'A Wider Europe—A Proximity Policy as the Key to Stability', speech at *Peace, Security and Stability International Dialogue and the Role of the EU*, Sixth ECSA–World Conference, Brussels, 5–6 December, available at: http://europa.eu/rapid/press-release_SPEECH-02-619_en.htm, accessed 10 January 2016.

Rehn, O. (2006) 'Europe's Next Frontiers', speech at European Policy Center, Brussels, 10 October, available at: http://europa.eu/rapid/press-release_SPEECH-06-586_en.htm, accessed 22 June 2015.

Rettman, A. (2009) 'EU–Russia Summit Ends With a Prickly Exchange Over Energy', *EUobserver.com*, 23 April, available at: https://euobserver.com/foreign/28173, accessed 22 June 2015.

Sakwa, R. (2015) 'The Death of Europe: Continental Fates after Ukraine', *International Affairs*, 91, 3.

Sasse, G. (2008) 'The European Neighbourhood Policy: Conditionality Revisited for the EU's Eastern Neighbours', *Europe-Asia Studies*, 60, 2.

Schiffers, S. K. (2015) 'A Decade of Othering: Russian Political Leaders' Discourse on Russia–EU Relations 2004–2014', *East European Quarterly*, 43, 1.

Schimmelfennig, F. (2003) *The EU, Nato and the Integration of Europe. Rules and Rhetoric* (Cambridge, Cambridge University Press).

Schimmelfennig, F. & Scholtz, H. (2010) 'Legacies and Leverage: EU Political Conditionality and Democracy Promotion in Historical Perspective', *Europe-Asia Studies*, 62, 3.

Smith, K. E. (1999) *The Making of EU Foreign Policy: The Case of Eastern Europe* (Basingstoke, Palgrave Macmillan).

Stewart, S. (2009) 'Russia and the Eastern Partnership. Loud Criticism. Quiet Interest in Cooperation', *SWP Comments*, 7 May (Berlin, Stiftung Wissenschaft und Politik).

Vachudova, M. A. (2005) *Europe Undivided: Democracy, Leverage, and Integration after Communism* (Oxford, Oxford University Press).

Van Elsuwege, P. (2008) 'The Four Common Spaces: New Impetus to EU–Russia Strategic Partnership', in Dashwood, A. & Maresceau, M. (eds) *Law and Practice of EU External Relations: Salient Features of a Changing Landscape*. (Cambridge, Cambridge University Press).

Walker, S. (2015) 'EU Eastern Partnership Summit Will Highlight Failure of Plan to Check Russia', *The Guardian*, 20 May, available at: http://www.theguardian.com/world/2015/may/20/eu-eastern-partnership-highlight-failure-plan-check-russia, accessed 13 July 2015.

White, B. (2001) *Understanding European Foreign Policy* (Palgrave, Basingstoke).

Wilson, A. (2014) *Ukraine Crisis. What It Means for the West* (New Haven, CT, Yale University Press).

German Foreign Policy towards Russia in the Aftermath of the Ukraine Crisis: A New *Ostpolitik*?

MARCO SIDDI

Abstract

This essay investigates the shift in Germany's *Ostpolitik* approach to Russia as a result of the latter's increasing domestic authoritarianism and assertive foreign policy, particularly its violations of international law in the Ukraine crisis. This prompted Germany to take the initiative in formulating EU sanctions against Russia. However, Germany has attempted to reconcile the sanctions policy with a diplomatic approach to resolving the Ukraine crisis by seeking ways of engaging Moscow on broader security and economic issues, as Russia is considered an essential factor in European and global security and a key energy supplier. Thus, *Ostpolitik* has not been abandoned altogether; it continues to play a role and shapes the long-term objectives of Germany's Russia policy.

THE RELATIONSHIP BETWEEN GERMANY AND RUSSIA IS considered to be an essential determinant of European politics and security. This perception was strengthened after 2013, when Germany emerged as the main economic and political power within the European Union and took up a leading role in shaping EU foreign policy. Following the onset of the Ukraine crisis, German chancellor Angela Merkel has led EU diplomatic efforts in conflict resolution. Germany has been the most influential EU country in the various negotiation formats concerning the crisis, from the Weimar triangle (including also France and Poland) to the Normandy group (comprising Germany, Russia, Ukraine and France). Moreover, Merkel led the shuttle diplomacy that negotiated the Minsk-2 agreement in February 2015.[1]

In addition to its current political influence, Germany's long-standing diplomatic relations with Russia have allowed the country to play a leading role in the negotiations. Berlin adopted a cooperative approach in its foreign policy *vis-à-vis* Moscow in the late 1960s (Krumm 2012, pp. 114–23; Schildt 2003, pp. 153–79). During the Cold War, this approach—known as *Ostpolitik*—was based on the idea that economic and political engagement with Moscow would lead to positive change, both within the Soviet Union and in bilateral relations.

---

[1]The agreement included a ceasefire between the Ukrainian army and the pro-Russian rebels fighting in Eastern Ukraine, the holding of elections in the regions of Donets'k and Luhans'k, the return of these regions to full Ukrainian government control and the decentralisation of powers in Ukraine through a constitutional reform that would recognise the special status of the Donets'k and Luhans'k regions. The full text is available at: http://www.ft.com/intl/cms/s/0/21b8f98e-b2a5-11e4-b234-00144feab7de.html#axzz42PSUGUCw, accessed 10 March 2016.

German governments adopted the same stance towards post-Soviet Russia, with an even stronger emphasis on promoting 'change through economic interlocking' (*Annäherung durch Verflechtung*). The political capital accumulated through decades of cooperation, as well as perceptions of its influence and trustworthiness both in Russia and the EU, enabled Germany to become the key mediator and Moscow's main interlocutor during the Ukraine crisis.[2]

However, Russia's violations of international law, notably its annexation of Crimea and military support for the separatists in the Donbas, have called into question the fundamental tenet of *Ostpolitik*, the pursuit of cooperation with Russia. Some analysts have claimed that, by supporting EU sanctions against Russia and condemning Russian policies in Ukraine, German leaders have abandoned *Ostpolitik* (Vestring 2014; Meister 2015). Others have argued that German policy towards Moscow has changed, but 'not as dramatically as some headlines have suggested' (Forsberg 2016, p. 23). At the other end of the spectrum, some pundits have contended that business interests determine German foreign policy, thereby implying that the logic of 'change through economic interlocking' will continue to guide Berlin's relations with Russia (Kundnani 2015; Szabo 2015).

This contribution explores the extent to which a shift has taken place in German foreign policy, and investigates the factors that help understand any such change. It argues that a shift of attitudes *vis-à-vis* Russia took place from late 2012 and became more noticeable during 2014, as the Ukraine crisis escalated. It was driven first by domestic developments in Russia (notably the deterioration of democracy and the rule of law since 2012) and, most significantly, by Russia's violations of international law in the Ukraine crisis. However, this change should not be interpreted as a major reformulation of German foreign policy. Although relations with Russia have cooled considerably, *Ostpolitik* has not been abandoned altogether; it continues to play a role in current developments and shapes the long-term objectives of Germany's Russia policy.

German foreign policy: key tenets and the challenge to Ostpolitik

Germany's foreign policy has been based on a set of tenets and values that could be reconciled with one another for several decades. In addition to *Ostpolitik*, these included the rejection of war as a means of resolving disputes, respect for human rights, support for democratic principles, transatlanticism (the post-war alliance with the US), multilateralism and European integration (Berger 1997; Banchoff 1999, pp. 259–89; Wittlinger 2011). While *Ostpolitik* dates back from the late 1960s, most of the other tenets were formulated in the first post-war years, when the Federal Republic regained its sovereignty.

The disastrous outcome of the dictatorial and militaristic policies of the Third Reich largely explains the rejection of war as a means to resolve disputes and the widespread support for a norm-based foreign policy among both German leaders and the public (Berger 1996). Germany's pacific security culture has often prevailed over other foreign policy tenets in circumstances when they contradicted each other. For instance, the rejection of the use of force and respect for international norms proved a stronger determinant of German foreign policy than transatlanticism when German leaders decided not to participate in the US-led war against Iraq in 2003 (Bjola & Kornprobst 2007). Moreover, cooperation and multilateralism

---

[2]Anonymous interview with official, Division for Russia, Belarus, Moldova and Eastern Partnership, at the Federal Foreign Office of Germany, Berlin, 28 October 2015.

in international relations are valued highly. European integration is seen as epitomising these norms and principles, and is therefore strongly advocated by the German political leadership.[3]

Reconciling the cooperative approach towards Russia with support for human rights and democratic principles was arguably one of the most difficult balancing acts for German politicians. Nonetheless, a solution was found in the idea that economic cooperation would have positive spill-over effects on Russian domestic political and economic developments. German foreign minister Frank-Walter Steinmeier has been one of the staunchest supporters of this approach: economic interlocking would bring about domestic change in Russia and lead to a rapprochement with the EU (Steinmeier 2007). In terms of policy making, the German–Russian Partnership for Modernisation (PfM) launched in 2008 reflected this stance.[4] Through the PfM, German leaders hoped to both promote Germany's economic interests and strengthen the rule of law in Russia, while their Russian counterparts were keen on economic consolidation and technology transfers from the West (Meister 2012; Makarychev & Meister 2015). The PfM was uploaded at the EU level in 2010, with the objective of promoting domestic reforms in Russia and enhancing bilateral trade, particularly through Russia's accession to the World Trade Organization (which eventually occurred in 2012). The PfM complemented previous agreements between the EU and Russia aimed at developing a strategic partnership, notably the Four Common Spaces, covering the economy and the environment; freedom, security and justice; external security; and research and education (EU & Russia 2010; David & Romanova 2015, p. 2).

However, the cooperative approach to Russia was increasingly challenged starting from the autumn of 2011. The irregularities in the Russian parliamentary and presidential elections in the winter of 2011–2012 and the authorities' repressive reaction to the ensuing protests signalled the judgement that economic partnership with the West had not led to improvements in democratic standards. Moreover, in the months after the elections, the Russian political establishment adopted several authoritarian measures, curtailing the rights of the LGBT community and compelling NGOs that received funding from abroad to register as 'foreign agents'. The authorities also adopted a more nationalistic and strongly conservative rhetoric, in an attempt to recover the support of part of the Russian electorate (Koesel & Bunce 2012; Gel'man 2013, pp. 3–10). These developments called into question the appropriateness of a policy of engagement and cooperation with the Kremlin.

The Ukraine crisis accelerated the deterioration of relations between Russia and the West. Russia's policies in Ukraine clashed with most tenets of German foreign policy. The Kremlin's annexation of Crimea in March 2014 and its military support of the separatists in Eastern Ukraine collided with the principle of rejecting the use of force and abiding by international law. Russia took unilateral action, to the detriment of a negotiated solution of the crisis, and its separatist allies in Ukraine prevented democratic elections in the area under their control.[3]

---

[3]In defence policy, German leaders tend to consider the EU's Common Security and Defence Policy (CSDP) as complementary to the transatlantic alliance; the CSDP is the preferred framework for civilian operations, whereas NATO is favoured for robust military engagement. However, due to the widespread opposition of the German public opinion to the use of military force, the civilian instruments of the CSDP are often seen as offering a more palatable option for German policy makers (Würzer 2013, pp. 28–9).

[4]See, 'Time for a German–Russian Modernization Partnership', Frank-Walter Steinmeier, Federal Minister for Foreign Affairs, at the Department of International Relations of the Urals State University in Ekaterinburg, 13 May 2008, available at: http://www.auswaertiges-amt.de/EN/Infoservice/Presse/Reden/2008/080513-BM-Russland.html, accessed 10 March 2016.

Moreover, Russian foreign policy overtly clashed with two of the pillars of Germany's positioning in the international arena, European integration and transatlanticism. The crisis in Ukraine was precipitated by the issue of Kyiv entering into an Association Agreement with the EU, which Russia fiercely opposed. It became clear that the Russian leadership considered further European integration in the post-Soviet space as a threat to its strategic interests. Putin explicitly rejected the Euro–Atlantic order, arguing that it was imposed by the West on Russia in the 1990s, and advocated a multipolar security architecture where Russia and the West recognise each other as equal partners and respect each other's strategic interests.[5] Furthermore, the US' strong condemnation of Russian actions in Ukraine and its pressure on Germany to follow suit created profound tension between Berlin's transatlantic alliance and its traditional policy of cooperation *vis-à-vis* Russia.

Under these circumstances, German leaders decided to support sanctions against Russia and accepted the costs that these would entail for the German economy. Policy makers in Berlin were particularly vocal in their criticism of Russia's violations of international law. Merkel defined the annexation of Crimea as 'criminal' (Merkel 2015), while Finance Minister Wolfgang Schäuble compared it to Hitler's annexation of the Sudetenland (Reiermann 2014). Russian reactions included both a firm repudiation of the accusations and attempts to ease tensions. The Russian foreign ministry issued a protest to the German embassy in Moscow about Schäuble's remarks, after which Schäuble was criticised by Merkel and backtracked.[6] On the other hand, despite Merkel's condemnation of Russia's annexation of Crimea, Putin conveyed to her that he remained interested in improving relations with the EU (MacFarquhar 2015). While voicing criticism of Russia, German leaders kept communication channels with the Kremlin open and came out strongly in favour of a negotiated solution to the crisis; Merkel repeatedly reiterated that there was no military solution. Despite having been weakened by developments on the ground and tensions with the other main German foreign policy tenets, the logic of *Ostpolitik* continued to play a significant role in decision making and in some influential parts of German society, notably in the business world and intellectual circles (Forsberg 2016).

Ostpolitik *revisited: agents and practice of Germany's Russia policy in 2014–2015*

German foreign policy towards Russia during the Ukraine crisis was shaped by the interaction of domestic and external factors. External factors pushed Berlin towards taking a critical stance. The US and several EU member states, particularly Poland and the Baltic states, immediately took a hard-line position *vis-à-vis* Russian policies. Initially, Merkel and Steinmeier attempted to resolve the Crimean crisis through talks. When this strategy failed, German leaders led efforts to impose sanctions on Russia.[7] Germany's position was seen as decisive for the overall EU stance *vis-à-vis* Russia. As the leading economic power in the EU and Russia's main European commercial partner, Germany steered EU foreign policy. In

---

[5]'Meeting of the Valdai International Discussion Club', The Kremlin, 24 October 2014, available at: http://en.kremlin.ru/events/president/news/46860, accessed 4 February 2016.

[6]*Deutsche Welle*, 3 April 2014, available at: http://www.dw.com/en/russia-protests-sch%C3%A4uble-comments-on-crimea-sudetenland-with-german-ambassador/a-17542060, accessed 3 February 2016.

[7]'Economic War with Russia: A High Price for German Business', *Spiegel Online*, 17 March 2014, available at: http://www.spiegel.de/international/europe/germany-to-play-central-but-expensive-role-in-sanctions-against-russia-a-959019.html, accessed 11 January 2016.

this role, its actions were also influenced by the desire to heed the transatlantic partnership and achieve consensus within the EU—and thus to act in accordance with the 'transatlantic' and 'Europeanist' foreign policy tenets. Practically, this meant reconciling the German foreign policy stance towards Russia with those of the US and eastern EU members states.[8] Nonetheless, German leaders rejected the proposal to send weapons to the post-Maidan Ukrainian government, as advocated by Republican congressmen in the US and treated as a possibility by Barack Obama,[9] since pursuit of a military solution to the conflict collided with Germany's post-war pacific security culture.

The forces at work in the domestic arena were more complex. Most mass media and public opinion surveys were very critical of Russia. In April 2014, over 50% of Germans interviewed in a survey conducted by the Allensbach Institute considered Russia as a threat to Germany, whereas before the Ukraine crisis two thirds thought that Russia was no threat to their country. In the same period, supporters of deeper cooperation with Russia diminished from over 50% to 32% of the interviewees.[10] The majority considered Putin and Russia responsible for the Ukraine crisis, but a sizeable minority (between 20% and 30% of interviewees) blamed the West and the new Ukrainian government. Moreover, the percentage of those considering Russia a 'world power' reached 67% in March 2015, compared to 45% in 2008 (Von Steinsdorff 2015, pp. 2–5).

Most politicians took a very critical stance towards Russia. Both parties in the governing coalition (the Christian Democrats and the Social Democrats) and the Green Party (in opposition) supported Merkel's policy of condemning and sanctioning Russia for its violations of international law. After initial hesitation, some of the main representatives of German business and industry (notably Markus Kerber, director general of the Federation of German Industries) also supported the government's line, arguing that gross violations of international law could not be tolerated and that peace and freedom stood above economic interests (Forsberg 2016, p. 34). This was particularly significant, as it refuted the argument that German foreign policy towards Russia is determined exclusively by national business interests (Kundnani 2015; Szabo 2015).

However, a closer look at the German domestic scenario reveals important nuances highlighting the persistence of *Ostpolitik* thinking in both the policy and business communities. While accepting the imposition of sanctions as a necessary evil, the associations of German industry remained sceptical of their effectiveness and appeared keen to see them lifted as soon as tensions with Russia started to de-escalate. Matthias Platzeck, head of the German–Russian Forum (an influential forum bringing together representatives of German and Russian civil society), repeatedly criticised the sanctions for being both counterproductive (Bidder & Schepp 2015) and fostering a siege mentality, thereby strengthening Putin's hold on power. Indeed, the surveys of the independent Russian polling organisation Levada showed that Putin's approval rating soared in 2014 and 2015.[11] Although other factors may have played

---

[8]Richard Sakwa argues that, following Russia's annexation of Crimea, 'German foreign policy lost some of its independence and swung behind Washington' (Sakwa 2015, p. 225).

[9]'Ukraine Conflict: US "May Supply Arms to Ukraine"', *BBC News*, 9 February 2015, available at: http://www.bbc.com/news/world-europe-31279621, accessed 11 January 2016.

[10]'Zunehmende Entfremdung', *FAZ-Monatsberichte*, 16 April 2014, available at: http://www.ifd-allensbach.de/uploads/tx_reportsndocs/FAZ_April_2014_Russland.pdf, accessed 3 February 2016.

[11]'Yanvar'skie reitingi odobreniya i doveriya', Levada Centre, 27 January 2016, available at: http://www.levada.ru/2016/01/27/yanvarskie-rejtingi-odobreniya-i-doveriya-4/, accessed 3 February 2016.

a more important role (notably the widespread patriotic enthusiasm following Russia's annexation of Crimea), it is plausible that Western sanctions contributed to rallying Russians behind Putin. This may change in the long run, as Russians feel the impact of the economic crisis. However, two years after the West imposed sweeping economic sanctions, despite the drastic depreciation of the ruble, Putin's approval rating has remained very high.

Platzeck was not the only prominent figure to criticise Merkel's stance towards Russia. Several former chancellors and foreign ministers—including Helmut Schmidt, Helmut Kohl, Gerhard Schröder and Hans-Dietrich Genscher—expressed strong reservations about Merkel's policy and argued for the resumption of dialogue and diplomatic cooperation with Moscow. Their criticism of Merkel's policy also highlighted the different stances of the current and the previous generations of German leaders *vis-à-vis* Russia. While the two German chancellors preceding Merkel (Helmut Kohl and Gerhard Schröder) had close personal relationships with Russian presidents, Merkel never developed similar ties with Putin (Krumm 2012). Their relationship is seen as having soured after Putin's denial of Russian military actions in Ukraine and Merkel's subsequent decision to impose sanctions on Russia (McGuinness 2015).

Even within the governing coalition, different points of view exist. The Social Democratic view of a policy of *détente* and engagement, following the *Ostpolitik* tradition initiated by Willy Brandt, remains one of the most influential. With Social Democratic leader Frank-Walter Steinmeier as head of German foreign policy, this view continues to play an important role in the foreign ministry, where negotiations (rather than confrontation) are seen as the only way of solving the current crisis, and partnership is still considered the long-term goal of relations with Moscow.[12] Prior to the Ukraine crisis, Steinmeier was a staunch supporter of cooperation with Moscow, particularly through the PfM; after the annexation of Crimea he has expressed moderate criticism of Russia, while appearing keen on upholding dialogue with Moscow (Belov 2015, pp. 6–11).

Despite the present tensions, the persistent influence of *Ostpolitik* thinking is discernible in current German foreign policy making, which has combined firm condemnations of Russian violations of international law with consistent support of diplomacy and dialogue. In February 2015, arguably the tensest moment of the Ukraine crisis so far, Merkel firmly rejected the idea of supplying weapons to Ukraine and initiated the diplomatic efforts that led to the Minsk-2 agreement. As the fighting in Eastern Ukraine lost intensity in the spring and summer of 2015, other political moves pointing to further dialogue and the resumption of German engagement with Russia took place. Angela Merkel was the only Western European leader who travelled to Moscow to commemorate the seventieth anniversary of the end of World War II. She declined the invitation to attend the military parade on the Red Square in Moscow, on 9 May, and only arrived in the city the day after. However, the fact that she travelled to the Russian capital to commemorate the anniversary, and held talks with Putin, highlighted her willingness to uphold both the historical reconciliation with Russia and direct diplomatic contacts with the Russian leadership.

Steinmeier also travelled to Russia to commemorate the anniversary. Together with his Russian counterpart, Sergei Lavrov, he attended an event in Volgograd, the site of a battle where the Soviet army gained a decisive victory against the German army. At the event, Steinmeier argued for reconciliation between Germans and Russians. He called Volgograd 'the city of heroes' who 'began Europe's liberation from Nazi dictatorship'. With implicit

---

[12]Anonymous interview with official, Division for Russia, Belarus, Moldova and Eastern Partnership, Federal Foreign Office of Germany, Berlin, 28 October 2015.

reference to the Ukraine crisis, he described the joint commemoration as 'an opportunity for us [Germans and Russians] to practise understanding and to peacefully resolve any antagonisms and conflicts between us' (Steinmeier 2015a).

Perhaps even more significantly, in the summer of 2015 German energy companies E.ON and Wintershall (together with Royal Dutch Shell, the French ENGIE and the Austrian ÖMV) restarted cooperation with Russian state energy company Gazprom on new joint energy projects. At the St. Petersburg International Economic Forum in June, E.ON, Shell and ÖMV signed a memorandum of intent with Gazprom for the expansion of the Nord Stream pipeline, which ships Russian gas to Germany *via* the Baltic Sea (Matalucci 2015). The expansion would double the capacity of the pipeline (from 55 to 110 billion cubic meters a year), thereby practically ending the dependency of EU–Russia gas trade on Ukrainian transit pipelines (Siddi 2015). Wintershall joined the Nord Stream-2 consortium in July and called for the end of sanctions against Russia. In September, the companies participating in the consortium pushed forward the project by signing a shareholders' agreement.[13]

German officials argue that Nord Stream-2 will contribute to European energy security.[14] In a meeting with Putin in October 2015, German Vice-Chancellor Sigmar Gabriel stated that building the pipeline is in the commercial interest of Germany and Europe.[15] This line of thinking was criticised by several European leaders, mostly from East-Central Europe. According to them, Nord Stream-2 would perpetuate the EU's energy dependence on Russia, disregard the interests of Ukraine and some East-Central European states (which would lose their strategic role as transit countries for Russian gas exports to Western Europe) and signal to the Kremlin that economic cooperation can resume before the Ukraine crisis is solved.[16] However, Merkel has minimised the political significance of the project, arguing that it is a commercial endeavour (Steinhauser 2015).

In fact, Nord Stream-2 is both a commercial and a political project. It is a commercial project because private Western companies are involved and have an interest in importing Russian gas through a route that appears more secure than the Ukrainian transit pipelines, particularly in the light of the current confrontation between Russia and Ukraine. The construction of the pipeline is estimated to cost nearly €10 billion; however, if Nord Stream-2 were to replace Ukrainian transit, it would eliminate the related transit tariffs ($3 billion in 2014) and the necessity of modernising Ukrainian pipelines, which would also be very costly.[17] On the other hand, the project has a strong political dimension because it is led by a Russian state company, Gazprom, and it would negatively affect the strategic significance of Ukraine and some East-Central European countries in energy trade. It may also reduce their energy

[13]'UPDATE 2-Gazprom, European Partners Sign Nord Stream-2 Deal', *Reuters*, 4 September 2015, available at: http://www.reuters.com/article/2015/09/04/russia-forum-nord-stream-idUSL5N11A0G420150904, accessed 11 January 2016.

[14]Anonymous interview with official, Division for Russia, Belarus, Moldova and Eastern Partnership, Federal Foreign Office of Germany, Berlin, 28 October 2015.

[15]'Meeting with Vice-Chancellor and Minister of Economic Affairs and Energy of Germany Sigmar Gabriel', The Kremlin, 28 October 2015, available at: http://en.kremlin.ru/events/president/news/50582, accessed 4 February 2016.

[16]'Seven EU Countries Oppose Nord Stream', *Euractiv*, 30 November 2015, available at: http://www.euractiv.com/sections/energy/seven-eu-countries-oppose-nord-stream-319933, accessed 4 February 2016.

[17]Gazprom estimates that this would cost nearly $20 billion. See 'Ukraine, Gazprom and Transit Issues—Factsheet', Gazprom, 20 March 2015, available at: http://www.gazpromukrainefacts.com/ukraine-natural-gas-facts/ukraine-gazprom-and-transit-issues-%E2%80%93-factsheet, accessed 4 February 2016.

security, at least until they diversify their energy imports and strengthen interconnections with Central and Western European markets (Dickel *et al*. 2014). However, Nord Stream-2 may also have positive political repercussions if, through energy cooperation, it helps improve the broader relationship between the EU and Russia. Incidentally, energy cooperation was one of the key drivers of German *Ostpolitik* towards both the Soviet Union and Russia and had a positive impact on political relations (Högselius 2013).

Despite the resumption of cooperation between some Western energy companies and Gazprom, German business associations have remained cautious about future prospects for EU–Russian and German–Russian trade. The *Ost-Ausschuss der Deutschen Wirtschaft*, the main representative of German industrial and commercial interests in Eastern Europe and Russia, estimates that the sanctions will remain in force until the Minsk-2 agreement is implemented. The *Ost-Ausschuss* claims that long-lasting damage has been done to economic relations with Russia, as mutual trust has been weakened and Moscow will try to diminish its dependence on business with the West in the future. Indeed, in 2015 German–Russian trade decreased by 35% compared to the previous year as a result of EU sanctions, Russian countersanctions and the economic crisis in Russia.[18] At the same time, the *Ost-Ausschuss* also argues that the sanctions against Russia are a driver for negative developments, as they reinforce Moscow's isolation and the radicalisation of its policies. The *Ost-Ausschuss* advocates the gradual lifting of sanctions during 2016.[19]

Its leadership claims that the policy of isolating Russia, rather than *Ostpolitik*, has failed. Eckhard Cordes (2015), chairman of the *Ost-Ausschuss* until the end of 2015, argued that, in the last ten years, *Ostpolitik* was a feature of German–Russian relations, but did not shape Western policy towards Russia sufficiently. According to Cordes, German policy makers were engaged in defusing crises that were caused by the policies of other countries, such as the plans of the US and East-Central European states to integrate Ukraine and Georgia into NATO and deploy ballistic missile defence in Eastern Europe. This view is corroborated by Germany's (and France's) opposition to offering NATO membership to Ukraine and Georgia at the 2008 NATO summit in Bucharest. The issue was a major irritant in relations with Russia, which perceives further NATO enlargement in Eastern Europe as a threat. Furthermore, as Cordes argued, the success of the German *Ostpolitik* in approaching Russia is highlighted by the fact that Berlin is the Western country with the best working relationship with Moscow. This allowed Merkel to play the role of mediator in the Ukraine crisis and achieve a diplomatic deal in Minsk. Cordes's successor as chairman of the *Ost-Ausschuss*, Wolfgang Büchele, is considered to be closer to Merkel than Cordes, who openly criticised the sanctions against Russia (Büschemann 2015). Nonetheless, Büchele believes that 'The most important concern of the *Ost-Ausschuss* must be improving relations with Russia in the medium term'.[20] *Ost-Ausschuss* support for *Ostpolitik*, which encompasses its political as well as economic dimensions, is partly explained by the very nature of the organisation, which was created

---

[18]'Bilateral Relations: Russian Federation', Federal Foreign Office, April 2015, available at: http://www. auswaertiges-amt.de/EN/Aussenpolitik/Laender/Laenderinfos/01-Nodes/RussischeFoederation_node.html, accessed 5 February 2016.

[19]Anonymous interview with senior manager, press and communication office, *Ost-Ausschuss der Deutschen Wirtschaft*, Berlin, 29 October 2015.

[20]'Wolfgang Büchele ist neuer Vorsitzender des Ost-Ausschusses der Deutschen Wirtschaft', *Ost-Ausschuss der Deutschen Wirtschaft*, 11 November 2015, available at: http://www.ost-ausschuss.de/node/1008, accessed 11 January 2016.

in the 1950s to facilitate the resumption of German trade with Eastern Europe and became one of the key instruments of Brandt's *Ostpolitik* in the 1960s and 1970s (Jüngerkes 2012).

To a large extent, the positive assessment of *Ostpolitik* is shared at the German foreign ministry. German foreign policy officials argue that the PfM with Russia has not failed, as projects continued to be implemented throughout the Ukraine crisis. A broader partnership with Russia, as well as cooperation with the Eurasian Economic Union, is portrayed as the long-term goal of EU–Russia relations, even if it is made conditional to the implementation of the Minsk-2 agreement.[21] German officials do not want further escalations of tensions with Moscow and attempt to keep diplomatic and trade channels open. Steinmeier's proposal, made in November 2015, to offer EU investment and energy concessions to Russia in order to prevent a clash over an EU–Ukraine trade deal is typical of this approach (Barker *et al.* 2015).

German officials saw their stance towards the Ukraine crisis vindicated when the Ministerial Council of the Organization for Security and Co-operation in Europe (OSCE) voted by consensus to entrust Berlin with the OSCE Chairmanship in 2016.[22] The OSCE is the only pan-European security organisation where both Russia and Western countries are represented and where the two sides have had regular contacts throughout the Ukraine crisis; its efforts to resolve the crisis have been praised by both Western leaders and Putin.[23] Moreover, the OSCE is playing an important role in monitoring the implementation of the Minsk agreement and the overall security situation in eastern Ukraine. The powers of the country holding the Chairmanship are limited and decisions in the organisation are taken by consensus. However, the choice of Germany can be interpreted as an act of confidence in the country's capabilities to mediate the Ukraine crisis and as an endorsement of its strategy—combining diplomacy with economic leverage—for future negotiations.

According to Steinmeier (2015b), Germany will use its OSCE Chairmanship to restore dialogue and trust in Europe, within the scope of OSCE principles such as the inviolability of borders. In his address to the OSCE Permanent Council in July 2015, Steinmeier unambiguously blamed Russia for the infringement of this principle and of international law. However, his call for dialogue, promoting economic exchanges and civil society cooperation, resonated with the tenets of German *Ostpolitik*. Steinmeier stressed the importance of civil society contacts within the OSCE framework, as part of the human dimension of the Helsinki Final Act. Significantly, civil society contacts are also a fundamental component of German *Ostpolitik*, and have been pursued consistently by the influential German–Russian Forum, with particular

---

[21]Anonymous interview with official, Division for Russia, Belarus, Moldova and Eastern Partnership, Federal Foreign Office of Germany, Berlin, 28 October 2015.

[22]Anonymous interview with senior official, Task Force for the 2016 OSCE Chairmanship, Federal Foreign Office of Germany, Berlin, 28 October 2015; see also 'German OSCE Chairmanship 2016', Ständige Vertretung der Bundesrepublik Deutschland bei der OSZE Wien, available at: http://www.wien-osze.diplo.de/Vertretung/wienosce/en/01a/DEU_20Vorsitz_202016.html, accessed 11 January 2016. The vote to entrust Berlin with the OSCE Chairmanship took place in December 2014; in the following weeks, Merkel took up a leading role in the negotiation of the Minsk-2 agreement.

[23]At a meeting of the Valdai International Discussion Club, Putin stated that 'even now, in trying to resolve the crisis in southeast Ukraine, the OSCE is playing a very positive role'. See 'Meeting of the Valdai International Discussion Club', The Kremlin, 24 October 2014, available at: http://en.kremlin.ru/events/president/news/46860, accessed 5 February 2016.

emphasis on youth exchanges, cultural cooperation and city partnerships.[24] Furthermore, Steinmeier's announcement that the German chairmanship will focus on 'common threats' such as 'international terrorism, radicalisation, cross-border drug trading, and risks in cyberspace' can be seen as an attempt to keep Moscow involved in security cooperation on issues where Western and Russian interests converge. During his visit to Moscow in October 2015, Sigmar Gabriel told Putin that Germany and Europe can be 'important partners' for Russia in discussing topics such as Syria and Ukraine, thereby implying that Germany wants to engage Russia in broad negotiations on global security issues.[25] Policy makers in Berlin consider cooperation between Russia and the US in these areas as particularly important for the improvement of East–West relations. For this reason, they see coordination between Washington and Moscow on their policies related to the Syrian crisis as a desirable outcome.[26] Following the terrorist attacks in Paris in November 2015, German officials viewed the incipient cooperation between Russia and the US-led coalition to fight the Islamic State as a positive development. In late November, Steinmeier proposed that Russia be allowed to return to the G-8 (from which it was excluded after the annexation of Crimea) if it continued to cooperate with the West over Syria and in the implementation of the Minsk-2 agreement.[27]

Conclusion: a new Ostpolitik*?*

Developments in German foreign policy during 2015 showed that the country has not entirely abandoned *Ostpolitik*. In German foreign policy circles, talk about the existence of a strategic partnership with Russia is muted, but this is still seen as a long-term objective that could be achieved when the current crisis is resolved and Russia restores its commitment to international law and OSCE principles in Europe. Meanwhile, German leaders have maintained a policy of diplomatic engagement with Moscow, which can also be seen as a legacy of *Ostpolitik*. This stance—together with Germany's rising influence in European foreign and security policy—has allowed Berlin to gain the trust of all sides in the Ukraine crisis and play the role of mediator. Significantly, countries that have taken a more militant stance in the crisis have been excluded from the negotiation process (notably Poland, after February 2014) or have not taken part in it (notably the US). Moreover, German leaders have supported energy cooperation with Russia, particularly through the Nord Stream-2 project, and have attempted to engage Moscow in negotiations concerning global security issues.

The policy of diplomatic engagement inherent in the philosophy of *Ostpolitik* has proven to be an important factor in achieving, for the time being, a negotiated path to de-escalate the crisis. What has evaporated, on the other hand, is the idea that economic ties alone are a

---

[24]Anonymous interview with executive board member, German–Russian Forum, Berlin, 29 October 2015; see also, Deutsch–Russisches Forum—Tätigkeitsbereiche, available at: http://www.deutsch-russisches-forum. de/index.php?id=taetigkeitsbereiche, accessed 11 January 2016.

[25]'Meeting with Vice-Chancellor and Minister of Economic Affairs and Energy of Germany Sigmar Gabriel', The Kremlin, 28 October 2015, available at: http://en.kremlin.ru/events/president/news/50582, accessed 4 February 2016.

[26]Anonymous interview with official, Division for Russia, Belarus, Moldova and Eastern Partnership, Federal Foreign Office of Germany, Berlin, 28 October 2015.

[27]'Steinmeier stellt Russland G-8-Rückkerhr in Aussicht', *Die Welt*, 22 November 2015, available at: http:// www.welt.de/politik/ausland/article149119201/Steinmeier-stellt-Russland-G-8-Rueckkehr-in-Aussicht.html, accessed 11 January 2016.

sufficient condition to achieve democratic domestic change in Russia, as well as the thought that Russian leaders would always prioritise economic interests over geostrategic goals (and hence avoid any confrontation with the West that may damage lucrative bilateral trade). In the past decade, *Ostpolitik* has focused excessively on an economic agenda, while overlooking the fact that its spill-over in terms of democratisation and rule of law was limited. Security issues hardly played any role in post-Cold War *Ostpolitik*. This meant that German foreign policy towards Russia did not adequately address a field that was considered crucial by the Russian counterparts. Until the Ukraine crisis, Berlin largely left the initiative on security and geopolitical issues to the US and other European partners in the Euro–Atlantic camp. Due to their long-standing mistrust of Russia and Moscow's threat perceptions, accompanied by aggressive foreign policy responses, relations between the West and Russia have become confrontational.

German policies during the Ukraine crisis suggest that a new type of *Ostpolitik*, combining diplomacy, economic engagement and a focus on the respect of norms, has gained momentum and will remain prominent in the foreseeable future. This approach is the result of an interplay between key tenets of German foreign policy: respect for international law, the rejection of war, multilateralism and the long-standing policy of engagement with Moscow. There may be tensions between the components of this approach, particularly if Russia does not cooperate in negotiations and escalates the military conflict in Ukraine. It is possible that German leaders will have to accept difficult compromises on issues where Russia or some of its Euro–Atlantic allies are unlikely to give in. For instance, they may have to relax Germany's drive for economic cooperation with Russia in areas where its East-Central European allies perceive it as threatening, or at least provide them with guarantees. On the other hand, if German leaders pursue reconciliation with Russia, they may have to decouple the extension of sanctions against Moscow from the full implementation of the Minsk-2 agreement, provided that ceasefire violations stop and Russia cooperates in de-escalating the crisis.

Despite these limitations, the German approach to Russia appears as the best available option for engaging Moscow and de-escalating both the Ukraine conflict and the current European security crisis. Berlin can use its considerable leverage to demand the respect of international law and offer the prospect of renewed economic cooperation to Russia, which is becoming more and more attractive to Moscow as its economy reels from low oil prices. Most importantly, Germany's refusal to supply weapons to Ukraine and seek a military solution to the crisis greatly reduces the probability of an all-out conflict between Russia and NATO, at least as long as Berlin remains at the helm of Western foreign policy towards Moscow.

References

Banchoff, T. (1999) 'German Identity and European Integration', *European Journal of International Relations*, 5, 3.

Barker, A., Wagstyl, S. & Olearchyk, R. (2015) 'Germany Pushes EU–Russia Deal to Avert Ukraine Trade Pact Tension', *Financial Times*, 1 December.

Belov, V. (2015) 'Zum Russland-Diskurs in Deutschland', *Russland-Analysen*, 300.

Berger, S. (1997) *The Search for Normality. National Identity and Historical Consciousness in Germany since 1800* (Oxford, Berghahn).

Berger, T. (1996) 'Norms, Identity and National Security in Germany and Japan', in Katzenstein, P. (ed.) *The Culture of National Security: Norms and Identity in World Politics* (New York, NY, Columbia University Press).

Bidder, B. & Schepp, M. (2015) 'Platzeck gegen Merkels Russland-Kurs: "Die Kanzlerin macht einen Fehler"', *Spiegel Online*, 5 June, available at: http://www.spiegel.de/politik/ausland/interview-platzeck-gegen-merkels-russland-kurs-a-1037400.html, accessed 12 January 2016.

Bjola, C. & Kornprobst, M. (2007) 'Security Communities and the Habitus of Restraint: Germany and the United States on Iraq', *Review of International Studies*, 33, 2.

Büschemann, K. H. (2015) 'Der Diplomat', *Süddeutsche Zeitung*, 9 November.

Cordes, E. (2015) 'Mehr Ostpolitik wagen!', 22 October, available at: http://www.ost-ausschuss.de/node/1001, accessed 11 January 2016.

David, M. & Romanova, T. (2015) 'Modernisation in EU–Russian Relations: Past, Present, and Future', *European Politics and Society*, 16, 1.

Dickel, R., Hassanzadeh, E., Henderson, J., Honoré, A., El-Katiri, L., Pirani, S., Rogers, H., Stern, J. & Yafimava, K. (2014) *Reducing European Dependence on Russian Gas: Distinguishing Natural Gas Security from Geopolitics*, OIES Paper 92 (Oxford, Oxford Institute for Energy Studies).

EU & Russia (2010) Joint Statement on the Partnership for Modernisation, EU–Russia Summit, 31 May–1 June, available at: http://www.consilium.europa.eu/uedocs/cms_data/docs/pressdata/en/er/114747.pdf, accessed 2 February 2016.

Forsberg, T. (2016) 'From Ostpolitik to "Frostpolitik"? Merkel, Putin and German Foreign Policy towards Russia', *International Affairs*, 92, 1.

Gel'man, V. (2013) 'Cracks in the Wall. Challenges to Electoral Authoritarianism in Russia', *Problems of Post-Communism*, 60, 2.

Högselius, P. (2013) *Red Gas. Russia and the Origins of European Energy Dependence* (Basingstoke, Palgrave Macmillan).

Jüngerkes, S. (2012) *Diplomaten der Wirtschaft: Die Geschichte des Ost-Ausschusses der Deutschen Wirtschaft* (Fibre, Osnabrück).

Koesel, K. & Bunce, V. (2012) 'Putin, Popular Protests and Political Trajectories in Russia: A Comparative Perspective', *Post-Soviet Affairs*, 28, 4.

Krumm, R. (2012) 'The Rise of Realism: Germany's Perception of Russia from Gorbachev to Medvedev', in Krumm, R., Schröder, H. & Medvedev, S. (eds) *Constructing Identities in Europe: German and Russian Perspectives* (Baden-Baden, Nomos).

Kundnani, H. (2015) *The Paradox of German Power* (Oxford, Oxford University Press).

MacFarquhar, N. (2015) 'In Talks with Merkel, Putin Calls for Improving Relations with Europe', *International New York Times*, 10 May, available at: http://www.nytimes.com/2015/05/11/world/europe/putin-urges-reconciliation-with-europe-in-talks-with-merkel.html?_r=0, accessed 23 February 2016.

Makarychev, A. & Meister, S. (2015) 'The Modernisation Debate and Russian-German Normative Cleavages', *European Politics and Society*, 16, 1.

Matalucci, S. (2015) 'Gazprom Signs Deals with E.ON, OMV, Shell for New Pipeline to Germany', *Natural Gas Europe*, 18 June, available at: http://www.naturalgaseurope.com/gazprom-signs-deals-with-e.on-omv-shell-for-new-pipe-to-germany-24262, accessed 12 January 2016.

McGuinness, D. (2015) 'Merkel and Putin: A Grudging Relationship', *BBC News*, 21 August, available at: http://www.bbc.com/news/world-europe-34009581, accessed 12 January 2016.

Meister, S. (2012) *An Alienated Partnership: German–Russian Relations after Putin's Return*, FIIA Briefing Paper 105 (Helsinki, Finnish Institute of International Affairs).

Meister, S. (2015) 'Politics Trump Economics', *IP Journal*, 5 February, available at: https://zeitschrift-ip.dgap.org/en/ip-journal/topics/politics-trump-economics, accessed 12 January 2016.

Merkel, A. (2015) 'Pressekonferenz von Bundeskanzlerin Merkel und Staatspräsident Putin am 10. Mai 2015 in Moskau', 10 May, available at: http://www.bundesregierung.de/Content/DE/Mitschrift/Pressekonferenzen/2015/05/2015-05-10-pk-merkel-putin.html, accessed 12 January 2016.

Reiermann, C. (2014) 'Fighting Words: Schäuble Says Putin's Crimea Plans Reminiscent of Hitler', *Spiegel Online*, 31 March, available at: http://www.spiegel.de/international/germany/schaeuble-compares-putin-moves-in-crimea-to-policies-of-hitler-a-961696.html, accessed 12 January 2016.

Risse, T. (2007) 'Deutsche Identität und Aussenpolitik', in Schmidt, S., Hellmann, G. & Wolf, R. (eds) *Handbuch zur deutschen Aussenpolitik* (Wiesbaden, Verlag für Sozialwissenschaften).

Sakwa, R. (2015) *Frontline Ukraine: Crisis in the Borderlands* (London, I. B. Tauris).

Schildt, A. (2003) 'Mending Fences: The Federal Republic of Germany and Eastern Europe', in Mühle, E. (ed.) *Germany and the European East in the Twentieth Century* (Oxford & New York, NY, Berg).

Siddi, M. (2015) *The EU–Russia Gas Relationship: New Projects, New Disputes?, FIIA Briefing Paper 183* (Helsinki, Finnish Institute of International Affairs).

Steinhauser, G. (2015) 'Germany's Merkel Defends Russian Gas Pipeline Plan', *The Wall Street Journal*, 18 December, available at: http://www.wsj.com/articles/germanys-merkel-defends-russian-gas-pipeline-plan-1450447499, accessed 4 February 2016.

Steinmeier, F. (2007) 'Verflechtung und Integration: Die neue Phase der Ostpolitik der EU', *Internationale Politik*, 1 March, available at: https://zeitschrift-ip.dgap.org/de/ip-die-zeitschrift/archiv/jahrgang-2007/maerz/verflechtung-und-integration, accessed 12 January 2016.

Steinmeier, F. (2015a) 'Speech by Foreign Minister Frank-Walter Steinmeier in Volgograd to Commemorate the End of the Second World War 70 Years Ago', 7 May, available at: http://www.auswaertiges-amt.de/EN/Infoservice/Presse/Reden/2015/150507_Wolgograd.html, accessed 12 January 2016.

Steinmeier, F. (2015b) 'Address to the OSCE Permanent Council', 2 July, available at: http://www.osce.org/pc/168376?download=true, accessed 12 January 2016.

Szabo, S. (2015) *Germany, Russia and the Rise of Geo-Economics* (London, Bloomsbury).

Vestring, B. (2014) 'For Steinmeier, the End of Ostpolitik', *Internationale Politik*, 12 March.

Von Steinsdorff, S. (2015) 'Zwischen Russlandverstehern und (neuen) Kalten Kriegern—Die Auswirkungen der Ukraine-Krise auf die Wahrnehmung Russlands in der deutschen Öffentlichkeit', *Russland-Analysen*, 300.

Wittlinger, R. (2011) *German National Identity in the Twenty-first Century: A Different Republic After All?* (Basingstoke, Palgrave Macmillan).

Würzer, C. (2013) 'A German Vision of CSDP: "It's Taking Part That Counts"', in Santopinto, F. & Price, M. (eds) *National Visions of EU Defence Policies: Common Denominators and Misunderstandings* (Brussels, Centre for European Policy Studies).

Between Dependence and Integration: Ukraine's Relations With Russia

RILKA DRAGNEVA & KATARYNA WOLCZUK

Abstract

Ukraine's policy towards Russia since independence in 1991 has been characterised by a predicament: how to preserve its statehood in the context of its heavy economic dependence on Russia, which was intent on Ukraine's participation in Russian-led integration projects. In this essay we argue that only by understanding the complexities and seeming contradictions in Ukraine's positioning *vis-à-vis* Russia can a full understanding of Ukraine's commitment to Russia's integration projects be attained. This essay systematically examines Ukraine's responses to Russia's initiatives and illuminates the strategy of the Ukrainian elites to extract economic benefits while minimising commitments.

THE SO-CALLED 'UKRAINE CRISIS' BROUGHT INTO SHARP FOCUS the relationship between Ukraine and Russia. Despite, or rather because of, their historical closeness, relations between the two states have been intermittently acrimonious ever since the collapse of the Soviet Union. The relations were extensively studied during a 'golden era' of academic research on Ukraine's foreign policy in the 1990s and early 2000s, when scholars explored fast moving and intricate developments as Russia and Ukraine sought a *modus vivendi* (Lester 1994; Sherr 1996; Garnett 1997; Kuzio 1998; D'Anieri 1999; Moroney *et al.* 2002; Wolczuk 2003). Interest waned by the mid-2000s, with Ukraine's foreign policy only coming back into focus with the eruption of the Ukraine–Russia crisis in late 2013.

The trigger of the crisis was the Ukrainian leadership's decision to postpone the signing of the free trade agreement with the EU and its acceptance of Russia's economic assistance. Thus, a full account of the causes of the crisis can only be provided by gaining an understanding of Ukrainian domestic politics as well as Ukraine's relations with the EU and Russia, along with the nature of Ukraine's international commitments with regard to these two actors. Too often, however, scholars have opted for a broad geopolitical explanation focussing on Russia's rivalry with the West. For example, for Sakwa:

> Washington … impeded the formation of some substantive Ukrainian–Russian alliance, which would have created a powerful market of some 200 million people and harnessed the dynamism of the two countries to purposes that may not always have served the interests of the Atlantic Alliance. (Sakwa 2014, p. 247)

Research for this essay has been facilitated by two research projects funded by the UK Economic and Social Research Council (ESRC): Grant No: RES-360-25-0096 and Grant No: ES/J013358/1.

In a variation of this, the EU has also been allocated blame for triggering the crisis. The EU–Ukraine free trade agreement is often seen as disruptive as it failed to take into account pre-existing economic ties, regional interdependencies and Ukraine's integration commitments *vis-à-vis* Russia—or, put simply, Russia's interests (Steinmeier 2013; Mearsheimer 2014; Braithwaite 2015; Tsygankov 2015). Such assertions are commonly based on Ukraine's 'pre-existing commitments' in relation to Russia, which the EU purportedly disrupted. However, as this essay argues, this contention is not supported by Ukraine's actual integration commitments, which are of particular interest in the light of Russia's integration agenda. This requires a suitable conceptual apparatus, going beyond the now-dated concept of 'multi-vector policy' (Kuzio 2005; Moshes 2006; Gnedina 2015). Given that Ukraine was confronted with a choice of economic integration with two different actors, namely the EU and Russia, the very nature of those 'integration offers' and Ukraine's engagement with them requires a more nuanced set of analytical tools. A full understanding of Ukraine's integration behaviour *vis-à-vis* Russia can only emerge from delving more deeply into the 'technocratic', legal nuances of their relations, which tended not to make headlines and, yet, which fundamentally contributed to the crisis of late 2013. This essay will explain Ukraine–Russia relations by focussing on why and how Ukraine reacted to, and engaged with, Russia-led projects for regional integration. To understand the why, we draw on Hirschman's seminal work (1980), according to which, first, an asymmetric economic relationship between two states (such as Russia and Ukraine) has political consequences, and second, economic relations influence the way in which governments define their interests, which in turn impacts on the foreign policy of the smaller state (in this case Ukraine). This latter aspect of Hirschman's work, which is much less appreciated, is of particular salience for Ukraine. In the highly asymmetric context with Russia, the Ukrainian incumbent elites defined national interests in terms of the benefits which accrued to them from perpetuating trade and energy dependence on Russia and only offered concessions to Russia in order to avoid the distress caused by the withdrawal of economic benefits.

This essay posits that only by understanding the complexities and seeming contradictions in Ukraine's positioning *vis-à-vis* Russia can a full understanding of Ukraine's commitment to Russia's integration projects be attained. In elaborating the how, we focus on three key episodes in Ukraine–Russia relations in the post-Soviet period. The first period relates to the economic integration projects within the framework of the Commonwealth of Independent States (CIS) in the mid-1990s. The second deals with the first half of the 2000s, during which two integration projects were launched by Russia (the Eurasian Economic Community in 2000 and the Common Economic Space in 2003). The third covers the period 2010–2013 and explores how Ukraine under President Yanukovych engaged with Russia's new Eurasian project launched in 2010. In each section, the discussion centres on the nature of Russia's offer and its exploitation of dependence on the one hand, and how Ukraine's elites engaged, while balancing dependence, sovereignty and commitment, on the other. In this context, relations with the EU will be touched on in order to highlight the extent to which Ukraine sought to engage with Brussels in order to resist Russia's demands.

Our analysis reveals that up to 2014 Ukraine was heavily dependent on Russia, with little done to reduce dependence. Russia exploited this economic dependence in pursuit of its own integration objectives in the post-Soviet space. This resulted in the Ukrainian leadership acting very cautiously when it came to entering into commitments with Russia. Our analysis reveals four key features. First, Ukraine's commitment to integration was highly functional and instrumental, with little interest in pursuing comprehensive and open-ended integration above and beyond seeking specific economic solutions to problems at hand (for example, achieving free trade). Second, driven by the need to balance dependence and sovereignty sensitivities, the Ukrainian elites avoided any open-ended, comprehensive, legally binding commitment to pursue 'deeper' forms of economic integration (such as economic unions). Third, the pattern of commitment was consistent for two decades, peaking at times of economic difficulties and/ or elections in Ukraine, when the political survival of the ruling elites was at stake. Finally, negotiations with Russia were conducted at the highest political level in a non-transparent, *ad hoc* and largely opportunistic engagement, invariably influenced by Russia's evolving integration plans and the Ukrainian elites' short-term political and economic objectives.

Conceptualising Ukraine's relations with Russia

The concepts and insights developed by Hirschman (1980) provide a useful starting point for conceptualising Ukraine's relations with Russia. From the very first days of its independence in 1991, these relations were dominated by a predicament: how to consolidate its independence in the context of an extensive economic dependence on Russia, which regarded Ukraine's independence as an aberration (Lester 1994; Kozakiewicz 1999; Bukkvoll 2001). On the one hand, upholding Ukraine's sovereignty was a key concern for Ukraine's elites, given that it was precarious and challenged (Wolczuk 2003, p. 28). On the other hand, Ukraine's economic interdependence with Russia was exceptionally high. Not only did many of its key industrial outputs emerge from cross-border production processes, but its manufacturing, which was highly energy intensive, was powered almost exclusively by Russian gas. At the same time, while Russia was heavily dependent on Ukraine's gas pipelines to transport hydrocarbons to customers further west, as a smaller, energy-poor state Ukraine's dependence was far greater on Russia with regard to trade and energy than *vice versa* (D'Anieri 1999; Balmaceda 2013).

As Hirschman (1980) has argued, such strong economic dependence has critical political implications. In the first place, for bigger states trade becomes an instrument of national power. Foreign trade not only enhances the potential military power of a country (the supply effect) but also may become a direct source of power in itself (the influence effect) of the larger country (country A) over its smaller partners. The influence effect derives from the fact that:

> the trade conducted between country A, on the one hand, and countries B, C, D, etc. on the other, is worth something to B, C, D etc. and that they would therefore consent to grant A certain advantages— military, political, economic—in order to retain the possibility of trading with A. (Hirschman 1980, pp. 14–5)

Exhibiting the trade asymmetry associated with 'the Hirschman effect', in 2011 Russia accounted for nearly 28% of Ukraine's trade, whereas Ukraine accounted for less than 5% of Russia's trade. Ukraine relied on energy supplies from Russia and, with its hugely inefficient energy use and energy-intensive industries, was one of the largest consumers of Russian gas in the world. Despite being an energy-poor state, Ukraine behaved like an energy-rich state and heavily subsidised gas prices for residential users, meaning that low gas prices were of the utmost importance for the Ukrainian economy and state budget (Balmaceda 2013). Such asymmetry gives the larger country coercive power over the smaller, because 'an interruption of the relationship would cause much greater distress in B than in A' (Abdelal & Kirshner 1999, p. 120). Furthermore, the economic dependence of Ukraine on Russia was exacerbated by Ukraine's unreformed economy and outdated technological capacity (especially with regard to more value-added goods, such as machinery), which made it difficult for Ukraine to capture other markets, including the EU's (Gnedina & Sleptsova 2012).

Hirschman's work helps explain how asymmetric economic relations result in larger states accruing political benefits: they can use economic means to advance their political goals *vis-à-vis* smaller states, something which 'makes the pursuit of power a relatively easy task' (Hirschman 1980, p. vi). Indeed, the history of post-Soviet regional economic integration provides abundant evidence of Russia's linkage of market access with energy supply, labour migration, provision of finance or other issues outside the scope of the integration projects. Notably, the provision of benefits to smaller countries have also depended on them agreeing to station military bases or cede control over strategic assets, such as energy transportation infrastructure (Gould-Davies 2016). In line with Keohane and Nye, we refer to this propensity as the linkage strategy (2000, pp. 25–6). We also note that Russia's linkage strategy with regard to Ukraine increased under President Putin. Russia's foreign policy, both in the near abroad and globally, was aimed at reclaiming its 'great power' status in the international arena (Lo 2015). Ukraine's participation in the Russia-led economic bloc formed an integral part of this plan (Dragneva & Wolczuk 2013, 2015a), reflecting Ukraine's pivotal geopolitical location (Kapusniak 2008, pp. 41–8).

The second powerful insight (less appreciated, but more significant in the case of Ukraine) provided by Hirschman relates to the way that economic dependence shapes domestic developments in the smaller state (country B). Dependence resulting from asymmetries in economic relationships shapes the preferences of smaller states: their very notion of 'national interest' is defined by economic dependence. Therefore, the difficulty for country B of dispensing with trade relations with A depends on several factors, the most salient being the strength of the vested interests which A has created by its trade with B (Hirschman 1980, p. 28). The smaller state's interests converge toward those of the dominant state, thanks to the incentives offered by the latter. As a result, economic dependence can have a profound and lasting effect: 'the pattern of economic relations, especially during periods of political transition when national interests are most malleable, will have a formative influence on their trajectories' (Abdelal & Kirshner 1999, p. 122).

In order to fully understand Ukraine's relations with Russia, we argue that it is pivotal to understand the key role and interests of Ukraine's political and economic elites. Many other studies of Ukraine attribute domestic and foreign policy outcomes to narrow elite preferences (Puglisi 2003, 2008; Bukkvoll 2004; Gnedina & Sleptsova 2012; Shumylo-Tapiola 2012). As in other post-Soviet states, the presidency, which was the locus of power in post-Soviet Ukraine (Wolczuk 2002), was the key institution for representing the interests of oligarchs— the powerful business tycoons who emerged in Ukraine in the 1990s. The Ukrainian presidents managed relations with Russia with a view to securing the economic benefits specifically sought by the oligarchs (such as access to the Russian market and lower energy prices for Ukraine's energy-intensive industries), who in return facilitated the political survival of the successive presidents.

As Åslund argues, for most of its independent existence, Ukraine's distorted economy was defined by a partial reform equilibrium, whereby the winners of early reform sought to preserve its features and block further modernisation, continuing to generate significant gains while imposing high costs on the population as a whole (Åslund 2009). The elites' management of dependence was critical in maintaining this equilibrium: market access and cheap energy resources, in particular, served to reduce the pressure for domestic reforms. Trade, and especially energy imports, from Russia were crucially important not only for the national economy but also served as a source of rents for the incumbent elites (Åslund 2009; Balmaceda 2013). The way the elites managed economic dependence on Russia was, in effect, a reform substitution strategy. While the Ukrainian elites lacked the incentives and capacity to embark on comprehensive and sustainable reforms, economic dependence on Russia became a proxy for reform.

At the same time, the lack of domestic reforms made Ukraine vulnerable to any deterioration of economic relations with Russia (Toritsyn & Miller 2002). In essence, the country's economic performance, and hence the elites' political survival, came to depend on the economic partnership with Russia. This also gives important insights as to why, up until 2014, Ukrainian elites took very limited steps to reduce the trade and energy dependence on Russia, despite distrusting Russia's intentions. In such a context domestic weakness increased the vulnerability to external demands. As noted by Sherr:

> the weaker Ukraine internally, the stronger the Russian factor—in internal affairs as well as international relations. For this reason, internal incapacity and external dependence have operated like the blades of a scissor, opening or closing in tandem. (Sherr 2006, p. 11)

This cycle repeated itself over the first two decades of Ukraine's independence. The approach served the interests of the Ukrainian elites relatively well, until President Yanukovych was confronted with its fateful consequences in late 2013.

Thus, Hirschman's framework helps to understand the influence that the larger state exerts over the smaller state and why a smaller dependent country is disinclined to rupture economic ties. Russia sought to use this dependence to entice Ukraine to join the Russia-led integration bloc. Therefore it is highly pertinent to explore how the smaller, dependent country reacts to the far-reaching political demands of the larger state. Admittedly, this is not a simple task—understanding the notion of integration commitments requires a venture into the specialised yet complex world of international law and its growing overlap with international relations and comparative studies of regional trade structures (Raustiala 2005; Duina & Morano-Foadi 2011). It is certainly known that there are different forms and stages on a continuum from economic cooperation to integration, involving different degrees of harmonisation of economic activity (from agreements on trade tariffs to ones dealing with complex regulatory issues such as, for example, phyto-sanitary control). It is less understood, however, that countries engage through different types of international commitments: not just bilateral or multilateral, but also commitments of a different kind of scope, precision and degree to which they bind signatory states. As a rule, free trade agreements entail a lower type of commitment than customs union and economic unions, but these forms/stages are often mixed and/or 'packaged' in various ways in legal agreements.

Given that economic integration choices and commitments are at the heart of the Ukrainian crisis, this suggests a fruitful avenue for exploration. The crisis of late 2013 can only be explained by focussing on the 'technocratic', legal nuances of Ukraine–Russia relations. With their unmistakable geopolitical underpinnings, international treaties are a key structural element of international relations (Chayes & Chayes 1993). Furthermore, as we argue in this essay, regardless of the reservations one may hold about the formality or limited relevance of legal commitments in the post-Soviet world, they provide a remarkably clear picture of Ukraine's preferences in response to Russia's objectives. Therefore, in the next empirical section we scrutinise Ukraine's integration behaviour since independence.

Ukraine's integration behaviour vis-à-vis *Russia (1992–2014)*

Reintegration within the CIS (1993–1995)

This first period focusses on the aftermath of the disintegration of the USSR, characterised by the pre-occupation with the search for a new legal framework for interactions between the former Soviet republics and Russia's first modest attempts at reintegration.

Initially, Russia proposed a new type of Union based around the Ukraine–Russia tandem, but Ukraine only agreed to the loose format of the CIS (Walker 2003) albeit very reluctantly. Ukraine clearly tried to balance its newly won sovereignty and independence with preserving economic ties with Russia in order to ensure its economic viability as a new state. Ukraine was a recalcitrant participant at best, only agreeing to engage with the CIS framework insofar as it did not threaten its sovereignty (Wolczuk 2003, 2007). For example, Kyiv refused to participate in the CIS Inter-Parliamentary Assembly agreed upon in March 1992 or in the Economic Court of the CIS set up a few months later; it also withdrew from signing the Charter of the CIS in January 1993. The Charter defined the notion of 'membership'; so declining to sign it sent a strong message regarding the limits of Ukraine's participation in the CIS (Wolczuk 2003).

Wary of contributing to the emergence of a strong CIS, the Ukrainian authorities prioritised bilateral relations with Russia. In June 1993 a bilateral free trade agreement was signed. This was a basic agreement to move relations from the system of planned deliveries to market principles and halt the decline in bilateral trade. Yet it was also a weak and patchy one, providing for limited trade liberalisation, (for example, exemptions to trade were defined in annual bilateral protocols) and containing no disciplines for breaches of its provisions (Dragneva & de Kort 2007). Ironically, given the weakness of the multilateral CIS framework in constraining Russia's hegemonic position in the 'near abroad', Ukraine was left more vulnerable to Russia's superior bargaining power in a bilateral context, as predicted by Hirschman.

The CIS Economic Union of 1993

While at first Russia's agenda for the CIS was modest, by 1993 President Yel'tsin sought to bolster Russia's position as a centripetal force for post-Soviet reintegration, developing plans for setting up a CIS economic union. A framework treaty was promptly signed in September 1993, to be followed by specific implementation agreements. The project envisaged EU-like economic integration, progressing from a free trade area to 'deep' economic integration, and sought to strengthen the institutional structure of the CIS. A dedicated regulatory body, the Inter-State Economic Commission, was planned, which entailed some supranational delegation (Dragneva & Wolczuk 2015a). However, Ukraine's room for manoeuvre was limited: while President Kravchuk of Ukraine favoured a pro-Western orientation, the Ukrainian elites lacked the single-mindedness and sound domestic policies to achieve this reorientation. With the country engulfed in a deepening economic crisis and rising popular discontent, including a miners' strike in Eastern Ukraine in 1993, improving relations with Russia acquired political urgency.

Facing domestic upheaval, Kravchuk committed to the CIS Economic Union by signing the joint declaration in May 1993 and participated in drafting its framework treaty. In the end, however, he agreed only on associated membership. The terms of this association were only clarified in April 1994, when a special agreement was signed with the Economic Union's founding members. Yet ironically this agreement never came into force as it was not ratified by most of the CIS countries, including Ukraine. As a result, Ukraine stayed out of what was viewed as a potentially open-ended commitment with some loss of sovereignty, preferring instead to sign selectively the specific implementing agreements within the Economic Union package (Dragneva & Dimitrova 2007). Concluding narrow, functional agreements to secure free trade in the post-Soviet space became a long-standing preference of Ukraine.

The CIS Customs Union of 1995

The CIS framework—involving 12 post-Soviet states with very different expectations— was, however, unwieldy and ultimately too costly for Russia. As a more feasible alternative, Moscow shifted its focus to a smaller and more committed group of states which could spearhead integration. To this end, Russia signed an agreement on a customs union with Belarus and Kazakhstan in January 1995, later joined by Kyrgyzstan and Tajikistan. Ukraine's participation in this project was perceived as crucial if it was to be a meaningful international body. Therefore, in addition to political persuasion, the Russian leadership used clear economic pressure to persuade the Ukrainian leaders to accede. Russia imposed excise duties on oil and gas imports, which were to remain in place until Ukraine joined the Customs Union, thus raising the cost of staying outside (Balmaceda 1998). This marked the Kremlin's emerging propensity to link energy and trade with achieving its aims in Ukraine, as predicted by Hirschman's influence affect, whereby economic dependence allows the larger state to pursue its own political objectives *vis-à-vis* the smaller, dependent state.

In 1994 President Kuchma came to power on a pro-Russian platform and decried the Ukrainian nationalism which ignored economic realities (Wolczuk 1997). However, while Kuchma persisted with a selective approach to agreements with Russia, during his two terms (1994–2004), he also perfected Ukraine's integration 'game' with Russia, aimed at maximising the benefits and minimising the commitments. Like his predecessor, Kuchma engaged in a dialogue on the CIS customs union, only to eschew participation in the new initiative. In line with the preferences of Kuchma's political and economic backers, namely regional elites in eastern and southern Ukraine (Bukkvoll 2004), Ukraine was concerned about achieving free trade with Russia/CIS but no more than that. The leadership was unclear if free trade would result from the new initiative, as the process was found to be driven by a top-down and hasty dynamic rather than attention to economic detail (Brzezinski & Sullivan 1997, p. 280), and Kuchma pulled back. Interested in the specified economic benefits and suspicious of the credibility of Russia's new promises, the President asked for the full implementation of the commitments already undertaken, such as the 1993 bilateral free trade agreement, before engaging in further integration steps.

However, the economic cost of staying outside was growing for Ukraine. In the late 1990s a build-up of protectionist measures led to trade wars between Ukraine and Russia. Ukraine complained about Russia's discriminatory and protectionist trade policy, the unpredictability of restrictions imposed and the manipulation of physical barriers, such as customs procedures, which were introduced on the demands of various Russian lobbies.[1] An attempt was made to resolve these accumulated problems in the context of a renewed attempt for a CIS-wide free trade agreement in April 1999, which Ukraine joined.[2] Ukraine's expectations were dashed as Russia refused to ratify it, as it did in the case of its 1994 predecessor. Instead, Russia preferred to deal with trade issues on a case-by-case basis in bilateral relations, something which provided the opportunity to link any trade-related concession to its own objectives. However, during the first ten years of Ukrainian independence Russia still lacked a coordinated political strategy *vis-à-vis* Ukraine (Bukkvoll 2001). This would change with the coming to power of Vladimir Putin, who would engage in issue-linkage in a more explicit and determined way.

Between 1993 and 1995, Ukraine's integration behaviour followed a very clear pattern: standing aside from Russia's open-ended, comprehensive integration projects but engaging in minimalist and flexible frameworks through bilateral and narrow-scope multilateral free trade agreements (mainly FTAs). However, Ukraine failed to achieve free trade because Russia was only ready to grant it as a stepping stone towards 'deeper' integration.

Seeking a modus operandi *during Putin's first presidency (2000–2004)*

Putin's first presidential term in 2000 led to a major upgrade of Russia's strategy towards Ukraine, backed by an enhanced capacity to implement it. In a clear demonstration of Hirschman's theory, the economic costs of supporting the states in the 'near abroad' became directly linked to the realisation of Russian foreign policy objectives. After the half-hearted and unsuccessful attempts to attract Ukraine in the 1990s, the new Russian leadership switched to a more 'pragmatic' approach by adopting explicit economic conditionality, namely stressing the economic benefits of integration bestowed onto the states willing to engage in 'deeper' integration. This way, multiple dependencies such as energy, trade, credits and labour migration became instruments for the reintegration of the post-Soviet space.

Russia's interest in integration intensified at a time when the Ukrainian authorities' domestic and external standing was at a low, making the Ukrainian leadership more reliant on Russia's support than in the 1990s. President Kuchma was facing a crisis at home in the aftermath of the Gongadze scandal of 2000–2001, when he was implicated in the murder of an opposition journalist. His standing was further compromised by the Kolchuga affair (in which he was implicated in the selling of radar systems to Iraq, thereby breaching the international embargo which was in place). This culminated in Kuchma's international isolation, as exemplified at the NATO summit in December 2002, to which he was not invited (but which he attended nevertheless). At the same time, economic reforms were largely abandoned following the ousting of the reformist government in 2001, something which further alienated Kuchma

---

[1]'Ukraine Finds Russia an Unreliable Partner', *Jamestown Monitor*, 15 November 1995, available at: http://www.jamestown.org/single/?tx_ttnews%5Btt_news%5D=9409&tx_ttnews%5BbackPid%5D=209&no_cache=1#.VuAqOf7cuA4, accessed 16 March 2016.

[2]Notably, and unlike the previous 1994 FTA project, the 1999 accord did not refer to free trade as a transitional step to deeper economic integration (Dragneva & de Kort 2007).

from the Western states and institutions (Toritsyn & Miller 2002). As a result he cautiously turned to Russia.

The Eurasian Economic Community (2001–2002)

The Eurasian Economic Community (EEC, or *Evrazes*) was the first major regional integration initiative launched by newly-elected President Putin. It represented a noteworthy shift in Russia's foreign policy, aimed at re-establishing Russia's place as a 'great power' in the international system (Lo 2002; Sherr 2002). The EEC comprised Russia, Belarus, Kazakhstan, Kyrgyzstan and Tajikistan. The institutional design of the EEC eradicated some of the problems plaguing the CIS by precluding a 'pick and mix' approach to integration. Russia's position in the new regime was strengthened institutionally, with the voting rules of its key body, the Integration Committee, giving it a decisive voice (Dragneva 2013).

For Russia, Ukraine's participation in the project was of great importance and this goal was pursued in a much more coherent and purposeful way in comparison to previous initiatives. For example, in various meetings and communications, Putin offered strong political support to the embattled Ukrainian President, for example by offering him the chairmanship of the CIS Council of Heads of State in 2003, even though Ukraine was not a full member of the CIS. Explicit economic conditionality was also deployed to incentivise Ukraine by offering to remove costly exemptions from its free trade with Russia and resolve standing anti-dumping and taxation disputes upon its membership. The benefits for Ukraine of such concessions were estimated at \$400–450 million.[3] Furthermore, Russia made clear that gas prices would be higher to the countries remaining outside the new grouping (Donaldson & Nogee 2009).

This combination of sticks and carrots led Kuchma to participate in Russia's regional plans. In March 2002, he declared Ukraine's interest in becoming an observer in the EEC, a decision which was finalised at a meeting with Putin in May 2002. In doing so, Kuchma hoped to secure specific economic benefits and boost his domestic popularity, while avoiding a general commitment to join Russia-led integration projects. Mindful of Russia's dominant position and far-reaching objectives, Kuchma signed up to nothing more than associated membership—a position with no formal definition or clear commitments. Perhaps reflecting the prevailing ambiguity when it came to integration, Kuchma used the terms CIS Economic Union, CIS Customs Union, CIS Free Trade Zone and EEC interchangeably.[4]

Common Economic Space (2003–2004)

As Ukraine's decision on the EEC fell short of the Kremlin's expectations, it soon proposed a new initiative. The plan for a new economic organisation of Russia, Kazakhstan, Belarus and Ukraine was announced in February 2003. The aim was to create a common economic space, overseen by a common regulatory body with supranational features. For Russia, this was a path to 'deep' economic integration, including a currency union (Kembayev 2009), modelled on the European single market (Dragneva & Wolczuk 2015a).

---

[3]'Sovmestnaya press-konferetsiya c Prezidentom Ukrainy Leonidom Kuchmoi', The Kremlin, 17 May 2002, available at: http://kremlin.ru/transcripts/21598, accessed 16 March 2016.

[4]'Kuchma—A CIS Integrator?', *Jamestown Monitor*, 20 March 2002, available at: http://www.jamestown.org/single/?tx_ttnews%5Btt_news%5D=24018&tx_ttnews%5BbackPid%5D=216&no_cache=1#.VuAzLf7cuA4, accessed 16 March 2016.

In Ukraine these proposals triggered a heated domestic debate, both within the political elites and the expert community.[5] Questions were raised over the potential consequences for Ukraine's independence (Silina 2003). With its vague objectives, accession to the Common Economic Space (CES) was seen as an open-ended commitment to reintegration with Russia. As Russia made free trade concessions dependent on Ukraine's commitment to deeper integration, which required pooling of sovereignty, this conditionality triggered concerns over ceding Ukraine's sovereignty, and thereby violating its 1996 Constitution, which explicitly prohibited this.

There were considerable differences in preferences. For the Ukrainian leadership the CES was a means of securing free trade with its partners and dealing with the pressing issues of trade exemptions and penalties, all of vital importance to Kuchma's oligarchic backers.[6] However, the oligarchs themselves disagreed on the risks of gaining access to free trade in exchange for a loss of 'economic sovereignty' (Bukkvoll 2004). More broadly, questions were raised about the consequences of participation in the CES for Ukraine's 'European vector' and its planned entry into the World Trade Organization. At this point participation would not violate any of Ukraine's commitments to the EU (see below). However, it was noted that CES membership would jeopardise future integration prospects, subject to Ukraine's lobbying with the EU at the time.[7] The CES was depicted as a 'return to the USSR' and relegation to 'the second division of Europe' by Roman Shpek, Ukraine's representative to the EU (Poliakova 2003).

However, domestic developments compelled the leadership to accept the invitation. Following the Gongadze affair, Kuchma's popularity was at rock bottom and, despite the formidable accumulation of formal and informal powers, Kuchma and his oligarchic backers were fearful of being ejected from power (D'Anieri 2006). In the 2002 parliamentary elections, the opposition 'Our Ukraine' bloc emerged as the most popular party, making it more difficult for the president to control the legislature. Demand for change was growing within the country and, with Kuchma approaching the end of his second term, the incumbent elites faced the uncertainty of the presidential contest in 2004. This vulnerability prompted Kuchma to enlist Russian support (Wilson 2005), and in exchange Kuchma agreed to show a greater readiness to accommodate Russia's demands, namely to participate in the newly proposed CES. He signed the joint declaration on the CES in February 2003, leading to a founding agreement in September 2003 which was ratified by the Rada in April 2004, just six months before the presidential elections. Ostracised in the West and faced with domestic uncertainties, the Ukrainian incumbent leadership was prepared to offer greater concessions in order to secure Russia's economic and political support and thereby ensure its political survival. This is evidenced in the manner in which the CES agreement was concluded. The process was led by Kuchma's special envoy, Deputy Prime Minister Azarov, known for his pro-Russian leanings, in an expedited process violating government procedure and alienating political

---

[5]For example, see Center for Peace, Conversion and Foreign Policy of Ukraine, Experts' evaluation on the Draft Agreement on the Single Economic Space, in *Ukrainian Monitor*, Policy Paper #13, September 2003. A study on Ukraine's Eurasian vector conducted by the Razumkov Centre was also reported in 'Ukraina-Evrazes: Nablyudenie? Sotrudnichestvo? Integratsiya?', *Zerkalo Nedeli*, 27 December 2002.

[6]See, 'Obsuzhdenie EEP v parlamente (stenogramma zasedaniya)', 16 September 2003, minutes available at: http://www.pravda.com.ua/rus/news/2003/09/16/4374340, accessed 9 March 2013.

[7]*Janes' Foreign Report*, 6 March 2003; *Oxford Analytica East Europe Daily Brief*, 13 June 2003.

opposition (Silina 2003, 2004). These violations caused ructions, resulting, for example, in the resignation of the Minister for the Economy, Valeriy Khoroshkovskyi.

In Bukkvoll's view (2004), the decision to sign up to Russia's project was primarily driven by the narrow political motivation of the Ukrainian leadership, rather than the balanced consideration of Ukraine's national interests, and it went against the spirit of public discussion in Ukraine at the time. But the incumbent elites were strongly interested in securing the election of Kuchma's anointed successor, Viktor Yanukovych. In return for lending support, the Kremlin wanted the CES deal finalised before the elections.

Nevertheless, Kuchma remained wary and signed up only to a framework agreement, which incorporated the principle of multi-level and multi-speed integration, which minimised the loss of sovereignty and allowed him (and his successor) to retain considerable flexibility and room for manoeuvre (Khokhotva 2003). Critically, Kuchma signed the agreement with an important reservation: subject to Ukraine's participation not contravening the country's 1996 Constitution. The leadership stressed that, despite signing a general framework agreement, Ukraine's actual commitment to future integration steps would be dependent on the free trade area being actually put in place (Bukkvoll 2004). Crucially, participation in CES was deemed compatible with Ukraine's 'European choice', as proclaimed by Azarov himself.[8]

The Ukrainian leader sought the economic benefits of lower trade barriers with Russia, remaining wary of committing beyond a free trade area. Nevertheless, Ukraine's more intensive engagement in the CES of 2003 (in comparison to that with the EEC in 2002) demonstrated that the Kremlin's linkage strategy—economic benefits for integration—was most effective, at a time when the political survival of the elites depended on Russia's economic and political support. The political calculus of the elites led them to adopt decisions on an *ad hoc* basis, without undertaking a transparent benefits analysis of pursing integration along different vectors or an overall assessment of the legal compatibility of simultaneous integration with the EU and CES (something which persisted until the next period, 2010–2013).[9]

However, even though embattled domestically, the Ukrainian leadership drew a fine line between 'strategic partnership' and integration with Russia, particularly in light of a renewed challenge to Ukraine's territorial integrity by Russia. In late 2003, Russia started building a dam by the Ukrainian island of Tuzla in the Kerch Straits, which was located within Ukrainian territorial waters in the Azov Sea (Woronowycz 2003). Russia appeared to be using the border issue in order to cement Ukraine's participation in the CES. As a result, the ratification of the CES agreement became part of a 'package' with two other agreements on borders, which delineated the terms of control over the Azov Sea and the Kerch Straits. While such a 'package' nominally secured Ukraine's engagement in the project, it once again impressed upon the Ukrainian political elite the threat presented by Russia. Confronted with this explicit disregard of Ukraine's territorial integrity, Kuchma announced that Ukraine had not made a firm commitment to integration and that future steps would be premised on the creation of a functioning free trade area (Bukkvoll 2004, p. 14).

---

[8]'Obsuzhdenie EEP v parlamente (stenogramma zasedaniya)', 16 September 2003, minutes available at: http://www.pravda.com.ua/rus/news/2003/09/16/4374340, accessed 9 March 2013.

[9]One of the very few cost–benefit analyses was undertaken in the report, 'Ukraine–EU on the Road to 4 Freedoms', 2003, Analytical Report ordered by the Ministry of Economy and European Integration of Ukraine, AHT Consulting Group (Kyiv), June.

The Eurasian project and Yanukovych's presidency (2010–2013)

The Orange Revolution of 2004 and the subsequent election of Viktor Yushchenko as President in 2005 represented a watershed in Ukraine–Russia relations. Up until that point, the incumbents' favourable disposition towards Russia could be relied on by Moscow: although they tended to be unwilling to comply fully with Russia's integration agenda, they did not dismiss Russian demands outright. However, following the Orange Revolution, the new Ukrainian leadership turned the country westward, explicitly looking for much closer relations with the EU through binding commitments leading to open-ended, comprehensive integration. While in the late 1990s, Kuchma had proclaimed EU membership as a strategic objective for Ukraine,[10] with little done beyond the proclamation, the intent of Yushchenko was notably more pronounced. This triggered a persistent demand for a new bilateral framework on the part of Ukraine commensurate with its membership aspirations (Zlenko 2002). Following the Orange Revolution, the EU acquiesced to Ukraine's demand for a new legal framework, albeit denying Ukraine a membership perspective (Dragneva & Wolczuk 2014, 2015b). The negotiations on the Association Agreement started in 2007, whereas the negotiations on the economic part of the agreement—which became known as the Deep and Comprehensive Free Trade Area (DCFTA)—were launched after Ukraine's accession to the World Trade Organization in 2008. Ironically, however, while Ukraine was a *demandeur* in relations with the EU, asking for 'deep' integration up to and including membership, its elites were unwilling to pay the high economic cost of moving away from Russia.

Yet the 'Orange elites' did little to prepare the economy for the consequences of reorientation through reform, with dependence on Russia actually growing in the late 2000s. At the same time, while Ukraine's exports to Russia increased, Russia did not deliver on its promise of free trade, continuing various *ad hoc* restrictions. In addition, Russia became more resolved to play the 'energy card' *vis-à-vis* Ukraine by attempting to raise gas prices almost five-fold following the Orange Revolution (Pirani 2012, p. 176). This triggered the first 'gas war' of 2006. A second gas war followed in 2009, in which Ukraine's vulnerability was exposed, resulting in a controversial and unfavourable gas contract with Ukraine (Balmaceda 2013). Because of a pricing formula linking gas to oil prices, by 2010 Ukraine was paying about 10% more than countries like Germany and Italy, something it could ill-afford; in the wake of the global financial crisis Ukraine's GDP had shrunk by 15% in 2009.

The economic crisis turned out to be a double-edged sword for Yanukovych's political fortunes. It facilitated his comeback in the presidential race of 2010, when his campaign was based on the promise of pulling the economy out of the crisis caused by the ineptitude of the Orange leadership, but at the same time his fate was dependent on economic recovery. The economic crisis reshaped the priorities of the newly elected authorities as, by 2009, the strategic outlook of the oligarchs shifted from investment and expansion to survival. Yanukovych reaffirmed integration with the EU as the strategic choice of Ukraine and continued with concluding negotiations on the Association Agreement (Yanukovych 2010). Yet, being premised on long-term modernisation, European integration did not offer an instant solution to Ukraine's accumulated problems (Delcour & Wolczuk 2013). Therefore, integration with the EU became a kind of luxury—desirable in the long-term but not an immediate priority (Gnedina & Sleptsova 2012). Moreover, in response to Yanukovych's authoritarian tendencies

[10]'On Approval of the Strategy of Ukraine's integration into the European Union', Decree of the President of Ukraine, No. 615, 11 June 1998.

and application of selective justice to political opponents, namely the imprisonment of key opposition figures such as Yulia Tymoshenko, the EU made the signing of the Association Agreement conditional upon democratic reforms in Ukraine.

Russia was seen as a solution to Ukraine's problems by Yanukovych and he set out to recalibrate relations with Moscow to help kick start the Ukrainian economy after the collapse of 2009. At the top of his political agenda was the restoration of the profitability of oligarchic enterprises through access to the Russian market and, especially, reduced gas prices. Immediately, Yanukovych sought to capitalise on Ukraine's geopolitical importance for Russia by making strategic geopolitical concessions in exchange for economic benefits (Sherr 2010). One of his first steps was to sign the 'Kharkiv Accords' in April 2010 which extended the lease of the Sevastopol naval base to the Russian Black Sea Fleet in exchange for a 30% discount on the 2009 pricing formula for gas. Despite the agreement Ukraine could still hardly afford to pay the price, which reached about $425 per thousand cubic metres (tcm) by 2013, an eight-fold increase since 2005.

The Customs Union membership offer (2011)

Recognising Ukraine's predicament, Russia made a renewed and extensive integration offer to Ukraine. As negotiations on the EU–Ukraine Association Agreement drew to a close, in 2011 the Russian leadership invited Ukraine to join the newly formed Customs Union between Belarus, Kazakhstan and Russia. This was an ambitious reintegration scheme, to be supported by a common regulatory space developed in conjunction with Russia's accession to the World Trade Organization. The deep and advanced nature of the integration was fixed *a priori*: the Customs Union was 'programmed' to evolve into a Single Economic Space (SES) in 2012 and, ultimately, into the Eurasian Economic Union (EEU) by 2015. Unlike all previous post-Soviet integration initiatives, this was to be a binding regime which did not allow flexible or partial commitment, and which entailed the delegation of significant regulatory powers to a supranational Commission (Dragneva 2013).

Ukraine's participation was vital for the project and, to this end, Russia tailored its incentives to play on Ukraine's dependency and offered not only free trade but also a marked reduction in gas prices (from $425 to $268 per tcm) if Ukraine joined the Eurasian project (EDB 2012). There is little doubt that Russia sought to appeal to Ukraine's rent-seeking elites: according to Åslund (2014), during Yanukovych's presidency the regime extracted rents of approximately $3 billion per year. In essence, sustaining energy and trade interdependence was a vital substitute for much needed domestic reform.

In contrast to the previous integration offers, the invitation to join the EEU was accompanied by a concerted campaign to demonstrate the advantages of this option as opposed to the European orientation. The campaign triggered extensive debates in Ukraine, which exposed the weakness of Russia's attraction as a pole of integration: its governance record hardly offered a solution to Ukraine's accumulated problems (Razumkov Centre 2013). The overall view was that joining the EEU was detrimental to Ukraine's national interests.[11] Yanukovych's position on membership reflected this domestic consensus: 'Ukraine has made its choice. It has entered the WTO and develops in line with the principles of this organisation. That is why joining the Customs Union is now impossible' (Solov'ev & Sidorenko 2010).

[11]For a more detailed discussion see Dragneva and Wolczuk (2015b, pp. 71–3).

Nevertheless, mindful of Ukraine's dependence, Yanukovych hoped to pursue a 'third way' by proclaiming a 'strategic economic partnership' with Russia, rather than full membership in Russia's integration project. The Ukrainian leadership proposed a '3+1' format (namely Russia, Belarus, Kazakhstan plus Ukraine) that would allow Ukraine to derive the benefits of improved trade terms with the Customs Union but without entering into the binding commitments resulting from membership. This was in the pragmatic and selective spirit of Ukraine's previous pattern of engagement with Russia's initiatives. Yet, on this occasion Ukraine's proposal was rejected swiftly because Russia wanted greater legal commitment in exchange for the specific economic benefits sought by Ukraine.

Ukraine's price for free trade

Since 1991, free trade with Russia had remained an elusive goal for Ukraine. Ukrainians hoped that, at last, it could be secured *via* the new CIS-wide FTA after two earlier attempts had failed (in 1994 and 1999). The economic crisis of 2008–2009 meant that the Ukrainian leadership and oligarchs were particularly sensitive to the recurring, unpredictable restrictions on trade with Russia and hence were looking for a legal framework curbing Russia's use of *ad hoc* protectionist measures. Thus, the leadership participated readily in the negotiations on the agreement, which was concluded in 2011 and signed by Ukraine in October. The focus of the CIS FTA was exclusively on trade issues, something which suited Ukraine well, particularly as it allowed Ukraine to pursue integration with the EU as the free trade area agreement was deemed compatible with EU DCFTA (Silina 2011). The fact that they initialled the DCFTA before ratifying the CIS FTA testifies to its importance to the Ukrainian elite.

However, from the Russian perspective, the offer of a CIS FTA was not intended to liberalise trade. It was in fact part of the broader strategy to draw Ukraine into the Customs Union. It was ironic therefore that the FTA concealed a 'trap' for the Ukrainian negotiators in the form of Annex 6, which in a highly asymmetrical way allowed Russia to raise tariffs in the case of increased volumes of Ukraine's imports.[12] The Annex made vague provisions about the preconditions and the process of activating it, allowing self-serving interpretations by Russia. Thus, Ukraine derived relatively few benefits from the new agreement but became vulnerable to the general threat stemming from Annex 6 (Dragneva & Wolczuk 2014).

Ukraine's search for a 'third way' with the EEU (2013)

Overall, by 2013 the Ukrainian leadership failed to achieve its goals of free trade or lower energy prices, as Russia offered these benefits only as part of the enticement to join the Eurasian integration bloc. In the spring of 2013, the Ukrainian leadership once again proposed vague cooperation formulas, resulting in the agreement to become an observer in the Eurasian project, embodied in a non-binding and succinct Memorandum for Cooperation between

---

[12]Annex 6 envisaged the unilateral right of the Customs Union member states to revert to less favourable tariffs, namely the Most Favoured Nation (MFN) regime, if a signatory state in the CIS FTA concluded an agreement with a third party, which resulted in higher volumes of imports from that country to an extent that caused harm or danger of harm to industry. This provision was subsequently used by Russia to punish Ukraine for concluding the Association Agreement. Russia also used this provision to revert to MFN terms with Ukraine in January 2016, even though Russia did not provide credible evidence of harm sustained as a result of the Association Agreement—hardly surprising given that the latter's implementation had not even begun (Dragneva & Wolczuk 2014, 2015c).

Ukraine and the Eurasian Economic Commission of May 2013.[13] Formally, Ukraine's commitment did not go beyond observer status, much in line with the long-standing pattern of avoiding commitment or a loss of sovereignty. But it was clearly part of the 'integration game', in which it sought to engage sufficiently to persuade Russia to fulfil its free trade promise and offer lower energy prices.

This did not satisfy the Kremlin, which was deeply frustrated by Ukraine's tendency to give vague undertakings (Glaz'ev 2011). To demonstrate Ukraine's vulnerability, Russia triggered a trade war in the summer of 2013, whereby Ukrainian exports were subjected to lengthy and detailed checks on the Ukrainian–Russian border, causing huge losses for the Ukrainian exporters. Yet even this was not enough to persuade Ukraine to join the Customs Union (Silna 2013).

However, Hirschman's view that 'harassed statesmen generally have a short-run view' would soon be confirmed in the case of Ukraine (Hirschman 1980, p. 27). The economic outlook of the Ukrainian economy deteriorated in the autumn of 2013 as the country slid into recession, and was expected to shrink further in 2014 with high gas prices crippling its unstructured economy. The failure of Yanukovych's presidency to deliver on his electoral promises of economic recovery did not bode well for his chances in the forthcoming presidential elections of 2015.

In the autumn of 2013 Yanukovych indicated his readiness to sign the Association Agreement during the Eastern Partnership summit in Vilnius in November 2013; in turn the EU relaxed its democratic conditionality. In turn Russia relaxed its economic conditionality as it sought to stop Ukraine's integration with the EU. As the Association Agreement was incompatible with membership of the planned EEU (der Loo & Van Elsuwege 2012), Moscow agreed to provide significant economic support for the Ukrainian leadership not to sign the Association Agreement with the EU. This deal was made during Yanukovych's secret meetings with Putin in October–November 2013, with Mykola Azarov, by then Prime Minister, hammering out the details with his Russian counterpart, Dimitrii Medvedev, in December 2013. However, by then the mass protests against Yanukovych's decision had started.

Yanukovych's bail-out and the Vilnius u-turn

Yanukovych 'postponed' the signing of the Association Agreement. In turn, Kyiv received from Russia a $15 billion financial loan, a reduction of gas prices to $268 per tcm and the promise of 'normalisation' of trade (that is, actual implementation of the previous legal commitments by Russia, such as the 2011 CIS FTA). However, reflecting the mistrust of Yanukovych in the Kremlin, these came with stringent conditions. The $15 billion loan was to be disbursed in instalments, enabling Russia to introduce its own conditionality for payment. The lowering of gas prices was discretionary, to be reviewed quarterly. Yanukovych was put on a short leash, which would have curtailed the scope for future 'game playing'. The Kremlin had learnt its lesson: having invested a great deal in the Eurasian project, it was making the full use of economic dependence to ensure Ukraine's participation.

Given their domestic weakness, the political survival of the incumbent elites in Ukraine made them prioritise the immediate deal with Russia over the longer-term benefits of integration

---

[13]'Memorandum ob uglublenii vzaimodeistviya mezhdu Evraziiskoi ekonomicheskoi komissiei i Ukrainoi', 31 May 2013, available at: https://docs.eaeunion.org/docs/ru-ru/0144009/ms_24072013_doc, accessed 19 March 2016.

with the EU. Like the case of the EEC in 2003, the decision to suspend the Association Agreement and accept the Russian offer was taken by a narrow circle of the President's closest associates—without appropriate deliberations with regard to this momentous foreign policy decision. It is noteworthy that the Ukrainian oligarchs, most of which were highly interested in access to the Russian market and lowering of energy prices, remained silent on Ukraine's integration choices. To the wider public, postponing the signing of the Association Agreement was presented as a technical delay on the grounds that it was a costly proposition for Ukraine, in contrast to the more beneficial economic package offered by Russia (Dragneva & Wolczuk 2015b).

The deal with Russia was presented as a success by the Ukrainian authorities, who clearly viewed it as such: Yanukovych had succeeded in extracting considerable benefits from Russia without making an official commitment to join the Eurasian regime. However, by postponing the signing of the Association Agreement, Yanukovych did offer *de facto* a major concession to the Kremlin—he had agreed to reduce Ukraine's relations with the EU to that of a function of Ukraine–Russia relations. As a result, Ukraine's 'European choice' became conditional upon Russia's relations with the EU, which had already been stagnant for some time. No other Ukrainian President had been asked to, or indeed, had had to make a concession on Ukraine's European choice. This is because during Kuchma's presidency (1994–2004), there was no integration 'offer' from the EU; during Yushchenko's presidency (2005–2009) there was no binding integration 'offer' from Russia.

Like his predecessors, Yanukovych sought short-term gains from Russia without actually committing to integration. But the leadership's readiness to mortgage Ukraine's 'European choice' to Russia on a short-term basis in pursuit of his political survival was met with mass protests.[14] Following his flight to Russia, Yanukovych was deposed from power, an event which triggered Russia's intervention in Ukraine, and which in turn represented a fundamental challenge to the European security order.[15]

No doubt, Russia's powerful reaction to the changes in Ukraine stemmed in no small measure from the frustration caused by Kyiv's reluctance since 1991 to reintegrate with Russia, despite repeated attempts and strong dependence. The importance of Ukraine accounted for Russia's readiness to indulge the notorious vacillation of Ukrainian elites in 1991–2004; however, in this later episode, during 2010–2013, lessons had been drawn from previous episodes and the use of dependence based on the linkage strategy aimed to curtail Ukraine's 'integration game'.

End of economic dependence

After two decades of failing to achieve its strategic objectives *vis-à-vis* Ukraine by using economic dependence, in 2014 Russia's strategy shifted to actual coercion. As Keohane and Nye argue 'employing force on one issue against an independent state with which one has a variety of relationships is likely to rupture mutually profitable relations on other issues' (Keohane & Nye 2000, p. 24). The use of military might disrupted long-standing patterns of complex interdependence, leading Ukraine to incur a hitherto unthinkable cost—even curtailing its trade and energy relationship with Russia—in order to preserve its sovereignty (Sidenko 2014).

---

[14]See the contribution by Onuch and Sasse in this collection and Wilson (2014).
[15]See Averre's contribution in this collection.

Inevitably, energy and trade dependence between the two states dropped precipitously. The value of Ukraine's imports to Russia decreased threefold between 2014 and 2015—from $12 billion to $4 billion.[16] By the autumn of 2015, Russia's share in Ukraine's trade fell to 18.2%, whereas the EU's grew to 31.5%.[17] Russia made an attempt to revise the terms of the Association Agreement in trilateral talks with the EU and Ukraine (or at least to postpone its implementation) using the threat of activating Annex 6 of the 2011 CIS FTA (Dragneva & Wolczuk 2015c). With the EU and Ukraine regarding Russian claims as baseless, Moscow unilaterally stopped applying the CIS FTA to Ukraine and introduced the MFA tariffs as of January 2016.[18] This brought to an end the free trade regime, however partial it was. Unable to agree on terms for purchasing gas with Russia (Varfolomeyev 2015), Ukraine purchased gas supplies from Slovakia, Hungary and Poland. While Moscow anticipated that Ukraine's economy would collapse and lead to a turn back to Russia (Trenin 2014), this scenario has not transpired.

Conclusion

The myths that have arisen since 2014 about the origins of the crisis between Ukraine and Russia have obscured a complex relationship that had progressively become more fraught. In simple terms, the objectives of the two states became increasingly incompatible: Russia wanted some form of reintegration of its near abroad; Ukraine increasingly wanted to be part of the prosperous and integrated West, however unattainable that may have been during the period studied.

Yet the realities of Hirschman's dynamics (1980) are evident: asymmetry confers power on the stronger power, forcing the smaller power to converge on the interests of the stronger. Russia used its economic might to influence Ukraine as 'such a relationship gives the larger country coercive power over the smaller, because an interruption of the relationship would cause much greater distress in B than in A' (Abdelal & Kirshner 1999, p. 120). The key phenomenon that this essay has sought to highlight is that the essence of Ukraine's vulnerability lay in the strength of the vested interests in Ukraine, which economic relations with Russia created and sustained. The willingness of the Ukrainian elites to exploit the energy dependence for their own personal gains accounts for Ukraine's prolonged and indeed increasing dependence on Russia. Russia used this dependence to secure Ukraine's participation in Russia-led integration regimes. However, Russia's far-reaching ambitions *vis-à-vis* Ukraine created room for manoeuvre which the Ukrainian elites exploited adroitly. Therefore, our analysis demonstrates that asymmetric economic dependence *per se* cannot explain actual bargaining outcomes between the larger and smaller state, without considering the nature of the demand placed on the smaller state.

The case of Ukraine–Russia relations also indicates that the use of economic dependence can trigger unintended consequences for the larger state, by creating the expectation that it can

---

[16]In 2014 trade with Russia declined by a third, consolidating the position of the EU as the largest trading partner of Ukraine. See the Ukrainian State Statistical Service, available at: http://www.ukrstat.gov.ua/.

[17]WTO Statistics on Ukraine, September 2015, available at: http://stat.wto.org/CountryProfile/WSDBCountry PFView.aspx?Country=UA, accessed 9 March 2016.

[18]'Trilateral Talks on EU–Ukraine DCFTA: Distinguishing between Myths and Reality', European Commission, DG Trade, 2015, available at: http://trade.ec.europa.eu/doclib/docs/2015/december/tradoc_154 127.pdf, accessed 22 March 2016.

influence the smaller state, something which is not addressed by Hirschman. Having defined Ukraine's participation as a *sine qua non* of the success of its integration projects, Ukraine became a pivotal country in asserting Russia's 'great power' status. As Garnett perceptively observed almost two decades ago, 'Russia's definition of itself as a state and international actor is significantly shaped by its long-term ties with Ukraine' (Garnett 1997, p. 7).

Ukraine's half-hearted but repeated engagement with Russian integration projects seems to have misled the Kremlin into believing that this would culminate in a wholehearted commitment to Russia-led integration at some stage in the future. It is perhaps this sense of betrayal which explains the powerful economic and military backlash from Russia which, ironically, is proving to be counter-productive. Not only has Ukraine's trade dependence on Russia collapsed, but perhaps more importantly, Russia has lost much of what leverage it had over Ukraine. Russia's actions in Ukraine have reverberated more widely and have had a profound impact on Russia's political relations and economic interdependence with the EU and the West in general.

Nevertheless, as the smaller, dependent state, Ukraine has clearly borne the brunt of the consequences of dependence. By hollowing out Ukraine economically, politically and militarily by a chronic failure to reform (Korablin 2015), the Ukrainian elites left the country exposed to Russia's punitive measures for failing to act on its political demands. As Russia still retains a powerful array of instruments to cripple the country in military, political and economic terms, Ukraine–Russia relations will remain profoundly antagonistic and unsettled and the resulting costs for Ukraine will continue to be very high, not least in terms of loss of life, dislocation and a protracted economic downturn. However, despite the massive level of distress inflicted and the slow pace of reforms in Ukraine, there are few indications that Ukraine is anything but determined to further lessen its economic dependence on Russia.

References

Abdelal, R. & Kirshner, J. (1999) 'Strategy, Economic Relations, and the Definition of National Interests', *Security Studies*, 9, 1–2.

Åslund, A. (2009) *How Ukraine Became a Market Economy and Democracy* (Washington, DC, Peterson Institute for International Economics).

Åslund, A. (2014) 'The Maidan and Beyond: Oligarchs, Corruption, and European Integration', *Journal of Democracy*, 25, 3.

Balmaceda, M. (1998) 'Gas, Oil and the Linkages between Domestic and Foreign Policies: The Case of Ukraine', *Europe-Asia Studies*, 50, 2.

Balmaceda, M. (2013) *Politics of Energy Dependency: Ukraine, Belarus, and Lithuania between Domestic Oligarchs and Russian Pressure* (Toronto, University of Toronto Press).

Braithwaite, R. (2015) 'Russian Federation', in *Europe's Neighbours: From Morocco to Moscow*, The Regent's Report 2015 (London, Regent's University), available at: https://issuu.com/regentscollege/docs/regents_report_2015, accessed 16 March 2016.

Brzezinski, Z. & Sullivan, P. (1997) *Russia and the Commonwealth of Independent States: Documents, Data and Analysis* (Armonk, NY, & London, M. E. Sharpe).

Bukkvoll, T. (2001) 'Off the Cuff Politics—Explaining Russia's Lack of a Ukraine Strategy', *Europe-Asia Studies*, 53, 8.

Bukkvoll, T. (2004) 'Private Interests, Public Policy: Ukraine and the Common Economic Space Agreement', *Problems of Post-Communism*, 51, 5.

Chayes, A. & Chayes, A. (1993) 'On Compliance', *International Organization*, 47, 2.

D'Anieri, P. (1999) *Economic Interdependence in Ukrainian–Russian Relations* (Albany, NY, SUNY Press).

D'Anieri, P. (2002) 'Constructivist Theory and Ukrainian Foreign Policy', in Moroney, D., Kuzio, T. & Molchanov, M. (eds) *Ukrainian Foreign and Security Policy* (Westport, CT, Praeger).

D'Anieri, P. (2006) *Understanding Ukrainian Politics: Power, Politics, and Institutional Design* (Armonk, NY, M.E. Sharpe).

D'Anieri, P. (2012) 'Ukrainian Foreign Policy from Independence to Inertia', *Communist and Post-Communist Studies*, 45, 3–4.

Delcour, L. & Wolczuk, K. (2013) 'Eurasian Economic Integration: Implications for the EU Eastern Policy', in Dragneva, R. & Wolczuk, K. (eds) *Eurasian Economic Integration: Law, Policy and Politics* (Cheltenham, Edward Elgar).

der Loo, G. V. & Van Elsuwege, P. (2012) 'Competing Paths of Regional Economic Integration in the Post-Soviet Space: Legal and Political Dilemmas for Ukraine', *Review of Central and East European Law*, 37, 4.

Donaldson, R. & Nogee, J. (2009) *The Foreign Policy of Russia* (4th edn) (Armonk, NY, M.E. Sharpe).

Dragneva, R. (2013) 'The Legal and Institutional Dimensions of the Eurasian Customs Union', in Dragneva, R. & Wolczuk, K. (eds) *Eurasian Economic Integration: Law, Policy and Politics* (Cheltenham, Edward Elgar).

Dragneva, R. & de Kort, J. (2007) 'Legal Regime for Free Trade in the CIS', *International and Comparative Law Quarterly*, 56, 2.

Dragneva, R. & Dimitrova, A. (2007) 'Patterns of Integration and Regime Compatibility: Ukraine between the CIS and the EU', in Malfliet, K., Verpoest, L. & Vinokurov, E. (eds) *The CIS, the EU and Russia: The Challenges of Integration* (Basingstoke, Palgrave Macmillan).

Dragneva, R. & Wolczuk, K. (2014) 'The EU–Ukraine Association Agreement and the Challenges of Inter-Regionalism', *Review of Central and East European Law*, 39, 3.

Dragneva, R. & Wolczuk, K. (2015a) 'EU Emulation in the Design of Eurasian Integration', in Lane, D. & Samokhvalov, V. (eds) *The Eurasian Project and Europe: Regional Discontinuities and Geopolitics* (London, Routledge).

Dragneva, R. & Wolczuk, K. (2015b) *Ukraine between the EU and Russia: The Integration Challenge* (Basingstoke & New York, NY, Palgrave Pivot).

Dragneva, R. & Wolczuk, K. (2015c) 'No Economic Bright Spot in Tensions between the EU, Ukraine and Russia', *Expert Comment*, Chatham House, 17 December.

Duina, F. & Morano-Foadi, S. (2011) 'Introduction: The Institutionalisation of Regional Trade Agreements Worldwide: New Dynamics and Future Scenarios', *European Law Journal*, 17, 5.

EDB (2012) *Kompleksnaya otsenka makroekonomicheskogo effekta sotrudnichestva Ukrainy so stranami Tamozhennogo soyuza i Edinogo Ekonomicheskogo prostranstv v ramkakh EvrAzEs* (St Petersburg, EDB Centre for Integration Studies).

Garnett, S. (1997) *Keystone in the Arch: Ukraine in the Emerging Security Environment of Central and Eastern Europe* (Washington, DC, Carnegie Endowment for International Peace).

Glaz'ev, S. (2011) 'Tamozhennyi soiuz—eto tol'ko pervyi etap integratsii', *Kommarsant Ukraina*, 18 April.

Gnedina, E. (2015) '"Multi-vector" Foreign Policies in Europe: Balancing, Bandwagoning or Bargaining', *Europe-Asia Studies*, 67, 7.

Gnedina, E. & Sleptsova, E. (2012) *Eschewing Choice: Ukraine's Strategy on Russia and the EU*, CEPS Working Document, No. 360, January.

Gould-Davies, N. (2016) 'Russia's Sovereign Globalization Rise, Fall and Future', Research Paper, Chatham House, January.

Hirschman, A. (1980) *National Power and the Structure of Foreign Trade* (expanded edn) (Berkeley, CA, University of California Press).

Kapusniak, T. (2008) *Ukraina jako obszar wplywow miedzynarodowych po zimnej wojnie* (Warsaw, Instytut Europy Srodkowo-Wschodniej).

Kembayev, Zh. (2009) *Legal Aspects of Regional Integration Processes in the Post-Soviet Area* (Berlin & Heidelberg, Springer).

Keohane, R. & Nye, J. (2000) *Power and Interdependence: World Politics in Transition* (4th edn) (New York, NY, Longman).

Khokhotva, I. (2003) 'Dead on Arrival', *Transitions On-line*, 26 September, available at: http://www.tol.org/client/article/10724-dead-on-arrival.html, accessed 15 January 2015.

Korablin, S. (2015) 'Vylka Depresiia. Ukraina', *Zerkalo Tyzhnia*, 21 August.

Kozakiewicz, J. (1999) *Rosja w polityce niepodlegej Ukrainy* (Warsaw, Instytut Studiów Politycznych PAN).

Kuzio, T. (1998) 'The Domestic Sources of Ukrainian Security Policy', *The Journal of Strategic Studies*, 21, 4.

Kuzio, T. (2002) 'To Europe with Russia! Ukraine's "Little Russian" Foreign Policy', *RFE/RL Newsline*, 6, 103, Part I, 4 June.

Kuzio, T. (2005) 'Russian Policy toward Ukraine during Elections', *Demokratizatsiya*, 13, 4.

Lester, J. (1994) 'Russian Political Attitudes to Ukrainian Independence', *Journal of Communist Studies and Transition Politics*, 10, 2.

Lo, B. (2002) *Russian Foreign Policy in the Post-Soviet Era: Reality, Illusion, and Mythmaking* (London, Palgrave).

Lo, B. (2015) *Russia and the New World Disorder* (London, Royal Institute of International Affairs, Chatham House).

Mearsheimer, J. (2014) 'Why the Ukraine Crisis is the West's Fault', *Foreign Affairs*, September/October.

Moroney, D., Kuzio, T. & Molchanov, M. (eds) (2002) *Ukrainian Foreign and Security Policy* (Westport, CT, Praeger).

Moshes, A. (2006) *Ukraine between a Multivector Foreign Policy and Euro–Atlantic Integration: Has It Made Its Choice?*, PONARS Policy Memo No. 426.

Pirani, S. (2012) 'Russo–Ukrainian Gas Wars and the Call on Transit Governance', in Kuzemko, C., Belyi, A., Goldthau, A. & Keating, M. (eds) *Dynamics of Energy Governance in Europe and Russia* (Basingstoke, Palgrave Macmillan).

Pirani, S. (2014) 'Ukraine Imports of Russian Gas: How a Deal May be Reached', *Oxford Energy Comment*, The Oxford Institute for Energy Studies, July, available at: https://www.oxfordenergy.org/wpcms/wp-content/uploads/2014/07/Ukraines-imports-of-Russian-gas-how-a-deal-might-be-reached.pdf, accessed 9 March 2016.

Poliakova, E. (2003) 'Nakanune EEP: Kuchma Protiv Diplomatov', *Ukrainskaia Pravda*, 17 September, available at: http://www.pravda.com.ua/rus/news/2003/09/17/4374367, accessed 12 February 2015.

Puglisi, R. (2003) 'Clashing Agendas? Economic Interests, Elite Coalitions and Prospects for Co-operation between Russia and Ukraine', *Europe-Asia Studies*, 55, 6.

Puglisi, R. (2008) 'A Window to the World? Oligarchs and Foreign Policy in Ukraine', in Fischer, S. (ed.) *Ukraine. Quo vadis?*, Chaillot Paper, no. 108, February (Paris, EU Institute for Security Studies), available at: http://www.iss.europa.eu/uploads/media/cp108.pdf, accessed 9 March 2016.

Raustiala, K. (2005) 'Form and Substance in International Agreements', *The American Journal of International Law*, 99.

Razumkov Centre (2013) 'Ukraine: Time for Choice', *National Security and Defence*, 4–5.

Sakwa, R. (2014) *Frontline Ukraine: Crisis in the Borderlands* (London, I.B. Tauris).

Sherr, J. (2002) 'Ukraine and Russia: A Geopolitical Turn?', in Lewis, A. (ed.) *The EU and Ukraine: Neighbours, Friends, Partners?* (London, The Federal Trust).

Sherr, J. (2006) 'Ukraine's Scissors: Between Internal Weakness and External Dependence', *Russie.Nei.Visions*, No. 9 (Paris, IFRI).

Sherr, J. (2010) 'The Mortgaging of Ukraine's Independence', *Briefing Paper*, 1 August (London, Chatham House).

Shumylo-Tapiola, O. (2012) 'Ukraine at the Crossroads: Between the EU DCFTA & Customs Union', *Russie. NEI.Reports*, April.

Sidenko, V. (2014) 'Degradation of the Ukraine-Russia Economic Relations: What Is Next?', *National Security and Defence*, 5–6.

Silina, T. (2003) 'Eepeiskii vybor', *Zerkalo Nedeli*, 19 September.

Silina, T. (2004) 'Souchastniki', *Zerkalo Nedeli*, 23 April.

Silina, T. (2011) 'Zona vid Zony Vidrizniayetsia', *Zerkalo Tyzhnia*, 21 October.

Silnia, T. (2013) 'Chy Vidkryyut' Soyuznyky "Druhyi Front"?', *Zerkalo Tyzhnia*, 22 August.

Solov'ev, V. & Sidorenko, S. (2010) 'President posovetovalsia s Evropoi', *Kommersant Ukraina*, 28 April.

Steinmeier, F. W. (2013) 'Speech at the Handover Ceremony in Canada', 17 December, available at: http://www.canada.diplo.de/Vertretung/kanada/en/__pr/2013/steinmeier-antritt/steinmeier-antrittsrede.html, accessed 1 March 2016.

Toritsyn, A. & Miller, E. A. (2002) 'From East to West, and Back Again: Economic Reform and Ukrainian Foreign Policy', *European Security*, 11, 1.

Trenin, D. (2014) 'Reconciliation between Kyiv and Donbass Looks Unlikely', *National Security and Defence*, 5–6.

Tsygankov, A. (2015) 'Vladimir Putin's Last Stand: the Sources of Russia's Ukraine Policy', *Post-Soviet Affairs*, 31, 4.

Varfolomeyev, O. (2015) 'Ukraine to Negotiate New Contract with Gazprom', *Eurasia Daily Monitor*, 12, 50, 18 March.

Walker, E. (2003) *Dissolution* (Lanham, CT & Oxford, Rowman & Littlefield).

Wilson, A. (2005) *Ukraine's Orange Revolution* (New Haven, CT, Yale University Press).

Wilson, A. (2014) *Ukraine Crisis. What it Means for the West* (New Haven, CT, Yale University Press).

Wolczuk, K. (1997) 'Presidentialism in Ukraine', *Democratization*, 4, 3.

Wolczuk, K. (2002) *The Moulding of Ukraine: The Constitutional Politics of State Formation* (Budapest, Central European University Press).

Wolczuk, R. (2003) *Ukraine's Foreign and Security Policy 1991–2000* (London & New York, NY, Routledge).

Wolczuk, R. (2007) 'Ukraine—A Partial but Reluctant CIS Member', in Dusseault, D. (ed.) *The CIS: Form or Substance?* (Helsinki, Aleksanteri Institute).

Woronowycz, R. (2003) 'Russian–Ukrainian Dispute over Tuzla Escalates', *The Ukrainian Weekly*, 26 October.

Yanukovych, V. (2010) 'Ukraine Will Be a Bridge between East and West', *The Wall Street Journal*, 17 February, available at: http://www.wsj.com/articles/SB10001424052748704804204575069251843839386, accessed 9 March 2016.

Zagorsky, A. (2011) 'Eastern Partnership from the Russian Perspective', *International Politics and Society*, 3 (Berlin, FES).

Zlenko, A. (2002) 'Ukraine and the EU: It Takes Two to Tango', in Lewis, A. (ed.) *The EU and Ukraine: Neighbours, Friends, Partners?* (London, The Federal Trust).

The Ukraine Conflict: Russia's Challenge to European Security Governance

DEREK AVERRE

Abstract

This essay uses the concept of security governance to explore the implications of Russia's intervention in Ukraine for the rules-based security order in Europe. It outlines key ideas in the literature about the post-Cold War European security order with respect to Russia's role and examines Russian debates on the Ukraine conflict. It then investigates European institutions' reaction to the conflict in order to understand to what extent Russia's exclusion (as a result of the West's policy of containment and deterrence) or self-exclusion now constitutes a structural factor in the security politics of the wider Europe. The essay concludes with the analysis of the challenges facing both Europe and Russia and considers the prospects for re-shaping this order to give meaning to partnership and shared security governance.

RUSSIA'S ROLE IN THE UKRAINE CONFLICT, IN PARTICULAR ITS intervention in eastern Ukraine and annexation of Crimea, appears to mark a turning point in the evolution of European security governance. Official Western statements claim that Russia's actions constitute a threat to regional and even global security. President Obama has stated that the US stands at the forefront of 'opposing Russia's aggression against Ukraine, which is a threat to the world' (Wintour 2014, p. 8). UK Prime Minister David Cameron, at an EU summit behind closed doors, compared the risk of appeasing Putin to the situation with Hitler prior to World War II (Traynor & MacAskill 2014). A UK Government report concluded that Russia's policies represent 'a strategic threat to NATO. … Member States must now be prepared to invest in NATO capabilities to enable the Alliance to deter, and if necessary counter, this threat' (House of Commons 2014, p. 7). The NATO Wales Summit Declaration declared that 'Russia's aggressive actions against Ukraine have fundamentally challenged our vision of a Europe whole, free, and at peace [with] long-term consequences for peace and security in the Euro–Atlantic region and stability across the globe'.[1] The European Parliament 'strongly condemns Russia's aggressive and expansionist policy, which constitutes a threat to the unity and independence of Ukraine and poses a potential threat to the EU itself' (European Parliament 2015). A leading commentator on European affairs summarises the widely held

---

The author is indebted to Natasha Kuhrt, Kataryna Wolczuk, Mark Webber and Stefan Wolff, as well as an anonymous reviewer, for very helpful comments on drafts of this essay.

[1]'Wales Summit Declaration', press release (2014) 120, NATO, 5 September 2014, p. 1, available at: http://www.nato.int/cps/en/natohq/official_texts_112964.htm, accessed 23 September 2014.

view: 'revisionist Russia emerges as a largely unpredictable player, which no longer gives prime importance to abiding (even in appearance) by international law, with a neo-imperial vision in the form of the Eurasian project and an across-the-board enmity for Western institutions in Europe and Western values in the world' (Heisbourg 2015, p. 34).

Western policy makers have promised a robust response. NATO has pledged to reverse the decline in Allies' military spending, improve its defence capabilities, bolster the NATO Response Force, conduct more regular live exercises and forward deploy air, ground and naval assets in the Baltics, Poland and Romania. These measures have been accompanied by US and European sanctions against the Putin regime. The US Freedom Support Act,[2] designed to assist the government of Ukraine in restoring its sovereignty and territorial integrity, has condemned Russian aggression and—rhetorically at least—lined European countries up behind a policy of containment. Official statements—in Obama's own words, aimed at the 'mobilization of world opinion and international institutions' to counter Russian claims[3]—have sought to marginalise alternative narratives by placing Russia 'on the wrong side of history' (Lewis *et al.* 2014) and dismissing any suggestion of appeasement (Charap & Shapiro 2015, p. 38). With Moscow responding in kind, as we shall see, the reciprocal delegitimation of the 'other' appears to have had a profound effect on the European security environment: Russia's relations with Europe are no longer based upon 'dependable expectations of peaceful change' (Webber 2007, p. 61) but appear to present an intractable security dilemma.

Yet there is uncertainty about Moscow's strategic objectives and disagreement among Western policy elites over the extent of the challenge posed by Russia. A report commissioned in advanced of the NATO Wales Summit concluded that the Ukraine conflict generates risks unprecedented since 1989 but 'does not presage a return to the Cold War. Russia and the West are not engaged in a global ideological contest for influence, nor are their differences the organizing principles of international politics'.[4] EU policy papers have indicated that the door remains open to reengagement with Russia if a resolution of the Ukraine conflict can be found.[5] The view that 'Putin surely has no place in the high councils of an international system whose rules and values he so blatantly subverts'[6] contends with the opinion of distinguished former practitioners that NATO and the EU have failed to understand Russia's security interests and that NATO's escalatory response 'amounts to more of the same, with little if any assurance of better outcomes'; they argue that a serious diplomatic effort to reestablish the core principles of the European political order must be sought (Matlock *et al.* 2014). One authoritative scholar

[2]'US Freedom Support Act of 2014', summary (S.2828), available at: https://www.congress.gov/bill/113th-congress/senate-bill/2828, accessed 25 January 2016.

[3]'Remarks by the President at the United States Military Academy Commencement Ceremony', 28 May 2014, available at: https://www.whitehouse.gov/the-press-office/2014/05/28/remarks-president-united-states-military-academy-commencement-ceremony, accessed 2 December 2015.

[4]'Collective Defence and Common Security—Twin Pillars of the Atlantic Alliance', Group of Policy Experts report to the NATO Secretary-General, June 2014, p. 2, available at: http://www.nato.int/nato_static_fl2014/assets/pdf/pdf_2014_06/20140606_140602-peg-collective_defence.pdf, accessed 23 September 2014.

[5]'Issues Paper on Relations with Russia', Foreign Affairs Council, 19 January 2015, available at: http://blogs.ft.com/brusselsblog/files/2015/01/Russia.pdf, accessed 17 February 2015.

[6]'Don't Let Putin Drag the World Back to the Past', Editorial, *The Observer*, 16 November 2014, p. 42, available at: http://www.theguardian.com/commentisfree/2014/nov/16/observer-editorial-world-leaders-must-stand-up-to-putin, accessed 15 March 2016.

warns of the danger of 'escalation dominance' and the need to resume diplomacy to dispel uncertainty about Russian decision making by seeking shared understandings about thresholds and boundaries (Freedman 2014, pp. 9–10).

The academic literature has seen a tendency for scholars to resurrect previous debates rather than offering a critical analysis of the security implications of the Ukraine conflict. Mearsheimer argues that the 'logic of realism' has trumped liberal interpretations of international affairs; in the absence of 'world government to protect states from one another' and the West's weakening structural and ideational power, Russia inevitably responds 'ruthlessly' to threats to its core interests: 'International law and human rights concerns take a back seat when vital security issues are at stake' (Mearsheimer 2014). His recommendation—to make Ukraine a neutral buffer and forego further NATO enlargement—echoes Kissinger's and Brzezinski's preference for the 'Finlandisation' of Ukraine (Brzezinski 2014; Kissinger 2014). Wohlforth also heralds 'the return of Realpolitik' to explain US–Russia confrontation, while arguing that a 'far more thickly institutionalized' international system constrains revisionist power and limits the chances of a power transition (Wohlforth 2015). Sakwa provides a much more subtle analysis, pointing to Europe's failure to 'deepen the structures and practices of liberal internationalism within the framework of a shared continental vision', but also concludes in realist vein that the EU's normative agenda is vitiated by the 'geopolitical aspirations of the new Atlanticism to extend its zone of influence to the east' (Sakwa 2015a, pp. 566–67).[7] Realism's preoccupation with geopolitics and material structures does not capture the multiple causal factors—political, ideational, identity—influencing the nature of this intra-European conflict. Prominent liberal scholars have rejected realist prescriptions as legitimising aggression against Ukraine and called on the West to respond to the challenge of Putinism, but offer little in the way of scholarly enquiry (Garton Ash 2015, p. 33). Empirical academic contributions have offered more interesting analyses of the legal aspects of Russia's intervention (Burke-White 2014; Kaminski 2014), domestic politics (Allison 2014) and the challenges posed to arms control and nuclear non-proliferation (Yost 2015).[8]

However, the existing literature has given much less consideration to the political and institutional consequences arising from Russia's challenge to the European order and to the belief systems that inspire Russian behaviour. This essay seeks to redress this shortfall through an explanatory framework based in the concept of security governance, as the most appropriate one for our empirical considerations: the response of NATO and the EU to Russia's revision of the rules-based order, and Russia's criticism of European institutional arrangements while claiming a bigger regional role, are crucial events in the evolution of the wider Europe. The problem we address revolves around two questions. First, to what extent is Russia's intervention in Ukraine shaped by a more assertive defence of its interests in its neighbourhood and inspired by a revisionist approach to the European rules-based system of security governance? Second, how do Western institutions and states respond to Russia's actions and manage the changing environment of European security governance?

This essay proceeds in five stages. We first outline key ideas in the security governance literature about the evolution of the post-Cold War European security order, particularly with respect to Russia's role. Second, we examine Russian debates on the Ukraine conflict,

---

[7]See also Sakwa (2015b, pp. 48–9).
[8]See also Survival Forum (2015).

highlighting conflicting trends in Russian thinking about the changing strategic and normative environment. Third, we consider European institutions' reaction to the conflict and to what extent the premise of Russia's exclusion, as a result of the West's policy of containment and deterrence, or self-exclusion now constitutes a structural factor in the security politics of the wider Europe. Fourth, we analyse the challenges facing both Europe and Russia and how the Ukraine conflict may impact on the European security order. In conclusion, we consider what the prospects are of re-shaping this order to give real meaning to partnership and shared security governance: is the institutionalised system of European security now aimed unambiguously at constraining Russia's purported revisionist intentions, or are there prospects for reengaging Russia?

A central aim in this essay is to interrogate the policies of the institutions and actors through which the practices of security governance are played out. Accordingly we adopt an interpretive approach to policy analysis, based on extensive research into official policy documents from Russia, sourced primarily from the Ministry of Foreign Affairs and President's websites, and into official NATO, EU and Organization for Security and Co-operation in Europe (OSCE) documents. This is backed up by secondary source material written by authoritative Russian and Western scholars and policy commentators on the political and security implications of the Ukraine conflict.

Russia and European security governance

The concept of security governance has developed as a framework to analyse 'the coordinated management and regulation' of European security arrangements by multiple authorities, acting both formally and informally and involving states and non-state actors, and the ways in which regulation is 'structured by discourse and norms, and purposefully directed towards particular policy outcomes'—the regulation of inter-state relations based on trust, the voluntary acceptance of common goals and collectively recognised norms of interaction that underpin order (Webber *et al.* 2004, p. 4; Webber 2007 pp. 62–3). Empirical analysis focuses on coordination, how actors interact and which of them leads policy making; on management, meaning risk assessment and negotiation to mitigate risk; and on regulation, and the motivation underpinning policy objectives. Much of the literature on security governance has centred on Europe,[9] and the institutional and normative regulation of security challenges by NATO and the EU. This reflects the fact that NATO and the EU became the preeminent actors in developing in Europe a system of regulation that can claim wider legitimacy; the institutional settlement following the end of the Cold War was predisposed to a Euro–Atlantic understanding of order and Russia, mired in domestic problems and much less influential than during the Soviet period, was unwilling or unable to challenge this order (Flynn & Farrell 1999). With time, however, the 'idea that global solutions to security problems can better be achieved through the existence and the practices of post-Westphalian states … spurred debates on the exportation of the European system of security governance', including to the EU's eastern neighbourhood (Christou *et al.* 2010, p. 344).[10]

---

[9]A notable exception is the 2010 edited volume by Emil Kirchner and James Sperling on patterns of global governance, which contains a chapter on Russia (see Averre 2010).

[10]See also Kirchner and Sperling (2007).

A closer look at this process is needed. In the closing years of the Cold War the Conference on Security and Co-operation in Europe (CSCE) encouraged the acceptance by all European states of what were at the time ground-breaking principles of inter-state cooperation, within a framework of sovereignty and non-intervention, to underpin the rules for co-existence in Europe (Pourchot 2011, pp. 180–81). States would refrain from the threat or use of force; aim at peaceful settlement of disputes; respect human rights and basic freedoms; ensure equal rights and self-determination of their peoples; and fulfil their obligations under international law. The principles enshrined in the Helsinki Final Act, a political declaration of intent, instituted a nascent security regime in which Europe's states recognised the indivisibility of European security. But the Helsinki principles also served 'to articulate shared aspirations as well as to codify formally extant practices', and shaped the views—including about human rights—of Soviet elites which inspired both Gorbachev's domestic reforms and 'new thinking' in foreign policy (Herman 1996, p. 290). The norms of inter-state and domestic behaviour were legitimised in the Charter of Paris for a New Europe and subsequently accepted by the Yel'tsin leadership. This laid the foundations for a pluralist European international society: with the emergence of the OSCE, the wider Euro–Atlantic space was institutionalised in an inclusive process of decision making, guided by 'change and adaptation to the shared values of the organization as a whole' (Pourchot 2011, p. 192). An underlying assumption was that this institutionalisation would become a causal factor for reform in Russia and the post-Soviet states.

However, this did not lead to the emergence—favoured by Moscow—of the OSCE as the central European security organisation. Within an evolving governance environment underpinned by CSCE/OSCE norms, NATO and the EU proceeded to take on the leading role in managing and regulating the security agenda in Europe. In successive Strategic Concepts NATO made a conceptual shift away from territorial defence and deterrence to encompass a broader, cooperative approach to security management (Webber *et al.* 2004, p. 9). The Partnership for Peace and the Euro–Atlantic Partnership Council, both of which included Russia, signalled the inclusive nature of the Alliance's thinking. The 1997 NATO–Russia Permanent Joint Council failed, largely due to Russian resentment over NATO's intervention in the Former Republic of Yugoslavia over Kosovo, but the NATO–Russia Council (established in 2002) provided a forum for bilateral consultations in recognition of Russia's unique role in European security. Nevertheless, NATO's overwhelming institutional power, encompassing many security-related issues and promoting a European security order firmly based in liberal values and norms, was perceived by Russia as marginalising it; at the same time, the Alliance's enlargements to the east were interpreted by Moscow as the actions of a powerful military organisation exploiting Russia's weakened position in regional security (Webber *et al.* 2004).

Even though NATO–Russia relations appeared to be moving towards partnership, for European elites the Alliance remained 'the organisation of reassurance should conditions deteriorate in the Balkans ... or tensions heighten with Russia'; Russia inherited 'the status of NATO's great power opposite' and 'continued to contest the notion that NATO in any way represents the legitimate expression of a pan-European international society' (Webber 2011, pp. 146, 155). Then President Dmitrii Medvedev's proposals for a European Security Treaty—focused on the principles of inter-state relations, arms control regimes, confidence and security building measures, conflict settlement and new security challenges—omitted any reference to the OSCE humanitarian 'basket' of relations;[11] it was not regarded as a suitable basis for negotiations by European states and was relegated to the OSCE Corfu process, where no consensus was reached (Evers 2011). Moscow's challenge to Europe to find a formula for shared management of the European security order was thus explicit well before the Ukraine conflict. The perceived danger to Russia of a NATO presence in eastern Europe, and particularly the 'open-door' pledge to Ukraine and Georgia made at the 2008 Bucharest summit (despite the reservations of influential member states), continued to vex Moscow.

The EU too, as reflected in its 1999 Common Strategy on Russia and the 2003 European Security Strategy, had a clear strategic goal of promoting European stability and security through deeper partnership with a Russia undergoing 'far-reaching transformation', including in their shared neighbourhood. This included 'a permanent policy and security dialogue', conducted both bilaterally and within the OSCE, on *inter alia* conflict prevention and crisis management.[12] The launch at the May 2003 EU–Russia Summit of a 'common space ... in the field of external security'—essentially a means of encouraging shared security governance rooted in common values—became part of the extensive institutional architecture of the relationship, bolstered by increasing bilateral links on trade, energy and internal security.[13] However, the EU's vision of a transformative foreign policy, promoting democratic reform, good governance, the rule of law and respect for human rights in the neighbourhood, and its growing authority in key areas of security governance—suggesting a readiness to project power further afield (Webber 2007, p. 132; Richter 2016, p. 48)—began increasingly to unsettle Russia's security establishment. Ukraine's 'Orange Revolution' in 2004 did much to trigger the shift in thinking in Russia's governing elite. Brussels' offer to Kyiv in 2008 of an Association Agreement and Deep and Comprehensive Free Trade Area (DCFTA)—which promised to bind Ukraine more closely into the EU's rules-based trade model and advance political and security cooperation—together with the subsequent launch of its Eastern Partnership (EaP) initiative, raised fresh concerns in Russia that its own interests and integration projects in the post-Soviet space were being challenged (Gretskiy *et al.* 2014, pp. 379–80). A German–Russian initiative for joint EU–Russia conflict resolution, the Meseberg Memorandum, was blocked by the EU; from 2011 there was no meeting of the Permanent Partnership Council, the main body for Russia–EU political cooperation at the ministerial level (House of Lords 2015, p. 27; Sakwa 2015b, p. 29).

The efforts of NATO and the EU to incorporate Russia as a partner in shaping a changing Europe, where the regulaton of complex security issues would be inspired by the logic of building an inclusive regional community of states committed to a collective purpose, went far beyond the nascent security regime embodied in the CSCE. As Flynn and Farrell have argued,

> the ordering process is not simply the consolidation of a larger Western sphere of influence in order to manage from a more advantageous position the balance of power with Russia ... the new normative framework is clearly not simply a reflection of power relationships or the imposition by Western states of their security interests and notions of social organization on weaker states. (Flynn & Farrell 1999, pp. 529–30)

[11]'The Draft of the European Security Treaty', President of Russia, 29 November 2009, available at: http://en.kremlin.ru/events/president/news/6152, accessed 29 November 2015.
[12]'Common Strategy of the European Union on Russia', 1999/414/CFSP, 4 June 1999, available at: http://trade.ec.europa.eu/doclib/docs/2003/november/tradoc_114137.pdf, accessed 15 March 2016.
[13]See, EU–Russia Summit, Joint Statement 9937/03 (Presse 154), St Petersburg, 31 May 2003, available at: http://www.consilium.europa.eu/uedocs/cms_data/docs/pressdata/en/er/75969.pdf, accessed 5 April 2016.

However, attempts by NATO and the EU to extend their form of order to the east—part of a broader vision of transformation in Europe—were perceived by Russia in terms of its own security logic: EU policy was 'hatched by the Brussels supranational and unaccountable bureaucracy, which was carried away by temptations of grandeur and geopolitical self-assertion … Russia continued to be contained' (Yakovenko 2014, p. 5). In Moscow's eyes, Brussels was effectively aiming to cement its own 'sphere of influence' (Christou 2010, p. 425). The OSCE was undergoing its own deepening systemic crisis stemming from Russia's, and other former Soviet states', resistance to the West's supposed attempt to 'dictate' its values and norms (Lavrov 2013b).[14]

It was thus already clear that the 'strategic, even visionary attitude' that characterised the 'grand project to consolidate the political, economic and security condition of post-communist Europe' was failing (Stivachtis & Webber 2011, pp. 103–4). The Euromaidan—in actual fact a popular uprising against Yanukovich's rapacious regime—was presented by Moscow as Europe 'trying to compel Ukraine to make a painful choice between east and west, further aggravating internal differences' (Lavrov 2014b, p. 28). The NATO/EU transformative mission in the east—whether in the form of enlargement or deeper engagement through the EaP—has come up firmly against Moscow's challenge to both the distributive and regulative components of the post-Cold War settlement (Webber 2007, pp. 43–4, 141–42): Russia's intervention has produced a sharp shift in the logic of relations that challenges many of the assumptions on which European security governance has been built. Can Europe now rely on institutionalised, normatively constituted forms of governance in the face of Moscow's different threat perceptions and adherence to sovereign national interests?

Russian debates on the Ukraine crisis

As highlighted in the previous section, the security governance literature focuses on how regulation is structured by discourse and norms and directed towards policy outcomes (Webber *et al.* 2004, p. 4). In this section we explore the discursive construction of security within Russia's domestic political environment, focusing in particular on Russia's behaviour in the Ukraine crisis, in order better to understand why its system of knowledge and beliefs clashes with European discourse and norms. Is there a structured set of ideas that Russia's governing elite draws on in its Ukraine policy and its interaction with other European security actors (Christou *et al.* 2010, pp. 345–46)? Here we draw on primary sources, together with analysis by the expert community, to examine the ideas which Russian elites have promoted in the Ukraine conflict.

The legal normative claims put forward by Moscow assert that Yanukovych's removal constituted an 'unconstitutional coup', endorsed by Western advocates of democracy promotion, by extremist nationalist forces which pose a serious threat to ethnic Russians and Russian-speakers. The intervention by Russian forces in eastern Ukraine—supposedly by invitation from Yanukovych as the 'legitimate' president, and initially denied but later admitted to by Moscow—was aimed at protecting and supporting the Russophone population. Crimea's secession was compared by foreign minister Sergei Lavrov to Kosovo's secession from Serbia; he defended it as being in line with international legal norms, invoking a 1970 UN General Assembly declaration on the right of peoples to self-determination, and declared

[14]See also Webber (2007, p. 211).

that the principle of territorial integrity should be observed in the case of states which allow self-determination and do not attempt to restrict that right, arguing that the Ukraine 'coup' deprived Kyiv of that authority (Lavrov 2015e).[15] Moscow also claimed that existing treaty arrangements with Ukraine over the strategic Black Sea Fleet base were invalidated by the unconstitutional coup, which meant previous commitments to respect Ukrainian sovereignty were unnecessary.

Moscow has launched a sustained information campaign, repudiating Western criticism in an often shrill diplomatic offensive, including scarcely veiled threats.[16] The litany of Russian grievances runs as follows. Europe backtracked on the agreement of 21 February 2014, brokered with Yanukovych and aimed at a political settlement with opposition groups to create a government of national unity, and has since been manipulated by the 'illegitimate' Kyiv authorities, which are pursuing an 'ultranationalist' agenda and perpetuating weak governance. Kyiv refuses to engage in direct dialogue with authorities in Donets'k and Luhans'k regions and is sabotaging the Minsk-2 Agreements—signed by Russia, Ukraine, France and Germany on 12 February 2015 and endorsed by UN Security Council resolution 2202 (UN 2015c)—which provide a framework to resolve the conflict with the involvement of the OSCE and the Trilateral Contact Group (Lavrov 2015a, 2015b). Moscow claims it is being penalised by Western sanctions and a freeze in relations, which will remain in force until it fulfils its part of the Minsk-2 Agreements; it insists that reinstatement of full control of the state border by the Ukraine government and the withdrawal of all foreign armed forces can only happen after constitutional reform, negotiated together with the Donets'k and Luhans'k regions, that includes decentralisation, an amnesty for separatists and a special status for the latter (Lavrov 2015c). Putin himself has repeatedly justified Russia's intervention in terms of both international law and 'truth and justice' (Putin 2014b, 2014c), deploring the longer-term damage to relations from what it perceives as a concerted attempt by the Poroshenko government to revise the history of World War II and rehabilitate fascist sympathisers, and to play down historical cultural and linguistic ties between Ukraine and Russia (Putin 2014e).

Russia's pursuit of its normative and political goals, if necessary at the expense of Ukraine's sovereignty, thus rests on its rejection of the legitimacy of the post-Yanukovych constitutional order. However, Russian statements have also gone beyond legal normative arguments to encompass political, economic and humanitarian dimensions of a broader confrontation between Russia and the West that traces its roots to well before the Euromaidan. Motivated by the belief of conservative elites that liberal reform under Yel'tsin left the country hostage to Western interests, Putin has asserted that Ukraine is only a pretext for attempts to contain Russia and undermine its sovereignty: 'Either we remain a sovereign nation, or we dissolve without a trace and lose our identity. ... They would gladly let Russia follow the Yugoslav scenario of disintegration and dismemberment' (Putin 2014a). Lavrov has stated that he has 'serious grounds to suppose'

---

[15]For a critical analysis see Allison (2014, pp. 1259–68).

[16]Vitalii Churkin, Russia's Ambassador to the UN, has warned that 'The representative of Ukraine would be well advised to choose his words more wisely ... if that path [Georgia's attempt to enlist US support in its 2008 conflict with Russia] is chosen, while using colourful words about the role of Russia, this will end very sadly for Ukraine—even more sadly than the events we have seen over the past year' (UN 2015b). The ongoing dispute at the OSCE between Russia's representatives on the one hand and the US and Ukraine, largely backed up by the EU, on the other can be followed in documents from the plenary meetings of the OSCE Permanent Council, available at: http://www.osce.org/resources/documents/decision-making-bodies, accessed 4 April 2016.

that sanctions are an attempt at destabilisation and regime change in Russia (Lavrov 2014a). Russia's Security Council also highlighted the likely use of 'the technology of "colour revolutions"' against Russia.[17] Moscow has repeatedly underscored Russia's refusal to accept the West's 'domination' of world affairs and its 'zero-sum' attempt to enlarge its 'geopolitical space' in Europe and spread Western civilisational models and norms; it argues that the diffusion of global power and influence favours a UN-centred 'polycentric' international system, with the collective management of global affairs based on the core principles of sovereign equality of states, respect for sovereignty and territorial integrity (Lavrov 2015c, 2015f). Russia's new military doctrine reflects Moscow's perception of the dangers it faces in a hostile external environment, in which military contacts with the West are downgraded to Cold War levels, so that 'a watershed has been passed' (Trenin 2014).[18]

Russian statements are not averse to misrepresentation. They play down the intervention of Russian forces in support of anti-government groups in eastern Ukraine, the factor that Western governments see as the main source of continuing instability. Moscow's defence of the annexation of Crimea was rejected in the UN General Assembly majority vote deeming the March 2014 referendum in Crimea and Sevastopol invalid and recognising Ukraine's territorial integrity (despite 11 votes against and a large number of abstentions) (Kaminski 2014; UN 2014; Yost 2015, p. 537). Rather than fomenting regime change, the West's response to the Euromaidan was in fact quite passive, and the EU in particular hoped that the 21 February agreement would produce a settlement; nor is there any evidence that Brussels coerced Kyiv into signing the Association Agreement (Dragneva & Wolczuk 2015, pp. 30–2, 96–7). A UN report has concluded that Russian minorities in Ukraine—though concerned that the Euromaidan movement would diminish the status of Russian language and culture—experienced no sense of political discrimination or exclusion, contrary to Moscow's claims that the local populations needed protection; tensions were escalated by extremist elements on both sides of a conflict marked by a deficit of good governance.[19]

The point we make here is that Moscow's arguments, borrowing selectively from narratives of national cultural identity, international legal norms and domestic political order (Zevelev 2014), are used instrumentally to promote Moscow's normative counter-offensive—what Allison calls the 'colour counter-revolution' (Allison 2014, p. 1290). With Russia's policy in Ukraine frustrated by the Euromaidan, the Putin regime is forced to turn to 'geopolitical' arguments and forceful promotion of conservative Russian values to claim legitimacy and discredit Western accounts. Putin's use of both normative and historical arguments to justify the annexation of Crimea and intervention in eastern Ukraine, with his promise to protect the rights and interests of Russians abroad (Putin 2014c), has also raised the suspicion—particularly among elites in eastern Europe—that Moscow is ready to carve out a larger

---

[17]'On the US National Security Strategy', Russian Federation Security Council, 25 March 2015, available at: http://www.scrf.gov.ru/news/865.html, accessed 13 July 2015.

[18]See also, 'Voennaya doktrina Rossiiskoi Federatsii', *Nezavisimaya gazeta*, 30 December 2014, available at: http://www.rg.ru/printable/2014/12/30/doktrina-dok.html, accessed 12 August 2015.

[19]Report of the Special Rapporteur on Minority Issues, Rita Izsak, United Nations General Assembly Human Rights Council, A/HRC/28/64/Add.1, 27 January 2015, pp. 1–2, 8–11.

sphere of foreign policy influence in its neighbourhood. One scholar argues that Russian narratives are now

> aimed at sustaining a broad domestic support base among political and security elites, bolstered by popular approval. ... The view of a right of acquisition over parts of the former Soviet state ... has been rhetorically justified in Putin's current discourse over Crimea and Ukraine by appeals to historic justice and historic rights, which is in essence a form of revanchism, even irredentism. (Allison 2014, pp. 1282, 1285–86)

Put simply, this represents a fundamental political challenge to Europe's rules-based order.

At the same time, Moscow has sought to portray a constructive approach that avoids confrontation or isolation. Lavrov has underlined Russia's attempts, through the Normandy quartet of Russia, Ukraine, France and Germany, to find a balanced resolution to the conflict: Russia will not 'shut itself away in its own "little world"' (Lavrov 2015d).[20] During the conflict Putin himself has periodically revived the narrative of interdependence and positive relations with Europe, albeit on the basis of equality (Putin 2014b, 2014d). This ambivalence has been a feature of Russian foreign policy for a decade or more. In 2007 Putin followed his notoriously hard-line speech at the Munich security conference (Putin 2007b) only weeks later with an article (also addressing a European audience) emphasising Russia's European choice: 'Our country is spiritually and culturally an integral part of European civilization ... in building a sovereign democratic state, we fully share the basic values and principles that form the world view of an overwhelming majority of Europeans' (Putin 2007a). In a leading Western academic journal published shortly before the Euromaidan, Lavrov similarly presented a more constructive Russian vision of a common economic and humanitarian space between the EU and Russia. In the same article, however, he highlighted how Moscow's perception of the changing global environment has reshaped Russian assumptions: a shifting global balance of power, aggravated by destabilising trends, means that 'Europe will no longer play a central role' in an international system in which the factors of 'civilizational identity' and 'the plurality of development models' are becoming prominent: 'one should not take the traditional system of international alliances for granted. It is obvious that history will make us reconsider a lot of things' (Lavrov 2013a, p. 9).[21] Moscow's resistance to a hegemonic European project is thus depicted not in terms of its own hegemony but as vital for survival of the Russian nation and state, the 'Russian world' (Lavrov 2015g). This may not preclude relations with Europe and the West; however, the core narrative is that external sources of political legitimacy, in the shape of Western norms and values, are no longer seen by Russia as a reference point. A process of self-reidentification is taking place in which Russia acts according to a different 'logic of appropriateness' as a source of 'social power' (Williams & Neumann 2000, pp. 363–64).

These official narratives frame the range of proposed policy options. But do they reflect a national consensus that ensures coherence between the policy process and the dominant ideas in Russia? In fact there have been fervent debates which exhibit a substantial plurality of opinion within the political class. Sergei Glaz'ev, a conservative economist and leading Putin adviser, merges economic and political arguments against the EaP—in his words, a geopolitical tool which 'deprives partners of their foreign economic sovereignty', with 'clearly expressed imperial features' that provoke colour revolutions and entrench civilisational

---

[20]See also Lavrov (2015f).
[21]See also Ambrosio and Vandrovec (2013, pp. 439–40, 447–51).

divisions (Glaz'ev 2013, p. 42)—with a rejection of Western institutions and liberal values in favour of a social model based on conservative–nationalist values (Glaz'ev 2014).[22] Other prominent Russian experts are also broadly in support of government views, arguing that '"limited systemic confrontation" between Russia and the West' is set to be 'a crucial factor in determining the future international order which will replace the protracted post-Cold War transition' (Suslov 2014).[23] One academic avers that, by promoting regime change in Kyiv 'through violent and unconstitutional means', the EU has damaged its reputation as a responsible actor and aligned its foreign policy with US interests, while NATO has gained 'new momentum on the current anti-Russian wave' (Gromyko 2014). The veteran commentator Sergei Karaganov (2014) writes that, in demanding change in the rules and norms of security, Russia 'speaks for the entire Non-West'; the liberal democracies' response to this new global competition is 'a new round of a policy of containment or rollback'. In short, the Ukraine crisis is symptomatic of the 'new normality' in which 'the current level of confrontation is not an aberration but a new norm in life' (Gromyko 2015).

There are sharply dissenting voices, however, which offer a different conception of Russian national interests. A number of experts argue that the main objective of foreign policy—creating a favourable external environment for domestic development—has been undermined by rejecting the 'European choice' of political, economic and social modernisation (Arbatov 2014). The territorial gains for Russia in eastern Ukraine and Crimea may serve to bolster support for Putin but are outweighed by a drain on Russia's resources and the loss of Ukraine from its regional integration initiatives. Leading specialists on Europe point to the ignorance in Russia's political establishment of social processes that are shaping a revival of national identity in Ukraine and criticise Moscow's reliance on the concept of 'limited sovereignty', which emphasises national interests and historical justice rather than accepted legal and normative rules (Institute of Europe 2014, pp. 14–6). A survey on Russian identity compiled by younger Russians and published by the government-sponsored Valdai Club is bold in its main assumptions: 'Modern Russia needs peacetime heroes, and not constant preparation for war with a real or imagined foe. … Enough threats and fortress mentality … the individual and his personal dignity takes precedence over the state, its dogmas and national ambitions'.[24]

The discursive shift towards a more conservative–nationalist paradigm at odds with the West is thus far from monolithic within Russia's political establishment: it still contends with a body of progressive opinion which differs in its assessment of Russia's core interests. While critical of the West for its refusal to negotiate collective security arrangements and its approach to the Ukraine crisis, moderate elites argue that Russia should reengage with Europe in order to modernise a stagnating system and remedy xenophobic complexes, thereby creating a viable polity which can take its place in the international system. One Russian scholar sums up the diversity of ideological trends: 'it is a mistake to understand Russian civil society in liberal or traditionalist terms only … it is composed of both … and their dialogue and struggle for ideological hegemony determine the evolution of civil society in this country' (Chebankova 2015, p. 251).[25]

---

[22]See also Rodkiewicz and Rogoza (2015), Chebankova (2015, p. 263).

[23]See also Bazhanov (2013).

[24]*National Identity and the Future of Russia*, Valdai International Discussion Club, Moscow, February 2014, p. 8, available at: http://vid-1.rian.ru/ig/valdai/Identity_eng.pdf, accessed 25 July 2014.

[25]See also Ambrosio and Vandrovec (2013, p. 451).

Western analysis has focused more on the impact of Russia's undemocratic and authoritarian political culture on policy making and much less on this ideational plurality. We emphasise here that the reality is much more complex: there are contending ideas that influence Russian foreign policy, resulting from a singular interplay between domestic political debates and elites' perceptions of the external environment. However, influential elements in the governing elite have succeeded in shaping narratives that marginalise more liberal policy preferences. This has a crucial bearing on the resolution of the conflict in eastern Ukraine and future relations between Russia and Europe. Whereas Moscow's rhetoric about sovereign autonomy has in the past masked a higher degree of normative and regulative commitment to shared security governance than was generally supposed, in which the legitimacy of European norms was partly accepted, this is now overshadowed by the governing elite's perception of Europe's weakness and lack of legitimacy and a consequent shift towards 'primitive' forms of multilateralism (Averre 2010, p. 284). We consider in the next section how NATO and the EU deal with Russia's self-exclusion from European security governance.

Europe's response to the Ukraine conflict

As suggested in our introduction, high-level Western statements in response to Russia's intervention in Ukraine have sought to develop a dominant narrative that discredits and marginalises Moscow's claims. We consider below how this informs the policies of NATO and the EU as the preeminent institutional actors in European security governance. We examine critically whether their response is informed by a clear and coherent purpose directed at feasible policy outcomes. We also assess the role of the OSCE and in particular the Special Monitoring Mission, and consider to what extent its monitoring of the conflict in Ukraine has contributed to managing the crisis and reviving a measure of cooperative security in line with the organisation's basic principles.

For many Western defence experts the lesson learned from Ukraine is that, given the non-transparent build-up of Russia's military capabilities near its western borders and 'a sufficient level of interest and perceived opportunity', Moscow is prepared to 'trigger a rapid escalation from the non-military to a military phase' in regional conflicts (Johnson 2015, p. 9). NATO's implementation of its Readiness Action Plan—which will effect 'a far-reaching adaptation of NATO military strategic posture' with a 'renewed emphasis on deterrence and collective defence capabilities'—centres on the 'spearhead' Very High Readiness Joint Task Force within the NATO Response Force, which has quickly reached operational status and is capable of rapid deployment to the Baltic states, Poland, Bulgaria and Romania.[26] Member states thus receive 'assurance' under the Article 5 collective defence guarantees. A further adaptation of overall NATO strategy is anticipated in the run-up to its July 2016 summit in Warsaw. A NATO White Paper has advocated 'a far-reaching transformation of the Alliance' to update its readiness 'by an order of magnitude, not just incrementally'; it explicitly refers to a Russia 'unconstrained by international law' posing a long-term threat to Allies and EU member states and recommends a 'strategic realignment' of the Alliance's core tasks to include a central role for deterrence, the pursuit of 'options for collective defence measures under

---

[26]'Statement by NATO Defence Ministers', NATO Press release (2015) 094, 25 June 2015, available at: http://www.nato.int/cps/en/natohq/news_121133.htm, accessed 3 July 2015.

the threshold of Article 5' in response to 'hybrid warfare' and 'factors beyond the traditional purview of NATO', and 'a more coherent strategy of engagement towards strategic neighbours in the East'.[27]

The driving assumption is of a long-term adversarial relationship with Russia that demands a return to collective defence. To what extent NATO's military preparedness is accompanied by an articulate political response is questionable, however. There is a considerable level of uncertainty over Moscow's intentions and a marked reluctance to slip back into direct confrontation and escalate tensions; even the White Paper talks of aspirations for a 'strategic partnership' with Russia. The US has committed additional forces to Europe but—given its numerous commitments elsewhere—has not effected a major shift in its strategic posture (Simon 2015, pp. 974–75). Germany has taken the lead in Europe's response to the Ukraine crisis but Berlin has been reticent about the military response and ruled out a permanent NATO deployment to the east as a violation of the 1997 NATO–Russia Founding Act,[28] thereby upsetting its eastern neighbours, who argue that it constitutes a weak deterrent capability which may embolden Moscow to test the Alliance further (Speck 2015).[29] The Very High Readiness Joint Task Force itself may be a 'powerful Allied symbol' but constitutes a relatively modest force; it has an uncertain political–military rationale and may face logistical problems which makes it unsuited for the potential challenges presented by Russia's 'hybrid warfare' (Zapfe 2015, pp. 9–10). The Defence Investment Pledge launched at the Wales summit, probably the minimum necessary to allow NATO to effect a reorientation to collective defence postures while retaining expeditionary capabilities, may not be realised by most member states unless serious escalation occurs; this would widen the transatlantic divide over security in Europe and exacerbate the differing threat perceptions among NATO member states.

Nor is it clear how NATO's response affects security governance with respect to Ukraine itself. Despite the Poroshenko government's commitment to Euro–Atlantic integration, Ukraine—still beset by domestic difficulties—is offered only 'strategic consultations' outside of the Article 5 provisions and cooperation on defence education, security sector governance, defence capacity-building and crisis management cooperation (Yost 2015, pp. 519–23), rather than robust military assistance. Political support to 'enhance Ukraine's ability to provide for its own security, and further improve the interoperability between Ukrainian and NATO Forces' appears to add up to little more than what was provided for in the 1997 'Distinctive Partnership'.[30]

NATO's emphasis on collective defence and deterrence does not address the central problem of the institutional decay in the NATO–Russia relationship and the vacuum in security governance in the neighbourhood. Indeed, it risks a return to a 'security dilemma' that may become a structural factor in the security politics of the wider Europe (Heisbourg 2015, p. 41). Moscow has, predictably, accused NATO of displaying 'the behavioural instincts of the

---

[27]*Next Steps in NATO's Transformation: To the Warsaw Summit and Beyond*, NATO/Atlantic Council White Paper, NATO Transformation Seminar, Washington, DC, March 2015, pp. 1–2, 5, 10, available at: http://www.atlanticcouncil.org/images/files/publication_pdfs/NATO_NTS_2015_White_Paper_Final.pdf, accessed 10 September 2015.

[28]See, 'Founding Act on Mutual Relations, Cooperation and Security between NATO and the Russian Federation, signed in Paris, France', 27 May 1997, available at: http://www.nato.int/cps/en/natolive/official_texts_25468.htm, accessed 4 April 2016.

[29]See also Forsberg (2016).

[30]'Joint Statement of the NATO–Ukraine Commission', NATO Press Release (2015)074, 13 May 2015, available at: http://www.nato.int/cps/en/natohq/news_112695.htm, accessed 28 October 2015.

Cold War years' and escalating tensions along its northwestern border in contravention of its commitments under the Founding Act (Grushko 2015), citing justification for its own large-scale military exercises due to concerns over NATO's ballistic missile defence posture and the US's space-based weapons and Prompt Global Strike capabilities. Even while accentuating its readiness to restore a partnership with Moscow, the Alliance's capacity-building efforts—heralded as 'containment' and 'deterrence' but without a clear political strategy that might motivate Moscow to initiate a fresh dialogue—does not resolve the conundrum of how to deal with Russia without provoking a Cold War-type confrontation that would threaten any shared approach to security governance.

A coherent foundation for security governance in the wider Europe is possibly even less in evidence when we consider the EU's policy.[31] All conceptions for its relationship with Russia—common spaces, strategic partnership and even partnership for modernisation—have failed to establish shared understandings over security. The EU is not involved in the Normandy format in support of the Minsk Agreements, in which Moscow deals with France and Germany (while at the same time demanding that the EU must put pressure on Kyiv to resolve the conflict in the Donbas). The only Common Security and Defence Policy (CSDP) instrument is the civilian EU Advisory Mission for Civilian Security Sector Reform Ukraine, tasked with supporting revised security policies and the rapid implementation of reforms in Ukraine. Russia's Ambassador to the EU has stated that Crimea is off the table in EU–Russia political dialogue other than with respect to talks on sanctions (Chizhov 2015). Brussels is locked into these sanctions and trade restrictions that narrow the basis for the relationship with Russia and may well be provoking a more *dirigiste* system of political economy (Connolly 2015) and a concerted attempt to diversify trade relations away from the EU.[32] Consultations between the EU and Russia on the Association Agreement and (following a delay in its implementation) the DCFTA, and negotiations over energy and other key trade issues, have kept contacts open. However, Russia's longer-term goal of a meaningful agreement between the EU and the Eurasian Economic Union (EEU)—possible only with compatible regulatory systems—appears unrealistic, particularly when the EU and Russia have not even been able to negotiate a successor to the Partnership and Cooperation Agreement, the legal basis of the relationship. The promise of maintaining stability and prosperity as the basis for security in a benign neighbourhood appears precarious.

Yet Russia remains a strategic priority for many EU member states. The High Representative for Common Foreign and Security Policy Federica Mogherini has harked back to the Common Strategy and spoken of restoring 'shared influence' by bringing Russia back to be a 'responsible power' (Mogherini 2015). She attracted criticism for an 'Issues Paper' from the EU Foreign Affairs Council which—while calling for strengthening the EU's and its neighbours' resilience to 'future Russian pressure, intimidation and manipulation' and maintaining sanctions as a response to 'violations of the rules-based international order'—spoke of interest-driven 'trade-offs' in a process of 'selective and gradual re-engagement', including between the EU and the EEU.[33] Any settlement that allows Russia to influence bilateral EU–Ukraine dialogue would reduce Ukraine 'to a mere subject of discussion [and] entail enormous adverse consequences

---

[31]For a critical analysis see Haukkala's essay in this collection.

[32]See Romanova's essay in this contribution.

[33]'Issues Paper on Relations with Russia', Foreign Affairs Council, 19 January 2015, available at: http://blogs.ft.com/brusselsblog/files/2015/01/Russia.pdf, accessed 17 February 2015.

for the country's internal stability and geopolitical consequences for the EU … [it would be] a strategic abdication made by the European Union in the East' (Eberhardt 2014, pp. 3–4). The Common Strategy is now wholly unacceptable to some European elites as a realistic intellectual framework for dealing with Moscow's challenge to European security governance.

The lack of an EU strategic framework, in terms of a set of core assumptions about how first-order security challenges should be dealt with, is evident. If Ukraine's sovereignty and independence is a crucial marker for the future of the European order, simply providing through the Association Agreement/DCFTA a credible alternative to economic dependence on Russia is insufficient. Yet the CSDP—designed to 'protect [the EU's] interests and project its values by contributing to international security, helping to prevent and resolve crises and including through projecting power'—was barely invoked as an appropriate policy instrument in the Ukraine conflict and there has been no discernible effort to coordinate the CSDP and the ENP or EaP; a lack of leadership, deriving from the overlapping competences among its institutions, weakens coordination among heads of state and governments over power projection and precludes effective strategic vision (Howorth 2014, pp. 134–40).[34] The EU and its member states have been involved in some form in all of the frozen conflicts in the former USSR countries but have been unable to force a resolution (Zagorski 2011, pp. 55–7). The CSDP, predicated on autonomy from NATO so that Europeans would provide for their own security, has not led to the crafting of a European strategic doctrine and has generated limited autonomous military capacity. Rethinking institutional arrangements between the CSDP and NATO post-Ukraine in order to establish a 'single regional capacity' for stabilising the wider European neighbourhood, with greater NATO–EU defence cooperation—as advocated in the NATO White Paper—would mean Europe reaching consensus over core security threats, committing resources and finding the political will to project power for conflict resolution in the east (Tardy 2015).

One commentator raises an important question: 'After Crimea and MH-17 [the Malaysian airliner disaster], how many red lines have to be crossed before the EU is able to overcome its cowardice and effectively counter such disdain for international law and the lives of innocent civilians in a conflict on its borders?' (Blockmans 2014). As it stands the EU, still riven by divisions among its member states and struggling to define its key strategic interests, is undermined as an effective security governance actor. The sanctions regime has largely held so far—not least in Germany, despite its substantial trade and continuing interest in energy cooperation through Nord Stream 2 (Forsberg 2016)—but there is little sign of Moscow's adopting a more constructive approach to security governance. Mogherini has been tasked with 'continu[ing] the process of strategic reflection with a view to preparing an EU global strategy on foreign and security policy … to be submitted to the European Council by June 2016'.[35] However, the EU is yet to set credible objectives with respect to Ukraine that can employ Brussels' extensive range of instruments and work within other multilateral mechanisms, including resolving the thorny issue of cooperation with NATO (Tocci 2014; Biscop 2015). In a situation where security governance in its vicinity is unravelling, in both the east and the south, there are calls for the ENP to be recalibrated into a pragmatic foreign policy able to give 'thicker substance to its proclaimed positive-sum, values-oriented version of geopolitics'

[34]See also Richter (2016, pp. 57–9).
[35]See European Council Meeting conclusions, EUCO 22/15, 25–26 June 2015.

in its dealings with Russia and with other neighbourhood states to guide the EU's external action (Youngs & Pishchikova 2013, pp. 3, 5).[36] Yet the 2015 Review of the ENP emphasises 'stabilisation as its main political priority', makes no real commitments in terms of CSDP activity and makes only cursory references to Russia (European Commission 2015a). The Joint Staff Working Document (2015) that accompanied the Review is similarly circumspect and pragmatic, stating that 'constructive cooperation with Russia could potentially be beneficial in terms of addressing the common challenges [and] would need to be consistent with EU's overall policy and relations with Russia and take due account of the state of relations between the ENP partners and Russia' (European Commission 2015b). The EU's normative concerns in Ukraine demand deeper engagement with Kyiv but clash with a policy—proper to a 'strategic actor'—of reengagement with Russia.

NATO and the EU have made little headway is reestablishing rules-based governance in the east of the continent. What does the OSCE offer? The Ukraine conflict is an important test for the latter's capacity for crisis management, as it became the principal multilateral platform on which cooperative measures to defuse the conflict were adopted. It has carried out much of the work on the ground in Ukraine, acting as a party in the Trilateral Contact Group along with Russia and Ukraine and mandated through the Special Monitoring Mission to monitor the movement of forces and exchange of prisoners, facilitate dialogue, aid civil society in conflict resolution and report on the humanitarian, social and economic situation to help guide political negotiations. Although excluded from Crimea, it has achieved some successes in mitigating the worst of the conflict in eastern Ukraine and supporting civil society's engagement in conflict resolution and reform (OSCE 2015b). It has formed an important link with wider international activities through the EU Advisory Mission for Civilian Security Sector Reform Ukraine, UN Human Rights monitoring mission and other international organisations. A powerful speech by foreign minister Frank-Walter Steinmeier, in advance of Germany taking over chairmanship of the OSCE in 2016, affirmed Berlin's aim of returning the OSCE to its basic principles and seeking a resolution of the Ukraine conflict, with a particular emphasis on the human dimension (Steinmeier 2015). An authoritative report calls for greater political support for the organisation from its member states, greater autonomy for its institutions, a long-term strategy for protracted conflicts and a permanent dialogue between Russia and the West to revitalise arms control and confidence and security building measures; it also appeals for adherence to the full package of its founding norms and for 'quiet diplomacy', backed up by an effective monitoring instrument, to impel all member states to observe human rights commitments (Tiilikainen 2015).

However, the OSCE has become an arena for political 'mud-slinging' over Ukraine rather than a credible forum for constructive political negotiations on security governance rooted in the traditional OSCE concept of comprehensive, cooperative and indivisible security to increase trust and transparency (Sammut & D'Urso 2015). The US and Ukraine accuse Russia of committing troops, arming rebels and supporting violations of ceasefires and restricting access of monitors, while Moscow in turn criticises Washington and Kyiv for interfering with the Special Monitoring Mission and preventing balanced reporting by OSCE observers (Lukashevich 2015). Moscow is accused of using the OSCE as a 'fig-leaf', appearing to agree to common endeavours but blocking reform of the organisation and manipulating the Special

[36]See also Kostanyan (2015).

Monitoring Mission and the border mission (Dehez & Rieck 2015). For its part, Moscow has decided not to participate in consultations on unusual military activities, complaining that confidence and security building measures under the OSCE Vienna document have been used instrumentally for purposes other than confidence-building. The Special Monitoring Mission is hindered by a lack of cooperation between the belligerent parties and by the fact that there is no undisputed factual basis on which opposing accounts of events can be effectively assessed. The divergence between Western and Russian interpretations of the conflict is reflected in a report by eminent persons which concluded that the Special Monitoring Mission and Trilateral Group have crucially lacked political support, with only modest progress made in implementing the Minsk Agreements (OSCE 2015a). With the sovereignty of Ukraine still to be effectively recognised by Moscow, the two sides are yet to find a common language that may allow the OSCE to take on responsibility for peaceful conflict resolution. The prospects for Russia, Ukraine and Europe agreeing on an implementable framework for a political settlement— designed to balance Ukraine's integration into Europe with a mutually acceptable partnership with Russia—appear remote.

Rethinking Russia's place in European security

We have outlined above the fundamental problems inherent in managing the changing environment of contemporary European security governance. Russia's policies point to an increasing institutional and normative separation from Europe. Moscow's apparent readiness to disregard the 'costs and consequences' of non-compliance with the Western-led normative order to pursue its own vital strategic interests in Ukraine goes hand in hand with its criticism of the West's own disregard of international norms, impelled by the perceived triumph of liberal values after the end of the Cold War. Moscow's perceptions are of an anarchic and unstable international system in which Russia's domestic legitimacy is continually questioned by the West and its leading role in the European order is challenged by the EU's promotion of its domestic norms and values in its foreign policy—unambiguously enshrined as a 'moral duty' in the Lisbon Treaty (Biscop 2015, p. 4). What are the broader strategic implications, for both Europe and Russia, arising from the latter's exclusion or self-exclusion from this order, and for rules-based security governance in the neighbourhood?

Michael Smith has argued that the securitisation of new areas of international life poses a critical challenge to Europe: that of managing the 'new geopolitics … in which the rising powers have taken a major role' (Smith 2013, p. 660). The EU's bilateral approach to institutionalising links with the emerging powers has been patchy and has not addressed major security concerns, diminishing expectations of it as a potential 'strategic' partner (Smith 2013, p. 665). Other experts agree that the EU's reliance on the legal constraints of treaties and permanent institutions, and on convergence with European legislation to integrate the wider Europe, has fallen short in terms of providing a comprehensive political vision that can enforce and maintain a regional order (Vimont 2015). The EU is unprepared for a major policy recalibration: 'In the context of a resurgent Russia and increasing enlargement fatigue within and outside the EU, the power of conditionality seems even more limited than was previously the case … [in a] new regional context [of] dislocation and instability' (Juncos & Whitman 2015, p. 213). As for NATO, while some experts suggest that the Ukraine conflict has consolidated Alliance members behind a new policy towards Russia (Freedman 2014,

p. 25), others argue that this does not constitute a genuine strategic approach due to differing views on Russia between the US and Europe and among European states (Dempsey 2014). The US, distracted by issues further afield, wants Europe to bear more of the burden of security in its eastern neighbourhood but will be forced to lead on 'traditional' security issues, with the CFE Treaty effectively defunct, reciprocal accusations over breaches of the INF treaty and NATO's US-designed ballistic missile defence system forcing Moscow to review its nuclear posture (Arbatov 2015; Kamp 2015). The political and diplomatic resources needed to tackle the challenges of arms control—not to mention 'hybrid' warfare—are considerable. Meanwhile Europe's leaders have to contend with financial and economic problems, the rise of Islamic State and the migrant and refugee crisis.

Transforming the post-Cold War European order is giving way to the priority task of containing the challenges to collective security governance. The West now faces the fundamental problem of preserving a liberal governance framework in its approach to Ukraine and the neighbourhood countries, complicated by 'domestic power struggles and entrenched illiberalism' there (Youngs & Pishchikova 2013) and Moscow's competing approach to politics and trade. The European focus on a rules-based order, closely bound up with the notion of an international society underpinned by shared values and common understandings, must deal with a Russia that insists on 'more flexible, non-bloc mechanisms of multilateral interaction' (Lavrov 2011) and respect for the 'national, cultural and historical peculiarities of each state' (Lavrov 2012). The Normandy format has had no conspicuous success to date in implementing the Minsk Agreements, with the Donbas effectively becoming a 'frozen' conflict. Russia wants to deal with the major European states at the expense of EU solidarity (Lavrov 2015i). Sanctions and containment measures aside, the EU's and NATO's professed belief in the possibility of reengaging with Russia—despite the political and security challenges posed by Moscow's policies—may ultimately encourage the partial defection of European countries where common interests with Russia predominate. As pointed out earlier, the vacuum of security governance is complicated by uncertainty over whether Russia will press further claims in the east of the continent.

There is also uncertainty over how resilient Russia will prove to be in terms of sustaining the costs of marginalisation in Europe. Sanctions and the slump in oil and commodities prices are depressing its economy. The Putin regime's attempt to narrow relations with the EU to the transactional level and rely on the EEU and the other BRICS states—which depend heavily on technology and trade links with the West and are facing economic problems of their own—undercut the imperatives of modernisation. The resources it can draw on to maintain its great power role and status as a legitimate regional actor—in terms of its political institutions, economic and social models and a clear normative commitment to contemporary international law (Urnov 2014, p. 306)—have suffered as a result of its actions in Ukraine.[37] Its strategic edifice, both in the regional and global contexts, is being built on preserving rather than transforming the international order, privileging authoritarian and/or corrupt regimes in states barely able to sustain sovereignty and in some cases not *de jure* recognised internationally. The preoccupation of the Putin regime with the maintenance of state order in Russia means that, beyond a search for great-power status and rhetorical appeals for partnerships with other leading powers, Moscow struggles to articulate progressive initiatives in the face of global political and social change and the break-up of the established order. There is only limited

[37]See also Freedman (2014, p. 14).

evidence, as suggested earlier, that officially-inspired conservative values are becoming the basis for Russia's social model or in any real way influencing its neighbours. Russia lacks a vision to sustain its influence in a rapidly evolving world; it risks regime delegitimation if the economy fails and threatens stability.

Putin's use of nationalist support for domestic legitimation of his political strategy, placing Ukraine at the heart of Russian identity, also faces problems. The regime has been criticised in the nationalist media over its reluctance to follow up the Crimea annexation by recognising the Novorossiya referendum. Moscow has distanced itself from calls for further expansion in Ukraine and the Donets'k and Luhans'k republics have not been recognised. Despite its assertive rhetoric, Moscow appears not to want to aggravate differences with the West and bear the burden of supporting the Donbas. Continuing attempts to justify intervention mask a reactive policy that stems from the absence of checks and balances in the decision-making *vertikal*. Russia's foreign policy ideology, based in a traditionalist political culture and historical ideas of a strong multinational state, is currently mediated by a regime which jealously monopolises political and information resources and tries to 'nationalise' the elites (Rodkiewicz & Rogoza 2015, p. 17). However, it is fearful of change and—as argued earlier in this essay—prey to divided opinions within these elites, some of which recognise the benefits of European political, economic and social models. Foreign policy is a function of a domestic political contest in which diplomacy is captured by nationalist-conservative narratives and tends to generate disproportionate expectations of Russia's influence. Churkin's call for the 'normalization' of Ukraine (UN 2015a) attests Moscow's ambition to restore something like the corrupt and ineffective pre-Euromaidan *status quo*; however, it offers no real normative content that can be convincingly defended intellectually and morally in terms that the West would understand.

There is thus a considerable degree of uncertainty about the future complexion of security governance in the wider Europe. Realist notions of a 'bipolar' Europe, with Ukraine as a neutral 'buffer', are inadequate to conceptualise the emerging situation. A less well-defined picture may be emerging in which a broader array of international actors create multiple and fluid sets of relations which are interest- rather than norms- and values-based, in an environment of 'ad hoc concert diplomacy' (Heisbourg 2015, p. 36). The Western-led rules-based order may be giving way to 'a multi-hub structure ... in which a growing number of states can and do play issue-specific leadership roles in a far more flexible and fluid legal system' (Burke-White 2014, p. 66).[38] Wohlforth's (2014) idea referred to earlier, of a 'thickly institutionalized' system constraining revisionist challengers, may underestimate the impact on security governance of Russia's challenge to this system. With some European elites recognising that Russian views over developments in the neighbourhood must be heeded, 'the [Eastern] partnership looks set to resemble a framework of negotiated order, within which Russia has a *de facto* if not a formal voice. The dynamics of assertively extending EU rules and norms are in retreat' (de Waal & Youngs 2015). Within this 'negotiated order' Russia resists incorporation into European security governance to reassert itself as the hub of an alternative legal-normative system within which it pursues its regional preferences; Crimea and the Donbas, like South Ossetia and Abkhazia—which recently signed a treaty with Russia on alliance and strategic partnership, establishing a 'common space' in areas of defence, security, social policy, economy and culture (Falkowski 2014)—claim their own sources

---

[38]See also Missiroli (2015).

of legitimacy despite their non-recognition by most of the international community. This alternative system is underpinnned by an information space in which 'alternative narratives … which act as a force multiplier in the conflict' are constructed (Seselgyte 2014), further reinforcing the governance divide in Europe.

Conclusions

Ukraine has highlighted the deep divisions in thinking between Russian and European political elites over fundamental principles of regional security governance. Russia's challenge to NATO and the EU—in particular their promotion of liberal norms in the eastern neighbourhood—has completed a paradigm shift debated for some time in the security governance literature. The current governing elite's view is that Russia must assert itself, in an unstable and inhospitable security environment, against the structural challenge presented by NATO and systemic challenges to the legitimacy of its domestic political model by the EU. These two organisations are unable to fill the governance vacuum that generates instability in the eastern neighbourhood. Moscow even contests shared norms in the OSCE due to the latter's perceived bias against Russia and other eastern member states. The Ukraine crisis has provoked the Putin regime to reject liberal interdependence in favour of illiberal sovereign statism as a guarantee of power and influence in the international system. The evidence appears to point to a 'negotiated order' in which Moscow can pursue its sovereign interests, characterised by divergent values and political outlooks, to the detriment of a common normative and institutional framework for security governance.

However, this essay raises an important caveat in relation to the above conclusion. There is uncertainty over to what extent 'the ideational influences of Russian nationalists marked by pronounced hostility to western powers and rather Manichean world-view' (Allison 2014, p. 1288) are likely to endure. These influences have always been present in post-Cold War Russian political thinking, driven by a great power complex and a 'realist' view of an anarchic global environment. As Renee DeNevers recognised early in the post-Soviet period, in the absence of agreement in Russia over national identity and national interests, 'the debate over foreign and security policy became a deeper one over the nature of the state itself' (DeNevers 1994, p. 23). We argue that Russian foreign policy is marked by a complex interplay between an attachment to sovereign autonomy on the one hand and interdependent approaches to regional and global security problems on the other. Domestic politics in Russia is influenced by moderate elites who are critical of the tendency to mark the country off in political and civilisational terms from Europe. Moscow's emphasis on cultural and civilisational pluralism in normative disputes stems more from a belief that the current institutional order is failing to meet the challenges of post-Cold War governance rather than a fundamental shift in national identity. Its desire to avoid isolation and calls for what amounts to co-management of the European security order—in Putin's words, 'a clear system of mutual commitments and agreements' (Putin 2014b)—suggest a reluctance to return to a détente-like co-existence of two hostile orders. Despite the overblown rhetoric often employed, the recognition that Russia's interests are closely bound up with Europe reflects an understanding of the limitations of its influence in regional affairs.

The evidence suggests that any resolution of the discord in European security governance is a long-term affair. A 'grand bargain'—'a durable compromise between liberal values and power politics' (Rynning 2015, p. 551), whereby NATO and the EU accede to demands for co-management of the European security order and accept *de facto* a Russian 'sphere of privileged interests'—would not address the root cause of the governance problem. An uneasy compromise between a commitment by Kyiv to real devolution in the east, Moscow's acceptance of Ukraine's control over its borders, Ukraine's agreement not to seek NATO membership and some kind of formula for Crimea would set a damaging precedent for Europe–Russia relations. Russia's continuing military involvement in the Donbas, as well as the use of political and economic levers against Ukraine (and elsewhere in the post-Soviet space), can not be accommodated within any shared rules-based governance in the wider Europe. NATO's rhetorically robust response is limited to assurance for the eastern European member states; striking a balance between a policy of deterrence and revitalising security dialogue with Russia—uncomfortably reminiscent of the debate surrounding the Cold War-era Harmel Report (Webber 2007, p. 83; Kuehn 2015)—leaves the question of stable security governance in the eastern neighbourhood open and NATO–Russia relations hostage to unforeseen events. The EU also faces squaring a stubborn circle: how to exert a transformative influence in the neighbourhood while rebuilding a functional and stable, if not fully strategic, relationship with Russia. Its response to Ukraine will be an important marker of its foreign and security policy ambitions. Important though the EU–Ukraine Association Agreement is to Kyiv, the EU's commitment is confined to partnership and (most likely limited) economic integration for the foreseeable future. Enlargement is no longer an option and even association for Ukraine and other EaP countries prompts divided opinions among EU member states. Russia itself puts forward no transformative concepts apart from poorly worked-out proposals for a European security treaty and the notion of an 'integration of integrations' between the EU and EEU, without any clear idea of its legal and regulatory basis. Indeed, Lavrov—implicitly recognising that a legal agreement is no longer possible—has called for 'open, unformalised dialogue on ways to form a single economic and humanitarian space from Lisbon to Vladivostok relying on the principles of equal and indivisible security' (Lavrov 2015h).

The present impasse may resolve itself in one of two ways. In the first, NATO and the EU face a semi-autarkic Russia that rejects engagement with Europe, with the possibility of further attempts to revise rules-based governance in the east of the continent. This means the emergence of a weakly-institutionalised Russia/Eurasia hub, with *ad hoc* informal or issue-specific contacts and transactional trade relations between Russia and Europe, and with the OSCE restricted to a crisis monitoring role complicated by Russia's ambivalent commitment to observing the Helsinki principles. In this negative-sum scenario Europe may once again increasingly rely on US military power at the expense of a coherent political approach. It already faces a new 'security dilemma', in many respects more complex than during the Cold War: to sustain its investment in reform and capacity-building in Ukraine as a prerequisite to deeper partnership and integration while devising a genuine strategy to face down the tensions and risks that may well arise with Russia. In other words, this would involve a long-term neo-containment approach, with none of the trust and accceptance of common goals and norms characteristic of security governance. In other words, managing insecurity.

A second, positive-sum scenario is to devise a long-term approach to manage interdependence. The inclusion of Russia into a Western-led system of security governance based on trust is a remote prospect. Both Russia and the West accept there is no early return to 'business as usual'. Moscow is not at present ready to accept normative constraints and reform its domestic political and economic order. However, as Flynn and Farrell (1999, p. 531) argue, states focus on recalibrating normative frameworks when the conditions and assumptions on which the previous structure of relations was based are in disarray. Russia can only be properly reengaged if norms are collectively legitimised and universally applied. It can not be ruled out that its longer-term interests—the need for modernisation and for stability and prosperity on its Western flank—will induce Moscow ultimately to retreat from self-exclusion. Russian elites, some of them sympathetic to Europe, have over two decades of experience of working with European institutions; in several EU member states there are political and economic elites more favourably disposed towards Russia. Existing platforms for dialogue on broader governance may underpin a resumption of state-level negotiations, with support from track-2 initiatives. The OSCE has an important role to play in cooperation on crisis management and as a forum for relegitimising the core principles of shared security governance on a pan-European basis. Sequencing a retreat from the current estrangement—a cooperative effort to broker and guarantee a constitutional settlement in Ukraine, easing sanctions and reviving trade and political–military links—demands a considerable investment of political will: Europe and Russia would have to address the cause, not the symptoms, of previous failures through negotiation over core principles and norms, and recalibrating security regimes and institutional arrangements, instead of relying on *ad hoc* agreements. There is a rich agenda here for scholars of security governance and Russia. The contours of a longer-term partnership are hard to discern but a sustained focus on positive-sum outcomes has a recent intellectual history, and support from some elites in Moscow, which Europe's policy makers may draw on.

References

Allison, R. (2014) 'Russian "Deniable" Intervention in Ukraine: How and Why Russia Broke the Rules', *International Affairs*, 90, 6.

Ambrosio, T. & Vandrovec, G. (2013) 'Mapping the Geopoliticsof the Russian Federation: The Federal Assembly Addresses of Putin and Medvedev', *Geopolitics*, 18, 2.

Arbatov, A. (2014) 'Collapse of the World Order?', *Russia in Global Affairs*, 23 September, available at: http://eng.globalaffairs.ru/number/Collapse-of-the-World-Order-16987, accessed 4 May 2015.

Arbatov, A. (2015) *An Unnoticed Crisis: The End of History for Nuclear Arms Control?*, Carnegie Moscow Center, 16 June, available at: http://carnegieendowment.org/files/CP_Arbatov2015_n_web_Eng.pdf, accessed 29 November 2015.

Averre, D. (2010) 'Russia: A Global Power?', in Kirchner, E. J. & Sperling, J. (eds) *National Security Cultures: Patterns of Global Governance* (London & New York, NY, Routledge).

Bazhanov, E. (2013) 'Rossiya i zapad', *Mezhdunarodnaya zhizn'*, 12.

Biscop, S. (2015) *Global and Operational: A New Strategy for EU Foreign and Security Policy*, Istituto Affari Internazionali, Working Paper 15/27, July.

Blockmans, S. (2014) *Ukraine, Russia and the Need for More Flexibility in EU Foreign Policy-Making*, Centre for European Policy Studies, Policy Brief No. 320, 25 July, available at: https://www.ceps.eu/publications/ukraine-russia-and-need-more-flexibility-eu-foreign-policy-making, accessed 10 September 2015.

Brzezinski, Z. (2014) 'Russia Needs to be Offered a "Finland Option" for Ukraine', *Financial Times*, 22 February.

Burke-White, W. W. (2014) 'Crimea and the International Legal Order', *Survival*, 56, 4.

Charap, S. & Shapiro, J. (2015) 'Consequences of a New Cold War', *Survival*, 57, 2.

Chebankova, E. (2015) 'Competing Ideologies of Russia's Civil Society', *Europe-Asia Studies*, 67, 2.

Chizhov, V. (2015) 'Interv'yu postoyannogo predstavitelya Rossii pri ES V.A. Chizhova agentstvu "Interfax"', *Interfax*, 17 June, available at: http://www.mid.ru/foreign_policy/news/-/asset_publisher/cKNonkJE02Bw/content/id/1457377, accessed 14 September 2015.

Christou, G. (2010) 'European Union Security Logics to the East: The European Neighbourhood Policy and Eastern Partnership', *European Security*, 19, 3.

Christou, G., Croft, S., Ceccorulli, M. & Lucarelli, S. (2010) 'European Union Security Governance: Putting the "Security" Back In', *European Security*, 19, 3.

Connolly, R. (2015) *Troubled Times: Stagnation, Sanctions and the Prospects for Economic Reform in Russia*, Chatham House Research Paper, February, available at: https://www.chathamhouse.org/sites/files/chathamhouse/field/field_document/20150224TroubledTimesRussiaConnolly.pdf, accessed 15 March 2016.

de Waal, T. & Youngs, R. (2015) *Reform as Resilience: An Agenda for the Eastern Partnership*, Carnegie Endowment for International Peace, 14 May, available at: http://carnegieendowment.org/2015/05/14/reform-as-resilience-agenda-for-eastern-partnership/i8k4, accessed 10 September 2015.

Dehez, D. & Rieck, C. E. (2015) 'Der deutsche OSZE-Vorsitz 2016', *Analyse und Argumente*, 171, June.

Dempsey, J. (2014) *Why Defense Matters: A New Narrative for NATO*, Carnegie Europe, June, available at: http://carnegieeurope.eu/publications/?fa=55979, accessed 10 November 2014.

DeNevers, R. (1994) 'Russia's Strategic Renovation: Russian Security Strategies and Foreign Policy in the Post-imperial Era', *The Adelphi Papers*, 34, 289.

Dragneva, R. & Wolczuk, K. (2015) *Ukraine between the EU and Russia: The Integration Challenge* (Basingstoke & New York, NY, Palgrave Macmillan).

Eberhardt, A. (2014) *Dialogue with the Eurasian Union on Ukraine—An Opportunity or a Trap?*, Centre for Eastern Studies Commentary No. 154, 1 December, available at: http://www.osw.waw.pl/sites/default/files/commentary_154.pdf, accessed 17 February 2015.

European Commission (2015a) *Review of the European Neighbourhood Policy*, Joint Communication to the European Parliament, the Council, the European Economic and Social Committee and the Committee of the Regions, JOIN(2015) 50 final, Brussels, 18 November, available at: http://eeas.europa.eu/enp/documents/2015/151118_joint-communication_review-of-the-enp_en.pdf, accessed 7 January 2016.

European Commission (2015b) *Towards a New European Neighbourhood Policy*, SWD(2015) 500 final, Brussels, 18 November, available at: http://eeas.europa.eu/enp/documents/2015/151118_staff-working-document_en.pdf, accessed 7 January 2016.

European Parliament (2015) *European Parliament Resolution of 15 January 2015 on the Situation in Ukraine*, 2014/2965(RSP), Strasbourg, 15 January, available at: http://www.europarl.europa.eu/sides/getDoc.do?pubRef=-//EP//TEXT+TA+P8-TA-2015-0011+0+DOC+XML+V0//EN, accessed 3 July 2015.

Evers, F. (2011) *The OSCE Summit in Astana: Expectations and Results*, CORE Working Paper 23, available at: https://ifsh.de/file-CORE/documents/CORE_Working_Paper_23.pdf, accessed 10 September 2015.

Falkowski, M. (2014) *Russia's 'Neighbourhood Policy': The Case of Abkhazia*, Centre for Eastern Studies Analysis, 26 November, available at: http://www.osw.waw.pl/en/publikacje/analyses/2014-11-26/russias-neighbourhood-policy-case-abkhazia, accessed 17 February 2015.

Flynn, G. & Farrell, H. (1999) 'Piecing Togther the Democratic Peace: The CSCE, Norms, and the "Construction" of Security in Post-Cold War Europe', *International Organization*, 53, 3.

Forsberg, T. (2016) 'From *Ostpolitik* to "Frostpolitik"? Merkel, Putin and German Foreign Policy Towards Russia', *International Affairs*, 92, 1.

Freedman, L. (2014) 'Ukraine and the Art of Limited War', *Survival*, 56, 6.

Garton Ash, T. (2015) 'There'll be no Peace while Putin is Squatting in Ukraine's Living Room', *The Guardian*, 17 February, available at: http://www.theguardian.com/commentisfree/2015/feb/16/peace-putin-ukraine-moscow-kiev, accessed 15 March 2016.

Glaz'ev, S. (2013) 'Takie raznye integratsii', *Rossiya v global'noi politike*, 6.

Glaz'ev, S. (2014) 'Ugroza voin i otvet Rossii', *Rossiya v global'noi politike*, 4.

Gretskiy, I., Treshchenkov, E. & Golubev, K. (2014) 'Russia's Perception and Misperceptions of the EU Eastern Partnership', *Communist and Post-Communist Studies*, 47, 3–4.

Gromyko, A. (2014) 'Smaller or Greater Europe?', *Revisti di Studi Politici Internazionali*, 81, 4, available at: http://www.ieras.ru/gromyko/Smaller%20or%20Greater%20Europe.pdf, accessed 10 November 2014.

Gromyko, A. (2015) 'Novaya normal'nost': ili novoe bol'shoe soglashenie', *Sovremennaya Evropa*, 2, available at: http://instituteofeurope.ru/images/stories/structura/gromyko/gromyko2.2015.pdf, accessed 29 November 2015.

Grushko, A. V. (2015) 'Vystuplenie postoyannogo predstavitelya Rossiiskoi Federatsii pri NATO A.V. Grushko na zasedanii Foruma po sotrudnichestvu v oblasti OBSE', Ministry of Foreign Affairs of the

Russian Federation, 18 March, available at: http://www.mid.ru/foreign_policy/news/-/asset_publisher/cKNonkJE02Bw/content/id/1104595, accessed 13 July 2015.

Heisbourg, F. (2015) 'Preserving Post-Cold War Europe', *Survival*, 57, 1.

Herman, R. G. (1996) 'Identity, Norms and National Security: The Soviet Foreign Policy Revolution and the End of the Cold War', in Katzenstein, P. J. (ed.) *The Cultuure of National Security: Norms and Identity in World Politics* (New York, NY, Columbia University Press).

House of Commons (2014) *Towards the Next Defence and Security Review: Part Two—NATO*, House of Commons Defence Committee, Third Report of Session 2014–15, 22 July (London, The Stationery Office Limited), available at: http://www.publications.parliament.uk/pa/cm201415/cmselect/cmdfence/358/358.pdf, accessed 15 March 2016.

House of Lords (2015) *The EU and Russia: Before and Beyond the Crisis in Ukraine*, House of Lords European Union Committee, 6th Report of Session 2014–15, 20 February (London, The Stationery Office Limited), available at: http://www.publications.parliament.uk/pa/ld201415/ldselect/ldeucom/115/115.pdf, accessed 15 March 2016.

Howorth, J. (2014) 'European Security Post-Libya and Post-Ukraine: In Search of Core Leadership', in Tocci, N. (ed.) *Imagining Europe: Towards a More United and Effective EU* (Rome, Istituto Affari Internazionali).

Institute of Europe (2014) 'Ukrainskii krizis: ekspertnaya otsenka', *Sovremennaya evropa*, 3, available at: http://www.sov-europe.ru/2014/3/Ukk.pdf, accessed 29 November 2014.

Johnson, D. (2015) *Russia's Approach to Conflict—Implications for NATO's Deterrence and Defence*, NATO Defense College Research Paper, Rome, No. 111, April, available at: http://www.ndc.nato.int/news/news.php?icode=797, accessed 10 September 2015.

Juncos, A. E. & Whitman, R. G. (2015) 'Europe as a Regional Actor: Neighbourhood Lost?', *Journal of Common Market Studies*, 53 Annual Review.

Kaminski, I. C. (2014) 'International Law Aspects of the Situation in Ukraine', in Bachmann, K. & Lyubashenko, I. (eds) *The Maidan Uprising, Separatism and Foreign Intervention* (Frankfurt-am-Main, Peter Lang).

Kamp, K.-H. (2015) *Nuclear Implications of the Russian–Ukrainian Conflict*, NATO Defense College Research Report 03/15, April, available at: http://www.ndc.nato.int/news/news.php?icode=789, accessed 25 July 2015.

Karaganov, S. (2014) 'Europe and Russia: Preventing a New Cold War', *Russia in Global Affairs*, 7 June, available at: http://eng.globalaffairs.ru/number/Europe-and-Russia-Preventing-a-New-Cold-War-16701, accessed 10 September 2014.

Kirchner, E. & Sperling, J. (2007) *EU Security Governance* (Manchester, Manchester University Press).

Kissinger, H. A. (2014) 'Henry Kissinger: To Settle the Ukraine Crisis, Start at the End', *The Washington Post*, 5 March, available at: https://www.washingtonpost.com/opinions/henry-kissinger-to-settle-the-ukraine-crisis-start-at-the-end/2014/03/05/46dad868-a496-11e3-8466-d34c451760b9_story.html, accessed 7 July 2015.

Kostanyan, H. (2015) *The Eastern Partnership after Riga: Review and Reconfirm*, Centre for European Policy Studies, European Neighbourhood Watch Issue 116, June, available at: https://www.ceps.eu/system/files/NWatch116.pdf, accessed 10 November 2015.

Kuehn, U. (2015) 'Deter and Engage: Making the Case for Harmel 2.0 as NATO's New Strategy', *New Perspectives*, 23, 1.

Lavrov, S. (2011) 'International Relations in a Turbulence Zone: Where are the Points of Support', *Diplomaticheskii ezhegodnik*, 29 December, available at: http://www.mid.ru/bdomp/brp_4.nsf/0/D126FA2FC8FF917B4425798200209721, accessed 9 May 2012.

Lavrov, S. (2012) 'Vystuplenie Ministra inostrannikh del Rossii S.V. Lavrova na Mezhdunarodnom parlamentskom forume "Sovremennyi parlamentarizm i budushchee demokratii"', Ministry of Foreign Affairs of the Russian Federation, 10 December, available at: http://www.mid.ru/foreign_policy/news/-/asset_publisher/cKNonkJE02Bw/content/id/131286, accessed 10 August 2015.

Lavrov, S. (2013a) 'State of the Union. Russia–EU: Prospects for Partnership in the Changing World', *Journal of Common Market Studies*, 51 Annual Review.

Lavrov, S. (2013b) 'Vystuplenie Ministra inostrannikh del Rossii S.V. Lavrova na 49-i Myunkhenskoi konferentsii po voprosam bezopasnosti', Ministry of Foreign Affairs of the Russian Federation, 2 February, Vienna, available at: http://www.mid.ru/foreign_policy/news/-/asset_publisher/cKNonkJE02Bw/content/id/124658, accessed 4 April 2016.

Lavrov, S. (2014a) 'Interv'yu Ministra inostrannikh del Rossii S.V. Lavrova telekanalu "Frans 24"', Ministry of Foreign Affairs of the Russian Federation, 16 December, available at: http://www.mid.ru/brp_4.nsf/newsline/29C0BA2F20252442C3257DB000502785, accessed 10 June 2015.

Lavrov, S. (2014b) 'It's Not Russia that is Destabilising Ukraine', *The Guardian*, 8 April, available at: http://www.theguardian.com/commentisfree/2014/apr/07/sergei-lavrov-russia-stabilise-ukraine-west, accessed 15 March 2015.

Lavrov, S. (2015a) 'Interv'yu Ministra inostrannikh del Rossii S.V. Lavrova avtorskoi programme "Vesti v subbotu s Sergeem Brilevym" na telekanale "Rossiya"', Ministry of Foreign Affairs of the Russian Federation, 21 March, available at: http://www.mid.ru/brp_4.nsf/newsline/2289F79A2C9CE38743257E0F002E980B, accessed 10 June 2015.

Lavrov, S. (2015b) 'Vstupitel'noe slovo i otvety na voprosy SMI Ministra inostrannikh del Rossii S.V. Lavrova v khode sovmestnoi press-konferentsii po itogam peregovorov s Ministrom inostrannikh del i mezhdunarodnogo sotrudnichestva Italii P. Dzhentiloni', Ministry of Foreign Affairs of the Russian Federation, 1 June, available at: http://www.mid.ru/brp_4.nsf/newsline/98FF38086C1EE30C43257E570047BFBD, accessed 10 June 2015.

Lavrov, S. (2015c) 'Interv'yu Ministra inostrannikh del Rossii S.V. Lavrova programme "Mezhdunarodnoe obozrenie" na telekanale "Rossiya 24"', Ministry of Foreign Affairs of the Russian Federation, 29 May, available at: http://www.mid.ru/brp_4.nsf/newsline/F462B34C4AA8893243257E5500220134, accessed 10 June 2015.

Lavrov, S. (2015d) 'Vystuplenie i otvety na voprosy Ministra inostrannikh del Rossii S.V. Lavrova v ramkakh "Pravitel'stvennogo chasa" v Sovete Federatsii Federal'nogo Sobraniya Rossiiskoi Federatsii', Ministry of Foreign Affairs of the Russian Federation, 20 May, available at: http://www.mid.ru/brp_4.nsf/newsline/7D5C10AE87AA6F9843257E4B003A396A, accessed 10 June 2015.

Lavrov, S. (2015e) 'Vystuplenie i otvety na voprosy Ministra inostrannikh del Rossii S.V. Lavrova v khode ezhegodnoi press-konferentsii po itogam deyatel'nosti rossiiskoi diplomatii v 2014 godu', Ministry of Foreign Affairs of the Russian Federation, 21 January, available at: http://www.mid.ru/brp_4.nsf/newsline/6631F30FBE1AB4B643257DD4003D0D59, accessed 10 June 2015.

Lavrov, S. (2015f) 'Vystuplenie Ministra inostrannikh del Rossii S.V. Lavrova na otkrytom zasedanii Soveta Bezopasnosti OON po voprosu "Podderzhanie mezhdunarodnogo mira i bezopasnosti: uroki istorii, podtverzhdenie priverzhennosti printsipam i tselyam Ustava OON"', Ministry of Foreign Affairs of the Russian Federation, 23 February, available at: http://www.mid.ru/brp_4.nsf/newsline/B31D502B22D103FE43257DF50058F38D, accessed 10 June 2015.

Lavrov, S. (2015g) 'Vstupitel'noe slovo i otvety na voprosy SMI Ministra inostrannikh del Rossii S.V. Lavrova v khode sovmestnoi press-konferentsii po itogam peregovorov s Ministrom inostrannikh del Latvii E. Rinkevichem', 12 January, available at: http://www.mid.ru/brp_4.nsf/newsline/E47437042173F9B643257DCB004C2386, accessed 10 June 2015.

Lavrov, S. (2015h) 'Vstupitel'noe slovo i otvety na voprosy SMI Ministra inostrannikh del Rossii S.V. Lavrova v khode sovmestnoi press-konferentsii po itogam peregovorov s Ministrom inostrannikh del Respubliki Belarus' V.V. Makeem', Ministry of Foreign Affairs of the Russian Federation, 8 June, available at: http://www.mid.ru/brp_4.nsf/newsline/BE236170AB02698643257E5E003AEF3E, accessed 10 June 2015.

Lavrov, S. (2015i) 'Interv'yu Ministra inostrannikh del Rossii S.V. Lavrova telekanalu "Zvezda"', Ministry of Foreign Affairs of the Russian Federation, 30 December, available at: http://www.mid.ru/foreign_policy/news/-/asset_publisher/cKNonkJE02Bw/content/id/2004143, accessed 13 January 2016.

Lewis, P., Ackerman, S. & Roberts, D. (2014) 'Obama: Russia's Actions in Ukraine put Putin "On the Wrong Side of History"', The Guardian, 3 March, available at: http://www.theguardian.com/world/2014/mar/03/russian-sanctions-likely-putin-ukraine-crimea, accessed 15 March 2016.

Lukashevich, A. K. (2015) 'Russian Permanent Representative to the OSCE Alexander Lukashevich's Interview with Rossiya Segodnya, September 16, 2015', Ministry of Foreign Affairs of the Russian Federation, available at: http://www.mid.ru/foreign_policy/news/-/asset_publisher/cKNonkJE02Bw/content/id/1756614, accessed 10 November 2015.

Matlock Jr, J. F., Pickering, T. R. & Collins, J. F. (2014) 'Give Diplomacy With Russia a Chance', The New York Times, 8 September, available at: http://www.nytimes.com/2014/09/09/opinion/give-diplomacy-with-russia-a-chance.html?_r=0, accessed 15 March 2016.

Mearsheimer, J. J. (2014) 'Getting Ukraine Wrong', The New York Times, 13 March, available at: http://www.nytimes.com/2014/03/14/opinion/getting-ukraine-wrong.html, accessed 15 March 2016.

Missiroli, A. (2015) The EU in a Multiplex World, EU–ISS Brief 7/2015, European Union Institute for Security Studies, March, available at: http://www.iss.europa.eu/uploads/media/Brief_7_ESS.pdf, accessed 4 May 2015.

Mogherini, F. (2015) 'Remarks by High Representative/Vice-President Federica Mogherini following the G7 Foreign Ministers' Meeting', European Union External Action Service, 15 April, available at: http://eeas.europa.eu/statements-eeas/2015/150415_02_en.htm, accessed 14 September 2015.

OSCE (2015a) Lessons Learned for the OSCE from its Engagement in Ukraine, Interim Report and Recommendations of the Panel of Eminent Persons on European Security as a Common Project, June, available at: http://www.osce.org/networks/164561?download=true, accessed 10 November 2015.

OSCE (2015b) Thematic Report. Civil Society and the Crisis in Ukraine, SEC/FR/125/15Corr.1*, 4 March, available at: http://www.osce.org/ukraine-smm/141046?download=true, accessed 4 May 2015.

Pourchot, G. (2011) 'The OSCE: A Pan-European Society in the Making?', *Journal of European Integration*, 33, 2.

Putin, V. (2007a) 'Vladimir Putin: Polveki evropeiskoi integratsii i Rossiya', 25 March, available at: http://www.c-society.ru/main.php?ID=289725&ar2=300&ar3=300, accessed 4 April 2016.

Putin, V. (2007b) 'Speech and the Following Discussion at the Munich Conference on Security Policy', 10 February, available at: http://archive.kremlin.ru/eng/speeches/2007/02/10/0138_type82912type82914type82917type84779_118123.shtml, accessed 10 August 2015.

Putin, V. (2014a) 'Presidential Address to the Federal Assembly', 4 December, available at: http://en.kremlin.ru/events/president/news/47173, accessed 13 April 2015.

Putin, V. (2014b) 'Meeting of the Valdai International Discussion Club', 24 October, available at: http://en.kremlin.ru/events/president/news/46860, accessed 20 November 2014.

Putin, V. (2014c) 'Address by President of the Russian Federation', 18 March, available at: http://en.kremlin.ru/transcripts/6889, accessed 15 August 2014.

Putin, V. (2014d) 'Russia–EU Summit', press conference, 28 January, available at: http://en.kremlin.ru/events/president/news/20113, accessed 5 March 2014.

Putin, V. (2014e) 'Interview to *Politika* Newspaper', 15 October, available at: http://eng.news.kremlin.ru/transcripts/23099, accessed 20 November 2014.

Richter, F. (2016) 'The Emergence and Evolution of CSDP', in Cladi, L. & Locatelli, A. (eds) *International Relations Theory and European Security* (Abingdon & New York, NY, Routledge).

Rodkiewicz, W. & Rogoza, J. (2015) *Potemkin Conservatism: An Ideological Tool of the Kremlin*, Centre for Eastern Studies Point of View No. 48, February, available at: http://www.osw.waw.pl/sites/default/files/pw_48_potemkin_conservatism_net.pdf, accessed 4 May 2015.

Ruehle, M. (2014) *NATO Enlargement and Russia: Die-Hard Myths and Real Dilemmas*, Research Report, NATO Defense College, 15 May, available at: http://www.ndc.nato.int/news/news.php?icode=676, accessed 25 July 2015.

Rynning, S. (2015) 'The False Promise of Continental Concert: Russia, the West and the Necessary Balance of Power', *International Affairs*, 91, 3.

Sakwa, R. (2015a) 'The Death of Europe? Continental Fates after Ukraine', *International Affairs*, 91, 3.

Sakwa, R. (2015b) *Frontline Ukraine: Crisis in the Borderlands* (London & New York, NY, I.B. Tauris).

Sammut, D. & D'Urso, J. (2015) *The Special Monitoring Mission in Ukraine: A Useful but Flawed tool*, European Policy Centre Policy Brief, 23 April, available at: http://aei.pitt.edu/63784/1/pub_5511_the_special_monitoring_mission_in_ukraine.pdf, accessed 10 September 2015.

Seselgyte, M. (2014) *Can Hybrid War Become the Main Security Challenge for Eastern Europe?*, Leadership Network, 17 October, available at: http://www.europeanleadershipnetwork.org/can-hybrid-war-become-the-main-security-challenge-for-eastern-europe_2025.html, accessed 10 November 2014.

Simon, L. (2015) 'Europe, the Rise of Asia and the Future of the Transatlantic Partnership', *International Affairs*, 91, 5.

Smith, M. (2013) 'Beyond the Comfort Zone: Internal Crisis and External Challenge in the European Union's Response to Rising Powers', *International Affairs*, 89, 3.

Speck, U. (2015) *German Power and the Ukraine Conflict*, Carnegie Europe, 26 March, available at: http://carnegieeurope.eu/2015/03/26/german-power-and-the-ukraine-conflict, accessed 4 May 2015.

Steinmeier, F.-W. (2015) 'Address to the OSCE Permanent Council on 2 July 2015', PC.DEL/919/15, available at: http://www.osce.org/pc/168376?download=true, accessed 29 November 2015.

Stivachtis, Y. A. & Webber, M. (2011) 'Introduction: Regional International Society in a Post-Enlargement Europe', *Journal of European Integration*, 33, 2.

Survival Forum (2015) 'NATO and Russia', *Survival*, 57, 2.

Suslov, D. (2014) 'For a Good, Long While', *Russia in Global Affairs*, December, available at: http://eng.globalaffairs.ru/number/For-a-Good-Long-While-17211, accessed 4 April 2016.

Tardy, T. (2015) *CSDP in Action—What Contribution to International Security?*, EU Institute for Security Studies Chaillot Paper, No. 134, 12 June, available at: http://www.iss.europa.eu/uploads/media/Chaillot_134_CSDP_missions.pdf, accessed 10 September 2015.

Tiilikainen, T. (ed.) (2015) *Reviving Co-operative Security in Europe through the OSCE*, OSCE Network, available at: http://www.osce.org/networks/188176?download=true, accessed 29 November 2015.

Tocci, N. (2014) *The Neighbourhood Policy is Dead. What's Next for European Foreign Policy Along its Arc of Instability?*, Istituto Affari Internazionali Working Paper 14/16, November.

Traynor, I. & MacAskill, E. (2014) 'Don't Appease Putin Like We Did Hitler, Cameron Warns', *The Guardian*, 3 September, available at: http://www.theguardian.com/politics/2014/sep/02/david-cameron-warns-appeasing-putin-ukraine-hitler, accessed 15 March 2016.

Trenin, D. (2014) *2014: Russia's New Military Doctrine Tells it All*, Carnegie Moscow Center, 29 December, available at: http://carnegie.ru/2014/12/29/2014-russia-s-new-military-doctrine-tells-it-all, accessed 17 February 2015.

UN (2014) 'Territorial Integrity of Ukraine', United Nations General Assembly, A/RES/68/262, 1 April, available at: http://www.securitycouncilreport.org/atf/cf/%7B65BFCF9B-6D27-4E9C-8CD3-CF6E4FF96 FF9%7D/a_res_68_262.pdf, accessed 10 November 2015.

UN (2015a) United Nations Security Council 7457th meeting, S/PV.7457, 5 June, available at: http://www. securitycouncilreport.org/atf/cf/%7B65BFCF9B-6D27-4E9C-8CD3-CF6E4FF96FF9%7D/s_pv_7457. pdf, accessed 10 November 2015.

UN (2015b) United Nations Security Council 7400th meeting, S/PV.7400, 6 March, available at: http://www. un.org/en/ga/search/view_doc.asp?symbol=S/PV.7400, accessed 10 November 2015.

UN (2015c) United Nations Security Council Resolution 2202, S/Res/2202, 17 February, available at: http:// www.securitycouncilreport.org/atf/cf/%7B65BFCF9B-6D27-4E9C-8CD3-CF6E4FF96FF9%7D/s_ res_2202.pdf, accessed 10 November 2015.

Urnov, M. (2014) '"Greatpowerness" as the Key Element of Russian Self-consciousness under Erosion', *Communist and Post-Communist Studies*, 47, 3–4.

Vimont, P. (2015) *The Path to an Upgraded Foreign Policy*, Carnegie Europe Policy Outlook, 30 June, available at: http://carnegieeurope.eu/2015/06/30/path-to-upgraded-eu-foreign-policy/ib7p, accessed 10 September 2015.

Webber, M. (2007) *Inclusion, Exclusion and the Governance of European Security* (Manchester & New York, NY, Manchester University Press).

Webber, M. (2011) 'NATO: Within and Between European International Society', *Journal of European Integration*, 33, 2.

Webber, M., Croft, S., Howorth, J., Terriff, T. & Krahmann, E. (2004) 'The Governance of European Security', *Review of International Studies*, 30, 1.

Williams, M. C. & Neumann, I. B. (2000) 'From Alliance to Security Community: NATO, Russia and the Power of Identity', *Millennium Journal of International Studies*, 29, 2.

Wintour, P. (2014) 'Cameron Warns Putin of More Ukraine Sanctions', *The Observer*, 16 November, available at: http://www.theguardian.com/world/2014/nov/14/putin-russia-oil-price-collapse-sanctions-g20, accessed 15 March 2016.

Wohlforth, W. C. (2015) 'The Return of Realpolitik', *Russia in Global Affairs*, 19 June, available at: http://eng. globalaffairs.ru/number/The-Return-of-Realpolitik-17536, accessed 29 November 2015.

Yakovenko, A. (2014) 'A Case Study in the Failure to Learn from History', *Russia Beyond the Headlines*, 26 August.

Yost, D. S. (2015) 'The Budapest Memorandum and Russia's Intervention in Ukraine', *International Affairs*, 91, 3.

Youngs, R. & Pishchikova, K. (2013) *Smart Geostrategy for the Eastern Partnership*, Carnegie Europe, 14 November, available at: http://carnegieeurope.eu/publications/?fa=53571, accessed 7 January 2014.

Zagorski, A. (2011) 'Eastern Partnership from the Russian Perspective', *Internazionale Politik und Gesellschaft*, 3.

Zapfe, M. (2015) *Efficacy, not Efficiency: Adjusting NATO's Military Integration*, NATO Defense College Research Paper, 118, August, available at: http://www.ndc.nato.int/news/news.php?icode=839, accessed 10 November 2015.

Zevelev, I. (2014) 'Russia's National Identity Transformation and New Foreign Policy Doctrine', *Russia in Global Affairs*, 7 June, available at: http://eng.globalaffairs.ru/number/The-Russian-World-Boundaries-16707, accessed 25 July 2014.

Russia's 'Governance' Approach:
Intervention and the Conflict in the Donbas

LANCE DAVIES

Abstract

This essay explores Russia's involvement in the conflict in the Donbas by examining the extent to which Moscow's contribution has demonstrated a governance approach. We argue that Russia's engagement has remained in a perpetual state of flux due to contradictions in its policy, shaped by the interaction of a complex set of competing security logics. Opposing the view that Russia's response is solely a policy of destabilisation, we put forward the view that Moscow's behaviour has not ruled out a positive engagement in the settlement through the selective practice of certain norms and processes underpinning a governance approach.

THE INTERNAL CONFLICT IN UKRAINE WHICH ERUPTED IN 2014 has initiated an external crisis in Russia's relations with the central actors of European security governance. One noted political commentator sums up the conflict's impact on relations as potentially marking 'the end of a generally cooperative phase in those relations [and opening] a new period of heightened rivalry, even confrontation, between former Cold War adversaries' (Trenin 2014, p. 3). The Russian leadership has looked askance at the broadening of Europe's system of security governance, believing it to be an attempt by the European Union (EU) to create a 'sphere of influence' on its borders by pressuring Ukraine to choose the way of the West at Russia's expense (Baczynska & Hudson 2014), and blaming many Western capitals for instrumentally inciting revolution in Kyiv.[1] Policy and academic communities alike in the West have agreed that Russia has, with the annexation of Crimea in March 2014 and intervention in the Donbas region, pursued a deliberate strategy of destabilisation in Ukraine through the dismemberment of the latter's sovereignty—in the words of US Secretary of State John Kerry, in order to 'change the security landscape of eastern and central Europe'.[2] This neighbourhood has been

The author would like to express his gratitude for the constructive feedback on a draft of this essay by Derek Averre and Kasia Wolczuk, both of CREES, University of Birmingham, and he would also like to thank the anonymous referees for their helpful comments.

[1]'Lavrov Accuses West of Using Ukraine as a Pawn', *The Telegraph*, 24 April 2014, available at: http://www.telegraph.co.uk/news/worldnews/europe/russia/10784310/Lavrov-accuses-West-of-using-Ukraine-as-a-pawn.html, accessed 12 March 2015.

[2]'John Kerry Rips into "Putin's Russia" over Ukraine Crisis', *The Guardian*, 30 April 2014, available at: http://www.theguardian.com/world/2014/apr/30/john-kerry-rips-into-putins-russia-over-ukraine-crisis, accessed 12 March 2015.

the main area of contention between Russia and the main European actors, with scholarly opinion pointing towards divergent interpretations between Moscow and Western capitals about what this space signifies for European security governance (Averre 2009; Webber 2009, p. 270).[3]

Existing research on conflict management in the neighbourhood has already criticised the legitimacy of Russia's approach. Western capitals claim that Moscow has utilised various instruments in a carefully calibrated strategy to safeguard its political aims in Ukraine. This has been reflected in much of the academic debate which views the methods Moscow has employed as a policy of destabilisation (Allison 2014; Freedman 2014; Wilson 2014; Giles 2015). The operational basis of Moscow's intervention—described as a form of hybrid warfare in support of the pro-Russian opposition in the Donbas—has been traced to an article authored by Russia's Chief of the General Staff, Valerii Gerasimov (2013). Confirming for many Moscow's calculated approach, Gerasimov (2013, p. 2) points out that this type of warfare emphasises 'the use of political, economic, information, humanitarian, and other non-military measures, implemented by taking advantage of the protest-making capabilities of the population' in addition to the use of 'special forces' under the pretext of 'peacekeeping' and 'crisis management' operations. Indeed, NATO's Supreme Allied Commander Europe, General Breedlove, has concluded: 'This is a 21st-century offensive employing 21st-century tools for strategic deception and calculated ambiguity to achieve Moscow's political goals' (Breedlove 2014). This is considered to be a replay and an escalation of previous tactics (Mankoff 2014, p. 214), embedded in a problematic regional legacy of interference, coercion and disproportionate force which fundamentally departs from the practices of a governance approach that have evolved in the system of European security governance (Crow 1992; Allison 1994, 2008, 2009, 2013; MacFarlane & Schnabel 1995; Jonson & Archer 1996; Baev 1997, 1998, 2003; Jonson 2000; Lynch 2000, 2002; Mackinlay 2003a, 2003b; Sagramoso 2003).

This essay situates the analysis in this framework of European security governance, which captures the evolutionary changes of policy and practice in European conflict management, as a means to interrogate the extent to which Russia's behaviour reflects the policies and practices of a governance approach towards the ongoing conflict. This framework will also help to embed the analysis in the wider debate on Russia and contemporary European security. We challenge the mainstream narrative by showing that Russia's involvement in the ongoing conflict in Ukraine demonstrates a complexity based on both convergence with and divergence from a governance approach, and that this has been expressed in Russia's regional legacy of conflict management. The essay specifically focuses on Russia's involvement in the Donbas,[4] rather than its intervention in Crimea, which was indeed more calculated and has already been dealt with elsewhere in the existing literature (Allison 2014; Wilson 2014). Crucially, shaping Moscow's participation in the Donbas—and its regional response towards intra-state conflict more generally—is the interaction between a conflicting set of security logics, in pursuit of what Russia considers as the maintenance of regional stability and security. These include a humanitarian justification for the protection of Russia's diaspora and other regional populations, which has been both promoted for genuine reasons and used instrumentally to

---

[3]This essay considers the term neighbourhood to include those regions which have had a direct impact on issues of European security governance, such as the Caucasus and states situated along Russia's western periphery, where the emergence of intra-state violence has been a consistent security problem.

[4]The Donbas is used throughout the essay and refers to the *oblasti* of Donets'k and Luhans'k where the conflict is predominantly situated.

secure economic interests and the key political aim of preventing the extension of European security governance to its immediate neighbourhood.

In the case of the Donbas, the tension between these security logics has been further exacerbated due to Ukraine's significance in Russian foreign policy thinking (Tsygankov 2015, p. 2). As a result, this has intensified the inconsistencies underpinning Russia's adoption of the norms and processes of a governance approach, which have been increasingly influenced by political expediency as well as by a genuine desire for stability in the neighbourhood. Russia's involvement in the conflict—by simultaneously increasing its support for the opposition forces and engaging in the peace effort—reflects a level of ambivalence in Russia's behaviour which has not been recognised by the existing literature and Western policymakers. Moscow's paradoxical policy of escalation and de-escalation is shaped by a duality which, although increasingly motivated by instrumental calculations in order to maintain Russia's voice in the political future of Ukraine, has not ruled out a positive engagement in the settlement through the norms and processes of a governance approach.

The essay draws on empirical sources, which include official Russian statements and expert commentary together with interviews conducted in Moscow (as part of the author's doctoral research) with former practitioners at the Ministry of Defence and Ministry of Foreign Affairs and with academic experts on foreign policy and conflict management.[5] The essay is divided into four sections. First, we provide an overview of conflict management in relation to the development of Europe's system of security governance. Second, we offer an analysis of the legacy of Russia's regional approach to intra-state conflict in the context of the practices inherent in this system. Third, we interrogate Russia's approach towards the conflict in the Donbas. Finally, we suggest how Russia's role in the current conflict may be better understood, and highlight key trends in Moscow's approach towards regional intra-state violence and its implications for the wider academic debate on European security governance.

European security governance and conflict management

The process of developing mechanisms of governance in the policy area of conflict management began in the early 1990s and has since developed quite remarkably. The parallel developments of doctrine and practice have contributed to the growth of structures for coordinated multilateral action in and between the central organisations of European security (Wagnsson & Holmberg 2014, p. 324). A governance approach towards the management of intra-state conflict is considered not only as the most effective way to deliver public goods, but is viewed as a public good in itself. The evolution of conflict management has directly reflected the progression of Europe's system of security governance, where the provision of security is based on

> the coordinated management and regulation of issues by multiple and separate authorities, the interventions of both public and private actors (depending upon the issues), formal and informal arrangements, in turn structured by discourse and norms, and purposefully directed toward particular policy outcomes. (Webber *et al.* 2004, p. 4)

[5]These interviews were conducted in two rounds of fieldwork in Moscow, in autumn 2014 with the support of the Institute of World Economy and International Relations (IMEMO) and spring 2015 with the support of the Institute of Europe, Russian Academy of Sciences (IERAS), and with funding provided by a European Union Marie Curie Action International Research Staff Exchange scheme (IRSES) entitled 'EU in Depth—European Identity, Cultural Diversity and Political Change'.

Besides the Organization for Security and Cooperation in Europe (OSCE) and the United Nations (UN), the EU and the North Atlantic Treaty Organisation (NATO) have emerged as the principal regional institutions where security policy is both formulated and implemented. The latter two actors have rapidly integrated much of the continent through deeper cooperation across a broad range of policy areas.[6] While in some sectors inter-institutional rivalry continues (Hyde-Price 2007), Europe—as a site of security governance—has witnessed an evident shift in policy towards pooling sovereignty in order to pursue collective forms of security provision (Winn 2003, p. 149). Security is associated with a much more fluid set of problems against which strictly military responses are of diminishing utility (Webber 2014, p. 26). Although states and international organisations have adapted to these changes, limited resources and a lack of experience in combating non-traditional threats facilitated the increasing fragmentation of authority in security policymaking (Krahmann 2003, p. 10). The proliferation of a variegated set of actors above and below the state has therefore contributed towards the complexity of the European milieu and has altered the way in which many state actors navigate this environment.

The management of conflict in Europe since the early 1990s has revealed a progressive engagement in post-Westphalian security provision, demonstrating that conflict management operations 'reflect the nature of the evolution of security needs and of the ways to tackle security issues' (Tardy 2004, p. 3). This approach, embedded in the consolidation of norms and values shaping Europe's system of security governance, has been crafted through a steep learning curve of bloody experiences and failures. Ramesh Thakur points out that 'A significant cost of the cascade of generations of peacekeeping within a highly compressed timeframe is that most of the major operations today have little real precedent to go by; each has to make and learn from its own mistakes' (Thakur 2006, p. 41). In the European context, this has culminated in a governance approach based on several evolutionary trends.

First, operations have progressively come to possess a humanitarian dimension. This is closely intertwined with the second trend, whereby the integrity of state sovereignty as a prevalent norm has become increasingly contested, particularly if a conflict threatens international peace. While this has gained traction at the UN, it was NATO's action in Kosovo in 1999 which demonstrated that sovereignty was no longer absolute if human rights were being violated. This has been further promoted through the responsibility to protect doctrine and the notion that a state has the sovereign responsibility to protect its own populace. Yet the dilemma regarding the balance between territorial integrity and self-determination has become increasingly fraught as a result of this focus on human rights, with decisions implemented on an increasingly pragmatic case-by-case basis. Third, the use of force has become recognised as an acceptable and necessary measure in specific circumstances by legitimising its strategic application for the protection of civilians (Holzgrefe 2003, p. 18). Fourth, the maintenance of security and the implementation of civil society initiatives and post-conflict reconstruction have become central to a self-sustainable peace (Drent 2011, p. 3). Fifth, operations have experienced the emergence of complex coordination and interaction through the pooling of sovereignty between multiple actors, where there is a consent-based culture of coordination between civil and military aspects of a mission. Crucially, however, these trends have not permeated the neighbourhood in their entirety due to contestation of the values and norms that now characterise European security governance.

---

[6]See Derek Averre's contribution in this collection.

Russia's regional legacy of conflict management

A core Russian interest has been the maintenance of stability in its immediate neighbourhood amidst the outbreaks of intra-state violence during the early 1990s and the fragile post-conflict situations that ensued. While Russia's experience of conflict management extends to Central Asia, the following analysis is based on an interrogation of the regional conflicts in Georgia and Moldova, as they provide the most informative cases of Russia's thinking and also have had a more direct impact on European security governance as they are situated in the neighbourhood. Prior to the mid-2000s Moscow made genuine attempts to settle the conflicts, aiming for an outcome acceptable to all actors involved. However, the enlargement of NATO and the Kremlin's changing perception of the EU from benign economic power to competitor—not to mention domestic political transformations in the former Soviet republics, particularly in Georgia—increasingly shaped Moscow's response to conflict settlement in the context of what it considered to be the threat posed by the extension of the system of European security governance to the east. The freezing of the conflicts changed from a means to implement a final political settlement to largely an end in itself. While this did not rule out Russia's participation in initiatives to settle the conflicts, the Kremlin began to exploit the *status quo* for political ends. On the other hand, the *status quo* did serve to maintain some form of stability along Russia's periphery.

During the early 1990s Moscow's initial approach lacked impartiality as it provided logistical and military support to the separatist forces. This was largely based on *ad hoc* responses, guided by the decisions of local Russian commanders (Mokhov 2001; Baev 2003, p. 140). In fact this initial behaviour was based on a limited knowledge of how to conduct and participate in peace operations, exacerbated by the disastrous Afghan experience which was still fresh in the thinking of the Russian army's high command and power ministries (Sagramoso 2003, p. 15). Once ceasefires had been achieved, peacekeeping operations were established based on the consent of the central governments in Transnistria and Georgia, although domestic nationalist opinion vehemently opposed Moscow's involvement. While Russia positioned itself as the dominant actor in the peacekeeping forces and settlement processes during this period (Allison 1994; Mackinlay 2003b, p. 207), Moscow requested financial support from the UN (Trenin 1996, p. 83), and even entertained the idea of including international troops in the operations.[7] Russia also made consistent and genuine requests for assistance from the Commonwealth of Independent States (CIS), only to be ignored.

At this stage, 'freezing' the conflicts was considered by the Russian Ministry for Foreign Affairs and the Ministry of Defence as a logical interim solution from which a comprehensive political settlement could be achieved. Peacekeeping operations were established through trilateral formats, and even though some of these arrangements departed from formal guidelines practised in European security governance by including belligerent forces in the peacekeeping operations, the aim was to provide further transparency premised on a strict interpretation of consent and impartiality.[8] The peacekeeping operations were specifically designed not to allow for the wider use of force, which Russia—notwithstanding its later systematic application of disproportionate force in Chechnya—considered a danger to regional stability due to its

[7]Russia would not, however, have relinquished control over the mission to an external UN commander. See *BBC Summary of World Broadcasts*, 30 April 1994.

[8]Interview with Professor Aleksandr Nikitin, Moscow State Institute of International Relations, Moscow, 1 October 2014.

impact on the notions of consent and impartiality in conflict management (Vorob'yev 1994; Lavrov 1996).[9] This thinking prevailed even in Russia's official pronouncements regarding the importance of defending the rights of its regional diaspora (Balmforth 1994). Moscow also relied on the initiatives of UN agencies and the OSCE, alongside local and international NGOs, to rehabilitate the conflict zones—although there was considerable room for improvement in the pro-activeness of Russian forces' coordination with these actors when implementing peacebuilding strategies.

Throughout Yel'tsin's tenure and Putin's first presidential term Russia proposed and constructively engaged in many rounds of negotiations. Although Moscow ensured its centrality in the diplomatic formats to shape the settlement processes, it sought a compromise, to be underwritten by both the UN and OSCE, premised on the greater autonomy of the separatist enclaves while preserving the territorial integrity of the states in question. Russian foreign policy thinking became more 'realist' as the 1990s progressed but this did not alter Russia's approach towards the management of the conflicts in a fundamental way: while Russia maintained a military presence in the former Soviet republics in order to retain a foothold in the region (Balmforth 1994), it made efforts to close many of its forward military bases, and in fact their impact on the settlement processes has been overstated. Maintaining a regional presence was largely driven by a goal of establishing itself as regional security guarantor which, while closely bound up in a 'great power' narrative, did not necessarily correspond to imperialist intent. Thus, Russia embraced certain aspects of a governance approach in managing the peace effort while remaining the central actor in the settlement processes.

The beginning of Putin's second term in office witnessed a shift in Russia's foreign policy, in response to the 'colour revolutions', and a deterioration in Moscow's relations with Washington and Brussels, which included its approach to the frozen conflicts. With the tension between its security logics inclining it towards more self-interested political aims, Russia became less inclined to commit itself to a solution. This reflected not only a degree of frustration in Moscow owing to the intransigence of the opposing parties, but also a desire to keep its neighbouring states relatively weak in the context of the potential widening and deepening of European security governance in the neighbourhood. While Russia continued to engage in certain elements of a governance approach when conducting the peace efforts, this became more driven by political expediency.

The use of force in conflict management was still viewed with scepticism by the Russian power ministries. Moscow consistently argued that a resolution of the conflicts could only be established through political means, premised on existing formats that provided for compromise-based solutions between the belligerents. This was particularly pertinent in the Georgian case, where Tbilisi began to argue for a change in the mandate and format of the existing missions to allow for the wider use of force based on the 'Bosnian model'. This was prompted by Russia's refusal to change the diplomatic frameworks to allow for further flexibility in decision making; as a result Moscow has been accused by many critics of deliberately attempting to freeze the settlement processes in order to serve Russian political aims (Popescu 2006, p. 7; 2012, p. 4). However, while the *status quo* did indeed serve Russia's political aims, there are strong grounds to suggest that its reluctance to alter the political

[9]Anonymous interview with a former Russian first deputy permanent representative to the UN, Moscow, 18 September 2014.

framework and allow more forceful methods derived from a doctrinal concern that such actions would be destabilising, as they might irrevocably change the shared understanding of consent (Lavrov 2004). This did not rule out the calculated distribution of passports that provided a pretext for Moscow to claim the protection of Russian citizens during the conflict in 2008. The sporadic supply of military equipment to the separatist enclaves, which gradually increased from the mid-2000s, also assisted in the consolidation of their *de facto* independence.

While Russia continued to engage in meaningful peace brokering through existing formats to solve the conflicts in Georgia, which began to include Western institutions such as the EU in the capacity of observers, by the time of the 2008 war Moscow's approach began predominantly to reflect 'realist' concerns in its policy towards NATO. Tbilisi's attack on South Ossetia and the Russian peacekeepers stationed in the region triggered a disproportionate military response from Moscow. The Russian political leadership attempted to legitimise this military action using humanitarian discourse and referred to responsibility to protect in order to protect civilians residing in South Ossetia (Lavrov 2008). The decision to use force in this instance was reactive and primarily based on a politically motivated decision to resist what Moscow considered as growing Western incursions into its regional space (Allison 2008, 2009), rather than signifying a long term revision in doctrinal thinking.[10] The prevalence of strategic necessity over a commitment to the rules and norms of security governance was also illustrated by Russia's recognition of Abkhazia's and South Ossetia's independence, which became a heated topic of debate between Moscow and its Western counterparts. Although independence was rejected by the UN Security Council and General Assembly, the Kremlin justified its decision by linking it to the controversy surrounding Kosovo's declaration of independence earlier in 2008 (Hughes 2013, p. 1012; Wolff & Rodt 2013, p. 812). Clearly, in the light of Medvedev's declaration that the former Soviet space was a sphere of privileged Russian interests, the spread of Europe's system of security governance had, in the Kremlin's eyes, limits in its immediate neighbourhood (Kramer 2008).

Moscow's delivery of humanitarian supplies and engagement in the peacebuilding effort, led largely by NGOs and international organisations such as the OSCE and EU,[11] increased considerably after the war in 2008. This followed existing Russian practice of distributing aid to the separatist regions and initiating economic projects in order to facilitate the settlement process (Yakovenko 2004; Orlova 2005). This humanitarian effort, alongside Russian diplomatic negotiation with the EU,[12] became more deliberate and coherent during Medvedev's presidency in the aftermath of the 2008 conflict as a means 'to have more soft power in the region'[13] and to cultivate an appearance of credibility and legitimacy.[14] However, this also coincided with the establishment of further military bases on the separatist territories. Abkhazia and South Ossetia have since been off the negotiating table and Moscow has deliberately strengthened its military presence and ties with the leadership of the two

---

[10]Interview with Dr Dmitrii Polikanov of the PIR Center, Moscow, 17 October 2014; interview with Dr Yuliya Nikitina, Moscow State Institute of International Relations, Moscow, 21 October 2014.

[11]Interview with the former Head of the OSCE Mission to South Ossetia, London, 3 June 2015.

[12]'Georgia and Russia Agree on Truce', *BBC News*, 13 August 2008, available at: http://news.bbc.co.uk/1/hi/world/europe/7557457.stm, accessed 17 April 2015.

[13]Interview with Dr Yuliya Nikitina, Moscow State Institute of International Relations, Moscow, 21 October 2014.

[14]Russia supported UN Security Council resolution 1808 (UN 2008) which called for post-conflict reconstruction in South Ossetia.

regions. Further military and border treaties were signed in 2014 and 2015, binding the two regions closer to Russia, in the context of the situation in Ukraine.[15]

The initial eruption of unrest in the Donbas

After the March 2014 referendum, Russia considered Crimea not to be a subject for negotiation. Kyiv, on the other hand, remained firm in its resolve to bring Crimea back under its rule, with support from an overwhelming vote in favour of Ukrainian territorial integrity at the UN General Assembly (UN 2014). In the wake of the euphoria over Crimea, nationalist tensions began to emerge in the Donbas with strong pockets of provocative and violent demonstrations. Amidst the maelstrom of diplomatic activity, Moscow was accused of attempting to replicate the Crimean scenario in these regions through the carefully crafted incitement of revolt. Ukrainian and US officials pointed out that many of the towns and cities seized were of strategic value, demonstrating that the events were not based on spontaneous uprisings.[16] During a mid-April meeting of the UN Security Council the British representative concluded that 'Contrary to Russian claims, the recent demonstrations in eastern cities are not organic. … Rather, what we are witnessing is a well-orchestrated campaign designed to destabilise the country' (Grant 2014a, p. 6). It was noted by officials in Kyiv and many Western capitals that the weapons and level of training of the opposition forces indicated that the latter were being led by or even formed part of the Russian military.[17] While the Russian political leadership initially denied allegations that its military and security services interfered during the initial unrest in the Donbas (Paniev 2014a), there is evidence to suggest that, alongside the transfer of small groups of armed men, Russia provided military intelligence and arms deliveries, with Ukrainian officials accusing Russian Special Forces (*spetsnaz*) and intelligence units of organising the seizure of public buildings (Blair 2014).

To deal with unrest in the Donbas, Kyiv launched what it framed as an anti-terrorist operation against the pro-Russian opposition on 14 April 2014 (Luhn 2014a). This was followed by a short interval in the fighting while diplomatic negotiations were taking place in the Trilateral Contact Group which led to the signing of the Geneva Agreement on 17 April 2014. The conflict quickly intensified within a week of signing the Agreement, however, with the pro-government armed group 'Right Sector' launching attacks on opposition checkpoints around the city of Slovyansk. Kyiv continued its anti-terrorist operation which Ukraine's acting president, Oleksandr Turchnyov, legitimised as part of a wider strategy to save innocent Ukrainian civilians from Russian *spetsnaz* and terrorist units (Oliphant 2014). A statement by the Ukrainian Ministry of Foreign Affairs declared that 'Special units of Ukraine engaged in anti-terrorist operations act professionally in order to neutralize subversive groups that

---

[15]The Agreement on Alliance and Strategic Partnership between Russia and Abkhazia was signed in Moscow in late 2014 and came into effect in March 2015. On the signing of the Treaty on the State Border in February 2015, see 'Remarks and Comments by Foreign Minister Sergey Lavrov at a Joint News Conference after Talks with South Ossetian Foreign Minister Dmitry Sanakoyev', 18 February 2015, available at: http://archive.mid.ru//brp_4.nsf/0/026279F6BC64E29C43257DF0005FE3DE, accessed 19 April 2015.

[16]'Pro-Russian Protests Appear in Strategic Towns in Ukraine's South and East', *Radio Free Europe/Radio Liberty*, 15 August 2015, available at: http://www.rferl.org/contentinfographics/pro-russian-protests-appear-in-strategic-towns-in-ukraines-south-and-east-/25334338.html, accessed 20 June 2015.

[17]'Kremlin: Putin Denies Russian Role in Ukraine Unrest', *Radio Free Europe/Radio Liberty*, 14 April 2014, available at: http://www.rferl.org/content/ukraine-russia-putin-anxiety/25333073.html, accessed 20 June 2015.

have illegally crossed the border of our state'.[18] Many Western diplomats supported this action, with the UK's permanent UN representative stating that Kyiv acted with restraint and used proportionate measures when combating the pro-Russian forces illegally occupying Government buildings: 'The Ukrainian Government has the right and responsibility to uphold the rule of law and protect both its citizens and its officials on Ukrainian territory' (Grant 2014b, p. 3). Refusal by the opposition forces to withdraw from the government buildings in the major population centres in the Donbas further exacerbated the violence.

This stage of the conflict posed an entirely new challenge and in some respects an opportunity for the Kremlin. Foreign Minister Lavrov called for an early political resolution of the violence based on a revision of Ukraine's constitution in order to protect the Russian-speaking population—a controversial justification which many critics argue lacks credibility—and to promote a nation-wide dialogue including all political actors and regions (Lavrov 2014a). Moscow attempted to justify its position further by pointing out the past failures of a unitary state in Ukraine, remarking that the 'Constitution changes after each election—it is changed to pro-presidential, pro-parliamentary or pro-government order. This leapfrog scheme cannot keep going on in this way' (Lavrov 2014a). This meant that each region would be able to choose its own government and legislative authorities and have the right to conduct its own economic affairs (Lavrov 2014a).[19] Elaborating on this arrangement, Lavrov suggested that candidates should be drawn from each of the leading parties and regions in Ukraine to participate in the multilateral talks, which included Russia, the US and the EU (Paniev 2014b). This coordinated multilateral action was developed in the Trilateral Contact Group which included Russia, Ukraine and other predominantly Western representatives from the OSCE. According to Moscow, this would create a space for mutual dialogue in order to promote transparency and an early stabilisation of the unrest (Lavrov 2014b). This did not indicate that Moscow was allowing external Western actors to monopolise the negotiating process; however, neither did it merely signify an instrumental use of diplomatic initiatives in order to provide a cloak of legitimacy. Rather, the Russian leadership aimed to pursue a compromise-based solution which took into consideration Moscow's vital regional interests. If this was impossible to achieve, as some Russian experts and Western policymakers have pointed out, the Kremlin would attempt to freeze the settlement process as a means to preserve a level of influence over the opposition regions.[20]

Moscow's call for a swift but comprehensive resolution of the conflict was thus an attempt to achieve the best possible outcome for Russia while at the same time securing a political settlement which was considered by Russia a rational compromise. Russia claimed that it aimed to prevent Ukraine from '[spiralling] into crisis with unpredictable consequences' (Lavrov 2014b). Russia's permanent representative at the UN, Vitalii Churkin, declared during a meeting of the Security Council in mid-April that 'Russia has never advocated aggravating

---

[18]'Comments on the Statement of Russian Deputy Minister of Defence', Ministry of Foreign Affairs, Ukraine, 16 April 2014, available at: http://mfa.gov.ua/en/press-center/comments/1032-omentar-departamentu-informacijnoji-politiki-mzs-ukrajini-u-zvjazku-iz-vislovlyuvannyami-zastupnika-ministra-oboroni-rf, accessed 25 January 2016.

[19]Certain Russian academics agree with the official opinion; interview with Professor Pavel Zolotarev, Deputy Director of the Institute for US and Canada Studies of the Russian Academy of Sciences, Moscow, 6 October 2014.

[20]Interview with Dr Nadya Arbatova, Institute for World Economy and International Relations (IMEMO), Moscow, 5 September 2014.

[the crisis] or destabilizing the country … for us Ukraine is too important as an economic and political partner and a country that is very close to us in many ways' (Churkin 2014a, p. 15).

Moscow's Western counterparts at the UN found this deeply problematic, however, with the French representative stating that, 'The only alternatives they [Moscow] are offering Kyiv are capitulation or partition' (Araud 2014a, p. 4). The Kremlin's preoccupation with maintaining its foothold in the conflict resolution process ran counter to the limited ceasefire many of the Western actors were attempting to promote in the negotiations, demonstrating a lack of mutual understanding on how to facilitate peace. The UK's representative to the UN spoke for many in the West and in Kyiv when he objected to Russia's proposals on the grounds that the most important concern was a cessation of the violence, from which a discussion on Ukraine's constitution would follow; he also noted that including the opposition leaders in the negotiations would provide them with legitimacy and credibility whereas they were no more than Russian puppets (Grant 2014b, p. 3). Crucially, it was also emphasised by the French representative at the Security Council that Ukraine's political future could only be decided by the Ukrainian people—effectively a rejection of any notion of 'limited sovereignty' (Araud 2014b, p. 5). The West and Kyiv wanted to deny Moscow, which was considered the main architect of the violence, the legitimacy and credibility it desired and were outraged at what they considered as Russia's duplicity. Indeed, Russia showed its readiness to put pressure on the authorities in Kyiv if its interests were being sidelined. Cutting off gas supplies and staging sizeable military exercises along Ukraine's border—the former justified by Putin as 'business' (Paniev & Tsilyurik 2014a) and the latter as routine 'snap' training exercises (Lavrov 2014a)—were evidently a means to intimidate and coerce Kyiv to peace. With Moscow's failure to participate in an OSCE ministerial meeting to justify its military build-up along the Ukrainian border, Kyiv viewed this as further evidence of Russia's intentions to use military force against Ukraine.[21]

Moscow's basic aim was the establishment of a diplomatic arrangement which combined its experiences in the Contact Group during the Balkan operations and the formats of its regional conflict management experience. Russia argued that only through painstaking negotiation and compromise-based solutions could a resolution of the conflict be found and pressed for what it considered as the logical inclusion of the opposition's political leadership in the talks (Lavrov 2014c). Although Russia pushed for multilateral action, it aimed to secure a compromise in Geneva that secured its own interests and those of the opposition forces, and this was reflected in the Geneva Statement of 17 April 2014. Besides mutual support for the implementation of an OSCE monitoring mission, Moscow recognised the dissolution and demilitarisation of all illegal armed units in the Donbas, began to pull back its forces from the Ukrainian border, and further promoted its views on any forthcoming political settlement.[22] This was accompanied by a pause in Ukraine's 'anti-terrorist' operation on 17 April and Kyiv's consideration for decentralising power in the country, in addition to an amnesty—except for

---

[21]'Comment on the Refusal of the Russian Federation to Participate in the Meetings within the OSCE', Ministry of Foreign Affairs, Ukraine, 10 April 2014, available at: http://mfa.gov.ua/en/press-center/comments/991-komentar-departamentu-informacijnoji-politiki-mzs-ukrajini-shhodo-vidmovi-rf-vid-uchasti-u-zasidannyah-obse, accessed 25 January 2016.

[22]'Joint Statement: Geneva Statement on Ukraine', European Union External Action Service, 17 April 2014, available at: http://eeas.europa.eu/statements/docs/2014/140417_01_en.pdf, accessed 20 March 2015.

those suspected of committing capital offences—for all persons who lay down their arms and withdrew from public buildings.[23]

Yet with the resumption of violence only a week after the signing of the Agreement, Russia considered the ceasefire breached, with a spokesperson for Putin declaring in late April that the Geneva agreement was no longer viable as a result of Kyiv's continued military offensive (Luhn 2014b). Russia's OSCE representative placed sole blame on Kyiv for the renewed military clashes, also declaring—as per the Geneva agreement—that all armed formations such as the Right Sector should disarm and an inclusive constitutional process should begin (Kelin 2014a). Foreign Minister Lavrov even drew a parallel with Russia's actions in Georgia in 2008, stating that 'If our interests, our legitimate interests, the interests of Russians have been attacked directly, like they were in South Ossetia, I do not see any other way but to respond in full accordance with international law' (Luhn 2014c).

A key problem preventing de-escalation was thus the divergent interpretation of the conflict. Moscow portrayed the increasing turmoil as a legitimate armed uprising against an ultra-nationalist Kyiv, while in Western capitals the central Ukrainian authorities were depicted as fighting for their sovereignty against external Russian aggression in support of a manufactured opposition. The vagueness of the Geneva statement showed this divergence and resulted in opposing arguments about which side should make the initial step towards disarmament. While Churkin stated at a UN Security Council meeting in mid-April that 'The [Geneva agreement] is so simple, there is nothing to interpret. There is nothing to be done but to implement it' (Churkin 2014b, p. 19), *Nezavisimaya Gazeta* suggested that 'In practice, it turns out that the signatories put different things in the same words—in accordance with its own picture of events' (Paniev 2014c). The circumstances surrounding the escalation of the conflict made both narratives plausible, with Moscow and Kyiv influencing public opinion through the manipulation of information. Lavrov (2014e) pointed out that people cannot be expected to negotiate when force is still being used against them. At the same time Kyiv demanded that Russia put pressure on the opposition to de-escalate and withdraw from public buildings.[24]

This raises a crucial point concerning the extent Moscow was able to direct the opposition's strategy and behaviour. Certain opposition forces made it clear that they would not be bound by any decisions made at the talks in Geneva, with one high-ranking opposition member in Donets'k stating that 'Lavrov and Kerry decided, but who are they to us? We are the Donets'k Republic. We have people who make their own decisions' (Gordon 2014).[25] This casts doubt on claims that Moscow had complete control over the opposition forces. Sir Rodric Braithwaite, a former British ambassador to Russia, has commented that 'It may be true that Putin is losing control over events in eastern Ukraine and that he fears being sucked into a situation which could turn out to be unmanageable' (Poole 2014). When commenting on the viability

---

[23]'Comment on the Steps of the Ukrainian Side, Aimed at Implementing the Geneva Agreements', Ministry of Foreign Affairs, Ukraine, 18 April 2014, available at: http://mfa.gov.ua/en/press-center/comments/1066-komentar-mzs-shhodo-krokiv-ukrajinsykoji-storoni-spryamovanih-na-vikonannya-zhenevsykih-domovlenostej, accessed 25 January 2016.

[24]'Comment on the Steps of the Ukrainian Side, Aimed at Implementing the Geneva Agreements', Ministry of Foreign Affairs, Ukraine, 18 April 2014, available at: http://mfa.gov.ua/en/press-center/comments/1066-komentar-mzs-shhodo-krokiv-ukrajinsykoji-storoni-spryamovanih-na-vikonannya-zhenevsykih-domovlenostej, accessed 25 January 2016.

[25]'Daily SMM Report', SMM, OSCE, 19 April 2014, available at: http://www.osce.org/ukraine-smm/117859, accessed 9 February 2016.

of the Minsk II talks at the annual Munich Conference, Lavrov claimed that 'We shouldn't pretend that those people [opposition] will readily obey. They live on their land, and they are fighting for it' (Lavrov 2015). While this argument has indeed been used by the Kremlin to distance itself from further involvement, especially during phases of increased Russian military escalation, the agency of the opposition has largely been overlooked as a central factor in the continuation of the conflict. One Russian scholar has pointed out that both the opposition and the authorities in Kyiv have been reluctant to compromise.[26] This does not suggest that Moscow is unable to influence the decision making of the opposition, but does show that there has not been a broad and consistent degree of control.

Russia's approach towards the initial stages of unrest in the Donbas has reflected complex motives, with Moscow occupying a grey zone between mediator and conflicting party. Its behaviour has—to an extent not often accepted by Western critics—been driven by a concern for the management and stabilisation of the conflict. Basing its military intervention on humanitarian justifications, Moscow drew on its regional legacy from the early 1990s, and more recently on its intervention in South Ossetia in 2008. However, tension between its competing security logics leads to fluctuating engagement with the norms and processes of a governance approach; promoting the safeguarding of human rights became bound up with the problematic notion of limited sovereignty. Moscow's involvement in the settlement process has consequently veered between consent-based coordination between multiple actors *via* the informal Trilateral Contact Group to address security problems collectively, and a determination to maintain its central position in the settlement process and steer negotiations in order to safeguard its political aims. Russia thus remains at the centre of efforts to determine Ukraine's political future, promoting the federalisation of Ukraine which would provide it with an opportunity to exercise influence through the cultivation of closer ties with the Donbas region. It also lays down a marker in the wider struggle against the establishment of Western-led European security governance models in the neighbourhood.

Russia's escalation: passing the point of no return?

With the continuation of the fighting after the failure of the Geneva Agreement in late April 2014, Ukrainian government troops conducted major offensive operations and managed to eradicate much of the opposition's power base, taking control of many strategically important sites such as Donets'k airport. Newly elected President Poroshenko's proposed peace plan in late June failed and the fighting continued in both the Luhans'k and Donets'k *oblasti* with both sides incurring casualties. In August, with direct Russian military support, the opposition forces were able to reverse many of Kyiv's military gains in the Donbas achieved throughout the previous months. This period included both the escalation of Moscow's military involvement and its participation in mitigating the humanitarian crisis.

The second major settlement plan was brokered in Minsk on 5 September 2014 and led to a brief stabilisation of the conflict. However, this was only a momentary pause. Major fighting broke out when opposition forces—with Russian military support—attempted to retake Donets'k airport in late September, culminating in a withdrawal of Ukrainian government troops in January 2015. Encouraged by these military gains, opposition forces continued their

---

[26]Interview with Dr Andrei Kortunov, Director of the International Affairs Council (RIAC), Moscow, 2 October 2014.

offensive operations to retake strategically important objectives such as the city of Debaltseve in the Donets'k *oblast'*. Amidst this period of fighting, a third settlement plan, the Minsk II agreement, was signed on 12 February 2015, although opposition forces continued their offensive and forced government troops to withdraw from the city in late February.[27] Since then there has been a relative stabilisation of the conflict, with both sides largely adhering to the ceasefire. While there have been sporadic clashes between the parties, there have been no major military offensives.

As Russia became more involved in the conflict the paradoxical pattern of escalation and de-escalation in Moscow's behaviour became more evident. Lawrence Freedman puts forward the notion of 'limited war' as a basis to understand the escalation of Russia's behaviour during this phase of its intervention; Russia's political leadership has endeavoured to keep the conflict 'restricted in terms of time taken and resources expended', premised on the logic 'that if the demands of a campaign exceeded the value of the objective, then an intervention could be drawn to a close' (Freedman 2014, p. 10). While the Russian power ministries had prepared for greater involvement this limited approach can be related to the tension between Russia's security logics. Moscow's strategic concerns relating to the wider struggle with the central actors of European security governance did not rule out concern over the widening humanitarian crisis and instability along its border.

After the failure of the Geneva talks and the continuation of the fighting in the Donbas, Moscow's focus on humanitarian issues became more frequent. In late May the Russian Foreign Ministry sent a communication to the Kyiv authorities expressing its readiness to supply humanitarian aid to the worst affected areas of the fighting and requested that Kyiv assist in securing safe conditions for its delivery.[28] When this was ignored by the Ukrainian government, which asserted that the proposal was nothing more 'than another element of propaganda' to demonstrate Russia's good intentions whilst taking advantage of the situation in order 'to serve its own shallow political interests',[29] Moscow pressed Kyiv to allow the provision of aid based on generally accepted humanitarian norms[30] and pressed its arguments through the OSCE and UN Security Council. A war of words followed, with Russia and its Western counterparts continually accusing each other of aiming to manipulate international opinion and destabilise the conflict. In early June Russia's delegation to the UN proposed a draft resolution in which it highlighted Moscow's concerns about the suffering of civilians and the damage to infrastructure and residential quarters (Lavrov 2014f). These humanitarian concerns were rebuffed, with the US declaring that 'Russian aid operations sends soldiers,

[27]'Ukraine Ceasefire: New Minsk Agreement Key Points', *BBC News*, available at: http://www.bbc.co.uk/news/world-europe-31436513, accessed 15 March 2015.

[28]'Comment Regarding the Provision of Humanitarian Aid to the Population in the Eastern Regions of Ukraine', Ministry of Foreign Affairs of the Russian Federation, 30 May 2014, available at: http://archive.mid.ru//bdomp/brp_4.nsf/e78a48070f128a7b43256999005bcbb3/22f387941232e03e44257cec00486fe1!OpenDocument, accessed 12 February 2014.

[29]'Comment on an Official Note of the Russian MFA Regarding the so-called "Russian Humanitarian Aid" in the Eastern Regions of Ukraine', Ministry of Foreign Affairs, Ukraine, 29 May 2014, available at: http://mfa.gov.ua/en/press-center/comments/1484-komentar-departamentu-informacijnoji-politiki-mzs-ukrajini-shhodo-oficijnoji-noti-mzs-rf-pro-tak-zvanu-rosijsyku-gumanitarnu-dopomogu-zhitelyam-skhidnih-oblastej-ukrajini, accessed 25 January 2016.

[30]'Comment Regarding the Provision of Humanitarian Aid to the Population in the Eastern Regions of Ukraine', Ministry of Foreign Affairs of the Russian Federation, 30 May 2014, available at: http://archive.mid.ru//bdomp/brp_4.nsf/e78a48070f128a7b43256999005bcbb3/22f387941232e03e44257cec00486fe1!OpenDocument, accessed 12 February 2014.

not doctors, it mans armoured personnel carriers, not relief tents. It provides surface-to-air missiles, not meals ready-to-eat' (Power 2014, p. 6). The rejection of the resolution provided Russia with the opportunity to claim that Washington's and Brussels' policy towards Ukraine was premised on 'geopolitical' rather than humanitarian interests.[31] During another session of the OSCE on 19 June Kelin even went as far as to declare that the 'Donbas is "cleansed" not of imaginary Russian saboteurs, but of the Russian-speaking population. It is close to ethnic cleansing' (Kelin 2014d).

These protestations were followed by Russia's delivery of humanitarian aid, albeit under controversial circumstances, to the worst affected areas of the Donbas region. Critics warned that 'Russia—and Vladimir Putin personally—is coming across less as a warmonger than as a humanitarian actor [and this] is likely aimed at improving Moscow's image and room for manoeuvre in any future peace talks' (Pugsley 2014). Lavrov commented in early June that Russia was serious about facilitating the humanitarian effort 'on a generally acceptable systemic basis' which the Ukrainian authorities must also be ready to implement (Lavrov 2014g). The mounting humanitarian crisis was linked to the Russian leadership's concerns about the complete destabilisation of Ukraine and the humanitarian spill over into Russia's southern regions. Moscow, through its Ministry of Emergency Situations, endeavoured to address the crisis by assisting with the accommodation of the mass refugee flows.[32] Kyiv has also had to manage substantial amounts of internally displaced people (Stern 2015) and has requested humanitarian assistance from international bodies and Western governments.[33] Moscow began to implement the delivery of aid to the Donbas region in August 2014.[34] However the initial convoy deliveries were not undertaken in cooperation with the International Committee of the Red Cross (ICRC), which had offered its support but stated that it did not receive the relevant information on the initial convoys, including the materials being delivered to the Donbas.[35] Although both Moscow and Kyiv agreed to the rules of consent and impartiality as stipulated by the ICRC (Nebenhay 2014), and while there have been sporadic inspections of aid convoys, transparency has continued to remain a key concern for Kyiv and its Western partners. The Kyiv authorities asserted that consent was a precondition for the delivery of humanitarian aid, which must gain the approval of the Ukrainian authorities and be delivered *via* the channels of the UN and/or ICRC.[36]

[31]'Comment on the Blocking of the Russian Draft of the UN Security Council Statement on the Provision of Humanitarian Aid to South Eastern Ukraine', Ministry of Foreign Affairs of the Russian Federation, 14 May 2014, available at: http://archive.mid.ru/bdomp/brp_4.nsf/e78a48070f128a7b43256999005bcbb3/fc216870be040e3c44257cd900491440!OpenDocument, accessed 17 February 2014.

[32]See, 'Over 40 Russian Regions Provide Shelter for Ukrainian Refugees—EMERCOM', *Tass*, 16 July 2014, available at: http://tass.ru/en/russia/740893, accessed 15 May 2015. At the time of writing 600,000 have left the country, mainly to Russia's south western regions (UNHCR 2015).

[33]'Statement on Attempts of the Russian Federation to Organize a Humanitarian Convoy', Ministry of Foreign Affairs, Ukraine, 8 August 2014, available at: http://mfa.gov.ua/en/press-center/comments/2118-zajava-mzs-ukrajini-u-zvjazku-zi-sprobami-rosijsykoji-federaciji-organizuvati-gumanitarnij-konvoj, accessed 25 January 2016.

[34]'Statement on the Beginning of the Delivery of Humanitarian Relief Aid to Residents of Southeastern Ukraine who have been Affected by the Hostilities', Ministry of Foreign Affairs of the Russian Federation, 21 August 2014, available at: http://archive.mid.ru/bdomp/brp_4.nsf/e78a48070f128a7b43256999005bcbb3/719009204c73849d44257d3c001e64e8!OpenDocument, accessed 5 April 2015.

[35]'Ukraine: ICRC Calls for Clarity on Aid Convoy', 12 August 2014, available at: https://youtu.be/X-X0melzLgI, accessed 15 December 2015.

[36]'Statement on Attempts of the Russian Federation to Organize a Humanitarian Convoy', Ministry of Foreign Affairs, Ukraine, 8 August 2014, available at: http://mfa.gov.ua/en/press-center/comments/2118-zajava-mzs-ukrajini-u-zvjazku-zi-sprobami-rosijsykoji-federaciji-organizuvati-gumanitarnij-konvoj, accessed 25 January 2016.

Russia has continued to dismiss the suggestion that the delivery of humanitarian supplies is a Trojan horse for the shipment of *materiel*, declaring at the Security Council (Pankin 2014, p. 19) that '[i]n the worsening circumstances, such accusations are simply amoral'. Some have suggested that Russian statements are credible, as Moscow has violated Ukrainian sovereignty by delivering military equipment without recourse to the subterfuge of humanitarian convoys (Pugsley 2014). Indeed, Stephen O'Brien, the UN Under-Secretary-General for Humanitarian Affairs, thanked Russia for providing substantial material assistance in alleviating the humanitarian crisis in the Donbas.[37] Moscow has consistently emphasised at the UN its attempts to be transparent and negotiate with Kyiv on the delivery of humanitarian assistance (Churkin 2015a, p. 9). Foreign Minister Lavrov has also continued to emphasise the pooling of humanitarian efforts by various internationally recognised organisations and actors such as the UN, OSCE, ICRC, the World Food Programme and the International Organisation for Migration (Lavrov 2014h). This has been accompanied by regular positive references to NGOs by Russia's then permanent representative to the OSCE, Andrei Kelin (Kelin 2014e). While NGOs had rarely featured in Russian discourse, even after the 2008 Georgian War and the increase of peacebuilding initiatives, Moscow's attitude towards NGOs in intra-state conflict settings was 'changing dramatically' because '[n]ow the state understands the positive role of NGOs'; reports on the humanitarian situation from Amnesty International have been received positively by the Russian power ministries, suggesting a more nuanced Russian perception and understanding of the role of NGOs in the current conflict.[38] Similar views have also surfaced in the Russian academic community where it is acknowledged that, while Russia lacks 'a culture of NGOs', the emergence of independent religious and political groups delivering aid has increased since the beginning of the conflict in the Donbas region.[39]

However, Russia's engagement in the peace effort has been vitiated by its resolute refusal to consider Kyiv's proposals to introduce an external UN or EU peacekeeping mission into the conflict zone (Ivzhshenko 2015). The Kremlin's reliance on the OSCE to prevent violence (Kelin 2014d) can be attributed to Moscow's preference for an institution of which it was a member. This decision was also premised on the realisation that the OSCE's Special Monitoring Mission in Ukraine was incapable of halting the violence and would thus be unable to obstruct Russia's mounting military support and intervention against government forces, which an international peacekeeping mission would have been able to do. Moscow's selective interaction with other participating actors is aimed at steering collective multilateral action at the operational level away from an exclusive reliance on Western actors, and instead towards a dependence on wider international institutions and agencies centred in or closely affiliated with the UN and OSCE. Moscow has engaged with these actors because it holds membership in these organisations and/or has confidence in their ability and impartiality, as long as this has not meant compromising its aims.

In Ukraine this has been accompanied by controversy over the credibility of the OSCE's Special Monitoring Mission as a result of Russia's involvement, as Moscow is considered an aggressor by Kyiv and many of the OSCE members (Sammut & D'Urso 2015). There is a

---

[37]'UN Official Thanks Russia for Contributing in Relief Efforts', *NEOnline*, 9 November 2015, available at: http://neurope.eu/article/un-official-thanks-russia-for-contributing-in-relief-efforts/, accessed 15 December 2015.

[38]Interview with a former Russian first deputy permanent representative to the United Nations, Moscow, 18 September 2014.

[39]Interview with Dr Vasilii Kashin, Center for Analysis of Strategies and Technologies, Moscow, 10 October 2014.

deep-set feeling in Kyiv and certain Western countries that the OSCE is biased towards Russia, although Moscow has only contributed a small percentage of the observers to the OSCE mission (Sammut & D'Urso 2015). During an OSCE meeting in early December Lavrov called for the organisation to intensify its efforts on the ground through the Special Monitoring Mission in Ukraine (Paniev 2014d), suggesting a commitment to collective multilateral action in the peace effort; at the same time, Russia continued to obstruct diplomatic efforts to expand the OSCE's zone of observation along its border with Ukraine, firmly denying accusations that Russian troops and supplies continued to flow into the Donbas (Kelin 2014f). Also, a decision by Moscow to increase the number of humanitarian convoys coordinated by the ICRC acted as a political ploy to draw attention away from Russia's military escalation.

By July 2014 Kyiv's unrelenting counter-terrorist operation had successfully pushed pro-Russian forces deep into the Donbas. Consequently, Russia began to escalate its military response to alter the balance of power in favour of the pro-Russian forces and 'get a grip on the situation' (Freedman 2014, p. 16). According to a briefing paper for the Royal United Services Institute, which provides a detailed overview of Russia's military involvement and troop movement in and along Ukraine's border, from mid-July onwards Russian artillery positions began to target advancing Ukrainian units from within Russia's territory in order to support the weakened opposition forces in the Donbas (Sutyagin 2015, p. 1). By mid-August the Russian military became directly engaged in combat operations with Ukrainian forces when the prospect of defeat had become a reality for the opposition (Sutyagin 2015, p. 1), and since then the presence of Russian troops on Ukrainian sovereign territory in eastern Ukraine has 'become a permanent feature of the conflict' (Sutyagin 2015, p. 1). Yet Lavrov has continued to declare that 'there will not be a military intervention' in the Donbas (Paniev & Tsilyurik 2014b).

Further complicating Moscow's involvement in the conflict was its engagement in the settlement process. Statements emanating from Moscow consistently advocated a cessation of hostilities based on its interpretation of the talks concluded in Geneva. The Russian leadership's position on the settlement process was further demonstrated by its acceptance of the OSCE Swiss Chairmanship's Roadmap, introduced in mid-May, Lavrov (2014g) stating that it 'is the foundation on which crisis settlement efforts should be built' since it adhered to the points mutually agreed on in Geneva, including a broad national dialogue (Burkhalter 2014). Officials in Kyiv were not convinced, stating that 'discussion of the peaceful settlement in Ukraine, but without Ukraine is senseless and unacceptable. Instead of statements we need real actions'.[40]

Moscow continued at this time with its narrative of the wider struggle against Washington's and Brussels' promotion of their geopolitical interests to the east. However, it also continued to engage in negotiations through the 'Normandy' format alongside France, Germany and Ukraine, which has become the main negotiating body for conflict resolution and has the backing of the OSCE and UN Security Council, ensuring wide political support for any agreements reached (Zagorski 2015, p. 51). The introduction of Kyiv's new initiative, the 'Poroshenko Plan', in late June was met with initial hesitation in the Kremlin, as Moscow

---

[40]'Statement of the MFA of Ukraine on De-escalation Intents Expressed by Presidents of the Russian Federation and the OSCE Chair Switzerland', Ministry of Foreign Affairs of Ukraine, 7 May, available at: http://mfa.gov.ua/en/press-center/comments/1251-zajava-mzs-ukrajini-z-privodu-vislovlenih-prezidentami-rosijsykoji-federaciji-i-shvejcariji-golovujuchoji-v-obse-namiriv-dejeskalaciji-situaciji-v-ukrajini, accessed 25 January 2016.

considered whether it should increase its assistance to a deteriorating opposition force in the hope that this would reverse any government military gains, or support the Plan and risk unfavourable terms for the opposition and impact on Russia's wider position; in the words of Lavrov (2014h), the Plan sounded more like an 'ultimatum' for the opposition to disarm than 'an appeal to an immediate and equal dialogue' as set out in Geneva. Its eventual rejection of Poroshenko's initiative did not completely signal a refusal to negotiate, but its military support for the opposition had a clear aim: to negotiate from a position of strength.

In early September 2014 President Putin issued an impromptu press statement where he proposed a relatively modest seven point peace plan (MacFarquhar 2014), precipitating negotiations in Belarus, where the wider concerns of a political settlement were discussed, and the Minsk Protocol of 5 September 2014. In response to frequent violations by both sides in the two weeks following the signing of the agreement, the Minsk Memorandum on 19 September was introduced to clarify the specifics of the Protocol. For the Russian leadership the significance of the agreements in Minsk stemmed from the inclusion of a concrete amnesty clause for the opposition forces. This was also based on the fact that, while the Minsk Protocol resembled the Poroshenko Plan, Moscow was now able to negotiate from a position of strength due to the military gains achieved over the summer months. Critics argued that Russia's involvement in the Minsk process was simply due to the need for a period of recuperation after the summer of intense fighting, after which a renewed military offensive would be initiated by pro-Russian forces (Kofman 2015).

There is merit in this argument, as there were no signs that Russia was going to relinquish its support for the opposition. A unilateral decision was taken to hold elections by the Donets'k and Luhans'k People's Republics on 2 November 2014. Amidst unanimous condemnation from the West and Kyiv, Moscow (Pankin 2014, p. 19) at the UN justified its support for the elections based on arguments of self-determination 'respect[ing] the will of the people of the south-east as they have expressed it', thus furthering Ukrainian federalisation. Although the other major actors engaged in the settlement process agreed that a certain form of autonomy for the provinces in the Donbas was now necessary for a long term political resolution, they held deep reservations about how this would enhance Russia's future regional posture and the unpredictable consequences that might ensue. At the UN Security Council Moscow justified this on a practical level, arguing that electing officials would assist in launching 'a sustainable dialogue between the central Ukrainian authorities and the representatives of [the] Donbas' (Churkin 2014c), but the Russian leadership's support for the unilateral elections led to a further deterioration of relations between Moscow and its Western counterparts.

Soon after the first Minsk agreements frequent sightings of troops and equipment moving into the Donbas region were reported by the UN and Special Monitoring Mission in Ukraine, with an escalation of fighting between the Russian-pro opposition and government forces throughout the last quarter of 2014. Indeed, the pattern of escalation and de-escalation continued with sustained Russian support for the opposition forces during phases of intense fighting for Donets'k airport in late 2014. Even with the second round of Minsk negotiations in February 2015 Russia continued to encourage the opposition forces, which became further emboldened in their fight against government forces. The battle for Debaltseve in February 2015, while revealing inadequacies in Minsk II over the specific modalities of the ceasefire line, showed the extent to which Moscow was willing to support the opposition in gaining its strategic objectives, even justifying these military operations at the UN as self-defence

(Churkin 2015c, p. 12). The conflict in the Donbas continued, with the opposition launching sporadic attacks in strategic places along the line of demarcation throughout the spring and summer of 2015, as did the humanitarian crisis.

By early 2016, a relative calm had been established along the ceasefire line and there was cautious optimism about moves towards a final resolution of the conflict in Western capitals (Copley 2016). Nevertheless, Russia's involvement is still viewed both by officials and by the majority of experts in the West as the main impediment to resolving the conflict. The US permanent representative, Samantha Power, asserted that

> We have gotten used to living in an upside-down world with respect to Ukraine. Russia speaks of peace and then fuels conflict. Russia signs agreements and then does everything within its power to undermine them. Russia champions the sovereignty of nations and then acts as if its neighbours' borders do not exist. (Power 2015, p. 3)

In response, Moscow has remained resolute that it is not a party to the conflict and has consistently denounced any claims to the contrary, with Vitalii Churkin even retorting at the UN that his colleagues have regularly 'employed fifty shades of black' when commenting on Russia's involvement (Churkin 2015b, p. 10). The Russian political leadership has argued that it has endeavoured to alleviate the humanitarian crisis and to facilitate a compromise resolution through Minsk II within the broader framework of a long term political settlement, which takes into consideration the legitimate interests of the Donbas region (Lavrov 2015).

Conclusion

By applying the framework of security governance to Russia's regional legacy of managing intra-state violence, this essay has explored the nature of Russia's involvement in the ongoing conflict in the settlement process in Ukraine's Donbas region. We have demonstrated that Russia's behaviour in the Donbas has both adopted and rejected certain features central to a governance approach, reflecting an uneven policy shaped not only by political expediency but also by a genuine desire for stability in its neighbourhood. Russia's behaviour has demonstrated inherent contradictions—not readily recognised by Western policymakers and commentators—which stem from the complex array of interests shaping its policy formulation. This duality is inherent in Russia's often paradoxical policy of military support for the opposition together with attempts to broker a solution to the conflict and mitigate the humanitarian crisis.

Russia's approach towards the current conflict in Ukraine, underpinned by the increasingly conservative foreign policy which emerged during Putin's second presidential term, has been shaped by a shift towards a more assertive engagement in its neighbourhood and is motivated by mistrust and resentment at what the majority of Russia's political class perceives as the marginalisation of Russia from the mainstream of European security governance and the undermining of its core national interests. The alternating pattern of escalation and de-escalation that characterises Russia's involvement in Ukraine stems from competing security logics: the struggle against Brussels and Washington co-exists with engagement in a governance approach that can be traced back to Russia's regional legacy. Russia's escalation of force in order to support the opposition forces is reflected in the 2008 war with Georgia, where Moscow demonstrated that it was prepared to use force when its regional interests were directly threatened. Moscow's selective interaction with other participating actors is aimed at steering collective action at the diplomatic and operational level away from an exclusive reliance on Western actors, and instead towards a dependence on international institutions and agencies centred in or closely affiliated with the UN and OSCE. This has allowed Russia to maintain its stakeholder position and thereby a degree of influence in both the conflict settlement and humanitarian processes. Russia's participation in the humanitarian effort may have served to provide a cloak of legitimacy for its more destabilising behaviour but it has also helped to mitigate the humanitarian crisis through the delivery of aid and management of the mass exodus of displaced people in Russia, in order to prevent Ukraine escalating into a spiral of violence.

As one scholar suggests, 'Russian policies towards the region are built upon the belief that internal security starts outside [its] borders and, thus, the countries in the shared neighbourhood emerge as lynchpins in [its] internal and regional security strategies' (Dias 2013, p. 257). This raises important questions regarding Moscow's future thinking and the extent to which it will be guided by the principle of the limited sovereignty of its regional neighbours when approaching intra-state conflict. The cases of Georgia in 2008 and Ukraine in 2014 may not be *sui generis*. Yet it is also necessary to consider Russia's engagement in certain aspects of a governance approach in its response to these conflicts and the influence it has on decision making in Moscow. While Russia has achieved its limited objectives of retaining influence over Ukraine's policy towards the Donbas, it has not attempted to destabilise Ukraine completely. Understanding the complexities conditioning Russia's behaviour may allow the external powers to open avenues of cooperation rather than confrontation over the current conflict as a basis for exploring a joint approach to Ukraine and negotiations over Russia's wider regional policy.

References

Allison, R. (1994) 'Peacekeeping in the Soviet Successor States', *Chaillot Papers*, 18, November, available at: http://www.iss.europa.eu/uploads/media/cp018e.pdf, accessed 14 February 2015.

Allison, R. (2008) 'Russia Resurgent? Moscow's Campaign to Coerce Georgia to Peace', *International Affairs*, 84, 6.

Allison, R. (2009) 'The Russian Case for Military Intervention in Georgia: International Law, Norms and Political Calculation', *European Security*, 18, 2.

Allison, R. (2013) *Russia, the West and Military Intervention* (Oxford, Oxford University Press).

Allison, R. (2014) 'Russian "Deniable Intervention" in Ukraine: How and Why Russia Broke the Rules', *International Affairs*, 90, 6.

Araud, G. (2014a) Statement at the United Nations Security Council, Report 7167 (S/PV. 7167), 2 May (New York, NY, United Nations), available at: http://www.securitycouncilreport.org/atf/cf/%7B65BFCF9B-6D27-4E9C-8CD3-CF6E4FF96FF9%7D/s_pv_7167.pdf, accessed 20 March 2015.

Araud, G. (2014b) Statement at the United Nations Security Council, Report 7165 (S/PV. 7165), 29 April (New York, NY, United Nations), available at: http://www.securitycouncilreport.org/atf/cf/%7B65BFCF9B-6D27-4E9C-8CD3-CF6E4FF96FF9%7D/s_pv_7165.pdf, accessed 20 March 2015.

Averre, D. (2009) 'Competing Rationalities: Russia, the EU and the "Shared Neighbourhood"', *Europe-Asia Studies*, 61, 10.

Baczynska, G. & Hudson, A. (2014) 'Russia Accuses EU of Seeking Ukraine "Sphere of Influence"', *Reuters*, 14 February, available at: http://www.reuters.com/article/us-ukraine-russia-eu-idUSBREA1D0PT20140214, accessed 7 March 2016.

Baev, P. (1997) 'Conflict Management in the Former Soviet South: The Dead-end of Russian Interventions', *European Security*, 6, 4.

Baev, P. (1998) 'Peacekeeping and Conflict Management in Eurasia', in Allison, R. & Bluth, C. (eds) *Security Dilemmas in Russia and Eurasia* (London, The Royal Institute of International Affairs).

Baev, P. (2003) 'The Impact of "Small Wars" on the Trajectory of the Russian Military', in Fedorov, Yu. E. (ed.) *Russian Military Reform and Russia's New Security Environment* (Stockholm, Swedish National Defence College).

Balmforth, R. (1994) 'Kozyrev: Moscow's Troops Should Stay in Ex-Soviet States', *Moscow Times*, 19 January.

Blair, D. (2014) 'Ukraine Crisis: We Are Now at War with Pro-Russian Rebels, States Kiev', *The Telegraph*, 3 May, available at: http://www.telegraph.co.uk/news/worldnews/europe/ukraine/10806477/Ukraine-crisis-we-are-now-at-war-with-pro-Russia-rebels-states-Kiev.html, accessed 7 March 2016.

Breedlove, P. (2014) 'The Meaning of Russia's Military Campaign Against Ukraine', *The Wall Street Journal*, 16 July, available at: http://www.wsj.com/articles/phil-breedlove-the-meaning-of-russias-military-campaign-against-ukraine-1405552018, accessed 7 March 2016.

Buchanan, R. T. (2014) 'Ukraine Crisis: Russian President Vladimir Putin Claims he Could "Take Kiev in Two Weeks"', *Independent*, 2 September, available at: http://www.independent.co.uk/news/ukraine-crisis-russian-president-vladimir-putin-claims-he-can-take-kiev-in-two-weeks-9705449.html, accessed 7 March 2016.

Burkhalter, D. (2014) 'A Roadmap for Concrete Steps Forward: The OSCE as an Inclusive Platform and Impartial Actor for Stability in Ukraine', OSCE, 12 May, available at: http://www.osce.org/cio/118509?download=true, accessed 20 March 2015.

Churkin, V. (2014a) Statement at the United Nations Security Council, Report 7154 (S/PV. 7154), 13 April (New York, NY, United Nations), available at: http://www.securitycouncilreport.org/atf/cf/%7B65BFCF9B-6D27-4E9C-8CD3-CF6E4FF96FF9%7D/s_pv_7154.pdf, accessed 14 May 2015.

Churkin, V. (2014b) Statement at the United Nations Security Council, Report 7311 (S/PV. 7311), 12 November (New York, NY, United Nations), available at: http://www.securitycouncilreport.org/atf/cf/%7B65BFCF9B-6D27-4E9C-8CD3-CF6E4FF96FF9%7D/s_pv_7311.pdf, accessed 18 May 2015.

Churkin, V. (2014c) Statement at the United Nations Security Council, Report 7167 (S/PV. 7167), 2 May (New York, NY, United Nations), available at: http://www.securitycouncilreport.org/atf/cf/%7B65BFCF9B-6D27-4E9C-8CD3-CF6E4FF96FF9%7D/s_pv_7167.pdf, accessed 18 May 2015.

Churkin, V. (2015a) Statement at the United Nations Security Council, Report 7365 (S/PV. 7365), 21 January (New York, NY, United Nations), available at: http://www.un.org/en/ga/search/view_doc.asp?symbol=S/PV.7365, accessed 18 May 2015.

Churkin, V. (2015b) Statement at the United Nations Security Council, Report 7384 (S/PV. 7384), 17 February (New York, NY, United Nations), available at: http://www.securitycouncilreport.org/atf/cf/%7B65BFCF9B-6D27-4E9C-8CD3-CF6E4FF96FF9%7D/s_pv_7384.pdf, accessed 20 April 2015.

Churkin, V. (2015c) Statement at the United Nations Security Council, Report 7400 (S/PV. 7400), 6 March (New York, NY, United Nations), available at: http://www.securitycouncilreport.org/atf/cf/%7B65BFCF9B-6D27-4E9C-8CD3-CF6E4FF96FF9%7D/s_pv_7400.pdf, accessed 20 April 2015.

Commonwealth of Independent States (1992) 'Polozhenie o Kollektivnykh silakh po podderzhaniyu mira v sodruzhestve Nezavisimykh Gosudarstv', available at: http://www.peacekeeper.ru/ru/?module=pages&action=view&id=74, accessed 12 May 2015.

Copley, C. (2016) 'Merkel Sees Progress on Ukraine Crisis in "Normandy Format" over Next Months', *Reuters*, 7 January, available at: http://af.reuters.com/article/worldNews/idAFKBN0UL27C20160107, accessed 16 March 2016.

Crow, S. (1992) 'Russian Peacekeeping, Defence, Diplomacy, or Imperialism?', *RFE/RL Research Report*, 1, 37.

Dias, V. A. (2013) 'The EU and Russia: Competing Discourses, Practices and Interests in the Shared Neighbourhood', *Perspectives on European Politics and Society*, 14, 2.

Drent, M. (2011) 'The EU's Comprehensive Approach to Security: A Culture of Coordination?', *Studia Diplomatica*, 64, 2.

Freedman, L. (2014) 'Ukraine and the Art of Limited War', *Survival*, 56, 6.

Garnett, S. W. (1998) 'Europe's Crossroads: Russia and the West in the New Borderlands', in Mandelbaum, M. (ed.) *The New Russian Foreign Policy* (New York, NY, Council on Foreign Relations).

Gerasimov, V. (2013) 'Novye vyzovy trebuyut pereosmyslut' formy i sposoby vedeniya boevykh deistvii', *Voenno-promyshlennyi kur'er*, 8, 476, available at: http://vpk-news.ru/articles/14632, accessed 8 February 2015.

Giles, K. (2015) 'Russia's Toolkit', in Giles, K., Hanson, P., Lyne, R., Nixey, J., Sherr, J. & Wood, A. (eds) *The Russian Challenge*, Chatham House Report, June, available at: https://www.chathamhouse.org/sites/files/chathamhouse/field/field_document/20150605RussianChallengeGilesHansonLyneNixeySherrWoodUpdate.pdf, accessed 7 March 2016.

195

Gordon, M. R. (2014) 'US and Russia Agree on Pact to Defuse Ukraine Crisis', *New York Times*, 17 April, available at: http://www.nytimes.com/2014/04/18/world/europe/ukraine-diplomacy.html?_r=0, accessed 16 March 2016.

Grant, M. L. (2014a) Statement at the United Nations Security Council, Report 7154 (S/PV. 7154), 13 April (New York, NY, United Nations), available at: http://www.securitycouncilreport.org/atf/cf/%7B65BFCF9B-6D27-4E9C-8CD3-CF6E4FF96FF9%7D/s_pv_7154.pdf, accessed 8 January 2015.

Grant, M. L. (2014b) Statement at the United Nations Security Council, Report 7165 (S/PV. 7165), 29 April (New York, NY, United Nations), available at: http://www.securitycouncilreport.org/atf/cf/%7B65BFCF9B-6D27-4E9C-8CD3-CF6E4FF96FF9%7D/s_pv_7165.pdf, accessed 8 January 2015.

Grove, T. & Strobel, W. (2014) 'Special Report: Where Ukraine's Separatists Get Their Weapons', *Reuters*, 29 July, available at: http://www.reuters.com/article/us-ukraine-crisis-arms-specialreport-idUSKBN0FY0UA20140729, accessed 16 March 2016.

Hill, W. (2012) *Russia, the Near Abroad, and the West: Lessons from the Moldova-Transdniestria Conflict* (Baltimore, MD, The Johns Hopkins University Press).

Holzgrefe, J. L. (2003) 'The Humanitarian Intervention Debate', in Holzgrefe, J. L. & Keohane, R. O. (eds) *Humanitarian Intervention: Ethical, Legal, and Political Dilemmas* (Cambridge, Cambridge University Press).

Hughes, J. (2013) 'Russia and the Secession of Kosovo: Power, Norms and the Failure of Multilateralism', *Europe-Asia Studies*, 66, 5.

Hyde-Price, A. (2007) *European Security in the Twenty-First Century: The Challenge of Multipolarity* (London, Routledge).

Ivzhshenko, T. (2015) 'Minskie Soglasheniya-2 na grani provaly', *Nezavisimaya Gazeta*, 23 March.

Jonson, L. (2000) 'Russia, NATO and the Handling of Conflicts at Russia's Southern Periphery: At a Crossroads?', *European Security*, 9, 4.

Jonson, L. & Archer, C. (1996) 'Russia and Peacekeeping in Eurasia', in Jonson, L. & Archer, C. (eds) *Peacekeeping and the Role of Russia in Eurasia* (Boulder, CO, Westview Press).

Kelin, A. (2014a) 'Speech by Russia's Permanent Representative to the OSCE, Andrey Kelin, at the Session of the Permanent Council of the OSCE, Vienna, 30 April 2014', Ministry of Foreign Affairs of the Russian Federation, available at: http://archive.mid.ru/bdomp/brp_4.nsf/e78a48070f128a7b43256999005bcbb3/c3ef672d615d2e6b44257cd0005b718b!OpenDocument, accessed 16 June 2014.

Kelin, A. (2014b) 'Speech by Russia's Permanent Representative to the OSCE, Andrey Kelin, at the Session of the Permanent Council of the OSCE, Vienna, 12 June 2014', Ministry of Foreign Affairs of the Russian Federation, available at: http://archive.mid.ru/bdomp/brp_4.nsf/e78a48070f128a7b43256999005bcbb3/dffea3c04ce2893d44257cfa005700d6!OpenDocument, accessed 16 June 2014.

Kelin, A. (2014c) 'Speech at the Session of the Permanent Council of the OSCE, 30 April 2014', Ministry of Foreign Affairs of the Russian Federation, available at: http://www.mid.ru/bdomp/brp_4.nsf/e78a48070f128a7b43256999005bcbb3/c3ef672d615d2e6b44257cd0005b718b!OpenDocument, accessed 30 August 2014.

Kelin, A. (2014d) 'Speech by Russia's Permanent Representative to the OSCE, Andrey Kelin, at the Session of the Permanent Council of the OSCE, Vienna, 19 June 2014', Ministry of Foreign Affairs of the Russian Federation, available at: http://archive.mid.ru/bdomp/brp_4.nsf/e78a48070f128a7b43256999005bcbb3/f795e99050d9d39044257d00005ca304!OpenDocument, accessed 18 February 2014.

Kelin, A. (2014e) 'Speech by Russia's Permanent Representative to the OSCE, Andrey Kelin, at the Session of the Permanent Council of the OSCE, Vienna, 12 June 2014', Ministry of Foreign Affairs of the Russian Federation, available at: http://archive.mid.ru/bdomp/brp_4.nsf/e78a48070f128a7b43256999005bcbb3/dffea3c04ce2893d44257cfa005700d6!OpenDocument, accessed 18 February 2014.

Kelin, A. (2014f) 'Russian Permanent Representative to the OSCE Andrei Kelin's Interview with ITAR-TASS News Agency, 4 September 2014', Ministry of Foreign Affairs of the Russian Federation, available at: http://archive.mid.ru/bdomp/brp_4.nsf/e78a48070f128a7b43256999005bcbb3/1d4ac6ebe8547d9d44257d4a0060186d!OpenDocument, accessed 18 February 2014.

Kellett, N. A. (1996) *Russian Peacekeeping. Part 1: The Soviet Experience*, Canadian Department of National Defense, Research Note 96/08, Ottawa, Canada, December.

Kirchner, E. & Sperling, J. (2007) *EU Security Governance* (Manchester, NH, Manchester University Press).

Kofman, M. (2015) 'Don't Doubt the Ceasefire: Minsk II Could Freeze the Conflict in Ukraine', *Foreign Affairs*, 22 February.

Kozyrev, Y. (1993) 'Peacemaking Costs a Lot. But Abandoning it is Even More Expensive', *Krasnaya Zvezda*, 1 October.

Krahmann, E. (2003) 'Conceptualizing Security Governance', *Cooperation and Conflict*, 38, 1.

Kramer, A. E. (2008) 'Russia Claims Its Sphere of Influence in the World', *New York Times*, 1 September, available at: http://www.nytimes.com/2008/09/01/world/europe/01russia.html?_r=0, accessed 7 March 2016.

Lavrov, S. (1996) 'The Russian View of Peacekeeping: International Activity for Peace', *The Brown Journal of World Affairs*, 3, 1.

Lavrov, S. (2004) 'Transcript of Remarks by Minister of Foreign Affairs of the Russian Federation Sergey Lavrov at Press Conference following talks with Georgian Parliament Speaker Nino Burjanadze', Press Release, Ministry of Foreign Affairs of the Russian Federation, 1 November, available at: http://archive.mid.ru//bdomp/brp_4.nsf/e78a48070f128a7b43256999005bcbb3/4bc5ed7e9985fa8bc3256f3f005928d4!OpenDocument, accessed 12 May 2015.

Lavrov, S. (2008) 'Interview by Minister of Foreign Affairs of the Russian Federation Sergey Lavrov to BBC Moscow', Ministry of Foreign Affairs of the Russian Federation, 9 August, available at: http://archive.mid.ru//bdomp/brp_4.nsf/e78a48070f128a7b43256999005bcbb3/f87a3fb7a7f669ebc32574a100262597!OpenDocument, accessed 15 May 2015.

Lavrov, S. (2014a) 'Interview by the Russian Foreign Minister Sergey Lavrov, Given to the Programme "Voskresnoye vremya" Moscow, 30 March 2014', Ministry of Foreign Affairs of the Russian Federation, available at: http://archive.mid.ru/bdomp/brp_4.nsf/e78a48070f128a7b43256999005bcbb3/ee4b80780ee88b2944257cad0056c74e!OpenDocument, accessed 10 March 2015.

Lavrov, S. (2014b) 'It's not Russia that is Destabilising Ukraine', *The Guardian*, available at: http://www.theguardian.com/commentisfree/2014/apr/07/sergei-lavrov-russia-stabilise-ukraine-west, accessed 3 March 2015.

Lavrov, S. (2014c) 'Phone Conversation between the Russian Foreign Minister, Sergey Lavrov, and the US Secretary of State, John Kerry', Press Release, Ministry of Foreign Affairs of the Russian Federation, 9 April, available at: http://archive.mid.ru/bdomp/brp_4.nsf/e78a48070f128a7b43256999005bcbb3/0561674f5582a31a44257cb7005407a5!OpenDocument, accessed 2 March 2015.

Lavrov, S. (2014d) 'Working Meeting of the Russian President, Vladimir Putin, with the Russian Foreign Minister, Sergey Lavrov, Moscow, 10 March 2014', Press Release, Ministry of Foreign Affairs of the Russian Federation, available at: http://www.mid.ru/bdomp/brp_4.nsf/e78a48070f128a7b43256999005bcbb3/8b903f6c12bd351a44257c9800239122!OpenDocument, accessed 7 February 2015.

Lavrov, S. (2014e) 'Interview of the Russian Foreign Minister Sergey Lavrov to "Bloomberg TV", Moscow, 14th of May 2014', Ministry of Foreign Affairs of the Russian Federation, available at: http://archive.mid.ru/bdomp/brp_4.nsf/e78a48070f128a7b43256999005bcbb3/fc216870be040e3c44257cd900491440!OpenDocument, accessed 10 February 2014.

Lavrov, S. (2014f) 'Answers to Questions from the Russian Mass Media by the Russian Foreign Minister, Sergey Lavrov, Moscow, 12 June 2014', Ministry of Foreign Affairs of the Russian Federation, available at: http://archive.mid.ru/bdomp/brp_4.nsf/e78a48070f128a7b43256999005bcbb3/e8642fba3c3f5a0344257cfa004b6583!OpenDocument, accessed 10 March 2015.

Lavrov, S. (2014g) 'Introductory Speech by the Russian Foreign Minister Sergey Lavrov before the Talk with the OSCE Secretary General, Lamberto Zannier, Moscow, 11 June 2014', Ministry of Foreign Affairs of the Russian Federation, available at: http://archive.mid.ru/bdomp/brp_4.nsf/e78a48070f128a7b43256999005bcbb3/3372965500602a4944257cfa0048955c!OpenDocument, accessed 10 March 2015.

Lavrov, S. (2014h) 'Answer to the Question from the Russian Mass Media on the Topic of the Ukrainian Crisis by the Russian Foreign Minister, Sergey Lavrov, Dushanbe, 30 July 2014', Ministry of Foreign Affairs of the Russian Federation, available at: http://archive.mid.ru/bdomp/brp_4.nsf/e78a48070f128a7b43256999005bcbb3/11415d9ca4e3f1b844257d27002064d6!OpenDocument, accessed 18 March 2014.

Lavrov, S. (2015) 'Foreign Minister Sergey Lavrov Delivers a Speech and Answers Questions during Debates at the 51st Munich Security Conference, Munich, February 7, 2015', Ministry of Foreign Affairs of the Russian Federation, available at: http://www.mid.ru/brp_4.nsf/0/4E7CDDD252FDEF1F43257DE60031E493, accessed 20 February 2015.

Luhn, A. (2014a) 'Ukrainian Troops Begin Military Operation to "Destroy Foreign Invader"', *The Guardian*, 15 April, available at: http://www.theguardian.com/world/2014/apr/15/ukrainian-troops-anti-terrorist-operation-kiev, accessed 7 March 2016.

Luhn, A. (2014b) 'Putin says Geneva Agreement no Longer Viable after Ukrainian Military Action', *The Guardian*, 2 May, available at: http://www.theguardian.com/world/2014/may/02/putin-geneva-agreement-not-viable-ukraine-military-action, accessed 7 March 2016.

Luhn, A. (2014c) 'Russia Warns it will Respond if Interests Attacked in Ukraine', *The Guardian*, 23 April, available at: http://www.theguardian.com/world/2014/apr/23/us-warns-russia-ukraine-moscow-snap-military-exercises, accessed 7 March 2016.

Lynch, D. (2000) *Russian Peacekeeping Strategies in the CIS: The Cases of Moldova, Georgia and Tajikistan* (Basingstoke, Macmillan).

Lynch, D. (2002) 'Separatist States and Post-Soviet Conflicts', *International Affairs*, 78, 4.

MacFarlane, S. N. & Schnabel, A. (1995) 'Russia's Approach to Peacekeeping', *International Journal*, 50, 2.

MacFarquhar, N. (2014) 'Putin Lays out Proposal to End Ukraine Conflict', *New York Times*, 3 September, available at: http://www.nytimes.com/2014/09/04/world/europe/ukraine-russia.html, accessed 7 March 2016.

Mackinlay, J. (2003a) 'Introduction', in Mackinlay, J. & Cross, P. (eds) *Regional Peacekeepers: The Paradox of Russian Peacekeeping* (New York, NY, The United Nations University Press).

Mackinlay, J. (2003b) 'Conclusion: The Paradox of Russian Peacekeeping', in Mackinlay, J. & Cross, P. (eds) *Regional Peacekeepers: the Paradox of Russian Peacekeeping* (New York, NY, The United Nations University Press).

Mankoff, J. (2014) 'Russia's Latest Land Grab: How Putin Won Crimea and Lost Ukraine', *Foreign Affairs*, May/June, available at: http://www.foreignaffairs.com/articles/141210/jeffrey-mankoff/russias-latest-land-grab, accessed 8 January 2015.

McNeill, T. (1997) 'Humanitarian Intervention and Peacekeeping in the Former Soviet Union and Eastern Europe', *International Political Science Review*, 18, 1.

Mokhov, V. (2001) 'Tyazhela golubaya kaska', *Krasnaya Zvezda*, 21 December.

Nebenhay, S. (2014) 'ICRC Lays Down Principles for Delivering Russian Aid to Ukraine', *Reuters*, 11 August, available at: http://www.reuters.com/article/us-ukraine-crisis-redcross-idUSKBN0GB1XA20140811, accessed 7 March 2016.

Oliphant, R. (2014) 'Ukraine Launches "Anti-Terrorist Operation" in the East', *The Telegraph*, 15 April, available at: http://www.telegraph.co.uk/news/worldnews/europe/ukraine/10767005/Ukraine-launches-anti-terrorist-operation-in-the-east.html, accessed 7 March 2016.

Orlova, N. (2005) 'V Tbilisi vse eshche zhdut normalizovat' gruzino-rossiiskie otnosheniya sposobina lish' vstrecha na vysshem urovne', *Nezavisimaya Gazeta*, 29 September.

Paniev, Yu. (2014a) 'Ukrainskii krizis na chetverykh', *Nezavisimaya Gazeta*, 18 April.

Paniev, Yu. (2014b) 'Moskva soglasilas' na peregovory s kievom', *Nezavisimaya Gazeta*, 22 April.

Paniev, Yu. (2014c) 'Pochemu zhenevskie soglasheniya slozheno vypolnit'', *Nezavisimaya Gazeta*, 18 April.

Paniev, Yu. (2014d) 'OBSE prokhodit ispytanie Ukrainoi', *Nezavisimaya Gazeta*, 5 December.

Paniev, Yu. & Tsilyurik, D. (2014a) 'Zapad v ozhidanii razvyazku', *Nezavisimaya Gazeta*, 16 April.

Paniev, Yu. & Tsilyurik, D. (2014b) 'Moskva nastaivaet na bezuslovnom prekrashchenii ognya v Ukraine', *Nezavisimaya Gazeta*, 2 September.

Pankin, A. (2014) Statement at the United Nations Security Council, Report 7311 (S/PV. 7311), 12 November (New York, NY, United Nations), available at: http://outreach.un.org/mun/files/2014/11/SPV7311_vc.pdf, accessed 25 April 2015.

Poole, O. (2014) 'Ukraine Crisis: Kremlin Insists it Cannot Control Pro-Russian Separatists and Calls for Dialogue with West', *The Independent*, 3 May, available at: http://www.independent.co.uk/news/world/europe/ukraine-crisis-kremlin-insists-it-cannot-control-pro-russian-separatists-and-calls-for-dialogue-with-9321412.html, accessed 7 March 2016.

Popescu, N. (2006) *'Outsourcing' de facto Statehood: Russia and the Secessionist Entities in Georgia and Moldova*, Centre for European Policy Studies, Policy Brief, 109, July, available at: http://aei.pitt.edu/11718/1/1361.pdf, accessed 18 May 2015.

Popescu, N. & Litra, L. (2012) *Transnistria: A Bottom-Up Solution*, European Council on Foreign Relations, Policy Brief, September, available at: http://www.ecfr.eu/page/-/ECFR63_TRANSNISTRIA_BRIEF_AW.pdf, accessed 18 May 2015.

Power, S. (2014) Statement at the United Nations Security Council, Report 7205 (S/PV. 7205), 24 June (New York, NY, United Nations), available at: http://www.un.org/en/ga/search/view_doc.asp?symbol=S/PV.7205, accessed 15 April 2015.

Power, S. (2015) Statement at the United Nations Security Council, Report 7384 (S/PV. 7384), 17 February (New York, NY, United Nations), available at: http://www.un.org/en/ga/search/view_doc.asp?symbol=S/PV.7384, accessed 15 April 2015.

Pugsley, S. (2014) 'Russia's Convoy to Eastern Ukraine and the International Committee of the Red Cross', European Council on Foreign Relations, Blog, 20 August, available at: http://www.ecfr.eu/blog/entry/russias_convoy_to_east_ukraine_and_the_international_committee_of_the_red_c, accessed 10 May 2015.

Renz, B. (2010) 'Crisis Response in War and Peace: Russia's "Emergencies" Ministry and Security Sector Reform', *World Defence Systems*, 16.

Sagramoso, D. (2003) 'Russian Peacekeeping Policies', in Mackinlay, J. & Cross, P. (eds) *Regional Peacekeepers: the Paradox of Russian Peacekeeping* (New York, NY, The United Nations University Press).

Sammut, D. & D'Urso, J. (2015) *The Special Monitoring Mission in Ukraine: A Useful but Flawed OSCE Tool*, European Policy Centre, Policy Brief, 23 April, available at: http://aei.pitt.edu/63784/1/pub_5511_the_special_monitoring_mission_in_ukraine.pdf, accessed 20 October 2015.

Stern, D. (2015) 'Ukraine Conflict: Refugees in Their Own Country', *BBC*, 15 August, available at: http://www.bbc.co.uk/news/world-europe-33880351, accessed 7 March 2016.

Sutyagin, I. (2015) *Russian Forces in Ukraine*, Royal United Services Institute, Briefing Paper, available at: https://www.rusi.org/downloads/assets/201503_BP_Russian_Forces_in_Ukraine_FINAL.pdf, accessed 18 March 2015.

Tardy, T. (2004) 'Introduction', in Tardy, T. (ed) *Peace Operations After 11 September 2001* (Oxford, Frank Cass).

Thakur, R. (2006) *The United Nations, Peace and Security: From Collective Security to the Responsibility to Protect* (Cambridge, Cambridge University Press).

Trenin, D. (1996) 'Russia', in Findlay, T. (ed.) *Challenges for the New Peacekeepers*, SIPRI Research Report No. 12 (Solna, SIPRI).

Trenin, D. (2014) 'The Ukraine Crisis and the Resumption of Great-Power Rivalry', *Carnegie Moscow Centre*, 9 July, available at: http://carnegie.ru/2014/07/09/ukraine-crisis-and-resumption-of-great-power-rivalry, accessed 7 March 2016.

Tsygankov, A. (2015) 'Vladimir Putin's Last Stand: The Sources of Russia's Ukraine Policy', *Post-Soviet Affairs*, 31, 4.

UN (2008) 'Security Council Resolution 1808', 15 April, available at: http://www.securitycouncilreport.org/atf/cf/%7B65BFCF9B-6D27-4E9C-8CD3-CF6E4FF96FF9%7D/Georgia%20SRES1808.pdf, accessed 20 June 2015.

UN (2014) 'General Assembly Adopts Resolution Calling upon States not to Recognise Changes in Status of Crimea Region', UN General Assembly, 27 March, available at: http://www.un.org/press/en/2014/ga11493.doc.htm, accessed 20 June 215.

UNHCR (2015) 'Ukraine Internal Displacement Nears 1 Million as Fighting Escalates in Donetsk Region', *United Nations High Commissioner for Refugees*, 6 February, available at: http://www.unhcr.org/54d4a2889.html, accessed 20 March 2015.

Vorob'yev, E. (1994) 'On Russia's Conceptual Approach to Peacekeeping', presentation given at Fort Leavenworth, Kansas, USA, available at: http://www.bits.de/NRANEU/docs/peacekeeping94.htm#concept, accessed 18 March 2015.

Wagnsson, C. & Holmberg, A. (2014) 'Conflict Management', in Sperling, J. (ed.) *Handbook of European Security Governance* (Cheltenham & Northampton, MA, Edward Elgar).

Webber, M. (2009) 'Russia and the European Security Governance Debate', in Gower, J. & Timmins, G. (eds) *Russia and Europe in the Twenty-First Century: An Uneasy Partnership* (London, Anthem Press).

Webber, M. (2014) 'Security Governance', in Sperling, J. (ed.) *Handbook of Governance and Security* (Cheltenham & Northampton, MA, Edward Elgar).

Webber, M., Croft, S., Howorth, J., Terriff, T. & Krahmann, E. (2004) 'The Governance of European Security', *Review of International Studies*, 30, 1.

Wilson, A. (2014) *Ukraine Crisis: What it Means for the West* (New Haven, CT, Yale University Press).

Winn, N. (2003) 'The European Union's External Face: The "Europeanisation" of JHA and CFSP', *Perspectives on European Politics and Society*, 4, 1.

Wolff, S. & Rodt, A. M. (2013) 'Self-Determination after Kosovo', *Europe-Asia Studies*, 65, 5.

Yakovenko, A. (2003) 'Alexander Yakovenko, the Official Spokesman of Russia's Ministry of Foreign Affairs, Answers a Russian Media Question Regarding Outcome of Regular Meeting of Expert Groups for Georgian–Ossetian Settlement', Ministry of Foreign Affairs of the Russian Federation, 21 October, available at: http://www.mid.ru/bdomp/brp_4.nsf/e78a48070f128a7b43256999005bcbb3/38629aa75f3ff17543256dc60042338a, accessed 12 September 2014.

Yakovenko, A. (2004) 'Alexander Yakovenko, the Spokesman of Russia's Ministry of Foreign Affairs, Answers a Question from RIA Novosti About the Course of the Settlement of the Georgian–Abkhaz Conflict', Ministry of Foreign Affairs of the Russian Federation, 4 May, available at: http://www.mid.ru/bdomp/brp_4.nsf/e78a48070f128a7b43256999005bcbb3/9bb10d61ebfdd2e5c3256e8b0038d5f8!OpenDocument, accessed 8 August 2014.

Yakovenko, A. (2008) 'Statement at the Security Council Meeting on Mediation and Settlement of Disputes', Ministry of Foreign Affairs of the Russian Federation, 24 September, available at: http://www.mid.ru/bdomp/brp_4.nsf/e78a48070f128a7b43256999005bcbb3/24209178bb380af5c32574ce0043a6ee!OpenDocument, accessed 20 June 2014.

Zagorski, A. (2015) 'The OSCE and the Ukraine Crisis', in Dynkin, A. & Oznobishchev, S. (eds) *Russia: Arms Control, Disarmament and International Security*, IMEMO supplement to the Russian edition of the SIPRI Yearbook (Moscow, IMEMO RAN).

The Empire Strikes Back: Economic Statecraft and the Securitisation of Political Economy in Russia

RICHARD CONNOLLY

Abstract

This essay considers the impact of economic statecraft, used by both Western countries and Russia in the aftermath of Russia's annexation of Crimea in March 2014, on political economy in Russia. The first part of the essay assesses the impact that economic statecraft had on the performance of the Russian economy in the period 2014–2015. The second half of the essay considers how economic statecraft has shaped the development of the system of political economy in Russia. It is argued that the available evidence indicates that economic statecraft has resulted in several unintended consequences, including the strengthening of elite cohesion, and a creeping 'securitisation' of economic policy in Russia.

ECONOMIC STATECRAFT HAS BEEN THE PRIMARY TOOL USED by Western powers and their allies in response to Russian involvement in the conflict in Ukraine. The term economic statecraft refers to a range of measures, including travel bans on individuals, asset freezes, trade embargoes, financial restrictions and other economic sanctions.[1] The objective of economic statecraft is not always clear; while effecting a change in the target country's foreign policy behaviour is desirable and is the ostensible objective of statecraft, in reality policy makers from sender countries often realise that the aims of statecraft should be more limited.[2] Imposing a cost on the target country to signal displeasure with its policies, for example, is a more limited objective. Imposing such a cost might then deter the target country from escalating its objectionable (in the eyes of the sender countries) behaviour.

In the context of the Ukraine conflict, the stated aims of Western economic statecraft are multiple. For example, certain measures were imposed in response to Russia's annexation of Crimea in March 2014. Later, wider ranging measures (so-called sectoral sanctions) were

The author would like to thank Julian Cooper, Philip Hanson and Silvana Malle for comments made on previous iterations of this essay. In addition, the insightful comments provided by two anonymous reviewers are gratefully acknowledged. Lucy Buckland also provided helpful research assistance. The usual disclaimers apply.

[1]For a broad discussion of economic statecraft, see Baldwin (1985); and for a discussion of the West's use of economic statecraft in relation to the Soviet Union during the Cold War, see Hanson (1988).

[2]The terminology of the statecraft literature refers to the country or countries imposing economic measures as 'sender' countries, while the country (or countries) that is the object of statecraft is described as the 'target' country.

imposed because of Russia's involvement in the conflict in south-eastern Ukraine. What is common to all these measures is a desire by the Western sender countries to impose a cost on the actions of the target country, Russia. These costs may then, at the very least, send a clear signal that Western countries are unhappy with Russia's actions in Ukraine, or possibly even deter Russia from escalating its activities. It is also possible, at least in theory, that if the costs of economic statecraft to Russia are sufficiently high, it might be persuaded to modify or reverse its policies towards Ukraine.

The focus of this essay is on assessing the costs imposed by Western economic statecraft on the Russian economy. The purpose of the essay is not to determine whether economic statecraft has achieved its political objectives—whether they are signalling deterrence or a demand for modification of Russia's foreign policy. While the economic impact and the effectiveness of economic statecraft are treated as analytically distinct, it is nevertheless true in practice that the magnitude of the costs imposed by economic statecraft is an important component in determining whether it will be effective as an instrument of foreign policy. After all, if the costs for the target country are modest, it is possible that the effectiveness of economic statecraft might be correspondingly low. In addition to assessing the costs of economic statecraft, this essay will also consider the Russian policy response and the impact that this response has exerted upon domestic political economy in Russia.

To address these two questions, the essay is organised as follows. The first section provides an assessment of the impact of Western economic statecraft on the performance of the Russian economy between March 2014 and spring 2015. This is done by first examining the importance of other conjunctural factors that also shaped the performance of the Russian economy during the period under examination, and then considering the direct and indirect effects of sanctions. It is argued that while some aspects of Western statecraft clearly imposed a significant cost to Russia—especially sanctions directed at the financial sector—the impact of the falling price of oil and the pre-existing slowdown in the economy complicate any attempt at explaining the sources of Russia's poor economic performance. Assessing the precise impact of economic statecraft is therefore extremely difficult. The second section considers the impact that Western statecraft has exerted on the domestic political economy in Russia. Here, it is argued that the Russian domestic policy response to the use of economic statecraft has thus far been consistent with the behaviour of many other countries that have been targeted by similar measures in the past. Perhaps the most important observation is that the system of political economy is becoming increasingly securitised, in other words defined by national security concerns rather than the demands of economic development. A third and final section concludes the argument.

The impact of economic statecraft on Russian economic performance

There are a range of estimates of the economic impact of Western statecraft imposed in the aftermath of Russia's annexation of Crimea and military involvement in Ukraine. In November 2014, the Finance Minister, Anton Siluanov, suggested that sanctions had cost Russia $40 billion.[3] In April 2015, President Putin stated that sanctions have cost Russia $160 billion

---

[3]'Anton Siluanov: iz-za sanktsii v 2014 godu Rossiya poteryayet $40 mlrd, iz-za padeniya tsen na neft'— okolo $100 mlrd', *Kommersant.ru*, 24 November 2014, available at: http://www.kommersant.ru/doc/2617993, accessed 20 August 2015.

(Latukhina 2015). Outside Russia, numerous politicians have assigned great importance to the impact of sanctions on the functioning and performance of the Russian economy during what turned out to be a very turbulent period.[4]

However, estimating the impact of economic sanctions on the Russian economy since March 2014 is fraught with even more difficulty than is normal when carrying out such estimates. In addition to the methodological challenges inherent in any such exercise under even 'normal' conditions, the performance of the Russian economy in the year subsequent to the imposition of sanctions was also affected by additional conjunctural, and therefore complicating, factors.

First, Russia was already in the grip of an economic slowdown that saw the country drift towards stagnation even before the imposition of sanctions. This slowdown was structural in nature and has been exerting a negative effect on a number of key economic indicators. Second, the dramatic decline in oil prices over the second half of 2014 was of profound importance to an economy that was, in 2013, the world's second largest producer and exporter of oil, and that relies on receipts from oil exports to provide around half of Federal government revenue (BP 2014).[5]

Consequently, disentangling the impact of statecraft from the other two, arguably more important, forces buffeting the Russian economy is nearly impossible. Healthy scepticism should therefore be exercised when presented with suspiciously precise estimates of the economic impact of Western statecraft. Rather than seeking to identify a precise cost to the Russian economy (in dollar terms, for example), it is perhaps more useful to examine how economic statecraft may have affected the economy in a step-wise fashion, assessing first the 'direct' impact on the targeted sectors of the economy, and then the less obvious 'indirect' impact that statecraft may have exerted on the functioning of the wider economy. Before doing so, however, it is first necessary to sketch out the importance of the economic context in which statecraft was imposed.

Context matters: slowing economic growth and the collapse in the price of oil

A truly accurate assessment of the macroeconomic impact of statecraft would require that the *ceteris paribus* condition be satisfied. However, during 2014 and 2015, all other things in the Russian economy were far from equal. It is important to be aware of two highly significant factors that influenced the performance of the Russian economy at the time that sanctions were imposed.

First, Russia's economic performance had been weakening for several years. This was probably due to the exhaustion of the economic growth model that served Russia well between

---

[4]David Cameron stated in November 2014 that sanctions were behind the poor economic performance of Russia at that time (Wintour 2014). US President, Barack Obama, went even further, claiming that sanctions had left the Russian economy 'in tatters'. See, 'Obama Says Western Sanctions Have Left Russia's Economy "In Tatters"', *The Moscow Times*, 21 January 2015, available at: http://www.themoscowtimes.com/business/article/obama-says-western-sanctions-have-left-russia-s-economy-in-tatters/514671.html, accessed 20 August 2015.

[5]In 2013, Russia produced an average of 10.3 million barrels per day (bpd). This compared to 11.5 million bpd in Saudi Arabia and 10 million bpd in the USA.

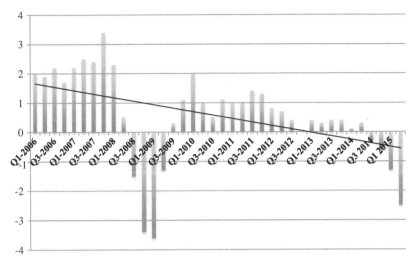

FIGURE 1. REAL GDP, 2006–2015, PERCENTAGE CHANGE FROM PREVIOUS QUARTER.
Source: Bank of Russia (2015, p. 63).

1999 and 2008.[6] As illustrated in Figure 1, annual real GDP growth was estimated to have slowed to just 0.6% in 2014, down from around 4% in 2012 and considerably slower than the 1999–2007 average of over 7%. This slowdown was probably caused by a combination of many factors, among which the most important were a shrinking labour force, the slowdown in government and consumer spending and, perhaps most importantly, a low share of investment in economic activity (Connolly 2011; Gaddy & Ickes 2014).

The second factor to note is the sharp decline in the price of oil which began in the second half of 2014 and continued into 2015. The average price for Urals crude oil hovered around $110 per barrel from 2011 to June 2014. Prices then plummeted to $47 per barrel at the end of January 2015. This resulted in a sharp decline in export revenues and tax receipts despite the fact that the volume of oil production in Russia reached a post-Soviet record level in 2014. Although oil prices later recovered somewhat in the first half of 2015—Urals crude was trading at around $65 per barrel in mid-May 2015—they fell again to below $40 per barrel in December 2015.

The simultaneous structural slowdown in economic growth in Russia and the decline in the price of oil make it difficult to isolate the economic impact of sanctions. To illustrate this point consider first the influence of the structural slowdown on economic performance. A large number of economic forecasts made immediately before the imposition of the first round of sanctions in late March 2014, or just after, predicted that annual GDP growth in 2014 would be very low (see Table 1). Yet the economy defied the expectations of the majority of forecasters and grew by an estimated 0.6% on an annual basis. All of these forecasts were unanimous in citing domestic factors, such as weak investment, as the primary drivers of weak performance. They did not take sanctions into account. If these forecasts had been

[6]Essentially, this model was based on the redistribution of fast-growing natural resource revenues to other parts of the economy. See, Zamaraev *et al.* (2013), Mau (2013, 2014), Kudrin and Gurvich (2014), Connolly (2015a), World Bank (2015). On the wider regional slowdown, see Prochniak (2011).

TABLE 1
SELECTED ECONOMIC FORECASTS MADE BEFORE THE IMPOSITION OF SANCTIONS

Forecaster	Month of forecast	Forecast	Difference between forecast and actual performance
Central Bank of Russia (Variant I)	December 2013	−1	−1.6
Development Centre (HSE)	December 2013	−0.1	−0.7
Bank of Finland	March 2014	0.5	−0.1
IMF	April 2014	1.3	0.7
EBRD	May 2014	0	−0.6
World Bank	June 2014	0.5	−0.1

Sources: Bank of Russia (2013); BOFIT (2014); EBRD (2014); IMF (2014); World Bank (2014); 'Opros professional'nykh prognozistov otnositel'no ikh videniya perspektiv rossiiskoi ekonomiki v 2013–2014 gg. i dalee do 2022 g.', Higher School of Economics Development Centre, Number 55, November 2013, available at: http://dcenter.ru/opros-professionalnyx-prognozistov-otnositelno-ix-videniya-perspektiv-rossijskoj-ekonomiki-v-2013-2014-gg-i-dalee-do-2022-g/, accessed 12 February 2016.

made with the knowledge that a range of significant economic sanctions would be imposed, or indeed that the price of oil would fall by around 50%, it is likely that the forecasts would have been even more pessimistic.

The Russian economy certainly did not perform well in 2014. But nor did it perform any worse than it was expected to, and, if anything, slightly surpassed pre-sanctions expectations.[7] This does not necessarily mean that the imposition of sanctions acted as a boost to the Russian economy (or to put it differently, that sanctions were a net benefit to the economy). Rather, what it does suggest is: first, that the initial negative economic impact of sanctions may have been modest; and second that some other factor that forecasters had not predicted may explain why the Russian economy performed slightly better than it was expected to.

It is likely that the other factor explaining Russia's economic performance was related to the sharp depreciation of the ruble that occurred over the course of 2014. Some commentators have suggested that this depreciation was caused at least partially by sanctions. It is, for example, intuitively appealing to suggest that sanctions may have led to a loss of business confidence in Russia, which in turn caused a rise in capital outflows, generating downward pressure on the exchange rate. However, closer inspection of the data reveals that daily movements in the price of oil act as a more reliable predictor of ruble–dollar exchange rate movements: between January 2013 and May 2015, the correlation in movements between the two was almost perfect (see Figure 2).[8]

Thus, the single best explanation for the depreciation of the ruble was the decline in oil prices. Most analysts did not expect the sudden and sharp decline in oil prices, and if it had been anticipated, they would probably have predicted dire consequences for the Russian economy. However, the impact on the Russian economy was mixed. On the one hand, the value of total exports, dominated by hydrocarbon sales, plummeted with a corresponding

[7]It should be noted that any conclusions derived from comparing actual performance with forecasts should be treated with caution. After all, the economic forecasts may not have been accurate in the first place.
[8]The Pearsons' *r* correlation coefficient is 0.96.

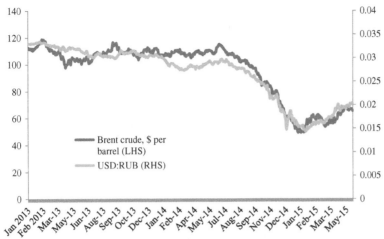

FIGURE 2. RUBLE–DOLLAR EXCHANGE RATE AND OIL PRICE (BRENT, $), 2013–2015.
Source: 'International Financial Statistics', International Monetary Fund, available at: http://data.imf.
org/?sk=5dabaff2-c5ad-4d27-a175-1253419c02d1, accessed 21 December 2015.

depreciation of the ruble. On the other hand, ruble depreciation helped cushion federal tax revenues from the fall in the price of oil. Russia's dollar-denominated oil revenues—which historically account for around half of total federal income—bought more rubles than they did in 2013. Consequently, Russia actually registered a modest federal budget surplus in 2014.[9]

Depreciation also raised the price of imported goods and services, resulting in a sharp decline in the value of imports. However, the weak currency also appeared to have boosted domestic production of goods and services through the import substitution effect. In simple terms, as the price of imported goods rose, Russian consumers and businesses switched to homemade substitutes. As is illustrated below, the impact of the weak ruble may well have cushioned the Russian economy from both the home-grown slowdown and the imposition of sanctions.

To sum up so far: the simultaneous nature of the shocks affecting economic performance in Russia over the course of 2014–2015 was highly significant from an analytical point of view. No single factor from the structural slowdown—the fall in oil prices or the imposition of sanctions—can solely explain economic performance over this period. Moreover, the interaction between each factor has resulted in some unexpected outcomes (such as the growth in GDP that exceeded most forecasts). It is therefore difficult to assign with any confidence a specific weight to the importance of Western economic statecraft on Russian economic performance during the period under examination.

Direct effects of Western statecraft on economic performance in Russia[10]

If the overall macroeconomic impact of economic statecraft is difficult to discern, it is nevertheless plausible to argue that it may have affected the performance of targeted sectors. In addition to asset freezes and visa bans on Russian individuals, companies or other entities in

---

[9]'O federal'nom byudzhete na 2013 god i na planovyi period 2016 i 2017 godov', Ministry of Finance of the Russian Federation, 2014.
[10]Passages from this section borrow heavily from Connolly (2015b).

Russia or Ukraine who are considered to be complicit in Russia's actions in Ukraine, sanctions were targeted at three main sectors: energy, defence and finance. They included, first, a ban on trading bonds and equity and related brokering services for products whose maturity period exceeds 30 days with some of Russia's largest state-controlled banks, including Sberbank and Gazprombank, and three Russian energy companies including Rosneft', Transneft' and Gazprom,[11] and numerous Russian defence companies, including United Aircraft Corporation, Uralvagonzavod and Almaz-Antei. There were also restrictions on loans to five major Russian state-owned banks by EU countries: Sberbank; VTB; Gazprombank; Vneshekonombank (VEB); and Rosselkhozbank, with the US ban also including Bank of Moscow. Further sanctions included an embargo on arms trade with Russia; a ban on exports of so-called dual-use items, comprising civilian industrial goods that can be used as (or to produce) weapons systems; and a ban on the provision, export or re-export of goods, services (not including financial services) or technology in support of exploration or exploitation of deep-water, Arctic offshore or tight oil projects.

In response, Russia imposed counter-sanctions in August 2014, which resulted in a one year ban on imports of fruit, vegetables, meat, fish, milk and dairy from a number of countries, including the EU, Japan and the USA. The initial impact of sanctions in each of these four sectors is discussed below.

The defence industry

Defence industry production rose in 2014–2015, despite sanctions, due to growing demand from abroad (with India the largest foreign customer) and from a surge in domestic orders that was explained by the rise in armaments procurement. The arms embargo affected some companies and high-profile projects within both Russia and the West. For example, France and Italy both had multi-billion dollar deals to supply Russian customers which were compromised by the imposition of sanctions. All future deals—and in the case of the French Mistral helicopter carrier, some past deals—were affected by the embargo. The aggregate effect of the arms embargo on Russia was, however, modest due to the fact that only a small proportion of Western arms exports go to Russia, and a correspondingly small proportion of Russian arms exports go to Western countries. As a result, despite the imposition of sanctions, Russia recorded well over $13 billion worth of arms exports in 2014 (see Figure 3), making Russia the world's second largest exporter of armaments.[12]

This robust export performance was achieved while domestic orders also rose to post-Soviet high levels. As part of the state armaments programme (*gosudarstvennaya programma vooruzheniya*—GPV) to 2020, which aims to re-equip and modernise Russia's armed forces, military spending as measured by SIPRI rose from 3.2% of GDP in 2000, to 4.5% in 2014.[13] Of this, half was spent on procurement and research and development. In 2015, military expenditure was expected to peak at 5.4%, with 60.5% of this amount earmarked for procurement and research and development. Given the strength of external and domestic

---

[11]Although Gazprom was excluded from EU sanctions, it was subject to US sanctions.

[12]The $13bn figure is as reported by the assistant to the Russian president, Vladimir Kozhin. See, 'Rossiiskii oboronnyi eksport otsenili v 13 milliardov dollarov', *lenta.ru*, 17 December 2014, available at: http://lenta.ru/news/2014/12/17/exports/, accessed 20 August 2015. The figure by Kozhin is expressed in current prices unlike data from the Stockholm International Peace Research Institute (SIPRI).

[13]All data on volume and composition of military expenditure are derived from Cooper (2015) (cited with permission of the author).

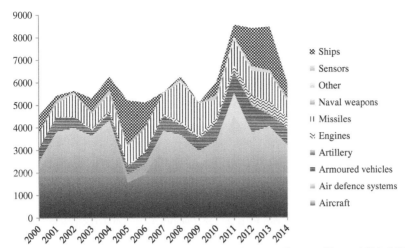

FIGURE 3. RUSSIAN ARMAMENTS EXPORTS BY WEAPONS SYSTEM TYPE, 2000–2014.
Note: SIPRI Trend Indicator Values (TIVs) expressed in US$ million at constant (1990) prices.
Source: 'International Arms Transfers Database', Stockholm International Peace Research Institute (SIPRI),
available at: http://www.sipri.org/databases/armstransfers/armstransfers, accessed 20 April 2015.

demand, there was little scope for further expansion of export deliveries due to domestic orders stretching the capacity of the Russian arms industry (*oboronnyi-promyshlennyi kompleks*—OPK) to fulfil all the orders placed.

The OPK did, however, encounter some problems in implementing production orders because of the Ukraine crisis. Some of these problems emerged not only as a result of Western sanctions, but also because of severed links with Ukrainian defence industry enterprises that were previously closely integrated with the Russian defence–industrial production network. The Ukrainian ban on arms exports to Russia has, for example, caused shortages of helicopter engines and power supply units for naval ships. The impact of Western sanctions was observed in the form of reduced access to some individual components used within weapons systems rather than in final weapon systems. To address these weaknesses, the Russian defence industry and Military–Industrial Commission developed an import substitution plan to replace embargoed products with domestically produced items. According to the deputy defence minister for armaments, Yurii Borisov, this import substitution plan for Ukrainian products should be fully implemented by 2017, although replacing Western components may take longer (Naberezhnov 2014; Mukhin 2015).

The hydrocarbons sector

The impact of sanctions on oil production over 2014–2015 was negligible, with post-Soviet record levels of oil production registered in 2014 (see Figure 4).[14] This is because Western sanctions target projects oriented to future rather than current production. This has been done by the imposition of restrictions on technologies related to Arctic and deep-water exploration,

[14]'Eksport rossiiskoi nefti za 4 mesyatsa 2015 goda vyros na 5,8%—do 79,49 mln tonn', Oil and Gas Information Agency, 6 May 2015, available at: http://www.angi.ru/news.shtml?oid=2824669, accessed 20 August 2015; 'Sanktsii okazalis' bessil'ny protiv energeticheskogo sektora Rossii', Oil and Gas Information Agency, 6 May 2015, available at: http://www.angi.ru/news.shtml?oid=2824627, accessed 20 August 2015.

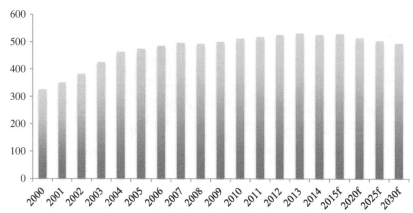

FIGURE 4. PAST AND PROJECTED FUTURE OIL PRODUCTION, MILLION TONNES PER YEAR,
2000–2030.
Sources: BP (2014); forecasts from: ERIRAS (2014, p. 134).

as well as onshore tight oil extraction (for example, from the giant Bazhenov formation). The
vast majority of Russia's current oil production comes from onshore deposits in Western and
Eastern Siberia, both of which continued to yield large volumes of hydrocarbons (IEA 2014,
p. 147). However, as illustrated in Figure 4, production from existing 'brownfield' deposits is
expected to decline over the next decade. Unless massive investment in 'greenfield' deposits
is undertaken—especially in the offshore deep-water, Arctic and tight oil deposits targeted
by sanctions—declining production may not be replaced. As a result, sanctions should only
be expected to affect Russian oil production over the medium term (of three to five years).

While aggregate production remained unaffected by sanctions, a number of high-profile
joint projects with Western international oil companies, such as Exxon-Mobil and Statoil,
were disrupted.[15] Perhaps the most high-profile example is the joint venture between Rosneft'
and Exxon's Kars Project to extract oil from the Kara Sea.[16] Without Western international
oil company participation, Russian firms lacked the technological capability to exploit this
or other similar deposits. While these projects are high profile, the short-term impact should
not be exaggerated. For example, a spokesperson for the French international oil company,
Total, stated in May 2015 that sanctions prevented it from proceeding with only one project
from its activities in Russia.[17]

As in the armaments industry, the Russian authorities developed a range of counter-
measures to prevent Western sanctions from constraining exploitation of technologically
demanding deposits. These included efforts to include equipment used for hydrocarbons
extraction in the wider import substitution strategy, as well as to source such equipment from

---

[15]A number of such joint ventures were formed in 2010–2011 to help Russian state-owned firms exploit
technologically demanding and hard-to-reach deposits offshore and in the Arctic. See Overland *et al.* (2013).

[16]"Rosneft" v sluchae okonchatel'nogo vykhoda Exxon iz proekta Karskogo morya ne budet iskat'
partnera—Sechin', 30 October 2014, available at: http://www.oilcapital.ru/company/255623.html, accessed
20 August 2015.

[17]'Investitsii Total v RF ne byli zamorozheny, kompaniya prodolzhaet proekty v strane', Oil and Gas
Information Agency, 20 May 2015, available at: http://www.angi.ru/news.shtml?oid=2825111, accessed 20
August 2015.

countries not involved in the sanctions regime, such as China (Barkov 2015). Elsewhere, Gazprom resorted to employing larger numbers of contractors to build smaller portions of the Power of Siberia pipeline in order to circumvent the constraints imposed by sanctions on the ability of Gazprom and several construction companies to acquire capital and technology (Sirov 2015).

While there was much uncertainty as to whether Russia could produce substitutes to a sufficiently high standard, early signs indicated that efforts to switch suppliers of imported equipment were bearing fruit. Trade data reveal that in 2014 imports of equipment used in oil and gas extraction including (drilling and tunnelling equipment, and pumps) from Western countries involved in the sanctions regime fell by around 50%.[18] By contrast, imports of similar equipment from China rose by 8%. This is even more noteworthy considering that total imports of such equipment fell by 24%, as the decline in oil prices caused oil producers to rein in investment (Yedovina 2015).

It is also worth noting that many consider the single biggest obstacle to future oil production in Russia to be the onerous tax regime currently in place. This is a claim made frequently by those in Russia's energy industry, including even by the minister for natural resources, Sergei Donskoi, who recently asserted that Russia's 'imperfect' taxation of the hydrocarbons sector is a bigger problem for the industry than Western economic sanctions.[19] It is thus possible, at least in principle, for Russian oil production to be maintained by changes to the taxation and regulatory system if it proves difficult to acquire substitutes for Western technology.[20]

In addition to restrictions on acquiring equipment, many Russian energy producers have been blocked from accessing capital. This is important for two reasons. First, and as stated previously, continued production requires massive volumes of capital investment (Henderson 2015). Financial sanctions have created a clear mismatch between projected investment and availability of capital to fund it. Second, many Russian energy producers—not least the state-owned Rosneft' and Gazprom—are highly leveraged, with high debt–revenue ratios, much of which is denominated in foreign currencies. Constrained in their ability to refinance existing stocks of debt, targeted Russian energy companies simply carried out scheduled repayments. Despite the decline in oil prices, foreign currency-denominated revenues, as well as existing cash assets, were used to finance these repayments. Some firms, such as Rosneft', also tapped into public foreign currency reserves (such as those managed by the Central Bank). Perhaps in a sign of financial distress, Rosneft was rumoured to be considering opening credit lines with state-owned banks, as well as applying for access to the country's sovereign wealth fund (Mordyushenko & Melnikov 2015). It has also been suggested that Rosneft' may sell a 19.7% share in the company to raise capital (Antonova 2015). Inevitably, high debt servicing costs have reduced the availability of capital to finance investment, although the low price

[18]'International Trade in Goods—Exports 2001–2014', International Trade Centre, available at: http://www.intracen.org/itc/market-info-tools/statistics-export-product-country/, accessed 20 August 2015.

[19]See, 'Sanctions against Russia already Affecting Production of Tight Reserves, Could Impact Shelf', *Interfax*, 10 September 2014, available at: http://www.interfax.com/newsinf.asp?id=535345, accessed 20 August 2015. See also Barsukov (2014).

[20]Several institutional changes have taken place, see '"Gazprom" obsuzhdaet s LUKOYLom vozmozhnost' raboty na uchastkakh shel'fa', *RIA Novosti*, 19 May 2015, available at: http://ria.ru/economy/20150519/1065301711.html#ixzz3aa6Lh33c, accessed 20 August 2015.

of oil caused a retrenchment in capital investment across the global energy industry, and not just in Russia.

In the event that the existing sanctions regime is maintained, the key issue is whether Russia can successfully replace existing Western technology and finance, either domestically (through import substitution or the use of state financial resources) or from 'friendly' states (in the form of equipment or loans). In this respect, much will depend on Russian government economic policy. At the time of writing, it appears that the Russian government would proceed with import substitution plans irrespective of whether the sanctions regime is relaxed. This is because Russia's leaders appear to have come to the conclusion that Russia should insulate itself from the threat of further sanctions in the future. Not to do so would represent a threat to Russia's national security, as stated after a meeting by the Russian National Security Council (Egorov 2015).[21]

The financial sector

Financial sanctions exerted perhaps the most observable influence over the Russian economy. Access to Western capital markets was effectively closed to a large number of Russian corporations, and not just those directly targeted by sanctions. Firms in sectors directly targeted by sanctions—such as those in the energy, defence and construction industries—suffered. But so did firms not directly sanctioned, due to a 'contagion' effect as lenders became reluctant to lend to Russian firms because of fears that sanctions may be extended in the future.

This resulted in many Russian firms being forced to repay, rather than refinance, their external debt obligations, causing a significant rise in net private capital outflows and a reduction in the pool of capital available to fund investment in the wider economy (see Figure 5). Indeed, the size of capital outflows in 2014 was more severe than the 'sudden stop' of capital inflows that accompanied the recession of 2008–2009. Total non-financial corporate (which includes many large state enterprises, such as Rosneft' and Gazprom) and financial sector external debt fell from around $715 billion in January 2014 to $597 billion at the end of 2014. The total stock of external debt has declined due to a combination of repayments (to Western banks), rescheduling of existing debt (to banks or other corporate entities that either own or are linked with the Russian debtors) or because of a reduction in the dollar value of ruble-denominated debt.

The surge in private capital outflows, at least partially driven by external debt repayments, contributed to the reduction in Russia's foreign exchange reserves (see Figure 6). It has been suggested that this threatened the financial stability of Russia because Russia's international reserves were not liquid enough to be used to meet external financial obligations, and also because Russia's foreign debt obligations in 2015 and 2016 exceeded the stock of reserves (Åslund 2014). However, upon closer examination, Russia's financial position appeared to be reasonably stable.

First, Russian reserves, including gold, which is normally held by central banks to provide emergency liquidity assistance should foreign assets suddenly depreciate, and reserves assigned to the two sovereign wealth funds—the Reserve Fund and the National Wealth Fund—could be utilised by the authorities, if required. Indeed, it should be noted that the domestic spending obligations attached to the Reserve Fund and the National Wealth Fund

---

[21]'Kto upravlyaet khaosom', *Rossiiskaya gazeta*, 10 February 2015, available at: http://www.rg.ru/2015/02/11/patrushev.html, accessed 20 August 2015.

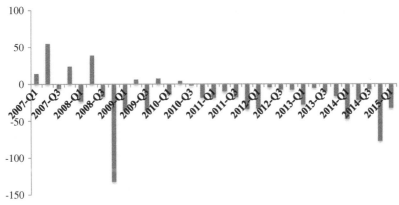

FIGURE 5. QUARTERLY NET PRIVATE CAPITAL FLOWS, 2007–2015 ($ BILLION).
Source: 'External Sector Statistics', Central Bank of the Russian Federation, available at: http://www.cbr.ru/Eng/
statistics/?PrtId=svs, accessed 20 August 2015.

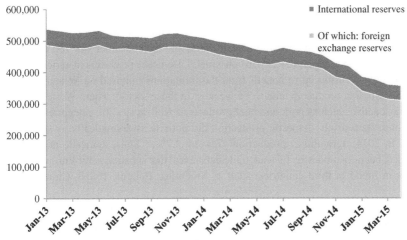

FIGURE 6. RUSSIA'S INTERNATIONAL RESERVES, 2013–2015 ($ MILLION).
Source: 'External Sector Statistics', Central Bank of the Russian Federation, available at: http://www.cbr.ru/Eng/
statistics/?PrtId=svs, accessed 20 August 2015.

are denominated in rubles. Consequently, domestic obligations could be met by simply instructing the Central Bank to print rubles to 'purchase' their holdings of foreign exchange reserves.

Second, Russia's external debt obligations were (and continue to be) exaggerated by financial arrangements employed by Russian corporate groups, which resulted in a substantial volume of 'intra-group' debt. These debts to 'parent' companies by subsidiaries were much softer loans than those taken out from Western banks. Indeed, many corporate groups postponed payments on such debt over 2014–2015. These intra-group debts accounted for nearly a quarter of Russia's total stock of external debt (that is, around $133 billion at the end of 2014). Moreover, intra-group debt repayments accounted for a proportionately larger share of scheduled external debt payments over 2015 (55% of all scheduled repayments) and 2016 (42%). In addition, Russian corporations also held significant cash reserves abroad (well over $100 billion in mid-2015).[22]

Third, as a country that consistently runs a large surplus on the current account of its balance of payments, Russia was in a position to be able to generate annual flows of dollar income in the region of at least 2–3% of GDP.

Thus, while it is clear that Russia was stretched by financial sanctions and saw the availability of capital dwindle, it possessed sufficient reserves, as well as the capacity to generate future earnings of foreign exchange, to ensure financial stability, at least in the short term. The ostensibly large external debt liability was also exaggerated by intra-group financing arrangements. As a result, Russia probably passed the peak of external financing pressure in late 2014. Because increased access to capital from alternative sources (such as Asian capital markets) had not materialised, sanctioned Russian firms began to reorganise their finance arrangements over 2014–2015 so that they relied more on domestic (usually state-owned) banks for funding.[23]

Agriculture

The effects of Russian counter-sanctions in the agricultural sector can be examined on the producer side (on Russian agricultural producers) and the consumer side (on the price and availability of food products to Russian consumers). Domestic producers of agricultural goods are seemingly well placed to benefit from the limitations imposed on Western producers. However, Russian producers tend to be weakest in those sectors where Western producers were most active, such as pork and beef products as well as specific categories of fruit and vegetables. As a result, domestic production did not rise as dramatically as some initially hoped. In 2014, agricultural production grew by 3.7%.[24] Thus, domestic production has expanded, but only modestly. Instead, trade data reveal that substitutes for European products have been found in third countries, such as Argentina, Belarus, Brazil, Chile, China and Turkey.[25]

The reduction in imports from Western countries, and the costs associated with seeking new suppliers, resulted in food prices rising above the average rate of consumer price inflation (CPI). Again, it is difficult to separate the impact of the food embargo from the ruble depreciation that contributed to a wider rise in prices for all imported products (see Figure 7). Food price inflation tended to affect those segments of society that consumed imported goods, that is, mainly the urban, middle classes. Poorer sections of Russian society were less affected for the simple reason that they tended to buy more domestically produced products, although the price of domestically produced food products also rose. It is also worth

[22]'External Sector Statistics', Central Bank of the Russian Federation, available at: http://www.cbr.ru/Eng/statistics/?PrtId=svs, accessed 20 August 2015.

[23]'External Sector Statistics', Central Bank of the Russian Federation, available at: http://www.cbr.ru/Eng/statistics/?PrtId=svs, accessed 20 August 2015.

[24]'Produktsiya sel'skogo khozyaistva po kategoriyam khozyaistv', Federal State Statistics Service, available at: http://www.gks.ru/free_doc/new_site/business/sx/tab-sel1.htm, accessed 20 August 2015.

[25]'International Trade in Goods—Exports 2001–2014', International Trade Centre, available at: http://www.intracen.org/itc/market-info-tools/statistics-export-product-country/, accessed 20 August 2015.

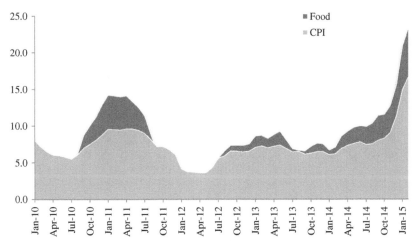

FIGURE 7. CONSUMER PRICE INDEX (CPI) AND FOOD (INCLUDING RESTAURANTS) PRICES, 2010–2015 (YEAR-ON-YEAR).
Source: Bank of Russia (2015, p. 63).

noting that historically it is not unusual for food prices to diverge from the headline rate of inflation in Russia.

Indirect effects

Sanctions may also have affected economic performance through indirect channels. For example, sanctions may have caused a diversion in the trade of certain goods or services, even if those goods or services were not explicitly sanctioned. For example, if there are expectations of future sanctions from certain countries, Russian firms may have sought to insulate themselves from any potential future disruptions by seeking out new markets or suppliers. The threat of future sanctions may also result in a higher perception of risk to those firms economically active in Russia. This may result in a deterioration of the business environment that may deter investment.

Impact on trade

Russia's trade with the world fell substantially in 2014. In 2014, exports amounted to $497.8 billion, down from $523.3 billion in the previous year (a drop of nearly 5%). Imports fell from $341.3 billion in 2013 to $308 billion in 2014 (a fall of 10%). Again, this decline in trade was largely driven by changes in the price of oil and the exchange rate.[26]

The composition of Russia's foreign trade also shifted.[27] The share of China in Russian exports rose from 6.7% in 2013 to 7.5% in 2014. However, total trade with the EU also rose. This included a decline in the EU's share of total Russian imports (from 42.5% in 2013 to 41.4% in 2014). The food embargo undoubtedly contributed to this decline. Perhaps

[26]'International Trade in Goods—Exports 2001–2014', International Trade Centre, available at: http://www.intracen.org/itc/market-info-tools/statistics-export-product-country/, accessed 20 August 2015.

[27]'International Trade in Goods—Exports 2001–2014', International Trade Centre, available at: http://www.intracen.org/itc/market-info-tools/statistics-export-product-country/, accessed 20 August 2015.

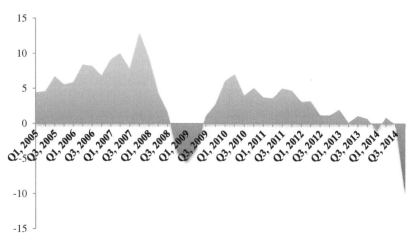

FIGURE 8. QUARTERLY GROWTH IN FIXED CAPITAL FORMATION, 2005–2014 (%).
Source: Bank of Russia (2015, p. 63).

unexpectedly, given both sanctions and the decline in the price of oil, the EU's share of total Russian exports rose from 45.7% to 52.2% in 2014. Thus, at this early stage, there was no evidence of a significant shift in trade from the EU to China. This demonstrates that caution should be applied when interpreting Russian official statements signalling a desire to 'pivot' away from economic integration with Western countries to non-Western countries. Any meaningful shift in the direction of Russia's external economic relations is likely to take decades.

Impact on investment

At around 20% of GDP, investment in fixed capital in Russia is, by the standards of many other middle-income countries, comparatively low. It is certainly too low to generate economic diversification and modernisation (Connolly 2011; Gaddy & Ickes 2014). There has been a clear trend towards declining investment growth since 2010, with a sharp contraction in investment observed in the final quarter of 2014 (see Figure 8). This was likely to have been caused by the drop in the oil price and the concomitant depreciation of the ruble.

Around 30% of total fixed capital formation in Russia takes place in extractive industries (that is, the extraction of metals and hydrocarbons).[28] Consequently, when sentiment in that sector takes a turn for the worse—as it did in 2008–2009, and again in the final quarter of 2014—aggregate investment also falls. Moreover, many of the capital goods and equipment used in investment activities are imported (Berezinskaya & Vedev 2015). This means that exchange rate depreciation of the sort observed in the second half of 2014 raises the cost of investment, leading to many firms postponing or cancelling planned investment.

There is also some evidence that the composition of investment shifted slightly. According to official statistics, the fastest growth in fixed investment data took place in the sectors associated with military production (aircraft, transport equipment and other machinery) and

[28]'Natsional'nye scheta', Federal State Statistics Service, available at: http://www.gks.ru/wps/wcm/connect/rosstat_main/rosstat/ru/statistics/accounts/#, accessed 20 August 2015.

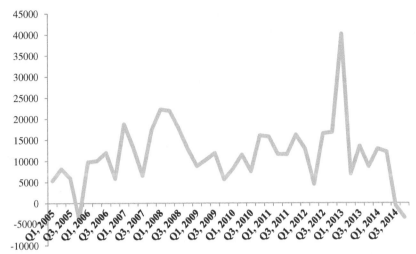

FIGURE 9. QUARTERLY NET INWARD FOREIGN DIRECT INVESTMENT FLOWS, 2005–2014 ($
MILLION).

Source: 'External Sector Statistics', Central Bank of the Russian Federation, available at: http://www.cbr.ru/Eng/
statistics/?PrtId=svs, accessed 20 August 2015.

food production. The sharpest decline in investment activity took place in extractive industries. This is to be expected given the downturn in energy prices. Because military spending and its associated investment was already scheduled before the imposition of sanctions, and because of the decline in energy prices, it is unlikely that sanctions contributed much to the overall trends described here.

Finally, as illustrated in Figure 9, foreign direct investment in Russia became a net outflow in the second half of 2014.[29] While this is not unprecedented (see 2005, for example), the fact that it accompanied a wider contraction in investment indicates that at the time of writing the prospects for investment in Russia appear bleak. It is likely that this was due to structural deficiencies in the Russian economy, as well as to the decline in oil prices, rather than as a direct result of sanctions. Nevertheless, sanctions added yet another reason for investors—Russian or foreign—to put off investment.

Summary of the economic impact of Western statecraft

As outlined above, the precise impact of sanctions is difficult to discern, and was complicated by the influence of Russia's own structural economic slowdown and the sharp decline in oil prices that began in the summer of 2014. The direct impact on targeted sectors has been mixed. In terms of output, the defence and energy industries performed relatively well in 2014. This appeared unlikely to change in the short term. Similarly, the Russian food embargo did not result in a change in fortunes—in either direction—for domestic producers. The sanctions that targeted the financial sector appeared to cause the most immediate disruption. The sizeable external debt repayments in 2014 made an important contribution to capital outflows, which in

[29]On recent patterns of FDI in Russia, see Brock (2005), Iwasaki and Suganuma (2007).

turn contributed to the depreciation of the ruble. However, Russia's overall financial position remained comparatively strong, and it is unlikely that sanctions will be sufficient to induce a financial crisis in Russia, at least in the short term.

In all instances where sanctions have been imposed, the Russian state has initiated a range of counter-measures, including a wide-ranging import substitution plan, as well as the provision of financial support to targeted firms and sectors. These counter-measures may succeed in insulating Russia from the threat of future sanctions due to the weakening of Russia's economic ties with those countries that imposed the current sanctions. As a result, if these measures are sustained—and the government made it clear that they will be—Russia may be much less susceptible to similar external pressure in the future.

The impact on Russian political economy

As well as affecting the performance of the Russian economy, Western economic statecraft has also generated a series of policy responses from the Russia government. In addition to the imposition of counter-sanctions in the agricultural sector, the Russian government has developed, and continued to further refine, a set of economic policies that emphasised self-sufficiency and a reassessment of Russia's pattern of integration with the global economy. Russia's response should not be a surprise. Past evidence from the use of economic statecraft—the economic instruments, such as travel bans, asset freezes, trade embargoes and sanctions employed by Western powers (and their allies) and Russia as instruments of foreign policy—reveals that those countries that are the 'target' of sanctions tend to respond in a relatively predictable manner.[30] This analysis highlights how Russia's response to sanctions confirms three hypotheses derived from the extant literature on sanctions.

H1. The impact of sanctions varies according to regime type of the target country

Sanctions affect leaders and populations in different political systems in different ways. As Risa Brooks argues, 'sanctions that harm the macro economy and thus hurt the "median voter" [are more likely to] be effective against democratic states', while authoritarian leaders, by contrast, 'tend to be insulated from aggregate or macro-economic pressures' and therefore cannot be expected to be as responsive to popular opinion as democracies (Brooks 2002, p. 2). Indeed, as Susan Allen suggests, the 'domestic political response to sanctions varies greatly by the regime type of the target. As states become more politically open, the domestic public can—and does, to some degree—create political costs for leaders who resist sanctions' (Allen 2008, p. 917). By contrast, in non-democracies, like Russia, leaders may in fact profit from sanctions. Without being accountable to the wider public, elites can do this relatively unchecked, as 'leaders may actually benefit from sanctions, as domestic publics are unable to impose political costs and the economic constraints of sanctions often allow leaders to extract greater rents while overseeing the trade of scarce goods' (Allen 2008, p. 917).

Russia's system of political economy is based on the redistribution of rent flows from its internationally competitive natural resource industries (Gaddy & Ickes 2005, 2010; Connolly 2013, 2015a). Revenues generated by oil, gas and metals exports are used to support high levels of social welfare spending, as well as Russia's recent rearmament programme. A system

---

[30]See, for example, Brooks (2002), Allen (2008), Peksen and Cooper Drury (2010), Portela (2010, 2014), Major (2012), von Soest and Wahman (2015).

such as this, based on the redistribution of rent flows, means that the Russian state was well equipped to insulate the elite to cushion it from the impact of sanctions. As a result, even if economic statecraft imposes costs on the bulk of a country's citizenry, what is most important from the perspective of the incumbent leadership is whether it can maintain the support of the elite. Over the course of 2014–2015, the Russian leadership was relatively successful in channelling resources to politically well connected allies. Sanctioned individuals—such as Gennadii Timchenko and Arkadii Rotenberg—received access to lucrative construction contracts, while systemically important firms, such as the state-owned oil giant, Rosneft', successfully lobbied for access to financial resources from the sovereign wealth fund.

In addition to the state support provided to key members of the elite, it is also instructive that the composition of the federal budget over the course of 2014–2015 also shifted to protect those constituencies that might be considered as integral to the prevailing system of political economy in Russia, including industries like defence, rail machinery, oil and gas machinery, and pipelines manufacturing, as well as people dependent on government spending (the so-called *byudzhetniki*, such as pensioners or those employed in the vast state bureaucracy).[31] Thus, even though the nominal ruble value of the revised federal budget for 2015 shrank by 5.7%, the budget chapter covering politically important social policy spending rose by 5.1%.[32] Although it is true that the chapters reserved for national defence and national security and the legal system declined (by 4.8% and 3.7% respectively), this was much less severe than the cuts applied to housing and municipal services (–10.8%), environmental protection (–16.1%), the national economy (–8.8%) and health (–8.3%). Therefore, despite challenging macroeconomic conditions, the Russian government was able to insulate its key constituencies from economic hardship.

H2. Sanctions can result in redistribution in target countries that strengthens the existing system

Not only can non-democratic regimes allocate scarce resources to allies of the incumbent regime in order to strengthen elite cohesion, they are also able to redistribute resources to important socio-economic constituencies that will ensure popular, as well as elite, support for the regime. Indeed, as Johan Galtung observes, sanctions can create the conditions for the rise of powerful constituencies in the target nation that benefit from international isolation (Galtung 1967). This is because, in the long run, sanctions often foster the development of domestic industries in the target country, thus reducing the target's dependence on the outside world and the ability of sender countries to influence the target's behaviour through economic coercion.

The economic policy climate in Russia since the imposition of sanctions emphasised support for precisely those industries that are targeted by sanctions. Import substitution (*importozameshchenie*)—popular among only a minority before 2014—became increasingly fashionable among policy makers, experts and many businesses in Russia. The longer Russia is isolated from the global economy, as will happen the longer sanctions persist, the more likely it is that these forces will grow to dominate economic policy making. Indeed, the

---

[31]See Connolly (2015a).
[32]'Poyasnitel'naya zapiska k proektu Federal'nogo Zakona "O vnesenii izmenenii v Federal'nyi zakon 'O Federal'nom byudzhete na 2015 god i na planovyi period 2016 godov', Ministry of Finance of the Russian Federation, 2015.

interruption of supply chains prompted a reallocation of resources to domestic industries through import substitution programmes, such as that designed to help build defence–industrial products previously imported from Ukrainian enterprises. In April 2015, Denis Manturov, the Minister for Industry and Trade, presented a plan for import substitution that envisaged the implementation of 2,059 projects across 19 branches of the economy between 2016 and 2020 (Yedovina & Shapovalov 2015).[33] The total cost was estimated to reach over RUB 1.5 trillion, with RUB 235 billion to be supplied by the federal budget. Over the course of 2014–2015, extra resources were allocated to the oil and gas equipment industry, the pharmaceutical industry, the agricultural machinery and production industries and, of course, the military–industrial complex. All of these are key economic constituencies that account for a large share of employment in Russia, and all are benefitting from friendly public policies taken as a direct result of the imposition of sanctions.

H3. Sanctions can cause a 'rally round the flag' effect

Finally, previous episodes of sanctions reveal that sanctions can also generate a 'rally round the flag' effect in target countries, in which sanctions lead to an increase in political cohesion within the target state. The imposition of sanctions enables targeted leaders to pinpoint a clear external threat, which can be used as a focal point for a leader to unify the state (Coser 1956; Downs & Rocke 1994; Smith 1996). Leaders can also place the blame for economic hardship on the sender state rather than on their own economic policies, suggesting that sanctioned populations might rally against the enemy or sender state (Galtung 1967; Mueller 1970, 1973; Ostrom & Job 1986).

In Russia, there is considerable evidence that such a 'rally round the flag' effect occurred over the course of 2014–2015. Not only did all opinion polls show public support for the leadership to be at near record high levels, with public support especially high for the President, but the Western sanctions regime also gave the leadership a convenient alibi for the structural downturn in the economy described earlier in this essay. Without sanctions, it is possible that the leadership would have come under much greater public scrutiny for its poor stewardship of the economy. However, the leadership was able to assign blame for any economic hardship to external enemies. On a broader level, there was also evidence that 'standing up to the West' gave many (although not all) Russian citizens a greater sense of pride in their country's standing on the international stage. Public approval ratings for President Putin, as measured by the respected Levada Centre, rose from 65% in January 2014 to 83% after the annexation of Crimea, and were as high as 89% in June 2015.[34] These were the highest approval ratings ever enjoyed by Putin. Time may erode this sense of pride felt by many, but in the short term at least, it was clear that most Russians had indeed 'rallied round the flag'.

Towards the securitisation of political economy in Russia?

The impact of Western economic statecraft was most observable at the domestic political level. Because statecraft tends to affect non-democracies in a different way to democracies, it was perhaps unsurprising that the Russian leadership was able to reallocate resources to its allies

[33]Of this total, 570 projects were said to be under way by November 2015.
[34]The Levada Centre Indexes, available at: http://www.levada.ru/indeksy, accessed 20 August 2015. The impact of the conflict with the West on Putin's popularity is discussed in Simes (2015).

within the elite, and also to key economic constituencies across Russia. Under the mantra of import substitution, economic policy began to take an increasingly introverted and *dirigiste* turn. Nevertheless, this blend of economic nationalism proved, at least at the time of writing, to be very popular among large swathes of the Russian population.

Taken together, the response to economic statecraft described above can be seen as evidence that Russia's economic policy debate was becoming increasingly characterised by an emphasis on self-reliance that was justified in the name of security, with economic policy subsumed within a wider effort to insulate Russia from a growing array of internal and external threats. This tendency can be labelled 'securitisation' and was affecting an increasingly wide range of areas of economic activity.[35] As of late 2015, official plans for economic securitisation in the form of public statements and government documents and decrees were inchoate and lacking in cohesion. There was no clearly formulated agreement on desired objectives or on the precise means that might be deployed to achieve those objectives. Also, a powerful array of constituencies remains opposed to rolling back many of the market reforms undertaken since the collapse of the Soviet Union. Yet the growing sense of insecurity felt by those in the Kremlin appeared to be leading to an increase in the relative power of those groups in and around the state apparatus that would like to see Russia adopt a new agenda for economic development. If, as this essay suggests, economic policy was increasingly defined by security concerns—if the process of economic securitisation was already under way—then the ramifications of this policy change may be profound.

Economic securitisation has the potential to change important aspects of Russia's political economy. For example, security concerns may result in the government taking measures that do not appear to be efficient in commercial or economic terms. This might involve the centralised allocation of resources to sectors considered vital to ensure national security—such as defence or agricultural production—at the expense of other sectors of the economy, such as health or education. To facilitate central control over key areas of the economy, the authorities may make greater use of large, state-owned or state-influenced firms rather than seek to improve the business environment for smaller enterprises.

Thus, given the ambiguity surrounding the efficacy of sanctions outlined in the previous section, it is reasonable to question whether Western sanctions exerted the effect that sender countries intended. Instead of causing elite dissatisfaction, elite cohesion appeared to have strengthened. And instead of imposing significant economic pain, sanctions merely gave the leadership a convenient alibi for what was already a poorly performing economy. Their senders surely did not intend these effects, which raises the question of whether more effective instruments could have been used in their place.[36]

---

[35]See Bacon *et al.*, who adapted Ole Waever's concept of securitisation to Russia's domestic politics; securitisation is what happens 'when normal politics is pushed into the security realm', and that the 'securitisation of an issue in a policy sector occurs when a political actor by the use of the rhetoric of existential threat … succeeds in justifying the adoption of measures outside the formal norms and procedures of politics' (Bacon *et al.* 2006, p. 10).

[36]More effective instruments could have included, for example, a greater emphasis on military responses to Russian assertiveness, or on intensified efforts to target Russian elite assets in the West.

Conclusion

The economic statecraft deployed by Western countries and their allies against Russia in response to its involvement in the conflict in Ukraine since March 2014 has the potential to shape profoundly the nature of Russia's future economic development. While economic statecraft was employed extensively throughout the Cold War, with only a modest impact on Soviet economic organisation and performance, the recent episode has been played out in a radically different context. Over the past two decades, the Russian economy has undergone historically unprecedented liberalisation at home, even if the quality and scope of that liberalisation remains weak relative to Russia's Western neighbours. Russia has also followed a path of deep, if somewhat distorted, integration with the global economy. As a result, the potential for at least the partial reversal of both domestic liberalisation and external integration is much greater than it was during the Soviet period when the degree of central economic control was much greater.

While the assessment offered here is only preliminary, there are signs that the configuration of Russia's system of political economy is changing. While the impact of economic statecraft on economic performance was, at the time of writing, difficult to discern, the impact on political economy appeared more pronounced. The economic policy debate in Russia was increasingly characterised by an emphasis on self-reliance in the name of security, with economic policy subsumed within a wider concern to insulate Russia from a growing array of external threats.[37] While the nature of the West's relationship with Ukraine is the most obvious security threat cited by Russian officials, these officials have been clear in stating that there are many other, potentially even more serious, threats to Russian national interests. It is in this context that Russia's reaction to Western economic statecraft can be more clearly understood: in a world that—from the vantage point of the Kremlin—appears increasingly menacing, many officials see economic security as an important component of Russia's wider security. The centralised management of Russia's external relations are, for many, a logical response to geopolitical uncertainty.

It is worth noting at this point that the geopolitical conflict with Western powers over Ukraine, in which economic statecraft has been the weapon of choice, did not cause the shift towards the securitisation of economic policy in Russia. For the past decade, the Kremlin's revealed preference for hands-on control across large swathes of the economy was clear. However, events subsequent to Russia's annexation of Crimea accelerated the process of securitisation and weakened those in the technocratic policy elite who traditionally guarded the progress made by Russia, in terms of both economic liberalisation at home, and its current pattern of close integration with the Western part of the global economy.

This should not be taken to mean that Russia is on the verge of resurrecting the centrally planned economy of the Soviet era. The demands of the twenty-first century economy would make such an endeavour self-defeating. Moreover, the nature of the global economy has changed dramatically since the collapse of the Soviet Union. During the Cold War there

---

[37]See for example, 'Strategiya natsional'noi bezopasnosti Rossiiskoi Federatsii do 2020 goda', Security Council of the Russian Federation, 2009, available at: http://www.scrf.gov.ru/documents/99.html, accessed 22 November 2009; and more recently, 'Kontseptsiya vneshnei politiki Rossiiskoi Federatsii', Ministry of Foreign Affairs, 2013. For a discussion of the evolution of the perception of threats to Russian national security, see Monaghan (2013).

were no economically significant 'third' powers. This is no longer the case. In addition to the obvious example of China, there are a number of other rapidly growing low and middle-income countries with which Russia could, in principle, develop closer economic ties. Nevertheless, it is plausible that a new type of system of political economy may be emerging in Russia, and one that satisfies the Kremlin's urge to deal with what it perceives to be an increasingly threatening external environment.

References

Allen, S. H. (2008) 'The Domestic Political Costs of Economic Sanctions', *Journal of Conflict Resolution*, 52, 6.

Antonova, E. (2015) 'Bloomberg uznal o vozmozhnoy prodazhe Surgutneftegazu 19,5% Rosnefti', *RBC.ru*, 12 May, available at: http://top.rbc.ru/business/12/05/2015/5551bc3d9a79475f722896e5, accessed 27 January 2015.

Åslund, A. (2014) 'There is Only One Cure for what Plagues Russia', *Financial Times*, 17 December.

Bacon, E., Renz, B. & Cooper, J. (2006) *Securitising Russia: The Domestic Politics of Russia* (Manchester, NH, Manchester University Press).

Baldwin, D. A. (1985) *Economic Statecraft* (Princeton, NJ, Princeton University Press).

Bank of Russia (2013) *Monetary Policy Report*, Number 4, December (Moscow, Bank of Russia), available at: http://www.cbr.ru/eng/publ/ddcp/2013_04_ddcp_e.pdf, accessed 12 February 2016.

Bank of Russia (2015) *Monetary Policy Report*, Number 4, December (Moscow, Bank of Russia), available at: http://www.cbr.ru/Eng/publ/ddcp/2015_04_ddcp_e.pdf, accessed 13 February 2016.

Barkov, M. (2015) 'Russia: Sanctions on the Oil Industry are Mostly Surmountable', *Rusmininfo*, 23 March, available at: http://rusmininfo.com/news/23-03-2015/russia-sanctions-oil-industry-are-mostly-surmountable, accessed 21 April 2015.

Barsukov, Yu. (2014) 'Pravila igry', *Kommersant''*, 18 September 2014, available at: http://www.kommersant.ru/doc/2607461, accessed 2 November 2014.

Berezinskaya, O. & Vedev, A. (2015) 'Proizvodstvennaya zavisimost' rossiiskoi promyshlennosti ot importa i mekhanizm strategicheskogo importozameshcheniya', *Voprosy Ekonomiki*, 1.

BOFIT (2014) *BOFIT Forecast for Russia 2014–2016*, Bank of Finland Institute for Economies in Transition, 25 March (Helsinki, BOFIT), available at: http://www.suomenpankki.fi/bofit_en/seuranta/ennuste/Documents/brf114.pdf, accessed 12 February 2016.

BP (2014) *BP Statistical Review of World Energy*, June (London, BP), available at: http://www.bp.com/content/dam/bp-country/de_de/PDFs/brochures/BP-statistical-review-of-world-energy-2014-full-report.pdf, accessed 7 February 2016.

Brock, G. (2005) 'Regional Growth in Russia during the 1990s—What Role Did FDI Play?', *Post-Communist Economies*, 15, 3.

Brooks, R. A. (2002) 'Sanctions and Regime Type: What Works, and When?', *Security Studies*, 11, 4.

Connolly, R. (2011) 'Financial Constraints on the Modernization of the Russian Economy', *Eurasian Geography and Economics*, 52, 3.

Connolly, R. (2013) *The Economic Sources of Social Order Development in Post-Socialist Europe* (London & New York, NY, Routledge).

Connolly, R. (2015a) *Troubled Times: Stagnation, Sanctions and the Prospects for Economic Reform in Russia* (London, Chatham House).

Connolly, R. (2015b) 'The Impact of EU Sanctions on Russia', in Dreya, I. & Luengo-Cabrera, J. (eds) *On Target? EU Sanctions as Security Policy Tools*, Report No. 25, September (Paris, EU-ISS).

Cooper, J. (2015) *Military Spending in the Draft Law Amending the Russian 2015 Federal Budget*, unpublished research note.

Coser, L. (1956) *The Function of Social Conflict* (New York, NY, Free Press).

Downs, G. & Rocke, D. (1994) 'Conflict, Agency, and Gambling for Resurrection: The Principal-Agent Problem Goes to War', *American Journal of Political Science*, 38, 2.

EBRD (2014) *Regional Economic Prospects*, European Bank for Reconstruction and Development, January, available at: http://www.ebrd.com/downloads/research/REP/rep-1401.pdf, accessed 11 February 2016.

Egorov, I. (2015) 'Kto upravlyayet khaosom', *Rossiiskaya Gazeta*, 10 February, available at: http://www.rg.ru/2015/02/11/patrushev.html, accessed 27 January 2016.

ERIRAS (2014) *Global and Russian Energy Outlook to 2040, The Energy Research Institute of the Russian Academy of Sciences* (Moscow, Energy Research Institute), available at: http://www.eriras.ru/files/2014/forecast_2040_en.pdf, accessed 16 February 2016.

Gaddy, C. & Ickes, B. (2005) 'Resource Rents and the Russian Economy', *Eurasian Geography and Economics*, 46, 8.

Gaddy, C. & Ickes, B. (2010) 'Russia after the Global Financial Crisis', *Eurasian Geography and Economics*, 51, 3.

Gaddy, C. & Ickes, B. (2014) *Bear Traps on Russia's Road to Modernisation* (London, Routledge).

Galtung, J. (1967) 'On the Effects of International Economic Sanctions with Examples from the Case of Rhodesia', *World Politics*, 19, 3.

Hanson, P. (1988) *Western Economic Statecraft in East-West Relations* (London, Royal Institute of International Affairs/Routledge).

Henderson, J. (2015) *Key Determinants for the Future of Russian Oil Production and Exports* (Oxford, Oxford Energy Institute).

IEA (2014) *Energy Outlook for Russia 2014* (Paris, International Energy Agency).

IMF (2014) *World Economic Outlook*, International Monetary Fund, October (Washington, DC, World Bank), available at: http://www.imf.org/external/pubs/ft/weo/2014/02/, accessed 11 February 2016.

Iwasaki, I. & Suganuma, K. (2007) 'Regional Distribution of Foreign Direct Investment in Russia', *Post-Communist Economies*, 17, 2.

Kudrin, A. & Gurvich, E. (2014) 'Novaya model' rosta dlya rossiiskoi ekonomiki', *Voprosy Ekonomiki*, 12.

Latukhina, K. (2015) 'Tsena bar'erov', *Rossiiskaya Gazeta*, 27 April, available at: http://www.rg.ru/2015/04/27/putin-site.html, accessed 27 January 2016.

Major, S. (2012) 'Timing is Everything: Economic Sanctions, Regime Type, and Domestic Instability', *International Interactions*, 38, 1.

Mau, V. (2013) 'Between Modernisation and Stagnation: Russian Economic Policy and Global Crisis', *Post-Communist Economies*, 25, 4.

Mau, V. (2014) 'Challenges of Russian Economic Policy: Modernisation or Acceleration? (Perestroika or Uskorenie)', *Post-Communist Economies*, 26, 4.

Monaghan, A. (2013) *The New Russian Foreign Policy Concept: Evolving Continuity* (London, Chatham House).

Mordyushenko, O. & Melnikov, K. (2015) 'Rosneft' nastrelyayet 10 trillionov', *Kommersant"*, 19 May, available at: http://www.kommersant.ru/doc/2729210, accessed 27 January 2016.

Mueller, J. (1970) 'Presidential Popularity from Johnson to Truman', *American Political Science Review*, 64, 1.

Mueller, J. (1973) *War, Presidents, and Public Opinion* (New York, NY, Wiley).

Mukhin, M. (2015) 'Sanktsii sryvayut gosprogrammu vooruzhenii', *Nezavisimaya Gazeta*, 30 January, available at: http://www.ng.ru/armies/2015-01-22/2_sanktsii.html, accessed 11 February 2016.

Naberezhnov, G. (2014) 'Minoborony zayavilo o riske snizheniya oboronzakaza iz-za oslableniya rublya', *RBC.ru*, 30 December, available at: http://top.rbc.ru/politics/30/12/2014/54a1ece59a79471c1ab9f13e, accessed 27 January 2016.

Ostrom, C. & Job, B. (1986) 'The President and the Political Use of Force', *American Political Science Review*, 80, 2.

Overland, I., Godzimirski, J., Lunden, L. P. & Fjaertoft, D. (2013) 'Rosneft's Offshore Partnerships: The Re-opening of the Russian Petroleum Frontier?', *Polar Record*, 49, 2.

Peksen, D. & Cooper Drury, A. (2010) 'Coercive or Corrosive: The Negative Impact of Economic Sanctions on Democracy', *International Interactions*, 36, 3.

Portela, C. (2010) *European Union Sanctions and Foreign Policy: When and Why Do They Work?* (London & New York, NY, Routledge).

Portela, C. (2014) *The EU's Use of "Targeted" Sanctions: Evaluating Effectiveness*, CEPS Working Documents No. 391, available at: https://www.ceps.eu/system/files/WD391%20Portela%20EU%20Targeted%20Sanctions.pdf, accessed 15 February 2016.

Prochniak, M. (2011) 'Determinants of Economic Growth in Central and Eastern Europe: The Global Crisis Perspective', *Post-Communist Economies*, 23, 4.

Simes, D. (2015) '5 Things You Need to Know about Putin's Popularity in Russia', *The National Interest*, 21 July, available at: http://nationalinterest.org/feature/5-things-you-need-know-about-putins-popularity-russia-13380, accessed 7 February 2016.

Sirov, M. (2015) 'Gazprom ne budet privlekat' genpodryadchika dlya stroitel'stva *Sily Sibiri*', *Vedomosti*, 2 February, available at: http://www.vedomosti.ru/business/articles/2015/02/02/silu-sibiri-v-odni-ruki-ne-davat, accessed 27 January 2016.

Smith, A. (1996) 'The Success and Use of Economic Sanctions', *International Interactions*, 21, 3.

von Soest, C. & Wahman, M. (2015) 'Are Democratic Sanctions Really Counterproductive?', *Democratization*, 22, 6.

Wintour, P. (2014) 'Cameron Warns Putin as Russian President Lashes Sanctions', *The Guardian*, 15 November, available at: http://www.theguardian.com/world/2014/nov/14/putin-russia-oil-price-collapse-sanctions-g20, accessed 27 January 2016.

World Bank (2014) *Global Economic Prospects*, January (Washington, DC, World Bank), available at: http://econ.worldbank.org/WBSITE/EXTERNAL/EXTDEC/EXTDECPROSPECTS/0,,contentMDK: 23578935~pagePK:64165401~piPK:64165026~theSitePK:476883,00.html, accessed 12 February 2016.

World Bank (2015) *Russia Economic Report. Balancing Economic Adjustment and Transformation*, September, No. 34 (Washington, DC, World Bank), available at: http://www.worldbank.org/en/country/russia/publication/rer, accessed 7 February 2016.

Yedovina, T. (2015) 'Neft' naidet kak prosochit'sya', *Kommersant"*, 23 March, available at: http://www.kommersant.ru/doc/2692593, accessed 27 January 2016.

Yedovina, T. & Shapovalov, A. (2015) 'Gossovet sobral plody importozameshcheniya', *Kommersant"*, 26 November, available at: http://www.kommersant.ru/doc/2862090, accessed 11 February 2016.

Zamaraev, B., Kiyutsevskaya, A., Nazarova, A. & Sukhanov, E. (2013) 'Zamedlenie ekonomicheskogo rosta v Rossii', *Voprosy Ekonomiki*, 8.

Sanctions and the Future of EU–Russian Economic Relations

TATIANA ROMANOVA

Abstract

The essay examines the qualitative changes in EU–Russian relations which resulted from the 2014 sanctions. Thematic, structural and institutional aspects of the issue are analysed through the 'level of analysis' approach. Thematically, policy-specific and implementation measures reinforced an EU–Russian 'divorce' both in energy and trade. Structurally, the scope of EU–Russian dialogue narrowed in favour of relations between Moscow and member states, and in multilateral fora; this dialogue also became dependent on Russia–US relations. Institutionally sanctions have led to the growing poverty of transgovernmental and transnational relations. As a result, achievements of previous years have been derailed, and reversal of the negative trends will prove difficult.

THE EU IMPOSED RESTRICTIVE MEASURES ON RUSSIA IN MARCH 2014 as a reaction to events in Crimea, which resulted in the peninsula acceding to Russia. It then further extended them. As of March 2014 the EU suspended high-level meetings and froze all negotiations on the visa regime and the new EU–Russian agreement. Furthermore, a number of Russian individuals and companies were blacklisted for being involved in the events in Crimea and later in eastern Ukraine. This list has been continually amended since then to reach 150 individuals and 37 entities (Council of the European Union 2014a, 2014b). In June 2014 the EU banned all commercial operations of EU companies in Crimea (Council of the European Union 2014c). Finally, severe restrictions on Russian financial, banking, oil and military sectors were approved in August 2014 and further tightened in September 2014 (Council of the European Union 2014d, 2014e, 2014f, 2014g). Russian business was blocked from long-term (exceeding 30 days) financing and from the purchase of oil exploration equipment, military technologies and dual-use goods. Hence sanctions against Russia have evolved from smart and targeted at individuals to blanket ones affecting all Russians. All these restrictive measures were extended in 2015.

Russia retaliated through its own sanctions. Initially they also affected only individuals. The EU's sectoral sanctions then provoked a more severe reaction: Russia introduced a ban on a wide range of EU (as well as US, Canadian and Australian) agricultural goods, including fruit and vegetables, milk and meat products (President of Russia 2014; Government of Russia 2014). These measures were also extended in summer 2015. Other restrictions, like the confiscation of foreign assets in Russia, advance prepayment of Russian gas supply, a ban on textile and automobile imports and the non-return of some Western equipment were also discussed but never approved.

The rich literature on sanctions most frequently discusses why sanctions (especially against authoritarian regimes) do not work. In particular, scholars demonstrate that sanctions barely affect the elite and their calculations, lead to a 'rally around the flag' (Galtung 1967) and rarely to big policy changes, and make the most disadvantaged part of the population suffer. At the same time they bring substantial economic losses to both sanctioned and sanctioning nations (Galtung 1967; Barber 1979; Mayall 1984; Baldwin 1985; Lindsay 1986; Doxey 1987; Wagner 1988; Damrosch 1993; Morgan & Schwebach 1997; Pape 1997; Cortright & Lopez 2000; Brooks 2002; Hufbauer *et al.* 2009; Peksen 2009). Others demonstrate that the goal is not necessarily to produce a policy change in the sanctioned nation but also to signal that something is done against a state which violates certain international norms, in order to prevent a worsening of the situation and to bring the sanctioned party to negotiations (Daoudi & Dajani 1983; Baldwin 1985, 1999–2000; Lindsay 1986; Martin 1992; Cortright & Lopez 2000, 2002; Hufbauer *et al.* 2009; Portela 2010; Giumelli 2013). These studies cover most arguments on the effectiveness of sanctions relevant to the present study.

This essay does not examine the question of whether the sanctions against Russia 'work', which depends in turn on the definition of 'work', nor does it provide a quantitative assessment of the effect of the sanctions, as studies of these issues are numerous by now (Havlik 2014; Bond *et al.* 2015; IMF 2015; EP Members Research Service 2015). Russian officials estimate Russian annual losses as US$40 billion while the EU is said to have lost about US$40 billion in 2014 and another US$50 billion in 2015 (or about 1.5% of its GDP).[1] The *EUobserver* has quoted unnamed EU officials as saying that Russia would lose €23 billion and €75 billion in 2014 and 2015 respectively, whereas the EU's losses would amount to €49 billion and €50 billion respectively.[2] However, current figures are not reliable (for example, many companies have rushed to buy needed goods and services in advance during summer 2014, foreseeing a tightening of the sanctions, while the increase in US–Russian trade in 2014 was due to contracts concluded beforehand). It is also difficult (if not impossible) to separate the effect of sanctions from the overall slow-down of the Russian economy, which started before the sanctions, and from the fall in oil (and thus, gas) prices and, consequently, export revenues of Russia.

This essay examines how sanctions are qualitatively transforming economic relations, how they reveal the problems already present and how they condition the long-term cooperation of the EU and Russia. Some qualitative economic effects of sanctions have been documented in earlier literature. In particular, scholars have paid attention to how sanctioned nations adapt to economic restrictions, change partners and circumvent various bans, develop import substitution and hence form a group of stakeholders interested in sanctions being maintained, and how the sanctioning nation is worse off as a result (Wallensteen 1968; Doxey 1987; Hoffmann 1967; Kirshner 1997; Rowe 1999; Brooks 2002; Morgan & Bapat 2003; Early 2009, 2011; McLean & Whang 2010; Bapat & Kwon 2015). This essay deepens this analysis

[1] 'Siluanov otsenil poteri Rossii ot sanktsii i desheveyushchei nefti v \$140 mlrd', *RBC*, 24 November 2014, available at: http://top.rbc.ru/finances/24/11/2014/5472ededcbb20f50f1970522, accessed 9 March 2015; 'Kudrin: Sanktsii negativno vliyaut na ekonomiku Rossii', *RIA Novosti*, 21 November 2015, available at: http://ria.ru/economy/20151121/1325569509.html, accessed 21 December 2015.

[2] 'Multi-billion Losses Expected from Russia Sanctions', *EUobserver*, 28 July 2014, available at: https://euobserver.com/economic/125118, accessed 9 March 2015.

by looking at thematic, structural and institutional aspects of EU–Russian economic relations and by applying the level-of-analysis approach. This approach entered international relations studies in the 1960s as a result of the wider discussion of levels in sciences in general (Bunge 1960), and on levels of analysis in understanding various social phenomena in particular (David Singer 1961). The key premise is that systemic or sub-systemic perspectives illuminate various aspects of the same phenomenon; and the totality of knowledge will only emerge from the combination of various perspectives. This essay treats levels of analysis as an instrument to examine the thematic, structural and institutional evolution of EU–Russian relations.

The study concludes that thematically the EU and Russia have *de facto* refrained from any close interaction or integration in both pillars of their economic relations: energy and trade relations in other goods and services. They have deliberately diversified away from each other, limiting interaction to straightforward exchange of energy resources for industrial goods. The difference between officially declared goals like openness to trade liberalisation or deeper energy cooperation and policy-specific measures and implementation mechanisms is stark. The roots of this 'divorce' lie in the inability of the EU and Russia to find a model of economic relations which would satisfy both the EU's liberalisation and external promotion of its rules and values and Russia's efforts to preserve its economic system and to ensure equality in its external relations.[3] The overall slow-down of the Russian economy was detrimental for EU–Russian economic relations. However, sanctions provided an excellent pretext for EU and Russian public bodies alike to disengage from the previous cooperative agenda and to shift to minimising mutual dependence. These goals are easily reinforced by policy-specific measures and their implementation mechanisms.

Structurally, economic relations between the EU and Russia are becoming more diverse. Faced with the EU's criticism and further disillusioned with contacts with Brussels, Russia increased its charm offensive towards member states. Moreover, Russia and the EU increasingly interact in multilateral fora like the World Trade Organization (WTO), and a new mechanism between the EU and the Eurasian Economic Union (EEU) is currently under discussion. The EU–EEU dialogue, multilateral organisations and contacts with member states compensate for a shortage of contacts between Moscow and Brussels caused by the sanctions, but also paradoxically allow Russia to multiply the venues of interaction with the EU, in line with the foreign policy preferences of Moscow. The evolution of structural levels of analysis is also a triumph of form over substance when compared with the growing poverty of thematic levels of analysis. Finally, because the EU introduced sanctions in cooperation with the US and because the 'hard' security agenda, dominated by the USA in the West, is increasingly important in Europe, EU–Russian economic relations become part of the Russian–US security agenda. The lack of EU–Russian interaction further facilitates politicisation of EU–Russian economic relations.

Finally, institutional relations between the EU and Russia are becoming poorer because the EU's sanctions policy destroys transgovernmental and transnational economic relations, which were meticulously created previously. Two strategies are identified here in the activities of EU officials and business; these are self-censorship and work-to-rule. Russian companies challenge EU sanctions in the European Court of Justice, and both Russian and some EU companies look for the ways to bypass sanctions, but these activities are not sufficient to offset the negative institutional consequences of sanctions. As a result, EU–Russian relations become

---

[3]For how Russian foreign policy concepts interprets this equality, see President of Russia (2013).

institutionally more primitive (that is mostly reduced to intergovernmental discussions) and, hence, even more prone to politicisation. This trend is reinforced by the thematic 'divorce' of the EU and Russia; the pressure to find a long-term agreement on what to do together and how to cooperate decreases, as does mutual socialisation of EU and Russian officials and business representatives. Hence, there is a clear link between the content of the thematic levels of EU–Russian economic relations and their poorer institutional levels. The change reinforces negative tendencies in EU–Russian economic relations.

In what follows, I first define thematic, structural and institutional levels of analysis, which are essential to organise an analysis of the complexity of changes in EU–Russian economic relations resulting from reciprocal sanctions. I then examine the evolution of thematic, structural and institutional aspects of EU–Russian economic relations through the prism of the levels of analysis to show the qualitative effect of sanctions and to deduce their long-term impact.

Thematic, structural and institutional levels of analysis

There are three aspects to any international relationship today. One is thematic, which is about what the parties want to do together, whether they integrate with each other or only cooperate on some global challenges and have limited trade, whether they construct a strategic partnership on the basis of shared values or see each other as rivals. In other words, the thematic aspect is about the substance of cooperation. The second aspect is concerned with how they interact, whether they do it bilaterally or multilaterally. In the case of the EU this question is particularly pertinent, given that the Union itself consists of sovereign states which, although they have agreed to cooperate with each other and to pool parts of their sovereignties, from time to time reaffirm their rights to construct independent relations with third parties. Finally, the third aspect concerns the institutional type of interaction, whether contacts are limited to intergovernmental level or whether they involve lower officials, or business and civil societies at large, at transgovernmental and transnational levels respectively. But what levels can be identified in each of these aspects?

International relations, integration studies and concepts of policy convergence illuminate thematic levels of analysis. Regime theorists talk about fundamental beliefs and concepts, which are the basis of more specific cooperation and modes of implementation (Krasner 1999). A similar 'levels' idea can be found in integration studies: visionary goals (like preventing future conflicts, enhancing the wellbeing of citizens or increased and diversified trade) are further developed through policy-specific proposals (like constructing a single market with certain legal approximation), and then are specified in detailed implementation measures. Finally, policy convergence is described as social learning, which 'usually involves three central variables: the overarching goals that guide policy in a particular field, the techniques or policy instruments used to attain those goals, and the precise settings of these instruments' (Hall 1993, p. 279). In sum, three thematic levels can be identified: fundamental long-term goals and principles of cooperation, policy-specific goals and implementation mechanisms. What is crucial is whether there is a coherence of the levels, whether fundamental goals are reinforced by policy-specific measures and implementation mechanisms, and what the sanctions changed in this respect.

The structural aspect (or how the parties interact) also involves numerous levels. The most obvious application of the level-of-analysis approach to the EU's external relations is linked to the specificity of the EU, which has been frequently described as a *sui generis* polity (Risse-Kappen 1996; Hix 1998; Phelan 2012), consisting of the EU's institutions and policies, and member states and their polities and policies. As a result, an external partner deals with it at the supranational and national levels (sometimes challenging the EU's coherence). Besides, Russia has always believed that the EU plays on various levels for the purpose of extracting the best possible outcome of negotiations (Sokolov 2007). It has therefore wished to recreate this situation on its side, and it finally succeeded through the Eurasian integration process, although the EU's recognition of the EEU is still pending and the involvement of the latter in EU–Russian relations remains limited. Finally, the interaction can also take part in the context of multilateral institutions where both the EU and Russia are members (like the UN, the WTO or the Energy Charter). It is interesting to see how the density of contacts at various levels changed as the sanctions were bolstered.

Finally, the institutional aspect is concerned with the quality of interaction; it is linked with the multiplication of channels of communication among member states. Keohane and Nye have described these relations as transgovernmental and transnational. The transgovernmental level denotes 'direct interactions among sub-units of different governments' (Keohane & Nye 1974, p. 43), which facilitate information exchange, harmonisation and control of the implementation of approved decisions (Slaughter 2004). The transnational level, for its part, is composed of non-state actors like business, civil society or epistemic communities. The denser the transgovernmental and transnational relations, the closer these relations are. The transgovernmental level contributes to the depoliticisation of relations because most issues are solved at the technical level. The transnational level is more ambiguous in this respect; business naturally prefers technical cooperation, while NGOs, especially acting in the field of human rights and democracy, politicise the agenda. Analysis of economic relations, however, naturally presupposes a focus on the business interaction in transnational relations. The quality of the interaction can, therefore, be assessed through the density of links at transgovernmental and transnational levels (Pollack & Shaffer 2001). The density of transgovernmental and transnational levels does not mean a rich agenda (which in itself is analysed through the thematic levels of analysis); however it provides an arena for the socialisation and, hence, for better mutual understanding. Again, the question is how the three institutional levels have evolved under the pressure of sanctions.

Thematic aspect: from cooperation to divorce and self-sufficiency?

The two pillars of EU–Russian economic relations are energy relations and trade or economic cooperation in other fields. Trade between the EU and Russia decreased in 2014 as a result of sanctions and a fall in oil prices from the 2012 record of €338.5 billion to €284.6 billion in 2014 and decreased further by €70 billion between January and November 2015 (Chizhov 2016). However, the EU remains Russia's biggest trade partner. Russia, for its part, still holds third or fourth place among the EU's most important trade partners. According to recent data, over 50% of Russia's natural gas and approximately two thirds of its oil exports go to the EU; the EU receives approximately 30% of its hydrocarbon imports from Russia (Russia & EU 2014).

The EU and Russia, in establishing their relations in the early 1990s, proclaimed that the long-term goal of their relations is partnership and cooperation; they also agreed on common values, like human rights, democracy, the rule of law and the market economy (EU & Russia 1994). In order to fill this long-term goal with content the parties explored a number of avenues in their economic cooperation: various scenarios of a free trade area (EU & Russia 1994), common economic space (EU & Russia 2005) and Partnership for Modernisation (EU & Russia 2010) are the best known. Between 2010 and early 2014 Moscow and Brussels held 13 rounds of consultations on a new agreement that would replace the 1994 Partnership and Cooperation Agreement (PCA).[4] The new text presupposed deepening economic relations.

The negotiations stalled because of discrepancies in legal approximation, on whether it had to be simply patterned after the EU, or designed together, including *inter alia* in the UN Economic Commission for Europe,[5] which would guarantee equality of the EU and Russia in defining the quality of their cooperation. Broadly, however, the question was how to reconcile an economic system substantially closed from external competition with the more liberal and open economic system of the EU. Eventually the issue of a free trade area was left to a separate agreement. On the energy side, the parties agreed on the Roadmap up to 2050, which presupposed a common market, defined as certain approximations of rules and enhancement of infrastructural connections (EU & Russia 2013). The issue of Russia's approximation to the EU's energy liberalisation policy was left unresolved and substituted with some technical approximation and mutually acceptable wording. Russian diplomats say that there was no progress on the negotiations on the post-PCA or free trade area agreement.[6] However, until early 2014 the long-term goals of EU–Russian economic cooperation were a continent-wide free trade area and a common market in energy, and work on defining policy-specific goals was under way. Some progress was reached, notably in energy.

The messages which the two parties currently send at the top thematic level are ambiguous. On the one hand, both parties continue to declare that, despite the sanctions, they aim at a common trade area from Lisbon to Vladivostok, possibly between the EU and EEA.[7] On the other hand, the EU classifies Russia as a strategic problem[8] while Russia stresses that Moscow will become more self-sufficient through import-substitution and will diversify its trade and

[4] The final, thirteenth round, has never been completed.

[5] Interview with a senior diplomat, Permanent Mission of the Russian Federation to the EU, Brussels, 5 February 2015.

[6] 'Peregovory po bezvizovomu rezhimu s ES i ran'she stoyali na meste', *RIA Novosti*, 1 August 2014, available at: http://ria.ru/politics/20140801/1018449690.html, accessed 25 July 2015. Interview with a senior diplomat, Permanent Mission of the Russian Federation to the EU, Brussels, 5 February 2015.

[7] See, for example, 'Russia Calls for EU Talks with Newly Born Eurasian Union', *EUobserver*, 2 January 2015, available at: https://euobserver.com/economic/127081, accessed 9 March 2015; 'Soglasno soobshcheniyam nemetskikh SMI, kantsler Angela Merkel i vitse-kantsler Zigmar Gabriel' predlozhili nachat' peregovory o svobodnom torgovom prostranstve ot Lissabona do Vladivostoka, ideyu sozdaniya kotorogo neskol'ko let nazad vydvinul rossiiskii president Vladimir Putin', *Rossiiskaya gazeta*, 23 January 2015, available at: http://www.rg.ru/2015/01/23/germany-site.html, accessed 9 March 2015; 'SZ: Germaniya predlagaet Evraziiskomy soyuzu druzhbu v obmen na mir na Ukraine', *Russia Today*, 23 January 2015, available at: http://russian.rt.com/inotv/2015-01-23/SZ-Germaniya-predlagaet-Evrazijskomu-soyuzu, accessed 9 March 2015; 'Ukraine Crisis: Angela Merkel "Offers Russia Free Trade Deal for Peace"', *Daily Telegraph*, 23 January 2015, available at: http://www.telegraph.co.uk/news/worldnews/europe/ukraine/11365674/Ukraine-crisis-Angela-Merkel-offers-Russia-free-trade-deal-for-peace.html, accessed 9 March 2015.

[8] 'Russia is a Strategic Problem for the EU—Tusk', *Reuters*, 18 December 2014, available at: http://www.reuters.com/article/2014/12/18/ukraine-crisis-russia-eu-idUSL6N0U253U20141218, accessed 9 March 2015.

energy markets by enlarging economic relations with BRICs and other partners. Which of the two versions of long-term goals is supported at the policy-specific and implementation levels?

In the energy field we can see a race towards mutual diversification of their partners. The EU intensified the race with its new energy security strategy (European Commission 2014a), where decreasing dependence on Russia in both natural gas and nuclear sectors is a key priority. The securitisation of the EU's dependence on Russia was bolstered through the so-called stress-test about the effect of the interruption of gas supply from Russia (European Commission 2014b), which reviewed scenarios of partial and total halt of gas supply from Russia to the EU. The final touch was provided by the Energy Union proposal (European Commission 2015), which makes energy security its first and main pillar. While recognising that the EU will depend on Russia, it calls for the diversification of partners and supply routes (through creating bypasses around Russia and liquefied natural gas terminals for alternative suppliers), for increased interconnection among EU member states, for negotiations on external gas purchase, coordinated at the EU's level, and for the development of renewable sources in the EU.

In essence, the EU does not believe any longer in Russian energy sector reform, in the liberalisation of the natural gas economy, or in relations on a market basis; rather the fear is that Russia could blackmail the EU (which has no precedent) and, hence, the EU chooses to limit its exposure to this unpredictable partner. That involves costly measures and it remains to be seen whether private companies will be willing to invest in it and what incentives have to be developed for them. However it is also certain that in this political climate Western companies will have little appetite to make additional investments that enhance EU–Russian energy cooperation. Moreover, for the first time the EU securitises not only its dependence on Russian natural gas but also its dependence on Russian nuclear energy supplies (European Commission 2014a, 2015). As a result the export market for Russian technologically advanced energy goods will potentially shrink.

The changes in the Russian strategy are also clear. Firstly, in May 2014 Russia concluded with China a 30-year contract to supply 38 billion cubic meters (bcm) of natural gas a year; a special pipeline, the Power of Siberia, is to be constructed for it.[9] Gazprom also plans to conclude another 30-year contract with China in 2015 for the supply of 30 bcm (with the possibility to augment the export to 100 bcm) through the so-called Western route, the Altai pipeline, yet to be completed.[10] Although the prospects of these deals are not certain, given the global prices and numerous divergences between Russia and China, both projects signify the wish of Russia to augment its share of the Asian market. Also, in December 2014 Russia abandoned the South Stream (a pipeline to link Russia and the south of the EU) in favour of a pipeline to Turkey, provisionally named Turkish Stream (Putin 2014a). (In November 2015 the fate of the latter was put into question as well, following the downing of a Russian military plane by Turkey and the consequent worsening of their relations.) Finally, Russia is developing liquefied natural gas facilities to export Russian gas to new markets like Latin America and India (Romanova 2015a).

All these facts signify not only diversification of export markets but also the refusal of Gazprom to move to the EU's gas distribution market, and hence to retreat from deeper energy

[9]'Power of Siberia', *Gazprom*, no date, available at: http://www.gazprom.com/about/production/projects/pipelines/ykv/, accessed 24 December 2014.

[10]'Altai Project', *Gazprom*, no date, available at: http://www.gazprom.com/about/production/projects/pipelines/altai/, accessed 24 December 2014.

market integration. To quote an official of the Russian Mission to the EU, the 'EU–Russian Roadmap is dead; the EU and Russia should now develop the means which would allow them to divorce peacefully and with minimal economic damage'.[11] Hence, Russia seems to be prepared to pay an additional price to be more immune to the EU's regulatory changes.

As a result Ukraine can potentially be deprived of gas transit between Russia and the EU. Already now the flows barely amount to 60 bcm whereas the capacity of the Ukrainian system is 288 bcm at the border with Russia and 178.5 bcm at the western border of Ukraine.[12] This poor use of the Ukrainian gas transport system might further decline as a result of the EU's and Russia's 'divorce' in energy, if not to zero then to an insignificant figure. It might bring an end not only to the ability of Kyiv to blackmail both parties with the stability of gas transit but also to its stable revenue and to becoming a bridge between the EU and Russia. Hence, the 'divorce' of Russia and the EU in energy does not do much good, not only to their energy relations but also to the reconstruction of the Ukrainian economy.

Changes in EU–Russian trade and economic cooperation are also huge. Russia is not a crucial market for the EU, but some member states and particularly business associations have complained about the decrease in exports to Russia.[13] Agricultural exports suffered the most because of the Russian retaliatory measures, whereas the flow of industrial goods is negatively affected by EU restrictions on energy and dual-use technologies, by financial sanctions (which make payments more difficult), as well as by the depreciation of the Russian ruble. Agricultural producers in the EU received some limited aid whereas the decrease in industrial export has gone unnoticed in policy terms. Overall, EU officials both publicly and in interviews tend to minimise the importance of Russia as an export market.[14]

The developments on the Russian side are more sophisticated. Faced with EU sanctions, Russia has initiated the strategy of import substitution in both agriculture and industrial goods. The choice is not for complete autarky but for a decrease in economic dependence (Putin 2014b). In particular, Russia has introduced a new law on industrial policy (Russian Federation 2014) which specifies means of support for Russian industries, including for the purpose of import substitution. Similar legislative acts for agricultural production were adjusted.[15] A series of legislative acts banned the purchase of foreign agricultural machinery and pharmaceutical goods for state procurement. Detailed programmes of financial support of various import substituting industries are being put in place. Finally, the resources of the Russian National Welfare Fund are directed to large-scale Russian projects in need of financing.[16]

[11]Interview with a senior diplomat, Permanent Mission of the Russian Federation to the EU, Brussels, 5 February 2015.

[12]'Gazotransportnaya sistema', *Neftegaz, Transportirovka i khranenie*, no date, available at: http://neftegaz. ru/tech_library/view/4344/, accessed 14 December 2015.

[13]See, for example, 'Germaniya poteryala iz-za sanktsii 60 tysyach rabochikh mest', *Rossiiskaya gazeta*, 5 February 2015, available at: http://www.rg.ru/2015/02/05/sankcii-site.html, accessed 9 March 2015; 'DW: Sanktsii protiv Rossii negativno vliyaut na evropeiskii biznes', *Regnum*, 22 February 2015, available at: http://www.regnum.ru/news/polit/1898144.html, accessed 13 March 2015.

[14]Interview with a deputy head of unit, DG Trade, European Commission, Brussels, 6 October 2014.

[15]'Plan deyatel'nosti Minselkhoza Rossii na 2013–2018 gody', Ministry of Agriculture of the Russian Federation, available at: http://www.mcx.ru/documents/document/show/24205.htm, accessed 14 March 2015.

[16]'Svedeniya o razmeshchenii sredstv fonda na depositakh vo Vneshekonombanke po sostoyaniyu na 1 marta 2015 goda', Ministry of Finance of the Russian Federation, available at: http://www.minfin.ru/ru/perfomance/nationalwealthfund/statistics/, accessed 14 March 2015.

The combination of these activities is increasingly conceptualised by politicians and experts alike as a Russian road to new industrialisation.[17] Vladimir Putin introduced this term in 2011 as an alternative to Dmitry Medvedev's modernisation.[18] Initially it was meant to send the signal that the state will concentrate on economic reforms (modernisation as a term was more ambiguous in this respect and allowed the EU to raise the issue of political reform (Romanova & Pavlova 2014)). Sanctions helped to fill new industrialisation with more substance, ranging from the patriotic goals of independence from the West through sector-specific mechanisms to very detailed implementation mechanisms.

Today's new industrialisation is clearly problematic. Russia lags behind in a number of technologies which can only be acquired in the West. The choice for import substitution can result in the production of outdated goods and bigger costs for consumers. Russia is also short of financial means and has chosen, because of limited resources, greater state interference in the economy, which provides a poor stimulus to entrepreneurial activities. Moreover, the scarce financial resources of the National Welfare Fund are used to support mostly oil and gas companies rather than industrial production. At the same time, import substitution and the new industrialisation illustrate that the Russian elite does not believe in prompt abolition of sanctions and thus creates policy-specific measures for 'divorce' from the EU. The changes in legislation and financial support also make some Russian agricultural and industrial producers interested in the maintenance of Russian and EU sanctions, so that their long-term investments have sufficient time to pay back. Thus an internal pro-sanction lobby in Russia has been formed.

In sum, the thematic levels of analysis demonstrate that in both the EU and Russia policy-specific measures and their implementation mechanisms strengthen the choice for 'divorce' and not for cooperation. EU–Russian mutual irritation emerged long before the 2014 Ukrainian crisis. It was due to the EU's wish to liberalise trade with Russia and open its economy (including the gas sector) for competition, and to the unwillingness of Russia to abandon its economic system and liberalise its gas sector and its economy in general. Central to the conflict was the EU's wish to export its legislation to Russia (demand for legal approximation), which contradicted the Russian demand for equality (as set in the 2013 Russian foreign policy concept) but also threatened some domestic economic interests (in energy, agriculture and industrial production). Hence, although the EU and Russia declared the goal of a shared energy space and a free trade area, policy-specific measures did not develop before 2014, not to mention implementation mechanisms.

Sanctions allowed them to match the rhetoric and the reality. Talks on shared cooperative solutions were frozen and alternative long-term goals were introduced. These involved mutual diversification away from each other to alternative partners, or in other words a 'divorce'. It also allows separate EU and Russian policy-specific solutions, which are finally in tune with the strategic long-term goal. These developments will lead to more shallow and primitive economic relations for years to come (straightforward trade in commodities rather than investments and cooperation in production). 'Divorce' as a strategic goal means that options acceptable to both parties are not even sought after any longer (in contrast to the period before

---

[17]'Russian New Industrialisation', *Regnum*, 26 February 2015, available at: http://www.regnum.ru/news/economy/1899555.html, accessed 9 March 2015.

[18]'Putin vydvinul programmu novoi industrializatsii', *Vestifinance*, 21 December 2011, available at: http://www.vestifinance.ru/articles/5365, accessed 25 July 2015.

2014). Both the EU and Russia are becoming more immune to the negative manipulation of their economic interdependence by the other side but at the same time more exposed to the politicisation of economic relations as the latter are not anchored in any policy-specific or implementation measures (or a search for these measures).

The structural aspect: towards a multiplication of venues?

In structural terms EU–Russian relations have never been easy. The EU is a complex polity where member states retain substantial competencies. Although institutional reforms have improved coordination and more is now done in Brussels, the divergence remains. Moreover, Russia has always been a very divisive topic for the EU. The spectrum of views on relations with Moscow broadened with every single enlargement. On the other hand, Moscow has always been annoyed by the lack of transparency in the division of competences between the EU and its member states; at times it viewed it as a negotiation tactic (Sokolov 2007) and looked for the possibility of emulating it on its own side as well (Chizhov 2012; Trenin 2014). Russia has also always tried to cooperate with national governments, especially where it could enhance relations compared to its dialogue with the EU. However, the consistency between EU and national levels of relations with Russia had improved by 2014; for example in cooperation on modernisation Moscow encouraged similar cooperation at the EU and member state levels (Romanova & Pavlova 2013; Romanova 2015b).

The EU was slow to introduce sectoral sanctions against Russia because of disagreement among EU member states. One group, dominated by Poland, the Baltic countries, Sweden and the UK, advocated further sanctions. Various reasons drove them: historical traumas in the case of Poland and the Baltic countries and concern about Russian violation of fundamental principles of the current world order and criticism of the lack of Russian progress towards democracy, human rights and the rule of law in the case of Sweden and the UK. Others, like France, Germany, the Central European states, Italy, Greece and Cyprus, were cautious, being deeply involved in economic relations with Russia, more pragmatic in relations with Moscow and also, in the case of Cyprus and Greece, because of cultural links. The third group consisted of member states with no clear preferences. Initially the sanctions were limited to a freezing of top-level contacts and ban on movement and assets of some individuals.

The situation changed significantly in the summer of 2014. Three factors contributed to the change. Firstly, the German political leadership grew increasingly disillusioned with the Kremlin. On the one hand, it was due to the perception that Vladimir Putin was not honest with Chancellor Merkel about Russian involvement in eastern Ukraine (Wagstyl 2014). On the other hand, Berlin strove to affirm its political leadership in the EU, which required taking seriously the preferences and fears of the Baltic countries and Poland. Secondly, the conflict in eastern Ukraine intensified and various evidence of Russian military presence was presented (Bidder *et al.* 2014; Spiegel *et al.* 2014),[19] although Russia insisted that those involved were volunteers and not regular members of the Russian army.[20] Finally, the downing

---

[19] 'NATO Releases Satellite Imagery Showing Russian Combat Troops Inside Ukraine', NATO, 28 August 2014, available at: http://www.nato.int/cps/en/natohq/news_112193.htm, accessed 21 February 2016.

[20] 'Kreml oproverg obvineniya Obamy o prisutstvii rossiiskikh voisk na territorii Ukrainy', *Newsru.com*, 3 September 2014, available at: http://www.newsru.com/russia/03sep2014/peskov.html, accessed 21 February 2016; 'Postpred Rossii pri OBSE oproverg vvod voisk na Ukrainu', *RBK*, 28 August 2014, available at: http://www.rbc.ru/politics/28/08/2014/945692.shtml, accessed 21 February 2016.

of the Malaysian civilian plane operating a regular flight MH17 from Amsterdam in July 2014 worsened the Russian image because the most popular explanation in the Western media was that the rebels shot the plane down with the help of Russian missiles, and possibly the Russian military (Cohen 2014; Davidson 2014; DeYoung 2014; Gregory 2014; Shear & Hirschfeld Davis 2014).[21] These events contributed to the feeling of the EU being under threat: the Baltic countries emphasised the threat of Russian 'green men' crossing the border, the Netherlands mourned their citizens killed in the plane. Hence a consensus emerged in the summer of 2014 in favour of demonstrating the EU's solidarity by introducing extensive sectoral sanctions against Russia. Unity in the face of an external threat has always been a characteristic of the EU.

This consensus among EU members then weakened during the winter of 2014–2015. Cyprus, Greece, the Czech Republic, Slovakia and Italy started to have doubts about sectoral sanctions because of the economic damage they caused to their economies. Given that the unanimity of all 28 member states was needed, Russia intensified its charm offensive. In the dialogue with Greece, where a new left government had come to power in January 2015, Russia alluded to the possibility to allow Greece to export some agricultural products despite Russian restrictive measures against the EU, and to create a gas hub (linked to the Turkish gas stream) in its territory and to assist Athens financially. During his visit to Hungary in February 2015 Putin tried to win Hungarian support by opening the Russian market to some Hungarian agricultural exports and also by confirming an agreement on the construction of a nuclear power station in Hungary. Economic cooperation was also discussed during the visit of Cypriot President Nikos Anastasiades to Moscow in February 2015.

In parallel Vladimir Putin ironically suggested that Bulgaria seek compensation from Brussels when announcing the cancellation of the South Stream on 1 December 2014 (Putin 2014a). Moreover, cases of economic losses (from the Russian agricultural ban and from the fall in the number of Russian tourists) in the Baltic countries and Poland (the most vehement critics of Russia) were meticulously documented in the Russian media (including its English speaking channels). Russia also raised the issue in early 2015 of suing Germany and France for the violation of contracts to supply military and related goods (Gavrilov 2014; Petrov 2015). By using economic language, quoting figures of bilateral trade and increasing unemployment in the EU and threatening economic fines, the Russian leadership demonstrated to EU member states the benefits of cooperation and the losses they incurred from the EU's policies.

Russian officials have stressed that it was the 'EU's bureaucracy in Brussels' which was guilty of worsening relations, that it 'consciously intensifies confrontation'.[22] In other words, Russia tried to detach 'good' member states from the 'bad' EU by playing on the theme of an unfair and bureaucratic Brussels wishing to augment its power rather than to solve problems. However, the game was much more intricate than frequently depicted in the mass media as 'divide and rule'. Russia did not engage in the abolition of sanctions for 'good' member states. Experts floated the idea of removing the restrictive measures on agricultural products, produced in Greece or Hungary. Russian phyto-sanitary and agricultural authorities held inspections in some EU states which would allow them to restart their export earlier

---

[21]'Ukraine Conflict: Russia Accused of Shooting Down Jet', *BBC News*, 17 July 2014, available at: http://www.bbc.com/news/world-europe-28345039, accessed 21 February 2016.

[22]'Lavrov nazval otvetstvennykh za nagnetanie konfrontatsii mezhdu Rossiei i ES', *RIA Novosti*, 10 March 2015, available at: http://ria.ru/tv_politics/20150310/1051805650.html, accessed 14 March 2015.

once the sanctions were lifted.[23] But Moscow stopped any further discussions on the partial abolition of sanctions.

Rather, Russian officials stated that restrictions could only be lifted for the whole of the EU, implying that Russia-friendly EU member states had to influence the position of the others in the Union. Dmitry Medvedev stated during his visit to Slovakia in June 2015 that sanctions were 'a collective responsibility of the EU ... all EU member states have to understand that'.[24] In fact, the EU's 'collective responsibility' became the Russian term for the EU's solidarity. That signified that Russian diplomats had learnt the way the EU functions. Having understood that no member state would veto anti-Russian sanctions in the EU because of collective pressure and the EU's internal institutional logics, Russia shifted from challenging the consensus within the EU (by having at least one member state against the renewal of the sanctions) to changing it in favour of Russia and making all member states 'prisoners' of their decisions. (In its own way, Russia currently promotes cohesion within the EU between national and supranational levels, rather than challenging it.)

In parallel, the structural aspect of EU–Russian relations has grown more complex. The first generation of EU sanctions (a ban on EU–Russian summits and negotiations on future relations) resulted in a vacuum in contacts between Moscow and Brussels. This vacuum was filled by developments in multilateral frameworks, which led to two new levels of interaction. Firstly, the EU and Russia intensified their cooperation in multilateral fora such as in the WTO and its dispute-resolution body. Russia brought a case against the EU about the third energy package, which limits Russian companies, while the EU challenged some Russian duties.[25] The possibility to challenge sanctions in the WTO was voiced. However, the EU opted not to do so because Russian sanctions were politically motivated. Russia, for its part, did not challenge the sanctions because it experienced difficulties in proving the case against them. Another example is the Energy Charter Secretariat where, despite Russian refusal to ratify the Energy Charter Treaty (ECT), it intensified work in some expert meetings of the Charter Secretariat in 2014.[26]

Multilateral organisations give Moscow an advantage in dealing with the EU because they limit the ability of the latter to impose its policies and legal solutions (especially in standardisation), and they thereby make the dialogue between Brussels and Moscow more 'equal' for Russia (in its foreign policy terms). For years Moscow has tried to make use of bodies like the UN Economic Commission for Europe (EU & Russia 2005; President of Russia 2013; Romanova 2013).[27] Surprisingly, it took the sanctions to finally activate the

[23]Phyto-sanitary authorities (Rosselhoznadzor in the case of Russia) work to ensure that various bacteria and infections do not arrive with imported agricultural products.
[24]'Resheniya o sanktsiyakh—kollektivnaya otvetstvennost' ES', *RIA Novosti*, 2 June 2015, available at: http://ria.ru/world/20150602/1067777514.html, accessed 2 June 2015.
[25]'Dispute DS476 European Union and its Member States—Certain Measures Relating to the Energy Sector', WTO, available at: www.wto.org/english/tratop_e/dispu_e/cases_e/ds476_e.htm, accessed 21 February 2016; 'Dispute DS479 Russia—Anti-Dumping Duties on Light Commercial Vehicles from Germany and Italy', WTO, available at: http://www.wto.org/english/tratop_e/dispu_e/cases_e/ds479_e.htm, accessed 21 February 2016; 'Dispute DS485 Russia—Tariff Treatment of Certain Agricultural and Manufacturing Products', WTO, available at: http://www.wto.org/english/tratop_e/dispu_e/cases_e/ds485_e.htm, accessed 21 February 2016.
[26]Energy Charter Treaty, 17 December 1994, available at: http://www.energycharter.org/process/energy-charter-treaty-1994/energy-charter-treaty/, accessed 21 February 2016. Interview with an official responsible for the relations with the EU, Russian Ministry of Energy, Moscow, 10 June 2014 and 16 June 2015.
[27]Interview with a senior diplomat, Permanent Mission of the Russian Federation to the EU, Brussels, 5 February 2015.

multilateral channel. However, the venues are the WTO and the Energy Charter Secretariat, whose aim is to further liberalisation, which is not in line with the current Russian economic system. The WTO is used mostly for EU–Russian dispute resolution and it takes time to resolve any conflict there. The Energy Charter is also limited by Russian withdrawal from the provisional application of the ECT and is compromised by the 2014 arbitration decision, requiring Russia to pay US$50 billion compensation to minority investors of Yukos for the confiscation of their assets. The EU also still refrains from using such channels as the UN Economic Commission for Europe. Hence, the potential of the multilateral channels is limited. However, the enhanced recourse to multilateral fora is an interesting development in the structural aspects of EU–Russian relations.

Second, despite the EU's non-recognition of the Eurasian Customs Union and Common Market, contacts between the EU and Eurasian institutions have intensified since 2014. The EU Delegation in Moscow is in contact with the Eurasian Commission in Moscow. An informal summit between the two organisations took place in Minsk in August 2014. The contacts were bolstered following the launch of the EEU in 2015; in particular, discussions on a wider free trade area were rhetorically shifted to the EU–EEU framework. On a more tangible level, the EU and EEU authorities hold regular consultations on the harmonisation of standards. Russia encouraged those contacts, arguing that it had already transferred a substantial part of its competences to the Eurasian structures. At the same time, when asked about the architecture of future EU–EEU relations, Russian diplomats had difficulties answering, arguing that most probably Russia would continue dealing directly with the EU on economic issues until the EEU was fully in place and complied with the WTO provisions.[28] That, in a way, confirms that at present the EEU serves Russian tactical interests of playing on the division of competences and of having an additional channel of economic contacts with the EU (Sokolov 2007).[29]

Lastly, the US connection must be mentioned in this discussion on structural levels. Russian media, political elite members and analysts were particularly vocal about the 'overseas friends' spoiling EU–Russian economic relations.[30] Coordination of sanctions between officials in Brussels and Washington contributed to numerous Russian conspiracy theories, as did the US legislation of December 2014 allowing it to punish all companies, irrespective of their location, for violating US sanctions against Russia (Shestakov 2014).[31] Many of these Russian messages convey a simplified picture, either aimed at the general public or in order to 'drive a wedge' between the USA and the EU (and to criticise the EU for not being independent and, as a result, incurring economic losses). However, the confrontation in Ukraine (and the depth of Russian involvement there) has increased the salience of military aspects in Europe; the EU has always been weak in this field and has relied on the US. Consequently, the role of the US in Europe has increased. The diminished importance of the cooperative agenda

---

[28]Interview with a senior diplomat, Permanent Mission of the Russian Federation to the EU, Brussels, 5 February 2015.

[29]See also, Trenin (2014).

[30]'Postpred RF pri ES: Evrosoyuz sokhranitsya, no ne bez shramov i izderzhek', *RIA Novosti*, 11 February 2016, available at: http://ria.ru/interview/20160211/1372526891.html, accessed 21 February 2016.

[31]'Postpred RF pri ES: Evrosoyuz sokhranitsya, no ne bez shramov i izderzhek', *RIA Novosti*, 11 February 2016, available at: http://ria.ru/interview/20160211/1372526891.html, accessed 21 February 2016; 'Putin nazval sanktsii SSHA protiv kompanii ES "otnosheniyami s vassalami"', *Rossiiskaya gazeta*, 22 October 2015, available at: http://www.rg.ru/2015/10/22/vassali-anons.html, accessed 21 February 2016; 'Zamglavy MID RF: Vashington davit na ES dlya sokhraneniya sanktsii protiv Rossii', *Russia Today*, 12 February 2016, available at: https://russian.rt.com/article/148194, accessed 21 February 2016.

and economic interaction, described in the previous section, has further contributed to the increase in the influence of the US as it remains the key security actor in Europe. As a result, economic cooperation between the EU and Russia is viewed increasingly, at least in Moscow, as dependent on the overall settlement in Europe, which in security terms will be mostly dealt with by Moscow and Washington.

In sum, as a result of the sanctions, the structural aspects of EU–Russian economic relations have become more complex. First, the dialogue between Moscow and Brussels is much narrower and is compensated for by Russian contacts with member states, by discussions in multilateral fora and by the dialogue between the EU and EEU. Second, Russia does not try to undermine the EU by dealing with member states (although some traces of these efforts can be identified in 2014). The current strategy is more sophisticated, targeted at changing the consensus on Russia at the EU level and at making even Russia-friendly member states prisoners of the EU's solidarity (or 'collective responsibility' in Russian terminology). Third, structural aspects became more complex. Given the deficit of direct EU–Russian contacts, the two sides intensified the use of multilateral fora (like the WTO or the Energy Charter Secretariat), which granted Russia more equality but also made it cooperate in the organisations, which are more liberal, or, in the case of the ECT Secretariat, where Russian membership is limited because of earlier decisions. Fourth, a dialogue between the EU and the EEU emerged, although without explicit recognition of the latter by the EU and with a limited mandate from Russia. Finally, EU–Russian economic relations are increasingly viewed not as softening confrontation and building stability but rather as a hostage of Russian–US strategic confrontation. Hence, traditional structural levels of EU–Russian relations are complemented by a series of new ones.

Paradoxically, as a result of the sanctions Russia obtained what it had long sought for in structural terms: bolstered multilateral frameworks, which allowed it to avoid the unilaterality of the EU in its legal approximation and policy transfer, and an additional—supranational— level on its side to play on the division of competences, mostly for tactical purposes. This multiplication, however, given the poverty of the shared economic agenda between the EU and Russia, signified a victory of form over substance.

The institutional aspect: increasing poverty of the dialogue?

EU–Russian economic relations, like many others, started as intergovernmental. Biannual summits, occasional Cooperation Council meetings and meetings between the President of the Commission and the Prime Minister of Russia drove the agenda. The Cooperation Committee and sub-committees rarely met and eventually the latter were disbanded.

The intensity of contacts started to increase at the turn of the century. First, an energy dialogue and then other dialogues were set up. They provided for closer and more frequent cooperation of junior and senior officials and experts. Thus a transgovernmental level emerged, mostly for the purpose of information-sharing (that is the very basic function of these structures (Slaughter 2004)). These dialogues facilitated information exchange but also limited policy convergence. The dialogues also fostered expert networking. Second, the EU–Russian Roundtable of Industrialists intensified its work. At the turn of the century it changed the way it recruited its members (from invitation to open application), enabling all those who were interested to participate. Russian companies also became members of various

EU associations. Furthermore, the work of the expert community on EU–Russian economic relations grew exponentially. Finally, the EU–Russian civil society forum was set up, providing for civil society interaction. Thus business, epistemic community and civil society contacts grew before 2014, making transnational interaction denser.

Transgovernmental and transnational links did not reach the level of EU–US relations. The Russian economic system limited the ability of Russian business to exert independent pressure on the intergovernmental level. Transgovernmental links were also constrained by the low level of delegation in Russian state institutions. However, both transgovernmental and transnational relations gradually matured to soften some strains of EU–Russian intergovernmental relations. The 2008 EU–Russian crisis, linked to the war in Georgia, became a good illustration of this phenomenon.[32] The move to limited policy convergence through transgovernmental and transnational interaction in the energy dialogue represents another positive example (Romanova 2014).

How did the sanctions influence the institutional aspect of EU–Russian relations? Already the first generation of sanctions, introduced in March 2014, had negatively affected it. Officially contacts were suspended only at the top level and the European External Action Service circulated a note advising other services to continue daily cooperation.[33] However, the Russian side soon discovered that most expert meetings were suspended and postponed indefinitely.[34] That affected not only transgovernmental structures *per se* but also related expert meetings (like the Gas Advisory Council and its working parties, which mostly consist of independent experts and business representatives). The working groups of these meetings eventually met but no plenary meeting of the Council has taken place since 2013. Moreover, in all cases EU officials did not attend meetings while EU experts refrained from discussing controversial issues like the Turkish Stream,[35] thus limiting information exchange and the socialisation function of this forum.

EU officials were extremely prudent when contacting their Russian counterparts from the Russian Mission to the EU in order not to show any bias. Merely inviting EU officials to academic events on EU–Russian relations became difficult because approval had to be sought at the top level of the Commission.[36] Thus, a certain self-censorship—defined here as a censoring of one's own behaviour, not engaging in any contacts or relations with Russian counterparts, even if the latter are not banned—emerged in the behaviour of EU officials as a result of the first generation of EU sanctions against Russia.

The only transgovernmental fora which functioned throughout 2014 and 2015 were those related to Ukraine. In relation to energy, representatives discussed first the winter package (conditions of gas supply to Ukraine in winter 2014–2015, which guaranteed the stability of

[32]Interview with a former official of the EU Delegation to Russia, DG RELEX, European Commission, Brussels, 19 November 2010.

[33]Interview with a head of unit, European External Action Service, Brussels, 5 October 2014.

[34]Interview with an official responsible for relations with the EU, Russian Ministry of Energy, Moscow, 10 June 2014; interview with an official responsible for cooperation with the WTO, Ministry of Economic Development, Moscow, 15 July 2014; interview with an official responsible for relations with the EU, Ministry of Foreign Affairs, Brussels, 3 February 2015.

[35]Interview with an official responsible for relations with the EU, Russian Ministry of Energy, Moscow, 10 June 2014.

[36]Interview with an official responsible for industrial dialogue with Russia, DG Industry and Entrepreneurship, European Commission, Brussels, 9 October 2014; interview with an official responsible for international relations, DG Energy, European Commission, Brussels, 6 February 2015.

supply to the EU), then gas supply for the summer of 2015 and—at the time of writing—for the winter of 2015–2016. These discussions were trilateral, involving the EU, Russia and Ukraine; their aim was to assist Gazprom and Naftogaz in reaching a deal. In overall EU–Russian trade relations, similarly, the only transgovernmental forum that functioned was the one responsible for identifying contradictions between the free trade zone, which links Russia and Ukraine, and the Association Agreement concluded by Brussels and Kyiv in 2014. Again, the issue was vital for the settlement in Ukraine (and for the overall climate of EU–Russian relations) but it did not advance EU–Russian relations.

Finally, the Commission took a long time to process its decisions. For example, nearly a year was required to translate from English into German several pages of its decision which allowed Gazprom to use additional capacities of the OPAL gas system, reserved for alternative suppliers and remaining idle (and without the translation it could not be sent to relevant German authorities). In the meantime Gazprom's request for the spare OPAL capacities expired. Similarly, the Commission treated Russia's case against the third energy package in the WTO as a reason to stop any expert meetings on the third liberalisation package, even though there is no rule that there can be no discussion on an issue if it is appealed in the WTO. Moreover, the EU, in parallel to its own complaint in the WTO about Russia's ban on the import of pork, requested expert consultations with Russia. Thus, we can identify a 'work-to-rule' strategy that EU institutions have used in areas of Russian concern. Its essence is to follow all the rules (even those that are most frequently ignored as a mere formality and certainly do not stop informal consultations), or make up additional ones, to minimise or delay contacts with Russian colleagues. These two strategies—self-censorship and work-to-rule—were preserved and intensified by EU institutions as the EU sanctions against Russia hardened. As a result, the efficacy of transgovernmental consultations on economic issues seriously deteriorated.

Transnational relations have not fared much better. Already the first and second generations of sanctions served as a caution for any EU company considering starting a business in Russia. Many of them decided to postpone new contracts because of the increasingly negative reputation of Russia, which did not encourage any deals with Russian counterparts, as well as because of the uncertainty of the future of sanctions. That change also affected financial institutions; thus even those companies that wished to continue cooperation with Russia found it difficult to secure banking services (Kalinovskii 2014). The lack of transparency of ownership of many Russian companies as well as a chain of deals in Russia, initiated by individuals and entities, which fell under sanctions also led to the decrease of contracts with EU partners. In many cases EU companies could not be sure any longer that they were allowed to deal with a particular entity or that this entity or its owners were not on the sanctions list (Ensign 2015).[37]

With the sectoral sanctions the situation further deteriorated. The financial resources dried up. Restrictions on the supply of dual-use goods meant that companies had to apply for permission, with the procedure frequently taking more than a month (Emmott 2014). Relevant public bodies at national level remained under-staffed whereas companies in many cases had to apply for permission twice (first to sell goods or services and then to settle the financial transactions). The US introduced a clause in December 2014 allowing it to punish

---

[37]'Fancy Footwork. How Businesses Linked to Blacklisted Oligarchs Avoid Western Sanctions', *The Economist*, 14 February 2015, available at: http://www.economist.com/news/business/21643122-how-businesses-linked-blacklisted-oligarchs-avoid-western-sanctions-fancy-footwork, accessed 25 July 15.

companies that violated American sanctions against Russia. A number of European banks had by then suffered from US fines for violating similar bans and European companies had little appetite to repeat that experience. As a result companies became even more inclined to self-censorship but also to clarifying as much as possible the terms of the deal and to obtain all possible permissions; hence paradoxically the work-to-rules approach emerged in business interactions as well. Finally, some deals with Russian companies were blocked pre-emptively, despite their not being in the sanctions list, out of a concern that they might find themselves in the sanctions list in future and cause problems for EU member states. The best known case is the unlucky purchase of RWE assets in Britain by LetterOne.[38]

One can attribute a decrease in deals to the Russian economic downturn, including falling household income, as well as the perception of Russia being prone to corruption and a lack of the rule of law. However, previous economic downturns (for example, in 2008) did not lead to similar developments as figures show (CBR 2015). Since the perception of relations with Russia involving risk is nothing new, most negative developments in transnational relations should be attributed to sanctions.

In sum, sanctions severely limited transgovernmental and transnational levels of EU–Russian economic relations, making them more vulnerable to politicisation and to the irregularities of intergovernmental discussions. The positive developments of the previous years of cooperation (growing intensity of transgovernmental and transnational links) were, therefore, neutralised if not destroyed. There are several reasons why this has happened. EU–Russian transgovernmental and transnational relations never became independent of intergovernmental ones, mostly because of the low level of delegation in Russian governmental and administrative systems and because of its economic system. Furthermore, the change in the thematic aspect of cooperation (in strategic long-term goals) also affected the situation at the transgovernmental level. In the light of this mutual divorce there was no incentive to cooperate.

Transnational relations turned out to be more durable than transgovernmental ones, clearly because of business interests. Two examples may be cited. First, when the Russian government decided not to submit a claim to the WTO against Western sanctions, a private way of challenging EU sanctions was chosen. Inspired by the previous success of Burmese, Belarusian and Iranian litigants, Russian banks (Sberbank, VTB, Vneshekonombank), oil companies (Rosneft, Gazpromneft) and physical persons submitted their claims to the European Court of Justice. The synchronicity of their claims in late 2014 led to speculation that they were being encouraged by the Kremlin. Little is known about the content of the claims except for the one from Rosneft, which challenged the legality of the sanctions (its contradiction with the PCA), denial of the right of self-defence and lack of clarity of some provisions.[39] Hence, Russian business is encouraged to pursue its interests not by uploading them to the intergovernmental level but rather by following the standard transnational or transgovernmental interaction with the EU. Although the claims might take several years and the outcome is not certain, the experience of judicial interaction with the EU will be positive for Russian business.

---

[38]UK authorities blocked the purchase of gas fields in the North Sea by Russian LetterOne due to potential future tightening of sanctions against Russia, which could affect LetterOne. See, Adams (2015); 'RWE Wraps Up EUR 5.1 bn Sale of Gas Unit to Russian-controlled Fund', *EUobserver*, 2 March 2015, available at: http://www.eubusiness.com/news-eu/germany-russia-rwe.100s, accessed 25 July 2015.

[39]'Russia's Rosneft Relies on Nine Pleas in Support of its Claim in ECJ', *RAPSI*, 12 December 2014, available at: http://rapsinews.com/judicial_news/20141212/272765797.html, accessed 25 July 2015.

Second, both EU and Russian companies developed ways to bypass the sanctions. Russian companies which were in the sanctions lists set up new independent entities, which can deal with EU counterparts because they are not covered by the sanctions list. EU companies can guess what is going on because newcomers know surprisingly well the technical side of their orders, which matches the frozen contracts. EU companies, for their part, shifted some production destined for Russia to third countries which did not introduce restrictive measures against Moscow (Hille *et al.* 2015). Belarus emerged as a channel of illegal transit of EU agricultural goods to Russia. New facilities were also constructed in Belarus to process EU agricultural goods, which allows further legal export to Russia, so that Russian consumers discovered 'Belarusian' shrimps, octopuses and bananas (Mel'nikov 2014; Samofalova 2014; Shokhina 2014). Businesses also exploit extensively the EU's interpretation that contracts concluded before sanctions can be implemented (the US, in contrast, bans all the deals, irrespective of the date of the contract). Both Russian judicial cases and exploitation of the loopholes in the sanctions' regime partially offset the destruction of transgovernmental and transnational relations described above. These transnational activities are driven by profit motives. However, they are nowhere near enough to make up for the durable institutional damage created by sanctions.

In sum, institutional levels demonstrate the narrowing of transgovernmental and transnational levels of EU–Russian economic relations as a result of sanctions. It has happened not as a direct consequence of sanctions but rather as a result of the self-censorship and work-to-rule strategies of EU officials and its business. The transgovernmental level of interaction was also discouraged by the poor shared EU–Russian economic agenda, by the 'divorce' in the strategic goals and policy-specific measures. Russian business was encouraged to search for judicial solutions to its problems rather than to upload these issues to the intergovernmental level. While transnational (business) relations on both sides have been more resistant to sanctions compared to transgovernmental relations, these activities were not sufficient to offset the negative consequences of the sanctions. As a result EU–Russian economic relations are being reduced mostly to the intergovernmental level, which makes them even more vulnerable to any sort of politicisation.

Conclusion

The level-of-analysis approach to the thematic, structural and institutional aspects of EU–Russian economic relations demonstrates the profound effect of reciprocal sanctions. Thematically, both the EU and Russia chose to 'divorce' each other. Despite their ambiguous declarations about long-term strategic goals, this 'divorce' manifests itself at the policy-specific level, both in energy and economic cooperation and trade. They diversify from each other in energy. In addition Russia pursues import substitution in other fields while the EU pays some compensation to farmers and rhetorically diminishes the importance of Russian export markets. The net result is a decrease in mutual economic dependence (and more immunity in the face of future attempts to use it as a political leverage). While the origin of this 'divorce' lies in conceptual contradictions between the EU and Russian economic systems as well as in the logics of building international relations (with the EU insisting on Russia's legal approximation to its rules and norms while Russia stresses the need for equality between the EU and Russia), sanctions freed the EU and Russia from any obligation to search for acceptable solutions at a policy-specific level. This allowed them to adopt unilateral solutions, which easily bring together strategic goals, policy-specific measures and implementation mechanisms.

Structural levels of analysis demonstrate that Russia tried to make up for the lack of interaction at the EU–Russian level by contacts with member states. The strategy is, however, not to 'divide and rule' but rather to foster a more favourable consensus on Russia within the EU. Russia uses economic language to demonstrate at the national level the benefits of cooperation, but at the same time it makes all member states 'collectively' responsible for the sanctions. So, paradoxically, Russia is interested in the EU's cohesion. Furthermore, structural levels also diversify because the EU and Russia intensified their economic interaction in international organisations and through the nascent dialogue between the EU and EEU. Finally, the level of Russian–US strategic dialogue increasingly conditions (or rather limits at present) any constructive advance in EU–Russian economic relations at all structural levels. This is mostly due to the return of hard security agenda in Europe.

Institutional levels of analysis demonstrate that EU–Russian relations became poorer because economic sanctions led to the dilution of transgovernmental and transnational relations. Both EU officials and companies are cautious about contacting their Russian counterparts, they exercise self-censorship and work-to-rule strategies. The poverty of the shared thematic agenda (or the 'divorce') also negatively affects transgovernmental relations. Increased interaction between Russian companies and the European Court of Justice, as well as EU and Russian companies exploiting sanctions loopholes to preserve some profit, are positive for transnational relations but they do not break the trend towards EU–Russian relations becoming institutionally poor. Nor can these trends offset the outflow of investments from Russia or new companies postponing deals with Russia.

The analysis of how sanctions influence thematic, structural and institutional levels of EU–Russian economic relations demonstrates that the drift of the partners away from each other is fundamental. It is a real 'divorce', even if the partners pretend that they have a shared long-term goal as an alternative. It does not mean that economic contacts between the two partners will cease to exist. The 'gravitational pull' of the EU and Russian economies remains large (given their proximity, trade flows, shared infrastructure, cultural links and various human contacts). However, present policy choices, reinforced by institutional evolution and structural changes, mean that economic relations will remain 'primitive' in the medium term, reduced to simplistic (and possibly falling) exchange of natural resources for processed goods. It is difficult to imagine any meaningful deepening, not to mention the construction of a free trade area between the EU and Russia for years to come (possibly until 2024, which would mark the end of a further term of Putin's presidency).

Furthermore, thematic, structural and institutional levels also point in the direction of politicisation of economic relations rather than these relations performing a stabilising, socialising and constructive role. Politicisation is, indeed, the purpose of the sanctions but the actual developments have outstripped most bold ideas, defying key premises of the liberal theory of international relations. Thematically it is because of the mutual 'divorce' and lack of shared long-term goals. Structurally, it is because, although venues of EU–Russian relations multiply, it is a triumph of form over substance; EU–Russian channels of communication remain closed while the real discussions are gradually reduced to the dialogue between Moscow and Washington. Institutional levels demonstrate openness to politicisation because sanctions dilute transgovernmental and transnational relations.

Finally, EU–Russian decreased interdependence does not offer any solution for a long-term settlement in Ukraine. It deprives it even potentially of its role as a bridge in EU–Russian relations. It also predetermines its remaining an arena of geopolitical confrontation with limited subjectivity.

References

Adams, C. (2015) 'Mikhail Fridman in Legal Threat over North Sea Block', *Financial Times*, 1 March, available at: http://www.ft.com/intl/cms/s/0/b66feb28-c015-11e4-a71e-00144feab7de.html, accessed 19 February 2015.

Baldwin, D. (1985) *Economic Statecraft* (Princeton, NJ, Princeton University Press).

Baldwin, D. (1999–2000) 'The Sanctions Debate and the Logic of Choice', *International Security*, 24, 3.

Bapat, N. A. & Kwon, B. R. (2015) 'When Are Sanctions Effective? A Bargaining and Enforcement Framework', *International Organization*, 69, 1.

Barber, J. (1979) 'Economic Sanctions as a Policy Instrument', *International Affairs*, 55, 3.

Bidder, B., Gathmann, M., Neef, C. & Schepp, M. (2014) 'Undeclared War: Putin's Covert Invasion of Eastern Ukraine', *Spiegel*, 2 September, available at: http://www.spiegel.de/international/world/russia-expands-war-in-eastern-ukraine-amid-web-of-lies-a-989290.html, accessed 21 February 2016.

Bond, I., Odendahl, C. & Rankin, J. (2015) *Frozen: The Politics and Economics of Sanctions Against Russia* (London, Centre for Policy Reform).

Brooks, R. A. (2002) 'Sanctions and Regime Type: What Works, and When?', *Security Studies*, 11, 4.

Bunge, M. (1960) 'Levels: A Semantical Preliminary', *The Review of Metaphysics*, 13, 3.

CBR (2015) 'Direct Investment of the Russian Federation by Institutional Sectors 1994–2014, Q1–Q2 2015', Central Bank of Russia, available at: http://www.cbr.ru/eng/statistics/?Prtid=svs&ch=ITM_14544#CheckedItem, accessed 20 December 2015.

Chizhov, V. (2012) 'Vliyanie evraziiskoi integratsii na otnosheniya s Evropeiskim soyuzom', Permanent Mission of the Russian Federation to the European Union, 15 June, available at: http://www.russianmission.eu/ru/intervyu/vliyanie-evraziiskoi-integratsii-na-otnosheniya-s-evropeiskim-soyuzom-vystuplenie-vachizhov, accessed 21 December 2015.

Chizhov, V. (2016) 'Russia–EU Trade Relations', Permanent Mission of the Russian Federation to the European Union, 20 February, available at: http://www.russianmission.eu/en/news/russia-eu-trade-relations, accessed 21 February 2016.

Cohen, T. (2014) 'Malaysian Plane Shot Down in Ukraine: What Happened?', *CNN*, 19 July, available at: http://edition.cnn.com/2014/07/18/world/europe/ukraine-malaysia-plane-questions/, accessed 21 February 2016.

Cortright, D. & Lopez, G. A. (2000) *The Sanctions Decade: Assessing UN Strategies in the 1990s* (Boulder, CO, Lynne Rienner).

Cortright, D. & Lopez, G. A. (eds) (2002) *Smart Sanctions: Targeting Economic Statecraft* (Lanham, MD, Rowman & Littlefield).

Council of the European Union (2014a) 'Decision 2014/145/CFSP of 17 March 2014, Concerning Restrictive Measures in Respect of Actions Undermining or Threatening the Territorial Integrity, Sovereignty and Independence of Ukraine', available at: http://eur-lex.europa.eu/legal-content/EN/TXT/?uri=CELEX%3A32014D0145, accessed 19 February 2016.

Council of the European Union (2014b) 'Regulation (EU) No. 269/2014 of 17 March 2014, Concerning Restrictive Measures in Respect of Actions Undermining or Threatening the Territorial Integrity, Sovereignty and Independence of Ukraine', available at: http://eur-lex.europa.eu/legal-content/EN/TXT/?qid=1455890881482&uri=CELEX:32014R0269, accessed 19 February 2016.

Council of the European Union (2014c) 'Decision 2014/386/CFSP of 23 June 2014, Concerning Restrictions on Goods Originating in Crimea or Sevastopol, in Response to the Illegal Annexation of Crimea and Sevastopol', available at: http://eur-lex.europa.eu/legal-content/EN/TXT/?uri=CELEX%3A32014D0386, accessed 19 February 2016.

Council of the European Union (2014d) 'Regulation (EU) No 692/2014 of 23 June 2014, Concerning Restrictions on the Import into the Union of Goods Originating in Crimea or Sevastopol, in Response to the Illegal Annexation of Crimea and Sevastopol', available at: http://eur-lex.europa.eu/legal-content/EN/TXT/?uri=CELEX%3A32014R0692, accessed 19 February 2016.

Council of the European Union (2014e) 'Decision 2014/512/CFSP of 31 July 2014 Concerning Restrictive Measures in View of Russia's Actions Destabilising the Situation in Ukraine', available at: http://eur-lex.europa.eu/legal-content/EN/TXT/?uri=uriserv:OJ.L_.2014.229.01.0013.01.ENG, accessed 19 February 2016.

Council of the European Union (2014f) 'Regulation (EU) No. 833/2014 of 31 July 2014 Concerning Restrictive Measures in View of Russia's Actions Destabilising the Situation in Ukraine', available at: http://eur-lex.europa.eu/legal-content/EN/TXT/?uri=uriserv:OJ.L_.2014.229.01.0001.01.ENG, accessed 19 February 2016.

Council of the European Union (2014g) 'Regulation (EU) No 960/2014 of 8 September 2014, Amending Regulation (EU) No 833/2014 Concerning Restrictive Measures in View of Russia's Actions Destabilising the Situation in Ukraine', available at: http://eur-lex.europa.eu/legal-content/EN/TXT/?uri=CELEX%3A32014R0960, accessed 19 February 2016.

Damrosch, L. F. (1993) 'The Civilian Impact of Economic Sanctions', in Damrosch, L. F. (ed.) *Enforcing Restraint: Collective Intervention in Internal Conflicts* (New York, NY, Council on Foreign Relations Press).

Daoudi, M. S. & Dajani, M. S. (1983) *Economic Sanctions: Ideals and Experience* (London, Routledge and Kegan Paul).

David Singer, J. (1961) 'The Level of Analysis Problem in International Relations', *World Politics*, 14, 1.

Davidson, H. (2014) 'MH17: Rebels Likely Shot Down Plane "By Mistake"', *The Guardian*, 23 July, available at: http://www.theguardian.com/world/2014/jul/23/mh17-rebels-likely-shot-down-plane-by-mistake-live-updates, accessed 21 February 2016.

DeYoung, K. (2014) 'Obama says Malaysian Plane Shot Down by Missile from Rebel-held Part of Ukraine', *Washington Post*, 18 July, available at: https://www.washingtonpost.com/world/missile-downs-malaysia-airlines-plane-over-ukraine-killing-298-kiev-blames-rebels/2014/07/18/d30205c8-0e4a-11e4-8c9a-923ecc0c7d23_story.html, accessed 21 February 2016.

Doxey, M. P. (1987) *International Sanctions in Contemporary Perspective* (New York, NY, St. Martin's).

Early, B. R. (2009) 'Sleeping with Your Friends' Enemies: An Explanation of Sanctions-Busting Trade', *International Studies Quarterly*, 53, 1.

Early, B. R. (2011) 'Unmasking the Black Knights: Sanctions Busters and Their Effects on the Success of Economic Sanctions', *Foreign Policy Analysis*, 7, 4.

Emmott, R. (2014) 'Europe Feels Sting in the Tail of Russia Sanctions', *Reuters*, 26 November, available at: http://www.reuters.com/article/2014/11/26/us-ukraine-crisis-eu-sanctions-insight-idUSKCN0JA0B620141126, accessed 25 July 2015.

Ensign, R. L. (2015) 'Russian Asset Sales Muddy Sanction Compliance. US Companies Already Have to Contend With Complex Rules', *The Wall Street Journal*, 12 February, available at: http://www.wsj.com/articles/russian-asset-sales-muddy-sanction-compliance-1423784903, accessed 25 July 2015.

EP Members Research Service (2015) 'Economic Impact on the EU of Sanctions over Ukraine Conflict', *European Parliament Briefing*, October, available at: http://www.europarl.europa.eu/RegData/etudes/BRIE/2015/569020/EPRS_BRI(2015)569020_EN.pdf, accessed 19 February 2016.

EU & Russia (1994) 'Agreement on Partnership and Cooperation Establishing a Partnership between the European Communities and their Member States, of one part, and the Russian Federation, of the other part', 24 June, available at: http://eur-lex.europa.eu/legal-content/EN/TXT/?uri=celex%3A31997D0800, accessed 19 February 2016.

EU & Russia (2005) 'Road Map for the Common Space of Freedom, Security and Justice', 10 May, available at: https://www.consilium.europa.eu/uedocs/cmsUpload/84815.pdf, accessed 19 February 2016.

EU & Russia (2010) 'Joint Statement on the Partnership for Modernisation', EU–Russia Summit, Rostov-on-Don, 31 May–1 June, available at: http://www.consilium.europa.eu/uedocs/cms_data/docs/pressdata/en/er/114747.pdf, accessed 19 February 2016.

EU & Russia (2013) 'Roadmap. EU–Russia Energy Cooperation until 2050', March, available at: https://ec.europa.eu/energy/sites/ener/files/documents/2013_03_eu_russia_roadmap_2050_signed.pdf, accessed 19 February 2016.

European Commission (2014a) 'Communication from the Commission to the European Parliament and the Council (Brussels) on European Energy Security Strategy', COM(2014) 330 final, 28 May, available at: http://eur-lex.europa.eu/legal-content/EN/ALL/?uri=CELEX%3A52014DC0330, accessed 19 February 2016.

European Commission (2014b) 'Communication from the Commission to the European Parliament and the Council (Brussels) on the Short-Term Resilience of the European Gas System. Preparedness for a Possible Disruption of Supplies from the East during the Fall and Winter of 2014/2015', COM(2014) 654 final, 16 October, available at: https://ec.europa.eu/energy/sites/ener/files/documents/2014_stresstests_com_en.pdf, accessed 19 February 2016.

European Commission (2015) 'Communication from the Commission to the European Parliament, the Council, the European Economic and Social Committee, the Committee of the Regions and the European Investment Bank, (Brussels) on a Framework Strategy for a Resilient Energy Union with a Forward-Looking Climate

Change Policy', COM(2015) 80 final, 25 February, available at: http://eur-lex.europa.eu/legal-content/EN/TXT/?uri=COM:2015:0080:FIN, accessed 19 February 2016.

Galtung, J. (1967) 'On the Effects of International Economic Sanctions, With Examples from the Case of Rhodesia', *World Politics*, 19, 3.

Gavrilov, Yu. (2014) 'Minoborony RF pred"yavit isk Rheinmetall za sryv kontrakta', *Rossiiskaya gazeta*, 19 December, available at: http://www.rg.ru/2014/12/19/mulino-site.html, accessed 13 March 2015.

Giumelli, F. (2013) *The Success of Sanctions. Lessons Learned from the EU Experience* (Farnham, Ashgate).

Government of Russian (2014) *Postanovlenie pravitel'stva Rossiiskoi Federatsii ot 7 avgusta 2014 goda No778 "O merakh po realizatsii Ukaza Presidenta Rossii "O primenenii otdel'nyh spetsial'nykh ekonomicheskikh mer v tselyakh obespecheniya bezopasnosti Rossiiskoi Federatsii"* (Moscow, Government of the Russian Federation).

Green, J. (1983) 'Strategies for Evading Economic Sanctions', in Nincic, M. & Wallensteen, P. (eds) *Dilemmas of Economic Coercion: Sanctions in World Politics* (New York, NY, Praeger).

Gregory, P. R. (2014) 'Here are the Intercepted Transcripts Indicating Russian Rebels Shot Down Malaysian Flight MH17', *Forbes*, 19 July, available at: http://www.forbes.com/sites/paulroderickgregory/2014/07/19/what-more-smoking-guns-are-needed-for-mh17-the-worlds-first-sam-terrorism/#b36001dd62f2, accessed 21 February 2016.

Hall, P. (1993) 'Policy Paradigms, Social Learning, and the State: The Case of Economic Policymaking in Britain', *Comparative Politics*, 25, 3.

Havlik, P. (2014) 'Economic Consequences of the Ukraine Conflict', *WIIW Policy Notes and Reports*, 14.

Hille, K., Farchy, J. & Weaver, C. (2015) 'Russia Exploits Loopholes in Sanctions', *Financial Times*, 15 June.

Hix, S. (1998) 'The Study of the European Union II: The "New Governance" Agenda and its Rival', *Journal of European Public Policy*, 5, 1.

Hoffmann, F. (1967) 'The Functions of Economic Sanctions: A Comparative Analysis', *Journal of Peace Research*, 4, 2.

Hufbauer, G. C., Schott, J. J., Eliott, K. A. & Oegg, B. (2009) *Economic Sanctions Reconsidered* (3rd edn) (Washington, DC, The Peterson Institute for International Economics).

IMF (2015) 'Russian Federation: 2015 Article IV Consultation—Press Release; and Staff Report', *IMF Country Report*, August, 15/211.

Kalinovskii, I. (2014) 'Bei svoikh', *Expert*, 26 November, available at: http://expert.ru/2014/11/26/bej-svoih/, accessed 25 July 2015.

Keohane, R. O. & Nye, J. S. (1974) 'Transgovernmental Relations and International Organizations', *World Politics*, 27, 1.

Kirshner, J. (1997) 'The Microfoundations of Economic Sanctions', *Security Studies*, 6, 3.

Krasner, S. (1999) *Sovereignty: Organized Hypocrisy* (Princeton, NJ, Princeton University Press).

Lindsay, J. M. (1986) 'Trade Sanctions as Policy Instrument: A Reexamination', *International Studies Quarterly*, 32, 2.

Martin, L. (1992) *Coercive Cooperation: Explaining Multilateral Economic Sanctions* (Princeton, NJ, Princeton University Press).

Mayall, J. (1984) 'The Sanctions Problem in International Economic Relations: Reflections in the Light of Recent Experience', *International Affairs*, 60, 4.

McLean, E. V. & Whang, T. (2010) 'Friends or Foes? Major Trading Partners and the Success of Economic Sanctions', *International Studies Quarterly*, 54, 2.

Mel'nikov, A. (2014) 'Kak belorusskie midii podryvayut rossiiskie sanktsii protiv ES i SShA', *Kapital strany*, 12 August, available at: http://kapital-rus.ru/articles/article/256306/, accessed 25 July 2015.

Morgan, T. C. & Bapat, N. A. (2003) 'Imposing Sanctions: States, Firms, and Economic Coercion', *International Studies Review*, 5, 4.

Morgan, T. C. & Schwebach, V. L. (1995) 'Economic Sanctions as an Instrument of Foreign Policy: The Role of Domestic Politics', *International Interactions*, 21, 3.

Onuf, N. (1995) 'Levels', *European Journal of International Relations*, 1, 1.

Pape, R. A. (1997) 'Why Economic Sanctions Do Not Work', *International Security*, 22, 2.

Peksen, D. (2009) 'Better or Worse? The Effect of Economic Sanctions on Human Rights', *Journal of Peace Research*, 46, January.

Petrov, I. (2015) 'RF v techenie polugoda podast isk k Frantsii iz-za "Mistralei"', *Rossiiskaya gazeta*, 15 January, available at: http://www.rg.ru/2015/01/15/mistral-site.html, accessed 13 March 2015.

Phelan, W. (2012) 'What is Sui Generis About the European Union? Costly International Cooperation in a Self-Contained Regime', *International Studies Review*, 14, 3.

Pollack, M. & Shaffer, G. (eds) (2001) *Transatlantic Governance in the Global Economy* (Lanham, MD, Rowman & Littlefield).

Portela, C. (2010) *European Union Sanctions and Foreign Policy. When and Why do they Work?* (Abingdon, Routledge).

President of Russia (2013) 'Concept of the Foreign Policy of the Russian Federation', Presidential Decree, 12 February, available at: http://archive.mid.ru//brp_4.nsf/0/76389FEC168189ED44257B2E0039B16D, accessed 23 February 2016.

President of Russia (2014) *Ukaz Prezidenta Rossiiskoi Federatsii ot 6 avgusta 2014 goda No 560 "O primenenii otdel'nyh spetsial'nykh ekonomicheskikh mer v tselyakh obespecheniya bezopasnosti Rossiiskoi Federatsii"* (Moscow, President of the Russian Federation), available at: http://kremlin.ru/acts/bank/38809, accessed 19 February 2016.

Putin, V. (2014a) 'Sovmestnaya press-konferentsiya s Presidentom Turtsii Redzhepom Tadgipom Erdoganom', The Kremlin, 1 December, available at: http://kremlin.ru/news/47126, accessed 24 December 2014.

Putin, V. (2014b) 'Poslanie Federal'nomu Sobraniyu', 4 December, available at: http://www.kremlin.ru/transcripts/47173, accessed 6 December 2014.

Risse-Kappen, T. (1996) 'Exploring the Nature of the Beast: International Relations Theory and Comparative Policy Analysis Meet the European Union', *Journal of Common Market Studies*, 34, 1.

Romanova, T. (2013) 'Faktor WTO v otnosheniyakh Rossii i Evropeiskogo soyuza', *Vestnik mezhdunarodnykh organizatsii*, 4.

Romanova, T. (2014) 'Russian Energy in the EU Market: Bolstered Institutions and their Effects', *Energy Policy*, 74, November.

Romanova, T. (2015a) 'LNG in the Baltic Sea Region in the Context of EU–Russian Relations', in Liuhta, K. (ed.) *Natural Gas Revolution and the Baltic Sea Region, BSR Policy Briefing*, 1.

Romanova, T. (2015b) 'The Partnership for Modernisation through the Three Level-of-Analysis Perspectives', *Perspectives on European Politics and Society*, 16, 1.

Romanova, T. & Pavlova, E. (2013) 'Modernization in Russian Relations with EU Member States: Conventional Goal, New Means, Unexpected Consequences?', in Makarychev, A. & Mommen, A. (eds) *Russia's Changing Economic and Political Regimes. The Putin Years and Afterwards* (New York, NY, Routledge).

Romanova, T. & Pavlova, E. (2014) 'What Modernisation? The Case of Russian Partnerships for Modernisation with the European Union and Its Member States', *Journal of Contemporary European Studies*, 22, 4.

Rowe, D. (1999) 'Economic Sanctions Do Work: Economic Statecraft and Oil Embargo of Rhodesia', *Security Studies*, 9, 1–2.

Russia & EU (2014) *Energodialog Rossiya-ES, Trinadtsatyi obobshchaushchii doklad* (Moscow), January, available at: http://minenergo.gov.ru/node/3377, accessed 19 February 2016.

Russian Federation (2014) *Federal'nyi zakon Rossiiskoi Federatsii ot 31 dekabrya 2014 g. No 488-FZ 'O promyshlennoi politike Rossiiskoi Federatsii'* (Moscow), available at: http://www.rg.ru/2015/01/12/promyshlennost-dok.html, accessed 19 February 2016.

Samofalova, O. (2014) 'Rossiya nachala bor'bu s belorusskoi kontrabandoi', *Vzglyad. Delovaya gazeta*, 25 November, available at: http://vz.ru/economy/2014/11/25/716514.html, accessed 25 July 2015.

Shear, M. D. & Hirschfeld Davis, J. (2014) 'Obama Says Plane Was Shot Down From Rebel-Held Ukraine Area', *New York Times*, 18 July, available at: http://www.nytimes.com/2014/07/19/us/obama-to-speak-about-downing-of-malaysian-plane.html?_r=0, accessed 21 February 2016.

Shestakov, E. (2014) 'Sami sebya vysekut. Evropa okonchatelno sela na amerikanskuyu iglu', *Rossiiskaya gazeta*, 28 July, available at: http://www.rg.ru/2014/07/27/evrosankzii-site.html, accessed 21 February 2016.

Shokhina, E. (2014) 'Kontrabanda po-bratski', *Expert*, 25 November, available at: http://expert.ru/2014/11/25/kontrabanda-po-bratski/, accessed 25 July 2015.

Slaughter, A.-M. (2004) *A New World Order* (Princeton, NJ, Princeton University Press).

Sokolov, S. (2007) 'Russia and the EU to Negotiate a New Cooperation Agreement', *Russia in Global Affairs*, 5, 3.

Spiegel, P., Buckley, N., Olearchyk, R. & Dyer, G. (2014) 'Russia has "Well Over 1,000 Troops" in Ukraine, Nato Warns', *Financial Times*, 29 August, available at: http://www.ft.com/intl/cms/s/0/8275bec4-2ea2-11e4-afe4-00144feabdc0.html, accessed 21 February 2016.

Trenin, D. (2014) 'Praktichnyi podkhod k otnosheniyam ES i Rossii', Carnegie Endowment for International Peace, January, available at: http://carnegieendowment.org/files/Article_EU_Russ_Trenin_Rus2014.pdf, accessed 21 December 2015.

Wagner, R. H. (1988) 'Economic Interdependence, Bargaining Power and Political Influence', *International Organization*, 42, 3.

Wagstyl, S. (2014) 'Merkel Rethink on Sanctions Reflects Loss of Trust in Putin', *Financial Times*, 30 July, available at: http://www.ft.com/intl/cms/s/0/a29dfa7e-17d5-11e4-a82d-00144feabdc0.html#axzz40km3P888, accessed 21 February 2016.

Wallensteen, P. (1968) 'Characteristics of Economic Sanctions', *Journal of Peace Research*, 5, 3.

Index

Note: Bold face page numbers refer to figures and tables. Page numbers followed by "n" refer to footnotes.